S0-ARO-855

INTERSTATE ECONOMIC RELATIONS

MONTGOMERY COLLEGE
ROCKVILLE CAMPUS LIBRARY
ROCKVILLE, MARYLAND

INTERSTATE ECONOMIC RELATIONS

Joseph F. Zimmerman

State University of New York Press

316828

APR 2 0 2006

Published by
State University of New York Press, Albany

© 2004 State University of New York

All rights reserved

Printed in the United States of America

No part of this book may be used or reproduced in any manner whatsoever
without written permission. No part of this book may be stored in a retrieval
system or transmitted in any form or by any means including electronic,
electrostatic, magnetic tape, mechanical, photocopying, recording, or otherwise
without the prior permission in writing of the publisher.

For information, address State University of New York Press,
90 State Street, Suite 700, Albany, NY 12207

Production by Diane Ganeles
Marketing Anne Valentine

Library of Congress Cataloging-in-Publication Data

Zimmerman, Joseph Francis, 1928–
    Interstate economic relations / Joseph F. Zimmerman.
      p. cm.
    Includes bibliographical references and index.
    ISBN 0-7914-6159-9 (alk. paper).
    1. United States—Economic policy. 2. Interstate commerce—United States. I. Title.

    KF1570.Z56 2004
    343.73'0815—dc22

                                                            2003066187

10 9 8 7 6 5 4 3 2 1

For Peggy

In appreciation of her support

Contents

Illustrations

Table

Figures

Preface

The drafters of the U.S. Constitution provided for both a flexible economic union and a flexible political union by granting Congress broad powers, including preemption ones, to be exercised as needed and by authorizing states to enter into interstate compacts with the consent of Congress to solve transboundary problems. The two unions were changed gradually in the nineteenth century by the U.S. Supreme Court's development of its dormant commerce-clause doctrine and occasional congressional enactment of preemption statutes that partially or totally displaced certain regulatory powers of the states. The twentieth century witnessed a sharp increase in the number and importance of preemption statutes and the use of interstate compacts, commencing in 1921, for purposes other than settling boundary disputes.

The economic union in the first decade of the twenty-first century differs significantly from the union established in 1789 by the newly ratified U.S. Constitution. States have lost a significant part of their regulatory authority, yet their reserved powers are vast and can be employed to promote interstate cooperation or competition or to generate interstate disputes. This book examines interstate economic relations in terms of disputes, state erected–trade barriers, competition for business firms and sports franchises, and cooperation.

The general reluctance of Congress to more fully exercise its power to regulate interstate commerce to remove state impediments to the commerce intercourse or to regulate interstate taxation has led the U.S. Supreme Court to play a very major role in umpiring the economic union. The court on occasion opines it is not the best forum for resolving contentious interstate disputes and urges Congress, the political branch directly representing the people, to enact statutes to resolve disputes.

Enactment of additional interstate compacts establishing common regulatory laws throughout the United States and/or a similar wide range of uniform laws by all states would promote the free flow of commerce within the United States. For a variety of reasons, the potential of compacts and uniform laws for solving impediments to interstate commerce have not been realized. In consequence, pressures upon Congress to more fully employ its preemption powers have led to the displacement of state economic regulation, thereby significantly changing the political union as well as the economic union.

One would assume the importance of interstate relations—general and economic relations in particular—would attract the attention of political scientists. In fact, relatively few political scientists have devoted their energies to researching interstate problems. This book has three major purposes. The first one is to examine and clarify the nature of major interstate economic problems. The second purpose is to encourage political scientists and others to conduct more research on relations between sister states that lead to a better understanding of interstate economic relations and possible solutions for old and emerging problems. The third purpose is to offer specific recommendations to Congress, the president, state legislatures, and governors for the strengthening of the economic union.

Acknowledgments

The relative lack of scholarly interest in interstate relations made the task of acquiring current information on the state of interstate economic relations difficult. In consequence, I relied heavily upon state and federal government officers, interstate compact administrators, associations of state administrators, and knowledgeable individuals who kindly responded to my requests for information. Respondents not only generally answered my specific questions, but also often provided additional valuable information and citations to reports and other materials not subject to location by standard library and nonlibrary searches—including computerized ones. Their cooperation is reflective of their professionalism and their desire to improve interstate relations.

A special debt of graditude is owed to my research associates—Dai Li, Christopher W. LaBarge, Michael A. Landsman, and Nicholas J. Parrella—for their conscientious and successful efforts to collect research materials through personal interviews of New York State government officers and library searches. I also compliment Addie Napolitano for excellence in preparing the manuscript. Any errors of fact or misinterpretations are naturally my sole responsibility.

CHAPTER 1

Interstate Economic Relations

The U.S. Constitution established an economic union as well as a political union of sister states in order to "establish justice, insure domestic tranquility, provide for the common defence, promote the general welfare, and secure the blessings of liberty to ourselves and our posterity."[1] Both unions have become more complex with continuous changes instituted in response to new challenges and emerging problems.

Much of the complexity is inherent in a federal system. Alexander Hamilton in the *Federalist,* number 82, explained:

> The erection of a new government, whatever care or wisdom may distinguish the work, cannot fail to originate questions of intricacy and nicety; and these may, in a particular manner, be expected to flow from the establishment of a constitution founded upon the total or partial incorporation of a number of distinct sovereignties. 'Tis time only that can mature and perfect so compound a system, can liquidate the meaning of all the parts, and can adjust them to each other in a harmonious and consistent whole.[2]

U.S. Supreme Court Chief Justice John Marshall in *Gibbons v. Ogden* in 1824 opined:

> In our complex system, presenting the rare and difficult scheme of one general government, whose actions extends over the whole, but which possesses only certain enumerated powers, and of numerous State governments, which retain and exercise all powers not delegated to the union, contests respecting power must arise.[3]

By delegating specific powers to Congress and reserving other powers to the states, the U.S. Constitution ensured there would be important daily interactions between the national and state governments, and between sister state governments. Many of these interactions were economic in nature and involved disputes or cooperation.[4] Our focus is interstate economic relations conducted under ground rules established by the U.S. Constitution and Congress as interpreted by the U.S. Supreme Court. Congress plays important roles in encouraging enactment of uniform state laws and interstate cooperation by regulating

1

relations between states and preempting regulatory powers of states if they are impeding the free flow of commerce in the nation.

The subject matter of interstate economic relations is broad and includes the allocation of river water; joint construction and operation of transportation facilities; erection and removal of interstate trade barriers; tax exportation; competition for industry, tourists, gamblers, professional sports team franchises, and federal government grants-in-aid and facilities; and numerous cooperative activities based upon interstate compacts and interstate administrative agreements.[5]

A review of economic and political conditions in the colonies prior to the Declaration of Independence in 1776, the prosecution of the Revolutionary War by the thirteen newly independent states, and experience under the Articles of Confederation and Perpetual Union will facilitate an understanding of the intergovernmental provisions included in the U. S. Constitution.

Development of the Constitution

Mercantilism was the prevailing economic and political policy in western Europe during the seventeenth century. England, the mother country of thirteen colonies in North America, sought to promote its political power in the world by developing strong home industries and a favorable balance of international trade.[6] The latter was to be obtained by the imposition of duties and tariffs on most imports, prohibition of other imports, and encouragement of exports. Gold, which was viewed as a major source of national power, would flow from nations with an export deficit to nations with an export surplus.

The seeds of revolt against the British crown were sowed in the Navigation Acts of 1660 and 1663 requiring colonists to purchase and sell goods only in England and to transport all goods in English ships. Eighteenth century mercantilist acts of Parliament sowed new seeds and fertilized the old seeds. A 1732 act forbade colonists to trade in woolen goods; the Molasses Act of 1733 imposed a duty on all molasses, rum, and sugar imported by a colony and thereby interfered with the colonies' trade with Spanish New World colonies; a 1750 act prohibited the manufacture of certain iron products and the shipment of pig iron to England; the Sugar Act of 1764 placed restrictions on trade in food, lumber, and other items with the West Indies; and a 1764 writ of assistance act empowered crown revenue officers combating smuggling to conduct searches and seizures, and required colonists to assist the officers. The Stamp Act of the following year was an attempt by Parliament to obtain revenue from the colonies to pay part of the cost of the French and Indian War by requiring an official stamp on various legal documents and newspapers. This act was viewed in particular as an attack on intellectual freedom. The Continental

Congress reacted by maintaining in 1765 taxes could be levied legitimately only by popularly elected colonial assemblies. Subsequently, the slogan "no taxation without representation" became popular.

The colonial break with the United Kingdom occurred in 1775 when New Hampshire declared its independence and representatives of the thirteen former colonies in 1776 signed the Declaration of Independence. Coincidentally, Adam Smith's famous book—*An Inquiry into the Nature and Causes of the Wealth of Nations*—was published in 1776 and constituted a blistering attack on the mercantilist system.[7] Emphasizing the law of comparative advantage, Smith wrote that it is best to purchase products from other nations if they can produce them at a cost lower than the cost of domestic manufacture and added ". . . in a mercantilist system, the interest of the consumer is almost constantly sacrificed to that of the producer. . . ."[8] His book represented a laissez-faire approach with respect to governmental intervention in the economy and this policy approach appealed to persons favoring individual liberties.

The Declaration of Independence produced thirteen new independent nations, but did not create a national government. Each state sent representatives to the second Continental Congress that prosecuted the Revolutionary War by borrowing funds, raising armies, and entering into treaties with certain other nations. This Congress recognized the need for a more formal national union and, in 1777, drafted the Articles of Confederation and Perpetual Union and transmitted them to the thirteen states for ratification.

Articles of Confederation

Four years were required for ratification of the articles primarily because of boundary disputes attributable to imprecise royal land grants. New Hampshire and New York, for example, claimed what today is Vermont; Massachusetts claimed the Rochester, New York, area; and Connecticut claimed present-day Illinois, Indiana, and northern Ohio. A solution to the disputes emerged in 1780 when the Continental Congress suggested the lands in dispute should be assigned to the new Congress, which would be created by the proposed Articles of Confederation and Perpetual Union, for settlement and formation as states of the proposed confederation.[9] In 1781, New York and Virginia ceded the lands they had been claiming and their lead was followed by the other states shortly thereafter. The Congress, created by the articles, enacted the Northwest Ordinance in 1787 and provided that each of the various parts of the Northwest Territory be admitted as a state when its population reached 50,000.[10]

Provisions. Article I titles the newly created confederacy "The United States of America," and Article II clearly reveals the nature of the new confederation:

"Each State retains its sovereignty, freedom and independence, and every power, jurisdiction and right, which is not by this confederation expressed delegated to the united States in Congress assembled." The absence of a reference to a newly established national government and the choice of the words "the united States in Congress assembled" were chosen deliberately and reflected the fear of centralized power. A new national government with legislative, executive, and judicial branches was not established.

Article III reemphasized the limited nature of the confederation by stipulating the thirteen states were entering

> into a firm league of friendship with each other, for their common defence, the security of their liberties, and their mutual and general welfare, binding themselves to assist each other, against all force offered to, or attacks made upon them, or any of them, on account of religion, sovereignty, trade, of any other pretence whatever.

Three important principles relating to harmonious interstate relations were incorporated in Article IV (see chapter 2). Citizens of each state were entitled to the privileges and immunities of citizens in the member states, fugitives from justice must be returned to the requesting state by the governor of the asylum state, and each state must give full faith and credit to the legislative acts, records, and judicial proceedings of sister states. These principles later were incorporated into Article IV of the U.S. Constitution.

Article V established a unicameral Congress composed of two to seven delegates from each state who were appointed annually in a manner prescribed by the state legislature and subject to the limitation that no delegate could serve in Congress for more than three years during any six-year period. Delegates could be recalled and replaced by a state at any time. Each state was allocated one vote in Congress regardless of the number of its delegates.

Although states were forbidden by Article VI to "lay any imposts or duties which may interfere with stipulations in treaties" entered into by Congress with foreign nations, no such prohibition was placed on states relative to imposts and duties being laid on products and raw materials that moved in interstate commerce. Furthermore, Article IX provided that treaties of commerce entered into by Congress may not prevent a state "from prohibiting the exportation or importation of any species of goods or commodities whatsoever . . ."

This article also authorized Congress to appoint a president as presiding officer for a period of one year during any term of three years, coin money, establish a standard system of weights and measures, regulate trade with Indians, establish post offices, and appoint "all officers of the land forces in the service of the United States excepting regimental officers . . . all the officers of the naval forces, and other officers of the United States." In addition, this article authorized Congress to appoint "a Committee of the States," composed of one delegate from each state, to sit during congressional recesses with authority to borrow funds, coin money, declare war, establish a postal system and standards of weights and measures, negotiate treaties, raise an army and a navy, and regulate relations with the Indian tribes. This committee was empowered to exercise additional powers provided that nine states agreed to their delegation.

One of the most interesting articles is Article XI:

> Canada, acceding to this Confederation, and joining in the measures of the United States, shall be admitted into and entitled to all the advantages of this Union, but no other colony shall be admitted into the same unless such admission be agreed to by the nine States.

The limited powers delegated to Congress by the Articles of Confederation and Perpetual Union predestined the failure of the Confederation. In 1974, Martin Diamond concluded "neither the friends nor the enemies of the Confederation regarded the articles as having created any kind of government at all, weak or otherwise."[11]

Defects. The defects of the Articles of Confederation and Perpetual Union became apparent within a period of four years. The first major defect was Congress' lack of authority to levy taxes and its reliance for funds upon states which often failed to contribute their quotas in full. The result was the inability of Congress to effectively implement the powers delegated to it by the articles.

The second major defect was the failure to authorize Congress to regulate interstate commerce. Alexander Hamilton in the *Federalist* number 11 reflected the views of Adam Smith: "An unrestrained intercourse between the States themselves will advance the trade of each by an interchange of their respective productions, not only for the supply of reciprocal wants at home, but for exportation to foreign markets."[12] He contended in the *Federalist* number 22 "[t]he interfering and unneighborly regulations of some States . . . have, in different instances, given just cause of umbrage and complaint to others, and . . . if not restrained by a national control, would be multiplied and extended till they became . . . injurious impediments to the intercourse between the different parts of the Confederacy."[13] Frederick H. Cooke in 1908 commented "[o]ne of the chief evils of the confederation was the power exercised by the commercial states of exacting duties upon the importation of goods destined for the interior of the country or for other states."[14]

The third major defect was Congress' inability to enforce its statutes and treaties with other nations because states were not obliged to respect them. James Madison reported in 1787 states had violated the Peace Treaty of 1783 with the United Kingdom, the Treaty with the Kingdom of France, and the Treaty with Holland, and added no foreign power had yet "been rigorous in animadverting on us."[15] Hamilton noted in the *Federalist* number 16 "[t]he measures of the Union have not been executed; and the delinquencies of the States have step by step matured themselves to an extreme, which has, at length, arrested all the wheels of the national government and brought them to an awful stand."[16]

The first defect was responsible for the fourth major defect: The lack of funds to raise and support an army and a navy during a period when the friendly French monarchy was in danger of collapse, Spain controlled the territory to the southwest and closed the Mississippi River, and Canada was under British control and excluded U.S. citizens from the St. Lawrence River. John Jay in the *Federalist* number 4 expressed concerns relative to the ability of the individual states to raise armies and navies and asked: "If one was attacked, would the others fly to its succor and spend their blood and money in its defense?"[17] Shays' Rebellion (1786–1787) in western Massachusetts demonstrated the inability of a state government to suppress a rebellion that was put down by a private army funded by wealthy citizens. Hamilton, a major supporter of the proposed U.S. Constitution, was convinced "[a] firm Union will be of the utmost moment to the peace and liberty of the States as a barrier against domestic faction and insurrection."[18]

The possible fracturing of the Confederation into a series of smaller confederacies was viewed as a distinct possibility. Madison wrote in 1787 "a breach of any of the Articles of Confederation by any of the parties to it absolves the other parties from their respective obligations, and gives them a right if they choose to exert it of dissolving the Union altogether."[19] Citing the historical division of Great Britain into three nations and constant wars between them, John Jay in the *Federalist* number 5 feared the "United States" would be divided into three or four nations and "they would always be either involved in disputes and war, or live in the constant apprehension of them."[20] Referring to commerce between states, Hamilton added a disunion "would occasion distinctions, preferences, and exclusions" on the part of individual states against other states.[21]

The 1787 Constitutional Convention

Observers were aware of the defects of the Articles of Confederation and Perpetual Union as early as 1785. In recognition of the importance of harmonious interstate relations, Maryland's and Virginia's state officers drafted, in 1785, a navigation and trade agreement for the Potomac River and Chesapeake Bay. In ratifying the interstate compact, the Maryland General Assembly suggested that Delaware and Pennsylvania be included in future negotiations on interstate-commercial relations. The Virginia General Assembly enacted the compact into law and invited the other states to send delegates to a convention—to be convened in Annapolis, Maryland—in 1786, for the purpose of developing a uniform system of interstate commerce.

Nine states appointed commissioners to attend the conference, but only twelve commissioners from five states participated. They endorsed a memorial, drafted by Alexander Hamilton of New York, requesting Congress to convene in May 1787 a convention to examine the Articles of Confederation and Perpetual Union and to propose amendments as needed. On February 21, 1787, Congress called such a convention to convene in Philadelphia on May 25, 1787, but let each state determine the method of selecting delegates. Seventy-four delegates were selected by the state legislatures or appointed by the governors under legislative authorization. Nineteen selected delegates either refused their appointments or did not attend the convention. An additional fourteen delegates, including New York delegates Robert Yates and John Lansing who objected to the approach taken by the majority of delegates, departed the convention prior to convention approval of the proposed U.S. Constitution. The State of Rhode Island and Providence Plantations failed to send delegates because it saw no need for a convention since Article XIII of the Articles of Confederation and Perpetual Union provided they could be amended by the concurrent affirmative actions of the Congress and each state legislature.

Four days after the convention opened. Governor Edmund Randolph of Virginia unveiled fifteen resolutions serving as the foundation for a national government possessing powers similar to those of the United Kingdom Government.[22] These resolutions generated a major debate relative to whether the Articles of Confederation and Perpetual Union should be amended or replaced. Prior to the arrival of delegates from five states, the convention voted, six to one, to replace the articles and draft a new national fundamental law.

A constitutional convention would be successful in drafting a new fundamental law only if the major regional interests were able to reach compromises on contentious proposals. There were sharp differences of opinion between the northern and southern states, the eastern and western states, and states with large populations or small populations. The latter, endorsed the New Jersey plan introduced by William Patterson, providing equal state representation in Congress, a continuation of the representation system established by the articles. The large states favored the Virginia Plan and argued equity demanded representation based upon population in view of the fact the large states would pay the bulk of the taxes levied by the proposed Congress. The issue was debated in the Committee of the Whole for several weeks prior to the so-called Connecticut Compromise solving the representational problem by providing equal state representation in the Senate and representation based upon population in the House of Representatives with the proviso that each state have a minimum of one representative.

Disputes over slavery and import and export duties threatened to produce a deadlocked convention. The southern states desired a provision allowing the importation of slaves, a provision opposed by the northern states. A compromise was reached in the form of Article I, §9, of the proposed constitution allowing the importation of slaves for a period of twenty years and granting Congress authority to impose a maximum tax of ten dollars on each imported slave. The northern states favored the levying of import and export duties to raise revenue for the proposed new national government, and southern states opposed such duties on the grounds that they imported most manufactured products and exported most of the products they produced. A logical compromise was reached in Article I, §8: Congress may levy only import duties.

A proposal to grant authority to Congress to disallow state statutes contravening the powers delegated to it provoked a major controversy. James Madison argued state legislatures could "pass laws which will accomplish their injurious objects before they can be repealed by the General legislature or be set aside by the national tribunals," hence a congressional negative was essential.[23] Not surprisingly, the convention rejected the proposal because the proposed constitution would significantly reduce the powers of the states, implementation of state laws would be delayed for several months while the statutes were reviewed by Congress, and the proposal would allow Congress—without constitutional criteria—to declare state statutes *ultra vires* and possibly convert the governance system into a unitary one.

The delegates fashioned the first federal constitution in the world that incorporated elements of a unitary system and elements of a confederate system by establishing an *Imperium in Imperio*. Specific powers were delegated by the supreme law to Congress which is forbidden to exercise specified powers. All other powers, unless prohibited, are reserved to the states. Most powers delegated to Congress are not exclusive and states possess concurrent authority to exercise these powers provided they do not violate the supremacy of the law provision of Article VI, which stipulated that all acts of Congress and treaties entered into by the United States were the supreme law of the land "any thing in the Constitution or Laws of any State to the contrary notwithstanding." As explained in chapter 4, the U.S. Supreme Court developed a dormant commerce clause doctrine under which the court in the absence of congressional legislation struck down state and/or local government laws as violative of the clause.

The proposed constitution established two branches of government that did not exist under the Articles of Confederation and Perpetual Union: an executive branch headed by the president and a judicial one consisting of a

Supreme Court. Congress was authorized to create courts inferior to the Supreme Court. The convention-produced document included a number of provisions, primarily ones governing interstate relations, contained in the articles. A major distinction between the two documents involved the source of governmental powers. Under the articles, Congress derived its powers from the thirteen states. The proposed constitution, reverting to the language of the Declaration of Independence, identifies the people as the source of the proposed new government.

Convention delegates were aware that the articles were popular with most citizens who feared a strong national government and to persuade all states to ratify the proposed constitution would be an impossible task. In consequence, they incorporated a provision in Article VII stipulating ratification by nine states would establish "this Constitution between the States," a provision that mirrored Article X of the Articles of Confederation and Perpetual Union, which permitted nine states in Congress assembled to delegate any or all of its powers to the Committee of the States for execution during recesses of Congress. The framers apparently were convinced that ratification of the proposed fundamental law by nine states would persuade the remaining four states to ratify it. The convention resolved on September 17, 1787, that each state should elect delegates to a convention to consider ratification of the proposed constitution.

Securing Ratification

Proponents faced a daunting task persuading nine states to ratify a document viewed by many citizens as a threat to their individual liberties because of the broad powers delegated to the proposed Congress. Article I, §9, of the proposed fundamental law contained three civil liberty provisions—prohibition of enactment of a bill of attainder and an ex post facto law, and suspension of the writ of habeas corpus except during an invasion by a foreign power. These guarantees did not satisfy opponents of the document who referred to colonial charters guaranteeing due process of law and right to petition for redress of grievances, levying of taxes only by approval of elected representatives, and prohibited of arrest and punishment without a specific charge. Certain critics also objected to the omission of any acknowledgment of God and to the requirement that all public offices be held by a Christian. The image of Oliver Cromwell was raised by the provision (Art. II, §2) designating the president as "commander in chief of the Army and Navy of the United States, and of the Militia of the several States, when called into the actual service of the United States. . . ." Furthermore, opponents maintained that the convention was called by Congress—created by the Articles of Confederation and Perpetual Union, for the sole purpose of amending the articles and the constitutional convention lacked authority to replace them.

The Federalist Papers. Opposition to the proposed constitution was particularly strong in New York where Alexander Hamilton enlisted John Jay and James Madison to join him in writing eighty-five letters to editors of New York City newspapers, all of which were signed *Publius* and collectively referred to as *The Federalist Papers,* which supported the handiwork of the convention during the winter and spring of 1787–1788. The first thirty-six letters were published in book form in late March 1788, and subsequently the remaining letters were published. Each letter, as noted, identified defects of the Articles of Confederation and Perpetual Union or explained and justified a provision of the proposed new fundamental document. These letters remain the best expositions on the unamended U.S. Constitution. The reader should be warned that the terms confederation and federation often were used interchangeably in the letters. Madison in the *Federalist* number 39 explained the proposed governance system would be "neither wholly national nor wholly federal" [confederate].[24]

The *Federalist* number 14, authored by Madison, sought to assure readers the proposed government would be one with limited powers and state governments would not be abolished.[25] In the *Federalist* number 45 he reiterated this point by writing "[t]he powers delegated by the proposed constitution to the federal government are few and defined. Those which are to remain in the State governments are numerous and indefinite."[26] Madison continued by maintaining the congressional delegated powers would concern external affairs, including the regulation of foreign commerce, and the reserved powers of the states would be broad.

Hamilton in the *Federalist* number 17 addressed the fear of a "too powerful" national government in the following terms:

> It will always be far more easy for the State governments to encroach upon the national authorities than for the national government to encroach upon the State authorities. The proof of this proposition turns upon the greater degree of influence which the State governments, if they administer their affairs with uprightness and prudence, will generally possess over the people.[27]

He repeated this argument in the *Federalist* number 31 and in number 32 assured readers each state would "possess independent and uncontrollable authority to raise their own revenues for the supply of their own wants" and an attempt by Congress to abridge this authority "would be a violent assumption of power, unwarranted by any article or clause of its Constitution."[28] He placed exclusive national powers in three categories:

> where the Constitution in express terms granted an exclusive authority to the Union; where it granted in one instance an authority to the Union, and in

another prohibited the States from exercising the like authority; and where it granted an authority to the Union to which a similar authority in the States would be absolutely and totally contradictory and repugnant.[29]

The Anti-Federalist Papers. Hamilton's, Jay's, and Madison's arguments were countered, generally by a series of letters termed the Anti-Federalist papers. Sixteen essays, signed Brutus, were published in the *New York Journal* in the period October 1787 to April 1788. These essays were not printed as a single document during the debates on ratification of the proposed U.S. Constitution. The identify of Brutus has not been proved conclusively, but available evidence suggests it was Robert Yates, a New York delegate to the Philadelphia Convention. Other letters opposing ratification of the proposed constitution were signed Cato who might have been Governor George Clinton of New York.

Brutus advanced several major objections to the work of the convention. He contended in his first letter a unitary system would develop in time because the proposed government would "possess absolute and uncontrollable power" inherent in the necessary and proper clause and the supremacy of the laws clause of the U.S. Constitution.[30] A second major objection, outlined in his sixth letter, was the authorization for the proposed Congress to levy and collect duties, excises, and taxes, which combined with the necessary and proper clause, would result in the states lacking "the power to raise one shilling in any way, but by the permission of the Congress."[31]

Brutus in his eleventh letter examined the proposed judicial system that was designed to be independent of Congress and the citizenry. He concluded: "That the judicial power of the United States will lean strongly in favour of the general government and will give such an explanation to the constitution as will favour an extension of the jurisdiction is very evident from a variety of considerations."[32] Brutus added that the Constitution's use of general terms combined with the necessary and proper clause suggests the constitution was not to be interpreted strictly.

Cato in his fourth letter took up the theme of the term of office of the proposed president and powers granted to the incumbent, and warned readers this combination "would lead to oppression and ruin."[33] Cato's fifth letter objected to biennial terms of office for proposed members of the House of Representatives on the ground annual terms are a democratic safeguard, and added the method of selecting members of the Senate will create an aristocracy, and emphasized "the slave trade is, to all intents and purposes, permanently established."[34]

In his seventh letter, Cato expressed in strong terms his distrust of "rulers."

Hitherto we have tied up our rulers in the exercise of their duties by positive restrictions—if the cord has been drawn too tight, loosen it to the necessary

extent, but not entirely unbind them—I am no enemy to placing a reasonable confidence in them; but such an unbounded one as the advocates and
framers of this new system advise you to, would be dangerous to your liberties; it has been the ruin of other governments, and will be yours, if you adopt
with all its latitudinal powers—unlimited confidence in governors as well as
individuals is frequently the parent of deception.[35]

Influenced in part by the promise of proponents, the first order of business of the new Congress would be the proposal of a series of constitutional
amendments collectively termed the Bill of Rights. The requisite number of
states ratified the proposed Constitution by June 1788, when the New York
convention convened. At this point in time, the New York delegates had to
make the decision whether the state should become a member of the union of
states. Hamilton and other supporters of the Constitution presented strong
arguments which were challenged by anti-Federalists and particularly by
Melancton Smith.[36] The proponents won the debate and also won the debate
in Virginia. The remaining noncommitted states—North Carolina and
Rhode Island and Providence Plantations—ratified the fundamental law in
the autumn of 1789 and spring of 1790, respectively.

The Framers' Motives

Charles A. Beard in a 1913 book addressed the question of the motives of
the framers of the U.S. Constitution.[37] His research uncovered the fact many
delegates to the constitutional convention were owners of government
bonds, land mortgages, and paper money that was nearly worthless, and suggested these delegates could benefit financially from the establishment of a
strong national government with taxation powers. The book was subjected
to strong criticism.

The author explained in 1935 the book had been criticized by former
president William H. Taft and a number of prominent historians, including
professor Albert Bushnell Hart who, in Beard's words, "declared that it was
little short of indecent."[38] Beard reported the text of the 1935 edition was the
same as the original text and denied the critic's charge the book accused the
delegates of seeking financial gain.

Writing in 1937, political scientist William Bennett Munro explained
the Declaration of Independence was drafted by men of wealth who clearly
were not motivated by economic gain and natural leaders would have been
excluded from the convention had wealthy persons not served in the constitutional convention.[39] Similarly, historian Robert E. Brown uncovered evidence a number of wealthy citizens in various states were opponents of the
proposed Constitution that was favored by relatively poor persons.[40] Political

scientist William H. Riker in 1964 endorsed Brown's views and suggested the
need for a strong army and navy to counteract potential threats from Great
Britain and Spain was the primary motive of delegates who favored a strong
national government.[41]

The evidence produced by the above and other scholars suggests the
delegates had multiple motives in drafting the Constitution with economic
considerations and the need for a strong military force the primary ones. Each
of these motives supported the other motive; that is, a strong army and navy
required a strong national economy and vice versa.

The Distribution of Powers

The framers of the U.S. Constitution, according to the *Federalist Papers*, did
not provide for a complete national government, but instead limited it to
expressed delegated powers and reserved all other powers not prohibited to
the states and the people including concurrent powers. The powers delegated
to this partial government, however, are substantial.

The Delegated Powers

Section 8 of Article I contained the following list of powers exercisable by
Congress:

To lay and collect taxes, duties, imposts and excises, to pay the debts
and to provide for the common defence and general welfare of the United
States, but all duties, imposts, and excises shall be uniform throughout the
United States;

To borrow money on the credit of the United States;

To regulate commerce with foreign nations, and among the several
States, and with the Indian tribes;

To establish an uniform rule of naturalization, and uniform laws on the
subject of bankruptcies throughout the United States;

To coin money, regulate the value thereof, and of foreign coin, and fix
the standards of weights and measures;

To provide for the punishment of counterfeiting the securities and current coins of the United States;

To establish post offices and post roads;

To promote the progress of sciences and useful arts, by securing for limited times to authors and inventors the exclusive right to their respective writings and discoveries;

To constitute tribunals inferior to the supreme court;

To define and punish piracies and felonies committee on the high seas, and offenses against the law of nations;

To declare war, grant letters of marque and reprisal, and make rules concerning captures on land and water;

To raise and support armies, but no appropriations of money to that use shall be for a longer term than two years;

To provide and maintain a navy;

To make rules for the government and regulation of the land and naval forces;

To provide for calling forth the militia to execute the laws of the Union, suppress insurrections, and repel invasions;

To provide for organizing, arming, and disciplining the militia, and for governing such part of them as may be employed in the service of the United States, reserving to the States respectively, the appointment of the officers, and the authority of training the militia according to the discipline prescribed by Congress;

To exercise exclusive legislation in all cases whatsoever, over such district (not exceeding ten miles square) as may, by cession of particular States, and the acceptance of Congress, become the seat of the government of the United States, and to exercise like authority over all places purchased by the consent of the legislature of the State in which the same shall be, for the erection of forts, magazines, arsenals, dock-yards, and other needful buildings; and

To make all laws which shall be necessary and proper for carrying into execution the foregoing powers, and all other powers vested by this Constitution in the Government of the United States, or in any department or officer thereof.

Relative to the sphere of economic activities, delegated powers authorizes Congress to tax and spend for the general welfare; borrow money; regulate interstate commerce, foreign commerce, and commerce with the Indian tribes; enact uniform bankruptcy laws; coin money; and establish copyright and patent systems.

Additional powers are delegated to Congress by constitutional amendments. The Thirteenth, Fourteenth, and Fifteenth Amendments grant powers to Congress to enforce their civil liberties provisions, the Sixteenth Amendment authorizes Congress to levy a graduated income tax, and the Nineteenth Amendment delegates to Congress the power to enforce the guarantee of the right of women to vote in elections. The reader should be aware Congress does not have to exercise any delegated power and did not enact a major statute based on the authority to regulate interstate commerce until 1887.

Implied and Resultant Powers. The "elastic" or "coefficient" clause of section 8 of Article I authorizes Congress to enact "all laws ... necessary and proper for carrying into execution" the powers specifically delegated to Congress "and all other powers vested by this Constitution in the Government of the United States, or in any department or officer thereof." This clause is the basis of the judicial doctrine of implied congressional powers first enunciated in *McCulloch v. Maryland* in 1819.[42] The broad judicial interpretation of the clause enlarged significantly the powers of Congress (see chapter 4).

A resultant power is one inferred from two or more specifically delegated powers. The U.S Constitution, for example, does not grant a specific power to Congress to regulate immigration, yet such a power can be inferred from the authority granted to Congress "to establish a uniform rule of naturalization" and to regulate commerce "among the several States."

The Reserved Powers

States surrendered part of their sovereignty when they ratified the U.S. Constitution which delegates several exclusive powers to Congress and the president, authorizes Congress to use its delegated powers in combination with the supremacy of the laws clause to preempt the regulatory authority of states, and prohibits the exercise of specified powers by states. To clarify that the U.S. Government is a limited government, the Tenth Amendment stipulates: "The powers not delegated to the United States, nor prohibited by it to the States are reserved to the States respectively, or to the people."

The reader should be aware the reserved powers of states are subject to preemption by treaties negotiated by the president with foreign nations and approved by a two-thirds vote of the U.S. Senate.[43] The constitutionality of a treaty entered into by the United States with the United Kingdom in 1916, which provided for the regulation of many bird species migrating between Canada and the United States, was challenged in 1920 on the ground the treaty violated the Tenth Amendment. Justice Oliver Wendell Holmes of the U.S. Supreme Court delivered its decision in *Missouri v. Holland* upholding the constitutionality of the treaty and opined:

> The treaty in question does not contravene any prohibitory words to be found in the Constitution. The only question is whether it is forbidden by some invisible radiation from the general terms of the Tenth Amendment. We must consider what this country has become in deciding what that Amendment has reserved.[44]

The North American Free Trade Agreement (NAFTA) of 1993—between Canada, the United Mexican States, and the United States—and the General

Agreements on Trade and Tariffs (GATT) of 1994 have significantly reduced the power of states to engage in economic regulation of interstate commerce.

The U.S. Constitution contains no specific references to the powers of states other than the small number of powers listed in section 10 of Article I, including entrance into interstate compacts, exercisable by states with the permission of Congress. These reserved powers may be placed in four categories, are undefinable except in the broadest of terms, and are important ones affecting the daily activities of citizens and business firms.

The Taxation Power. States possess wide discretion in designing their respective systems of taxation. They may impose any type of tax and determine the rate of taxation. Two constitutional limitations are placed on the taxing authority of states. First, no tax can be levied that significantly burdens interstate commerce. Chapter 3 explains the congressional ground rules for state taxation and chapter 4 examines judicial review of state taxes allegedly burdening interstate commerce. Second, the Constitution requires states to obtain the permission of Congress prior to levying import and export duties that may be imposed only for the expressed purpose of financing the execution of their inspection statutes with any surplus revenue dedicated to the U.S. Treasury (Art. I, §10).

The Police Power. Justice Oliver Wendell Holmes of the U.S. Supreme Court in 1911 opined this "power extends to all great public needs. It may be put forth in aid of what is sanctioned by usage, or held by the prevailing morality or strong and predominant opinion to be greatly and immediately necessary to the public welfare."[45] State legislatures have delegated this regulatory power in broad terms to general purpose local governments who employ it to regulate persons and property in order to protect and promote public health, safety, welfare, and morals.

A state or local government may exercise the police power summarily in emergency situations, but in all other situations must exercise the power in accordance with the due process of law guarantee of the Fourteenth Amendment to the U.S. Constitution that requires advance notice of a proposed governmental action, an opportunity for a hearing before the concerned governmental department, and the right to appeal the department's decision.

Chapter 5 explains that the use of the police power, along with other reserved powers, to erect interstate trade barriers. Decisions by the U.S. Supreme Court, based upon the First Amendment as incorporated into the Fourteenth Amendment, have placed nearly insurmountable obstacles in the path of subnational governments desiring to utilize the police power to suppress nude dancing, obscene literature, and pornographic films and videos.

Provision of Services. The U.S. Constitution authorizes Congress to provide only one service—the postal system—directly to citizens within states with the exception of provision of services on federally owned properties such as military installations. Subnational governments provide a wide variety of services to their respective citizens with most services provided by local governments.

These services may be grouped into six broad types. The first is public protection and involves police, fire, and emergency services. The second type is education provided by independent school districts and cities ranging from kindergarten to secondary schools. State governments operate universities and specialized schools such as a agricultural school, ceramic institute, fashion institute, or maritime academy.

The third type is public welfare services that have expanded greatly since they first were provided in the seventeenth century by towns in the Massachusetts Bay Colony. Historically, these services were the responsibility of local governments, but three states—Delaware, Massachusetts, and Vermont—assumed complete responsibility for the services.

Public health services are the fourth type and, in common with welfare services, have expanded greatly in scope. Although most such services are provided by local governments, the State of Rhode Island and Providence Plantations assumed complete responsibility for public health services in 1966.

The fifth type is transportation services. The U.S. Constitution authorizes Congress to construct post roads, yet it has not done so and has provided grants-in-aid to state governments to construct such roads. Most highways in cities, towns, and villages are the responsibility of local governments with the exception of major state and interstate highways. Many local governments operate bus systems and large cities or state public authorities operate subway systems. A number of authorities also operate bus systems.

Agricultural, conservation, and recreational services are the final type of service. Each state conducts agricultural research, promotes soil conservation, and provides assistance to farmers and citizens; develops water resources including reservoirs of drinking water; operates parks and recreational facilities; and engages in fish and game stocking.

The Local Government System. The newly independent states possessed complete control over their respective local government system as a unitary relationship existed between the two planes of government. Courts applied the *ultra vires* rule and defined local governments as creatures of the state subject to modification at will by the state legislature or even abolished.[46] A reform movement, termed "home rule," developed strength in the latter half of the nineteenth century and most state constitutions were amended to place one or more restrictions upon the power of the state legislature to intervene in the affairs of general purpose local governments.

Constitutions in a number of states were amended, commencing in the 1920s, to establish an *Imperium in Imperio* or federal system within a state. Depending upon the state, the state constitution granted cities and other specified local governments complete control over their organizational structure, property, and local affairs. Constitutional amendments, commencing in the 1950s, were adopted in many states devolving broad powers upon general purpose local governments subject to preemption by general law. The "home rule" movement has achieved considerable success. Nevertheless, the state legislature continues to exercise significant supervisory powers over local governments in all states.

An Overview

Interstate economic relations date to the Declaration of Independence in 1776 and apparently were generally cooperative during the prosecution of the Revolutionary War. As noted, such relations degenerated under the Articles of Confederation and Perpetual Union, and pressures grew for the amendment of the articles, among other purposes, to address the problems created by interstate-trade barriers. To resolve these problems, the U.S. Constitution grants Congress broad regulatory authority over commerce among the several states, with foreign nations, and with the Indian tribes. Congress has not fully exercised its interstate-commerce regulatory authority and interstate-trade barriers continue to be erected by states. On the other hand, Congress has employed incentives to encourage states to cooperate with each other on many matters.[47]

Chapter 2 examines seven provisions in the U.S. Constitution, as interpreted by the U.S. Supreme Court, which establish ground rules for interstate economic relations and an eighth ground rule promulgated by the U.S. Supreme Court.

Chapter 3 focuses on the interstate economic relations ground rules enacted by Congress, examines the limits of congressional powers, and addresses the question of why Congress has not employed its interstate-regulatory powers more fully.

The subject of chapter 4 is judicial ground rules for interstate economic relations. The U.S. Supreme Court annually is called upon to resolve a number of disputes between states involving economic matters.

Chapter 5 reviews direct and indirect interstate trade barriers based upon the police power, licensing, and taxation power of the states, the importance of the barriers, and their removal by interstate reciprocity agreements, congressional preemption statutes, and court decisions.

Interstate tax revenue competition is described and analyzed in chapter 6. Congress could play a greater role in curbing certain types of revenue competition while the U.S. Supreme Court, by default, is requested by plaintiffs to strike down certain types of competition as violative of the U.S. Constitution.

Chapter 7 focuses on interstate competition for business firms, professional sports franchises, tourists, and gamblers. Competition by states to attract tourists commenced with the development of railroad passenger service and accentuated with the advent of the motor vehicle. Interstate competition for business firms began in earnest shortly after the conclusion of World War II. Competition for professional sports franchises and gamblers is a more recent development.

The subject of chapter 8 is direct and indirect interstate economic cooperation, by means of interstate compacts and interstate administrative agreements, involving all subjects within the constitutional competence of the states.

The concluding chapter is a prescriptive one offering recommendations to Congress to play a more significant role as a innovator and facilitator of cooperative interstate economic relations. Additional recommendations are directed to the president and state governments, and a note is made of the important role played by national associations of state government administrators in promoting cooperative interstate economic relations.

CHAPTER 2

Constitutional Economic Relations Rules

Chapter 1 briefly noted that the U.S. Constitution contains seven provisions—equal protection of the laws, full faith and credit, interstate compacts, interstate free trade, interstate rendition, interstate suits, and privileges and immunities—that serve as ground rules governing relations between sister states and include ones borrowed from the Articles of Confederation and Perpetual Union. The legal equality of states—an eighth rule—was established by the U.S. Supreme Court. The constitutional ground rules are expressed in general terms and necessitate clarification by Congress and/or the U.S. Supreme Court.

Interstate economic relations during the confederacy suffered from two principal defects. The Articles of Confederation and Perpetual Union contained no mechanism for resolving major legal disputes between sister states and Congress was not authorized to regulate interstate commerce. Disputes at the time involved primarily conflicting state territorial claims. Although colonists resented British mercantilistic policies, the newly established state governments erected many trade barriers within three to four years of the end of the Revolutionary War. The U.S. Constitution seeks to overcome these defects by authorizing the U.S. Supreme Court to conduct an original trial if one state sues another state and by delegating power to Congress to regulate interstate commerce.

Equal Protection of the Laws

The U.S. Constitution did not contain this guarantee until 1868 when the Fourteenth Amendment was ratified by the requisite three-fourths of the states. Congress proposed and states ratified three reconstruction amendments subsequent to the Civil War. The Thirteenth Amendment, ratified in 1865, was designed to protect African-American citizens by guaranteeing "[n]either slavery nor involuntary servitude, except as a punishment for crime whereof the party shall have been duly convicted, shall exist within the United States, or any place subject to their jurisdiction."

It soon became evident the amendment did not offer adequate protection for the former slaves. In the south, African Americans were excluded from a number of towns unless they were engaged as menial servants, often not allowed to purchase or own land they cultivated, were ineligible to present testimony in court if the case involved a white person, and faced with large fines if convicted of loitering or vagrancy. Congress reacted by proposing in 1866 the Fourteenth Amendment that forbids states to "deny to any person within its jurisdiction the equal protection of the laws."

The amendment also contains two other guarantees protecting citizens—due process of law and privileges and immunities. The latter provision has been held by the U.S. Supreme Court to offer protection only to persons and not corporations, which nevertheless can file suit against a state if its statutes or administrative regulations allegedly deny them equal protection of the laws.[1]

A state legislature, however, is free to treat corporations differently provided the statute is based upon a reasonable classification and all corporations of the same class are treated in the identical manner. Owners of residential property are taxed on an ad valorem basis, whereas the constitutionality of state taxation of railroad companies based upon their gross income has been upheld against equal protection challenges. Similarly, a 1892 state statute prohibiting mining companies from operating stores for the benefit of their employees was invalidated on the equal protection grounds because the restriction applied to no other employers.

The U.S. Supreme Court in 1886 decided *Santa Clara County v. Southern Pacific Rail Road* on state-law grounds, but opined corporations are "persons" protected by the equal protection of the laws clause of the Fourteenth Amendment.[2] Subsequently, the court opined "[I]t is well settled that corporations are persons within the provisions of the Fourteenth Amendment. . . . A state has no more power to deny corporations the equal protection of the law than it does individual citizens.[3] In 1923, the court ruled that the arbitrary assessment of the property of a bridge company at full value while other property is assessed at a lower percentage of full value is a denial of equal protection of the laws.[4]

The clause, nevertheless, for decades played a relatively minor role in protecting nonresident citizens and foreign corporations (chartered in a sister state) from discriminatory statutes and administrative rules and regulations. Relief typically was sought by foreign business corporations on the ground that state action violated the interstate commerce clause because of the court's decision in 1886 holding a foreign corporation could not use the equal protection clause to challenge a state imposed tax on the privilege of conducting business in the state.[5] In 1981, the court overturned this decision in a case involving retaliatory state tax in which the plaintiff insurance company alleged a California tax violated the interstate commerce and equal protection clauses of the U.S. Constitution. The court held the tax could not be challenged on the ground of violating the interstate commerce clause because Congress in the *McCarran Ferguson Act of 1945* authorized state regulation of the insurance industry.[6] Subsequently, the equal protection of the laws clause has been cited in a number of alleged discriminatory tax cases (see chapter 5).

Full Faith and Credit

This nationalizing clause, extending the geographical reach of the legal documents of a state, is traceable in origin to letters of credence, based upon the principle of comity or reciprocity, employed in diplomatic practice during the Middle Ages. Nation states have to decide whether they should accord legal recognition to the statutes, official records, and judicial proceedings of other nations. In general, a nation extends such recognition provided other nations reciprocate in extending recognition to its legal documents. States in a confederal or federal system, unless mandated by a constitution, similarly have to decide whether to recognize the statutes, records, and proceedings of sister states.

The use of full faith and credit in the United States dates to a small number of Colonial legislative acts. The 1659 Connecticut Legislature extended full faith and credit to other states provided they reciprocated, the 1715 Maryland Legislature recognized fully court judgments on debts in sister states, the 1731 South Carolina Legislature granted full faith and credit to bonds, deeds, and records of other colonies, and the 1774 Massachusetts General Court accorded similar full faith and credit to debt judgments of courts in sister colonies.[7]

Following independence, the Second Continental Congress endorsed a resolution providing "full faith and credit shall be given in each of these states to the records, acts, and judicial proceedings of the courts and magistrates of every other state" and included a full faith and credit provision (Article IV) in its proposed Articles of Confederation and Perpetual Union which became effective in 1781.

The drafters of the U.S. Constitution included a nearly identical clause in Article IV, applicable only to sister states and not foreign nations, and authorized Congress to prescribe by general law "the manner in which such acts, records, and proceedings shall be proved, and the effect thereof." The grant of enforcement power to Congress was described by James Madison in *The Federalist Number* 42 as "an evident and valuable improvement on the clause relating to this subject in the Articles of Confederation.[8] This clause was viewed by delegates as essential for the economic and political success of the proposed union and appears to mandate each state to fully recognize the civil actions of sister states, but the conflict of laws of the member states of the Union makes essential judicial determination in a specific case of which law applies.

In 1928, Henry J. Friendly discovered evidence the assignment of diversity of citizenship jurisdiction to U.S. courts had the purpose of protecting creditors in a state "against legislation favorable to debtors" in a sister state.[9] He found, however, that the domestic party won only two of nine such court cases in Connecticut courts during the confederacy.[10]

The complexity and importance of the guarantee can not be appreciated fully unless it is read in conjunction with the grant of diversity of citizenship jurisdiction to U.S. courts in section 2 of Article III of the U.S. Constitution. A state or a federal court in addressing a conflict between the statutes of two states is directed by a literal reading of the full faith and credit clause to displace the law of state A with the law of state B. The semi-sovereignty of each state is infringed whenever a court applies to the state the law of a sister state. The U.S. Supreme Court in 1818 opined the clause requires federal courts to give the same full faith and credit to judgment of state courts that the latter courts are required to give to judgment of sister state courts.[11]

Congressional Clarification

Congress somewhat surprisingly seldom employs its authority to expand the constitutional provision and enforce the full faith and credit guaranty. Congress in 1790 and 1804 enacted statutes prescribing the method to be utilized in authenticating public acts and records with respect to their extrastate effect. The first statute stipulates "records and judicial proceedings authenticated shall have such faith and credit given to them in every court within the United States, as they have by law or usage in the courts of the states from where the said records are or shall be taken."[12] The second statute extends full faith and credits to acts of state legislatures and establishes a second method of exemplification of nonjudicial records by prescribing their effect in terms similar to those employed in the first statute.[13]

Congress did not enact a new statute relating to the guarantee until a full faith and credit provision relating to child custody determinations was included in the *Parental Kidnapping Prevention Act of 1980*.[14] Fourteen years later, Congress enacted a statute establishing standards state courts must following in determining whether they have jurisdiction to issue a child support order and the effect they must give to such orders issued by sister state courts.[15] The 1994 Hawaiian Supreme Court's interpretation of the state constitution as permitting the marriage of two persons of the same sex generated controversy throughout the United States and resulted in Congress enacting the *Defense of Marriage Act of 1996* defining a marriage as "a legal union between one man and one woman as husband and wife" and the term "spouse" as "a person of the opposite sex who is husband or a wife," and authorizing states to deny full faith and credit to a marriage certificate of two persons of the same sex.[16] In 2000, Congress included in the *Violence Against Women Act* a full faith and credit enforcement of protection orders section.[17] Congress to date has enacted no additional full faith and credit statutes.

A statute may be enacted by a state legislature containing less stringent standards than the ones established by Congress for authentication of judicial proceedings, but may not deny its courts jurisdiction over cases involving rights and duties created under the statutes of a sister state. Civil judgments of sister state courts have automatic validity in all states, but a state court may conduct an inquiry for the purpose of determining whether the sister state court had jurisdiction to issue the decision. If a ruling was obtained by fraud or a court lacked jurisdiction to render a ruling, its decision is not subject to the full faith and credit guarantee. *Lex loci contractus* provides the law of the state in which a contract or deed is witnessed and executed is binding in all states regardless of the fact states require a varying number of witnesses. Similarly, a state may not recognize a debt that is the result of gambling, yet the state must accord full faith and credit to a court judgment on a gambling debt incurred in a sister state.

Supreme Court Clarification

The early full faith and credit cases decided by the U.S. Supreme Court related only to decisions of courts of sister states. The court in 1813 opined foreign state judgments had conclusive effect in the courts of sister states.[18] The court often has invalidated choice of law decisions as illustrated by a 1866 decision striking down New York's application of its law in determining the effect to be given to an Illinois court judgment.[19] The importance of the clause to interstate economic relations was highlighted in 1897 when the court opined a Louisiana statute could not be applied to a contract entered into by a Louisiana citizen covering his property in the state and a New York chartered insurance company because the contract was made in New York.[20]

The court's rulings were attacked by a number of legal experts in the 1930s who maintained individual states had legitimate claims with respect to interstate events and the court's opinions infringed the semi-sovereign powers of states. The court, in a 1935 case involving employees of a California firm injured in Alaska, noted the need for accommodation of the respective interests of the two states when their respective statutes on a given subject were in conflict. The issue was whether the Alaska or California workmen's compensation statute should be applied. The court opined "every state is entitled to enforce in its own courts its own statutes" and the challenger had the burden of proof to demonstrate, on a rational basis, the conflicting interests of the sister state are superior to the conflicting interests of the forum state.[21]

A literal interpretation of the clause would mandate courts of one state to replace the statutes enacted by its legislature in favor of the statutes of a sister state in full faith and credit cases. The court in 1939 held judicial forums in one state were not required to consider the conflicting interests of other states since the federal system does not allow the use of the full faith and credit clause to compel "a state to substitute the statutes of other states for its own statutes dealing with a subject matter concerning which it is competent to legislate."[22] In 1951, the court explained "the principal purpose of the clause still remains to facilitate enforcement of judgments rendered in another jurisdiction, rather than to give effect to statutes enacted in other states."[23] Reviewing these decisions in 1987, James R. Pielemeir commented there had been "a vast expansion of the scope of personal jurisdiction and a noticeably increased tendency by the states . . . to apply their own law in conflicts settings. The combination of these developments has dramatically heightened the opportunities for plaintiffs to shop for favorable forums and laws."[24]

The full faith and credit clause applies only to civil matters. The U.S. Supreme Court in 1985 ruled the dual sovereignty doctrine allows separate prosecution in Alabama and Georgia for the murder of the same individual.[25] Nevertheless, an individual occasionally invokes the clause in a criminal case. Ronald Gillis, was indicted, tried, and acquitted of a murder charge in Delaware, but latter was convicted in Maryland of murdering the same individual. He argued the Maryland prosecution violated the full faith and credit clause by failing to accord recognition to his Delaware acquittal. The Maryland Court of Appeals in 1993 rejected the argument by applying the dual sovereignty rationale.[26]

The absence of congressional statutes, except in child support cases, mandating in other than general terms the effect of the full faith and credit clause has led to the U.S. Supreme Court fashioning a new common law in its decisions interpreting clause. The U.S. Constitution (Art. IV, §4) guarantees each state will have a republican or representative form of government. This guarantee conflicts with the command of the full faith and credit clause that the statutes of each state be extended *extraterritorum* in certain court cases because the laws of one state will be displaced by the laws of a sister state. A constitutional charge has been placed by the constitution upon Congress to "prescribe the manner in which . . ." the "acts, records, and proceedings shall be proved, and the effect thereof" (Art. I, §1). If Congress exercises this power more fully, states and their citizens would be accorded the opportunity of employing the political process to influence congressional acts prescribing the manner.

Interstate Compacts

Constitutional authorization (Art. I, §10) for states to enter into permanent or temporary interstate agreements and compacts has proven to be effective in resolving many disputes, including boundary ones, between sister states and promoting cooperation by sister states on a regional and a national basis that often has great economic benefits (see chapter 8). Similar to Article IV of the Articles of Confederation and Perpetual Union, the constitutional compact clause by negative implication allows states to enter into legally binding contracts subject to congressional approval. Such compacts are protected by the constitution's prohibition of state impairment of contracts (Art. I, §10). Congress in 1949 granted consent to the Northeastern Interstate Forest Fire Protection Compact which has the distinction of being the first compact to authorize a Canadian province contiguous to a compact to join the compact.[27] Subsequently, several compacts were entered into by groups of states with several or all Canadian provinces.[28]

The clause potentially is of great economic and political importance, yet delegates to the Philadelphia Constitution Convention did not debate it. James Madison in the *Federalist* no. 44 commented on the constitutional restriction on the power of states over imports and exports (Art. I, §10) and added: "the remaining particulars of this clause," including interstate compacts, "fall within reasonings which are either so obvious, or have been so fully developed, that they may be passed over with remark."[29]

A literal interpretation of the authorizing constitutional clause makes any execution of an interstate compact or agreement conditional upon the consent of Congress. The U.S. Supreme Court in 1893 clarified the clause by opining it only applies to political compacts that increase "the political power or influence" of the compacting states or intrude "upon the full and free exercise of federal authority."[30] A further clarification was made in 1939 when the court ruled a reciprocal sales tax agreement between Kentucky and Ohio was a nonpolitical agreement not needing congressional consent.[31] The United States Steel Corporation challenged the constitutionality of the Multistate Tax Compact, but in 1978 the U.S. Supreme Court rejected the challenge by ruling the compact does not "authorize the member states to exercise any powers they could not exercise in its absence. . . ."[32]

The Constitution is silent relative to the timing of congressional consent. Congress has granted such consent prior to and subsequent to the enactment of a compact by state legislature, and may grant consent-in-advance to states to enter into specified types of compact. In 1911 Congress gave its first consent-in-advance to states to enter into covenants to conserve "the forests and water supply" of the compacting states.[33] Although the *Resource Conservation and Recovery Act of 1976* grants consent-in-advance to states to enter into solid waste compacts, such compacts do not become effective until they are submitted to and receive the consent of Congress.[34]

The Constitution also is silent relative to whether or not congressional consent makes a compact federal law. Until 1981 federal courts were bound by a 1874 decision of the U.S. Supreme Court, which held that they must accept the interpretation of state law by the state's highest court.[35] In 1981 the court opined a compact became federal law upon receipt of congressional consent.[36] Hence, the court is free to ignore the interpretation of a state enacted compact by a state's highest court.

Today, there are a significant number of interstate compacts of great economic importance, such as the two Colorado River compacts, and an exceptionally large number of formal and informal interstate administrative agreements executed without congressional consent (see chapter 8). Many of the agreements promote economic development.

Interstate Free Trade

The spectacular success of the economic union established by the U.S. Constitution is attributable in large measure to the grant of power to Congress to "regulate commerce with foreign nations, and among the several States, and with the Indian tribes . . ." (Art. I, §8). The effectiveness of this power has been enhanced substantially by the U.S. Supreme Court's broad definition of interstate commerce and the court's development of the dormant commerce clause doctrine.

As noted in chapter 1, one of the gravest defects of the Articles of Confederation and Perpetual Union was the inability of the unicameral Congress to regulate commerce among the several states and remove state erected trade barriers. Writing in the *Federalist* number 15, Alexander Hamilton emphasized, "[I]t is indeed evident, on the most superficial view, that there is no object, either as it respects the interest of trade or finance, that more strongly demands a federal superintendence. The want of it has already operated as bar to the formation of beneficial treaties with foreign powers, and has given occasions of dissatisfaction between the States."[37] Hamilton, among other things, was referring to restraints on interstate commerce illustrated by the State of Rhode Island and Providence Plantations raising adequate revenues to finance its operations from duties levied at a single port on goods entering from sister states.

The broad congressional power to regulate interstate commerce (Art. I, §8) is supplemented by the clause (Art. I, §10) forbidding states to levy tonnage duties on marine ships or to impose import and export duties except to raise funds to finance their inspection program with any surplus funds dedicated to the U.S. Treasury. Congress has been slow in exercising its economic intercourse power and waited nearly 100 years to enact an *Act to Regulate Commerce* popularly known as the Interstate Commerce Act of 1887.[38] The U.S. Supreme Court, in the absence of congressional regulation of interstate commerce, developed its dormant commerce clause doctrine in 1824 by invalidating mercantilistic state statutes burdening commerce among sister states on the ground they offended the interstate commerce clause of the U.S. Constitution (see chapter 3). Impediments to interstate free trade also can be removed by state legislatures enacting parallel, reciprocity, and uniform statutes.

Interstate Rendition

A confederal or a federal system must establish procedures for the interstate rendition of fugitives from justice to prevent criminals or individuals charged with crimes, including economic ones, from escaping justice by fleeing to another state. Such nonself-executing procedures were contained in Article IV of the Articles of Confederation and Perpetual Union and were incorporated into Article IV of the U.S. Constitution which does not explicitly authorize Congress to determine the manner of rendering a fugitive to the demanding state.

Congressional Clarification

Congress enacted a 1793 statute, based on the full faith and credit and rendition clauses, providing only the governor of the state, district, or territory may request the governor of the asylum state, district, or territory to apprehend and return the fugitive to the demanding governmental unit and the constitutionality of the act, which lacks an enforcement provision, was upheld by the U.S. Supreme Court in 1842.[39]

The governor of the asylum state has the duty of determining who is a fugitive from justice and a fugitive rendered to the demanding state can be tried for any offense he committed even if it was not in the demanding state governor's requisition.[40] Furthermore, it is immaterial whether the offense in the demanding state is an offense in the asylum state. The requesting state is responsible for collecting and transporting the fugitive and for all associated costs incurred in the fugitive's arrest, incarceration, and transportation. The arrest and detention of a fugitive from justice may be regulated by a state statute provided it does not conflict with the national rendition act.

Congress utilized its power to regulate interstate commerce to enact the *Fugitive Felon and Witness Act of 1934* to assist states to regain custody of fugitives from justice.[41] The act makes it a federal crime for a person to travel in foreign or interstate commerce to avoid confinement after conviction or prosecution for specified crimes or testifying in a criminal court in a case where the offense is punishable by incarceration in a state prison.

Supreme Court Clarification

The U.S. Supreme Court did not interpret the rendition clause until the court issued its famous 1861 "run away slave" decision in *Kentucky v. Dennison* noting the clause was designed to promote harmonious relations between states by providing mutual assistance.[42] The court's decision, based upon its original jurisdiction, involved a petition for issuance of a writ of mandamus directing the Ohio governor to return to Kentucky a freed slave charged with the crime of assisting a Kentucky slave to escape. The state attorney general advised the governor the constitution's rendition clause applied only to actions defined as crimes by the Ohio General Assembly. This interpretation was rejected by the U.S. Supreme Court whose decision opined it was the clear intent of the clause "to include every offense made punishable by the law of the state in which it was committed."[43]

　　The court, however, added the constitutional words—a fugitive "shall on demand of the executive authority of the state from which he fled, be delivered up, to be removed to the state having jurisdiction of the crime"—were "not used as mandatory and compulsory, but as declaratory of the moral duty" of the asylum state governor to return the fugitive.[44] This precedent led to governors occasionally refusing to return a fugitive on various grounds including the refusal of the governor of the demanding state at an earlier date to render a fugitive. The court did not reverse its 1861 decision until 1987 when it held "there is no justification for distinguishing the duty to deliver fugitives from the many other species of constitutional duty enforceable in the federal courts. . . . Because the duty is directly imposed upon the states by the Constitution itself, there can be no need to weigh the performance of the federal obligation against the powers reserved to the states under the Tenth Amendment."[45]

Interstate Suits

The 1787 constitutional convention addressed one of the great defects of the Articles of Confederation and Perpetual Union—the lack of an impartial judicial form to resolve interstate disputes—by including in the U.S. Constitution (Art. III, §2) a nonexclusive grant of original (trial) jurisdiction to the U.S. Supreme Court in all cases involving interstate suits. Boundary disputes in particular were common following the Declaration of Independence and no mechanism other than direct state negotiations was available to resolve the disputes until the U.S. Constitution was ratified. Today, many interstate disputes involve issues of great economic as well as political importance.

The *Judiciary Act of 1789* made the constitutional grant of authority to the U.S. Supreme Court to try interstate suits exclusive and authorized it to promulgate rules for the conduct of business in all U.S. courts.[46] The court determined the constitutional grant of original jurisdiction would be exercised on a discretionary basis even though the grant appears to make exercise of the jurisdiction mandatory. In 1905, the court announced it would not exercise original jurisdiction over a suit by one state against a sister state unless the case was of serious magnitude.[47] The court reiterated in 1976 its original jurisdiction would be invoked sparingly and disputant states should engage in negotiations to reach a settlement.[48]

Rule 17, promulgated by the U.S. Supreme Court, establishes the procedure to be followed by a state seeking to invoke the court's original jurisdiction. The state is required to file, with the clerk of the court, a motion and supporting brief requesting permission of the court to file an original jurisdiction suit. A respondent brief is filed by the allegedly offending state. At this point, the court typically appoints a special master charged with collecting evidence from the disputing states and developing recommendations pertaining to case facts and the law that may persuade the party states to reach a settlement out of court.

Should the disputing states fail to negotiate a settlement, each state submits a brief to the court that will hold an oral hearing prior to its determination of whether to conduct a trial. Three court established criteria serve as the basis for the court's determination. First, each disputant state must be a genuine party and may not act on behalf of a private or a municipal corporation. The court in 1976, for example, rejected a challenge by Pennsylvania of the New Jersey commuter income tax because the petition was "nothing more than a collectivity of private suits against New Jersey" seeking the refund of income taxes.[49]

Second, the court will not exercise its original jurisdiction unless evidence reveals the controversy between the states is justiciable and requires adjudication by a law court. In 1939, the court explained there must be evidence one state has suffered a wrong as the result of the action of another state or "is asserting a right against the other state which is susceptible of judicial enforcement" in accordance with the common law or equity.[50]

The third criterion is appropriateness. In 1971, the court enunciated this doctrine to relieve a crowded docket in *Ohio v. Wyandotte Chemicals Corporation*.[51] The court extended the criterion to suits between states. In deciding whether or not a case is appropriate, the court considers the involved parties, the seriousness of the subject matter, and the availability of another judicial forum. The court invokes its original jurisdiction if the contending states are acting in their sovereign capacity, the dispute is a major one, and there is no alternative judicial forum. Relative to the later, in 1976 the court rejected a motion by Arizona to invoke the court's original jurisdiction and adjudicate the state's controversy with New Mexico because Arizona's public utilities had filed a similar suit raising the identical question in a New Mexico court.[52]

In adjudicating interstate disputes, the U.S. Supreme Court acts as an international tribunal and noted in 1902 that it applies "federal law, state law, and international law, as the exigencies of the particular case may demands."[53] The court has effectively established an interstate common law by synthesizing the common law and international law.

Privileges and Immunities

This clause appears twice in the U.S. Constitution in Article IV, §2 and the Fourteenth Amendment, §1. The guarantee first appeared in the 1606 royal charter granted to the Virginia Company and a similar guarantee subsequently was included in the Articles of Confederation and Perpetual Union (Art. IV). A nearly identically worded privileges and immunities clause was incorporated into the U.S. Constitution (Art. IV, §2) and the general terms of the clause suggest that each citizen is entitled to equal privileges and immunities. Alexander Hamilton advocated the establishment of a national judiciary and specifically referred to the role it would play in impartially interpreting and enforcing the guarantee of interstate privileges and immunities.[54] Brutus, on the other hand, contended the guarantee will mean a "citizen of one state . . . will be a citizen of every state."[55]

The Article IV full faith and credit guarantee and the privileges and immunities guarantee seek to establish an interstate citizenship by preventing a state legislature from favoring its citizens over citizens of sister states. The purpose of the Fourteenth Amendment's privileges and immunities clause is protection of individuals and groups of citizens of a state against discrimination by their state legislature.

Congress is not granted authority by the U.S. Constitution to clarify the Article IV guarantee, and courts are called upon to provide the needed clarification. This guarantee, in common with the full faith and credit guarantee, involves a conflict of laws necessitating judicial clarification since each state is free to define privileges and immunities provided they do not abridge the ones guaranteed by the Fourteenth Amendment. The U.S. Supreme Court in 1856 expressed the opinion "it is safer and more in accordance with the duty of a judicial tribunal to leave its meaning to be determined, in each case, upon a view of the particular rights asserted and denied therein."[56]

Presiding over a trial in the Circuit Court for the Eastern District of Pennsylvania, U.S. Supreme Court Justice Bushrod Washington described in 1823 the guarantee as a fundamental one and listed examples of privileges—acquisition and possession of property, right to travel, tax equity, among others—protected by the constitutional guarantee and his decisions was cited subsequently in a number of court decisions.[57] The U.S. Supreme Court in 1868 issued a major decision holding nonresidents possess only the privileges and immunities granted to the residents of the state of sojourn.[58] The court specifically held:

> It was undoubtedly the object of the clause in question to place citizens of each State upon the same footing with citizens of other States, so far as the advantages resulting from citizenship in these States are concerned. It relieves them from the disabilities of alienage in other States; it inhibits discriminating legislation against them by other States; it gives them the right of free ingress into other States; it insures to them in other States the same freedom possessed by citizens of those States in the acquisition and enjoyment of property and in the pursuit of happiness; and it secures to them the equal protection of the laws.[59]

However, a person visiting a state, under this ruling, has no constitutional basis for demanding the state extend all privileges and immunities extended by the person's home state. Furthermore, only privileges attributable to citizenship are secured by the clause and rights attached by law of the state where contracts are made or executed are not privileges of a citizen protected by the constitutional clause. It is important to note the court opined in 1948 the clause does not prevent a state from treating persons differently provided "there are perfectly valid independent reasons" for the different treatment.[60]

Corporations

The privileges and immunities clause (Art. IV) of the Articles of Confederation and Perpetual Union protected "all the privileges of trade and commerce. . . ." No such protection is offered to trade and commerce by the privileges and immunities clause of the U.S. Constitution. The drafters of the fundamental law apparently concluded the grant of power to Congress to regulate interstate commerce made unnecessary such a guarantee.

The U.S. Supreme Court, in interpreting the constitutional clause in 1839, emphasized the clause applies only to natural persons and a corporation is not entitled to privileges and immunities since it dwells only "in the place of its creation, and can not migrate to another sovereignty."[61] In addition, the court has held associations are not entitled to the privileges and immunities guaranteed to citizens.[62] A state in general may discriminate against foreign and alien corporations (chartered in another nation), including prohibiting them to conduct business within the state, without violating the privileges and immunities clause, but might be subject to retaliation by other states. State license fees imposed and tax rates levied on these corporations tend to be higher than ones imposed and levied on domestic corporations.

Foreign and alien corporations are not without constitutional protection against fee and tax discrimination if it violates the equal protection of the law clause and/or the interstate commerce clause. In 1985 the Metropolitan Life Insurance Company sued Alabama on the ground the state imposed a substantially higher gross premium tax rate on foreign and alien insurance companies than the rate imposed on domestic insurance companies, which was in violation of the equal protection of the laws clause.[63] The company was barred from suing the state on the ground of violation of the interstate commerce clause because the *McCarran-Ferguson Act of 1945* devolved the power to regulate the insurance industry to the states.[64]

Taxation

State legislatures and Congress possess the concurrent power of taxation essential for them to be viable political entities. The systems of taxation employed by the various states are inherently complex and differ substantially from state to state depending upon the ingenuity of the state legislature, which, in its attempts to maximize state revenues, accidentally or deliberately may utilize its taxation power to discriminate against citizens of sister states.

The fact nonresidents have no influence in a sister state legislature has led the U.S. Supreme Court, in exercising its appellate jurisdiction, to examine more closely the allegations that a privilege tax levied on residents of a sister state to engage in a business violates the guarantee of interstate privileges and immunities. The first major decision in such a case was rendered by the court in 1870 when it struck down a Maryland license fee imposed annually on nonresidents for the privilege of trading in non-Maryland manufactured goods. The $300 fee imposed on nonresidents was held to be discriminatory as the fee imposed on Maryland residents was $15 to $150 depending upon the respective size of their inventory.[65] In rendering its verdict, the court noted "[a]n attempt will not be made to define the words 'privileges and immunities,' or to specify the rights which they are intended to secure and protect beyond what may be necessary to the decision of the case before the court."[66]

A New York State nonresident income tax was held by the U.S. Supreme Court in 1920 to be in violation of the clause because nonresident taxpayers were not granted the same personal exemptions as resident taxpayers.[67] In 1948, the court reiterated its determination to protect nonresidents from discrimination in violation of the privileges and immunity clause by invalidating a significantly higher license fee imposed on nonresident owners of shrimp boats compared to the fee imposed on resident owners of such boats.[68]

In 1975 the court struck down on privileges and immunities grounds a New Hampshire commuter-income tax that also allegedly violated the equal protection of the laws clause of the U.S. Constitution. The New Hampshire statute was an ingenious one containing the following provisions:

> A tax is hereby imposed upon every taxable nonresident, which shall be levied, collected and paid annually at the rate of four percent of their New Hampshire derived income . . . less an exemption of two thousand dollars; provided, however, that if the tax hereby imposed exceeds the tax which would be imposed upon such income by the state of residence, if such income were earned in such state, the tax hereby imposed shall be reduced to equal the tax which would be imposed by such other state.[69]

Although the statute imposed an identical tax on residents, they were exempted from paying the tax if their income was "subject to a tax in the state in which it is derived . . ." or "such income is exempt from taxation because of statutory or constitutional provisions in the state in which it is derived, or . . . the state in which it is derived does not impose an income tax on such income. . . ."[70] This wording exempted residents from paying the New Hampshire tax on their domestic and foreign income.

The commuter income tax was defended by the New Hampshire Attorney General who maintained Maine residents employed in New Hampshire did not have an onerous burden placed on them since their home state grants a tax credit to residents for income taxes paid to other states. The Maine State Legislature could have, but did not repeal the tax credit that was diverting tax revenues from Maine to New Hampshire. The court dismissed the New Hampshire argument that no onerous burden was placed on Maine taxpayers by observing the Maine tax credit did not cure the constitutional discriminatory defect of the New Hampshire statute.[71]

Beneficial Services

Does the privileges and immunities clause of the U.S. Constitution entitled nonresidents to share in the beneficial services and economic resources of a state. Although U.S. Supreme Court Justice Bushrod Washington interpreted the guarantee as encompassing a wide variety of privileges, he rejected the proposition "the citizens of several states are permitted to participate in all the rights which belong exclusively to the citizens of any other state, merely upon the ground that they are enjoyed by those citizens; much less, that in regulating the use of the common property of the citizens of such state, the legislature is bound to extend to the citizens of all the other states the same advantages as are secured to their own citizens."[72]

Acting in its appellate capacity, the U.S. Supreme Court in 1876 applied Justice Washington's decision to a specific case involving the constitutionality of a Virginia law forbidding nonresidents to plant oysters in the waters of the Commonwealth. The court opined nonresidents "are not invested by this clause of the constitution with any interest in the common property of the citizens of another state . . ."[73]

The court in the early 1970s reviewed two lower court decisions upholding the constitutionality of state durational residency requirements as a condition for students to qualify for in-state tuition at state-operated colleges and universities. These decisions were affirmed summarily on the ground students from sister states did not pay taxes in the state where the university is located prior to attending it and taxes paid subsequently do not equal the differential between resident student and nonresident student tuition.[74]

In 1978, the court similarly upheld the constitutionality of a state nonresident hunting license fee that was significantly higher than the resident license fee by opining nonresidents do not have a fundamental right to a license to hunt Elk in Montana.[75]

Political and Other Privileges

Are nonresidents of a state eligible to be elected by its voters? The answer to this question is provided in part by sections 2–3 of Article I of the U.S. Constitution, which specifies that a member of the U.S. House of Representatives or Senate must be a resident of the state he/she is representing. In 1898, the U.S. Supreme Court upheld the right of a state, by a uniform constitutional or statutory provision, to establish a durational residency requirement as a condition for voting or election to public office.[76] The court in 1972 opined a state may restrict the voting franchise to residents and in 1978 upheld the right of a state to limit elective public offices to residents.[77] Although the court had typically struck down residency requirements for appointive officers, it ruled in 1978 a New York law restricting appointment of members of the state police to U.S. citizens did not violate the privileges and immunities clause of the U.S. Constitution.[78]

Over the years, state legislatures have established a durational residency requirement as a condition of eligibility to being granted the privilege of practicing a profession such as law or medicine and courts have validated the requirement. In general, state courts have ruled a state may utilize its police power to protect public health by regulating the practice of dentistry or medicine and such practice is not a privilege guaranteed by Article IV of the U.S. Constitution.[79] In a concurring opinion, Justice Joseph P. Bradley of the U.S. Supreme Court explained in 1872 that state legislatures possess the prerogative to prescribe regulations founded in nature, reason, and experience for the due admission of qualified persons to professions and callings demanding special skill and confidence. This fairly belongs to the police power of the state."[80]

Durational requirements obviously have an effect on interstate commerce in a number of instances. The U.S. Supreme Court in 1919 upheld the constitutionality of a state statute permitting the licensing as insurance agents of only residents of the state who have been licensed insurance agents in the state for a minimum of two years.[81] In 1948, Chief Justice Fred M. Vinson of the U.S. Supreme Court explained the constitutional guarantee is relative, not an absolute, and does not prevent a state from discriminating against citizens of sister states if "there are perfectly valid independent reasons" for the discrimination.[82]

The U.S. Supreme Court, however, issued a major decision on the subject of such requirements in 1985 when it ruled "the practice of law falls within the ambit of the Privileges and Immunities Clause."[83] A Vermont attorney, who resided within 1,200 feet of the New Hampshire boundary, met all requirements for admission to the New Hampshire bar except residency. She argued that New Hampshire deprived her of privileges and immunities guaranteed by the U.S. Constitution and the court agreed with her by rejecting New Hampshire's contention she would be less familiar with the state's legal procedures and rules and less available for court proceedings and performance of the required pro bono work.[84]

Equality of States

The legal equality of states was guaranteed by Articles II and III of the Articles of Confederation and Perpetual Union, which declared that each state retains "its sovereignty freedom, and independence, and every other power, jurisdiction, and right which is not by this Confederation expressly delegated to the United States in Congress assembled" and stipulated the thirteen states have entered into "a firm league of friendship with each other." Although no explicit provision guaranteeing the equality of states appears in the U.S. Constitution, the provisions for equal representation in the U.S. Senate and equal participation in the process of amending the Constitution suggests the legal equality of each state.

Article IV of the U.S. Constitution authorizes Congress to admit territories into the Union as states. Congress may establish preconditions for the admission of a territory. On March 4, 1791, Vermont was admitted to the Union "as a new and entire member of the United States of America."[85] In 1796 Congress admitted Tennessee to the Union as a state and stipulated it was "on an equal footing with the original states in all respects whatsoever."[86] Subsequently, the "equal footing" language was included in all congressional resolutions admitting territories to the Union including the admission of Alaska and Hawaii in 1958.[87]

The Oklahoma Territory accepted a congressional precondition that the state capitol must be located in Guthrie. The Oklahoma State Legislature subsequently ignored the precondition and authorized the relocation of the capitol to Oklahoma City. This action was challenged and in 1911 the U.S. Supreme Court opined the federal Union "was and is a union of states, equal in power, dignity, and authority, each competent to exert that residuum of sovereignty not delegated to the United States by the Constitution itself."[88]

A proposed state constitution, ratified by voters in the Territory of Arizona, contained a provision authorizing the electorate to employ the recall to remove state judges from office. Congress admitted the Arizona Territory and the New Mexico Territory into the Union by House Joint Resolution No. 14 containing a requirement that a constitutional amendment repealing the recall provision must be submitted to Arizona voters. President William H. Taft, a firm opponent of the recall, approved the admission of New Mexico to the Union because New Mexico voters had earlier removed the recall of judges from its proposed constitution as he had demanded, but vetoed the admission of Arizona on the ground subjecting state judges to the recall was pernicious and would destroy the independence of the judiciary.[89]

Summary and Conclusions

The general adequacy of the principles governing interstate relations, established by the U.S. Constitution, has been demonstrated by experience. These principles have guaranteed the United States is an economic and a political union more perfect than the very limited league of friendship established by the Articles of Confederation and Perpetual Union. Interstate competition for various resources, interstate disputes, and tax exportation continue to this day and their effects have been moderated by Congress and the U.S. Supreme Court. The latter, in particular, has been effective in employing the full faith and credit clause and the privileges and immunities clause to establish a type of interstate citizenship. Perhaps one of the greatest achievements of the court has been its invalidation of state erected interstate trade barriers and the resulting guarantee of generally free internal commercial intercourse.

Chapter 3 focuses on Congress and the actions it has or has not initiated to promote cooperative interstate economic relations. The chapter in particular notes that Congress often prefers to leave issues involving alleged state barriers to internal free trade to the courts.

CHAPTER 3

Congress and Interstate Economic Relations

The U.S. Constitution grants four important powers to Congress enabling it to act as superintendent of interstate economic relations. First, section 8 of Article I delegates plenary powers to Congress to regulate commercial intercourse "with foreign Nations, and among the several States, and with the Indian Tribes. . . ." Second, Congress is granted broad powers of taxation by the same section. Third, each state is required by section 1 of Article IV to give full faith and credit (see chapter 2) "to the public acts, records, and judicial proceedings of every other State" and Congress is authorized to "prescribe the manner in which such acts, records, and proceedings shall be proved, and the effect thereof." It is apparent there would be no economic union in the United States without such a guarantee. Fourth, section 10 of Article I authorizes states to enter into cooperative compacts with each other (see chapter 8) subject to the grant of congressional consent.

These powers are supplemented by the constitutional necessary and proper clause (Art. 1, §8) and the supremacy of the laws clause (Art. VI). The latter stipulates: "This constitution, and the laws made in pursuance thereof, and all treaties made, or which shall be made, under the authority of the United States, shall be the supreme law of the land. . . ." A literal reading of this clause suggests any state constitutional provision or statute conflicting directly with a congressional statute based upon a delegated power when challenged in a law suit is subject to invalidation by a court.

It is important to note Congress' exceptionally broad powers over interstate economic relations are latent ones. In other words, Congress can not be forced to exercise any of its delegated powers and, as explained below, has not fully exercised its commerce and taxation powers with the result states deliberately or inadvertently utilize their reserved police and taxation powers to create barriers to extrastate commerce in order to favor domestic business firms, and use their financial powers to engage in tax exportation and competition for industrial and commercial firms. Frequent references were made to the silence of Congress during most of the nineteenth century. The *Interstate Commerce Act of 1887* was the first major statute, other than ones regulating steam ships using navigable waters, based upon Congress' interstate commerce regulatory power and was followed by the *Sherman Antitrust Act of 1890* evidencing a proclivity of Congress to employ the power more actively in the future.[1]

Chapter I described the Anti-Federalists fear that the exceptional powers delegated to Congress combined with the necessary and proper and supremacy of the laws clauses would lead to the development of a federal Leviathan. This type of fear was accentuated by decisions of the U.S. Supreme Court early in the nineteenth century interpreting the interstate commerce clause broadly as illustrated by the development of the doctrine of implied powers in *McCulloch v. Maryland* in 1819 and the doctrine of the continuous journey in *Gibbons v. Ogden* in 1824 (see chapter 4).[2] Congressional employment of its delegated powers, however, remained relatively limited until the Great Depression. The replacement of John Marshall as chief justice of the U.S. Supreme Court by Roger B. Taney in 1835 ushered in a 100–year period typically described as dual federalism during which the court generally respected the rights of states by interpreting more narrowly the delegated powers of Congress. Nevertheless, in 1885 Woodrow Wilson wrote "Congress must wantonly go very far outside the plain and unquestionable meaning of the Constitution, must bump its head directly against all right and precedent, must kick against the very pricks of all well-established rulings and interpretation, before the Supreme Court will offer its distinct rebuke."[3]

The Great Depression revealed the inherent inability of states to respond effectively to newly emergent problems of crisis proportion. Predictions were soon made the states would or should disappear. Director Luther Gulick of the Institute of Public Administration was convinced in 1933 "the American State is finished" and added:

> The States have failed; the Federal Government has assumed responsibility for the work. The Constitution and the law must be made to conform to avoid needless complications, judicial squirmings, and great waste of time and money . . .
>
> All essential powers affecting economic planning and control must be taken from the States and given to the Nation . . .
>
> What would the States then become? They would become organs of local government. They would abandon their wasteful and bungling endeavors and pretense of competency in the field of national economics and settle down to perform honestly and successfully their allotted tasks in creating and maintaining the organs of local government and service.[4]

Writing in a similar vein, in 1939 Harold J. Laski pontificated federalism was obsolete and in 1948 added that "the States are provinces of which the sovereignty has never since 1789 been real."[5] In 1959 Felix Morley agreed with the prediction of Alexander Hamilton that political power would shift to Congress if states fail to "administer their affairs with uprightness and prudence."[6] Professor D.W. Brogan, an English observer, concluded in 1960 that the states' reserved powers included few important ones

Of the division of powers, probably the least important today is that between the Union and the States. There is, of course, an irreducible minimum of federalism. The States can never be reduced to being mere counties, but in practice, they may be littler more than mere counties . . . in a great many fields of modern legislation, States' rights are a fiction, because the economic and social integration of the United States has gone too far for them to remain a reality. They are, in fact, usually argued for, not by zealots believing that the States can do better than the Union in certain fields, but by prudent calculators who know that the States can do little or nothing, which is what the defenders of States' rights want them to do.[7]

It is particularly noteworthy these prognostications were written prior to 1965 when Congress commenced frequently to exercise its delegated powers to totally or partially remove regulatory powers from states and, by implication, local governments, thereby reducing significantly their discretionary authority (see below). The forecasts have proven to be fallacious as states continue to be viable polities exercising their reserved regulatory, service provision, and taxation powers in a manner revealing they possess very significant powers.[8]

This chapter examines congressional devolution of powers to states, employment of its spending, taxation, interstate commerce, and other preemption powers to establish other ground rules governing interstate economic relations, and promotion of uniform state laws.

Congressional Devolution of Powers

The reader should be aware that Congress has devolved some of its delegated powers to the states. In addition, the silence of Congress on a number of subjects has, in effect, devolved regulatory powers upon states that would be preempted if Congress chose to enact statutes on these subjects.

The first congressional devolution of power dates to 1789 when power was devolved upon states to regulate marine port pilots.[9] The *Shipping Statute,* revised in 1983, contains an almost identical provision: "pilots in the bays, rivers, harbors, and ports of the United States shall be regulated only in conformity with the laws of the States."[10] To resolve interstate disputes relative to pilots, the *Boundary Water Act of 1984* allows the master of a vessel entering or leaving a port in waters that serve as the boundary between two states may employ a pilot licensed by either state.[11]

The U.S. Government brought suit against thirteen states bordering the Atlantic Ocean to determine whether the United States has exclusive rights to the seabed and ocean's subsoil in the area beyond three miles of the coastline of each of the states. The suit, which included supplemental proceedings to determine the coastline of Rhode Island, reached the U.S. Supreme Court which appointed a special master to collect facts. The master allowed New York to participate in the proceedings. In 1985, the court established the boundary lines between the two states by ruling Block Island, Rhode Island, was too far removed from the headlands of the juridical bay (Long Island Sound) to determine the closing of the bay and the boundary line.[12] Based upon this decision, in 1985 New York State Attorney General Robert Abrams issued a formal opinion holding a New York licensed pilot "may navigate vessels from the sea through Block Island Sound to Long Island Sound when in so doing he initially must proceed through waters over which the State of Rhode Island claims jurisdiction for pilotage purposes."[13]

In 1991, the U.S. District Court for the Middle District of Florida noted the provisions of the *Boundary Water Act*, but upheld Florida's authority to require a vessel to employ one of its license pilots to guide a vessel because the Port of Fernandina is located on the Amelia River, which is distinct and separate from the St. Mary's River, which serves as the Florida-Georgia boundary line; the decision was affirmed by the U.S. Court of Appeals for the 11th Circuit in 1993.[14] The U.S. District Court for the Eastern District of New York in 1991 addressed a similar suit challenging the determination of the New York State Commissioners of Pilots that only pilots licensed by New York could guide vessels into and out of New York harbors on the boundary waters of Long Island Sound. The court concluded a pilot licensed by Connecticut and the U.S. Government may "(1) pilot a vessel through the New York waters of Long Island Sound; and (2) pilot a vessel from a Connecticut port to Execution Rocks in western Long Island Sound."[15]

Congress in 1945 devolved its authority to states to regulate the insurance industry.[16] The U.S. Supreme Court in 1868 ruled insurance was not commerce and could be regulated by the states, but reversed this decision in 1944.[17] The court's decision resulted in intensive lobbying of Congress by states, concerned by the loss of revenue, to reverse the decision. Congress responded favorably by enacting the *McCarran-Ferguson Act of 1945* devolving authority to states to regulate the insurance industry.[18]

The *Interstate Horseracing Act of 1978* devolves powers to states, including limited ones to preempt the federal prohibition of interstate off-track wagering.[19] Under the act, interstate simulcasts of horse races require the consent of the concerned state agency and a horsemen's association. The act was challenged on the ground it restricts commercial free speech. The U.S. District Court in 1993 agreed with the plaintiff by granting summary judgment holding that the act violates the First Amendment's guarantee of freedom of speech, is unconstitutionally vague, and is an irrational means to achieve a permissible goal.[20] The U.S. Court of Appeals for the 6th Circuit in 1994 reversed the decision by opining the act does not regulate commercial speech since off-track wagering can occur in the absence of simulcasting, the act regulates a very narrow subject and hence a "less strict vagueness test" is applicable to the act, and "the act does not delegate legislative power to private parties."[21]

In addition to devolving powers upon states, Congress enacted a number of statutes, including early ones, directing federal officers to cooperate with state officers. A 1796 statute, pertaining to marine foreign and interstate commerce, authorized the president to direct fort commanders and revenue officers to cooperate with state officers in the enforcement of state quarantine and health laws.[22] A 1799 amendment similarly authorized the Secretary of the Treasury to give direction to federal officers to cooperate with state officers in the enforcement of the same laws.[23] In 1878, Congress enacted a statute stipulating vessels carrying passengers with a contagious disease may enter into ports only in accordance with the quarantine laws of the several states.[24] And Congress in 1890 decided to assist states in enforcing their antilottery laws by enacting a statute banning lottery materials from the U.S. mail.[25]

Congressional Regulation of Commerce

During its first ninety-eight years, Congress refrained from enacting statutes regulating interstate commerce with the exception of "statutes regulating steamboats and their occupation upon the navigable waters of the country."[26] The silence of Congress relative to interstate commerce was broken definitively two years short of the centennial of the U.S. Constitution with enactment of the *Interstate Commerce Act of 1887* which established the Interstate Commerce Commission and sought to eliminate discriminatory actions—favoring certain cities over other cities, or large shippers over small shippers—and unreasonable transportation rates.[27] The commission, however, was not initially authorized to regulate rates. Such authority was granted to the commission by the *Hepburn Act of 1906*, which also brought express companies, pipelines, and sleeping-car companies under the act, and forbade transportation companies to transport their own commodities.[28] With the passage of time, Congress extended the jurisdiction of the commission to cover interstate telephone and telegraph companies, transoceanic cable companies, bus and trucking firms, and electric power transmission lines.

Continuing technological developments led to Congress to enact the *Federal Radio Act of 1927* establishing Federal Radio Commission.[29] In 1934, Congress created the Federal Communication Commission and made it responsible for the telephone, telegraph, and transoceanic cable functions of the Interstate Commerce Commission and the functions of the Federal Radio

Commission.[30] Congress in 1976 enacted the *Railroad Revitalization and Regulatory Reform Act of 1976* to economically deregulate railroads in order to promote greater competition.[31] The act also prohibits discriminatory state taxation of railroads.[32]

Public hostility toward monopolies dates to the Colonial period and is reflected in the following clause in the Maryland Constitution adopted in 1776: "Monopolies are odious, contrary to the spirit of free government and the principles of commerce, and ought not to be suffered." The clause appears in the current constitution.[33]

The *Sherman Antitrust Act of 1890* was a reaction to the unregulated growth of business trusts that lead to the domination of an industry by a few major firms.[34] Section 1 of the act declared: "Every contract, combination in the form of trust or otherwise, or conspiracy, in the restraint of trade of commerce among the several States, or with foreign nations, is hereby declared to be illegal" and section 2 added: "Every person who shall monopolize, or attempt to monopolize, or combine or conspire with any other person or persons, to monopolize any part of the trade or commerce among the several states, or with foreign nations, shall be deemed guilty of a misdemeanor." This act was the start of a series of congressional acts promoting free interstate commercial intercourse by means of regulating business firms through antitrust and antiunfair-trade practices, including the *Clayton Antitrust Act of 1914* and the *Federal Trade Commission Act of 1914*.[35] The latter act was designed to prevent discrimination in prices between different purchasers of commodities or to accord preferential treatment to one person over another.

Congress enacted the *Public Utility Holding Company Act of 1935* to curb abuses stemming from the formation of a new corporation for the single purpose of buying and holding stock in individual public utility companies that were often located in different states and hence were not subject to state regulation.[36] Holding companies sold shares of their own stock to the public at inflated prices and forced their operating companies to enter into contracts for the benefit of the holding companies. The 20,000-word act requires such companies to register with the U.S. Securities and Exchange Commission, and subjects their activities to detailed regulation, including accounts and records, advertising, contracts between holding companies and their subsidiaries, dividends, inter-company loans, sale of utility assets, and use of proxies at meetings of the board of directors.

Although a significant number of statutes regulating interstate commerce were subsequently enacted, Congress has continued to be silent on certain subjects and courts are called upon to mark the boundary line between congressional authority and state authority by determining whether certain state actions violate the dormant-commerce clause.

Spending As a Regulatory Power

Congress possesses broad taxing and spending powers subject to the constitutional limitation (Art. I, §8) all import duties and export duties must be uniform throughout the nation, the constitutional prohibition of the imposition of a tax or duty on articles exported from any state (Art. I, §9), and due process of law required by the Fifth Amendment. The U.S. Supreme Court in 1796 ruled the power of taxation is not be construed in a restricted manner and in 1936 noted "the power of Congress to authorize expenditure of public moneys for public purposes is not limited by the direct grants of legislative power found in the Constitution."[37]

The court, however, opined in 1987 "[t]he spending power is of course not unlimited" and listed four general restrictions: The spending must promote the general welfare; conditional grants-in-aid must be unambiguous; conditional grants must be related "to the federal interest in particular national projects or programs"; and conditional grants-in-aid may be barred by other constitutional provisions.[38] In practice, these restrictions have not proven to be major restraints on the spending power of Congress.

Grants-in-Aid

Conditional financial assistance enables Congress to influence the policies of states and dates to enactment of the *Morrill Act of 1862* authorizing land grants to states to establish colleges of agricultural and mechanical arts.[39] Similarly, the *Hatch Act of 1887* authorized grants to states to establish agricultural experiment stations at colleges of agriculture.[40]

The first condition attached to a congressional grant-in-aid, other than the purpose for which aid could be spent, was incorporated in the *Carey Act of 1894* and required a state to prepare a comprehensive irrigation plan for arid land as a eligibility requirement.[41] State matching funds requirements and federal inspection of state programs financed in part with federal funds date to the *Weeks Act of 1911,* which authorized grant funds for state forestry programs.[42]

Conditional grants, including land grants, were controversial. In 1866, the U.S. Supreme Court ruled the acceptance of a congressional grant by a state restricting the purpose for which funds could be expended is a binding legal contract protected by the U.S. Constitution against impairment by a state.[43] The controversy involving whether Congress could attach conditions to grants-in-aid to states continued with opponents maintaining these grants separate the spending power from the taxing power, are a bribe to states to execute congressional policies, and allow unelected federal bureaucrats to require sovereign states to initiate specific actions. In 1923 the controversy was settled when the U.S. Supreme Court upheld the conditions attached to a 1921 maternity act requiring states accepting a grant to comply with the conditions by exercising their reserved powers as constitutional.[44]

The first federal grant-in-aid program to have a significant impact on interstate economic relations and the national economy in general was the *Federal Road Aid Act of 1916* designed to expedite the transportation of farm crops to markets by providing grants of up to fifty percent of the cost of constructing designated highways.[45] The *Transportation Act of 1920,* another grant-in-aid act, also authorized the Interstate Commerce Commission to control intrastate freight rates whenever it found unreasonable rate differentials between interstate and intrastate commerce.[46] Subsequently, Congress enacted hundreds of conditional grants-in-aid and many have a direct or indirect impact on interstate economic relations which underwent a substantial expansion subsequent to the enactment of the *National Defense and Interstate Highway Act of 1956,* which authorized grants to states of ninety percent of the cost of constructing interstate highways conforming to federal standards and provided for a bonus of one percent if states banned billboards within a specified distance of these highways.[47]

Congress also enacted a series of statutes containing cross-over sanctions threatening states failing to comply with a congressional statute with the loss of national grants-in-aid. The *Hatch Act of 1939* is the first act containing a cross-over sanction; a state accepting federal grants-in-aid must employ the merit principle to select and promote state personnel.[48] In 1974, Congress responded to the Arab nations' embargo of shipments of oil to the United States by enacting a cross-over sanction statute designed to promote conservation of diesel fuel and gasoline by encouraging states, except Vermont which had a fifty miles per hour maximum speed limit, to lower their maximum highway speed limit to fifty-five miles per hour by threatening to withhold ten percent of the state's annual federal highway aid.[49] The following year Congress enacted a second cross-over sanction statute to promote conservation of motor fuels by permitting motorists stopped at a red traffic light to make a right turn on red if no vehicle is approaching from the left.[50]

Concerned with alcohol-related traffic deaths and injuries involving drivers under twenty-one years of age, Congress enacted a statute in 1984 directing the Secretary of Transportation to withhold five percent of a state's highway grant-in-aid effective in fiscal year 1986 if a state lacks a statute prohibiting the purchase or possession of alcoholic beverages by persons who have not reached their twenty-first birthday with the penalty increasing to ten percent in each subsequent year.[51] The U.S. Supreme Court upheld the constitutionality of the conditional grant-in-aid in 1987.[52]

Still concerned about alcoholic-related traffic accidents, Congress included a provision in the *Transportation Equity Act of 1998* threatening states with the loss of two percent of their annual federal highway grants-in-aid if they fail to lower the blood alcohol content (BAC) standard for determining drunk driving to 0.08 percent by 2004.[53] Congress also appropriates funds for federal programs promoting enactment of uniform state laws and assisting states in exercising their regulatory powers. The *Hotel and Motel Fire Safety Act of 1990* encourages each state to adopt national fire-safety standards by stipulating federal government employees may stay only in hotels and motels meeting the national standards.[54] Furthermore, the act allows federal grants to be spent for a conference, convention, meeting, or training seminar provided the meeting hotel or motel conforms to the national standards.

A congressional spending alternative to a grant-in-aid program is a federal program designed to assist states in the exercise of their reserved regulatory powers such as the National Driver Register (NDR) established in 1982.[55] Currently, each state and the District of Columbia on a voluntary basis send to NDR information on drivers convicted of major traffic offenses and revocation of licenses. NDR enables states to contact electronically the register prior to issuing an operator's license to determine whether an applicant has been convicted of motor vehicles offenses in other states, thereby helping to ensure dangerous drivers are not allowed to operate on the nation's highways.

Taxation As a Regulatory Power

The value of taxation as a regulatory tool has long been recognized. High excise taxes have been levied by state legislatures on certain commodities—alcoholic beverages, tobacco products in particular—considered to be harmful to public health if consumed in large quantities in order to discourage consumption.

Congress also may use its power of taxation for regulatory purposes and in 1886 enacted a statute restricting the sale of oleomargarine by requiring manufacturers, wholesalers, and retailers of the product to pay an annual license tax, and levying a two cents per pound tax.[56] The constitutionality of the act was upheld in 1898 when the U.S. Supreme Court invalidated a Pennsylvania statute prohibiting the sale of oleomargarine.[57] This decision allowed states to license the manufacture and sale of oleomargarine, thereby protecting domestic butter producers.

Subsequently, Congress discovered tax credits and tax sanctions are powerful incentives that may be employed to encourage states to adopt national policies including administration of a congressionally established program.

Tax Credits

Congressionally authorized tax credits, also known as tax expenditures, have been employed to achieve several national goals. Each of two major tax credit statutes impacts interstate economic relations by promoting a nationally uniform program. *The Revenue Act of 1926* authorized the first tax credit to encourage states without an estate or inheritance tax to levy one identical to the federal estate tax and to persuade the other states to amend their tax laws to incorporate the provisions of the federal estate tax.[58]

States with no or low inheritance taxes attracted wealthy citizens as residents who desired to preserve their estates for their heirs. Eligible taxpayers are granted by the 1926 act an eighty percent credit against the federal estate tax up to a specified amount for estate taxes paid to a state. The entire tax revenue would flow to the U.S. Treasury if a state lacks a state estate tax.

Congress in 1935 decided to persuade each state to operate a nationally uniform unemployment insurance program by incorporated tax credit in the *Social Security Act of 1935.*[59] Employers are granted a ninety percent credit against their federal unemployment insurance tax for a similar tax paid to a state provided its statute is identical to the national one. This act resulted in the establishment of a nationally uniform unemployment compensation system administered by the various states.

Tax Sanctions

In 1982 Congress employed a tax sanction for the first time as a mechanism for persuading all states to enact a uniform law providing all state and local government issued long-term bonds—termed municipal bonds—must be registered and not traditional bearer bonds.[60] Under the statute, interest received by holders of newly issued bearer bonds is subject to the federal income tax and investors will not purchase such bonds unless they carry a higher rate of interest. The U.S. Supreme Court in 1988 opined the act does not violate the U.S. Constitution.[61]

A second tax sanction, incorporated in the *Tax Reform Act of 1986,* mandates state and local governments issuing long-term tax-exempt bonds to deposit any arbitrage profit in the U.S. Treasury.[62] The proceeds of such bond issues are commonly invested in the U.S. Treasury notes and other conservative securities until needed for paying various construction projects and arbitrate profits may be large if there is a wide spread between the interest received from treasury notes and the interest rate on the municipal bonds.

Preemption As a Regulatory Power

Congress, based upon the supremacy of the laws clause, may employ a delegated power to remove totally or partially a regulatory power of the states.

Congress first exercised its preemption power in 1790 when it enacted two total preemption statutes relating to copyrights and patents.[63] Congress, of course, has modified these acts to bring them up-to-date in the electronic age as illustrated by the *Digital Millennium Copyright Act of 1998.*[64]

The silence of Congress may prevent the invalidation of a state statute. Writing for the court, Chief Justice William H. Taft in 1926 opined:

> In the absence of any action taken by Congress on the subject-matter, it is well settled that a state, in the exercise of its police power, may establish quarantines against human beings, or animals, or plants, the coming in of which may expose the inhabitants, or the stock, or the trees, plants, or growing crops, to disease, injury, or destruction thereby, and in spite of the fact such quarantines necessarily affect interstate commerce.[65]

The case involved a challenge of a 1921 Washington statute authorizing the state director of agriculture, with the approval of the governor, to impose a quarantine to prevent infestation of trees and plants by disease and/or plant insects.[66] The director ordered a quarantine to prevent the spread of a weevil that damages alfalfa and his action was challenged. The U.S. Supreme Court invalidated the quarantine because Congress enacted a statute in 1912, amended in 1917, authorizing the Secretary of Agriculture to quarantine any state or territory.[67] The court stressed the fact the secretary did not impose a quarantine was evidence there was no need for a quarantine and the existence of the federal law invalidated the state law.

A total of only twenty-nine preemption statutes were enacted through the year 1899 and a number of these statutes subsequently were repealed.[68] One hundred eleven preemption statutes were enacted between 1900 and 1959. Several statutes, enacted between 1912 and 1923, established standards for agricultural products as illustrated by the *Standard Apple Barrel Act of 1912, Grain Standards Act of 1916,* and *Cotton Standards Act of 1923.*[69] Other statutes included a wide variety of topics. The pace of enactment of preemption statutes accelerated subsequent to 1959 and peaked during the 1970s and the 1980s. A slight reduction in the number of such statutes coincided with the Republican Party capture of control of Congress effective in 1995.

A constitutional paradox developed subsequent to 1965 when Congress began to exercise its partial preemption powers removing specified regulatory powers from states and simultaneously encouraging states to exercise reserved powers they previously had not exercised or exercise certain other powers more fully. As explained in a subsequent section, one type of congressional partial preemption statute establishes national minimum regulatory standards and authorizes a national department or agency to delegate regulatory primacy to states provided they establish regulatory standards meeting or exceeding the national ones and possess the necessary qualified personnel and equipment to enforce the standards.

A congressional preemption statute may contain one or more mandates requiring state and local governments to initiate specific courses of action that may be costly. Not surprisingly, there is strong subnational governmental opposition to expensive mandates.[70] The United States Supreme Court has invalidated only one major mandate to date. The Court in *New York v. United States* in 1992 examined provisions of the *Low Level Radioactive Waste Policy Act of 1980*, upheld the constitutionality of the monetary incentives and access to disposal sites incentives offered to states for complying with the act, but struck down the incentive requiring states to accept title to such waste on the ground "the Framers explicitly chose a Constitution that confers upon the Congress the power to regulate individuals, not States."[71] The first set of incentives was held to be within Congress' commerce and spending powers and the second set of incentives was termed a condition employed in Congress' exercise of its commerce power. The take title provision was declared to be unique as no other congressional act gave states no option other than to adhere to the congressional mandate.

A preemption statute also may contain one or more restraints. The *Surface Transportation Assistance Act of 1982*, for example, imposed a restraint on states by forbidding them to regulate the size and weight of trucks operating on interstate highways and on sections of the national-aid highway system as determined by the Secretary of Transportation.[72] This restraint did not result in increased state operating costs.

The *Ocean Dumping Ban Act of 1988*, on the other hand, imposed a restraint that has had costly implications for a number of coastal municipalities which previously dumped sewage sludge in an ocean.[73] New York City, for example, daily generates a huge amount of sewage sludge, which prior to 1988 was barged and dumped in the New York Bight located outside New York Harbor in the Atlantic Ocean. The sludge presents a sanitation hazard and the city was faced with two costly alternatives. The sludge could be incinerated, but would add pollutants to the atmosphere, or the sludge could be shipped to a landfill. New York City signed contracts with five companies to ship sewage sludge to sites in other states. In 2001, the city exercised its option to withdraw from its contract with Merco, a Long Island company, which had been shipping up to 250 tons of the city's sludge daily, via dedicated trains 2,065 miles to Sierra Blanca, Texas, where the company had purchased a 81,000-acre site.[74] The city estimated the withdrawal from the contract would produce a savings of approximately three million dollars annually and was motivated by the fact the city could not generate sufficient sewage sludge for the five companies shipping the city's sludge to other states.

The 1989 murder of actress Rebecca Schaeffer by a stalker, who obtained her home address from the California Department of Motor Vehicles, induced Congress to include a restraint in the *Violent Crime Control and Law Enforcement Act of 1994;* i.e., states are forbidden to release specified types of information pertaining to motor vehicle owners and operators.[75]

A congressional restraint also may reduce the revenues of a state or a local government while aggravating existing problems. A 1986 preemption statute requires motor vehicle tolls on any bridge connecting Brooklyn and Staten Island in New York City must be collected as vehicles exit the bridge in Staten Island.[76] This restraint on the location of toll booths has resulted in the Triborough Bridge and Tunnel Authority losing several million dollars in toll revenues annually because motorists who exit the Verrazano Narrows Bridge in Brooklyn return to Staten Island by using Holland Tunnel under the Hudson River, toll free for vehicles traveling west, to reach New Jersey and return by another bridge to Staten island. The restraint has increased traffic congestion at the entrance to the tunnel and the idling vehicles contribute to air pollution.

Total Preemption

Congress possesses complete discretion whether or not to exercise a delegated power to remove regulatory authority totally from states. The sharp increase in the number of total preemption statutes during the previous three decades is attributable to the general recognition that major public problems often have an interstate dimension, failure of federal conditional grants-in-aid to spur adequate state action to solve problems viewed as national ones by Congress, lack of effective cooperative interstate programs to address important problems, and aggressive lobbying by economic interest groups and newly organized environmental and public-interest groups.

Do state government officers and their associations always oppose total preemption statutes? The answer is no because a national association of state government officers occasionally will urge Congress to assume complete responsibility for a regulatory function. The National Governors' Association in 1980, for example, recommended congressional establishment of national weight and length standards for trucks.[77] Similarly, the association urged Congress to enact the *Commercial Motor Vehicle Safety Act of 1986* because interstate cooperation was not successful in removing from state highways truck drivers whose operator's licenses were revoked or suspended by a state motor vehicle department because each driver typically held licenses issued by several states.[78] The act makes it a federal crime for a truck operator to hold more than one commercial operator's license.

A surveyed governor expressed mixed views relative to the various federal preemption statutes:

> As a general rule, I have been opposed to federal preemption of state law. I have always supported the concept of having decisionmaking at levels closest to the people. Yet I do understand that there are circumstances which dictate the use of preemption. For example, I support the use of preemption in areas of voting rights and air quality. . . . Conversely, I do not support the preemption doctrine as it has been used to limit state and local governments' abilities to regulate wages and hours of their employees.[79]

Congressional statutes may or may not contain an expressed total preemption provision. Congress can make its intent clear by including a stipulation, illustrated by the *Flammable Fabrics Act*, "this Act is intended to supersede any law of any State or political subdivisions thereof inconsistent with its provisions."[80] This intent declaration, however, may not eliminate the need for judicial clarification because a controversy may erupt over the question of whether a state statute is inconsistent with the federal statute.

Congressional intent was made explicit in the *United States Grain Standards Act of 1968:* No state or local government is allowed to "require the inspection or description in accordance with any standards of kind, class, quality, condition, or other characteristics of grain as a condition of shipment, or sale, of such grain in interstate or foreign commerce, or require any license for, or impose any other restrictions upon the performance of any official inspection function under this act by official inspection personnel."[81]

It is not unusual for a total preemption statute to contain an exception for a named state. Congress enacted in 1866 a statute regulating the transportation of certain types of explosives, including nitroglycerine, and stipulating that the act was not to be interpreted to prevent, states, territories, and local governments from regulating such transportation or prohibiting the introduction of such explosives within their respective jurisdiction.[82] Similarly, a 1978 statute provides "no State or political subdivision thereof and no interstate agency or other political agency of two or more States shall enact or enforce any law, rule, regulation, standards, or other provision having the force and effect of law relating to interstate rates, interstate routes, or interstate services of any freight forwarder."[83] The statute also provides "nothing in this subsection . . . shall be construed to affect the authority of the State of Hawaii to continue to regulate a motor carrier operating within the State of Hawaii."[84]

A total preemption statute may be limited in its scope. The *Gun Control Act of 1968* contains a savings clause allowing limited state regulation: "No provision of this chapter shall be construed as indicating an intent on the part of the Congress to occupy the field in which such provision operates to the exclusion of the law of any State on the same subject matter, unless there is a direct and positive conflict between such provision the law of the State so that the two can not be reconciled or consistently stand together."[85]

A number of congressional statutes lacking an explicit preemption provision have been interpreted by courts to be preemptive. Chapter 4 describes the criteria employed by the U.S. Supreme Court to determine whether a congressional statute totally or partially preempts state and local laws.

The federal government possesses adequate resources to administer successfully a number of total preemption statutes including the *Bankruptcy Act of 1933* and the *Clean Air Act Amendments of 1970,* which established emission standards for motor vehicles.[86] Other federal statutes forbid states to engage in economic regulation of airline, bus, and motor carrier, companies with respect to fares and routes, but allow states to continue to regulate buses and trucks to ensure the vehicles are safe.[87]

The success of a congressional total preemption statute may be dependent upon the assistance of state and local governments. The U.S. Nuclear Regulatory Commission has been granted complete responsibility for the regulation of civilian nuclear electric power plants by the *Atomic Energy Act of 1946* as amended.[88] The commission, however, lacks the qualified personnel and equipment to respond immediately to an incident at a plant and must rely upon the assistance of state and local governments. By enacting a total preemption statute on occasion, Congress notes the need for the assistance of subnational governments. The *United States Grain Standards Act* specifically authorizes the administrator of the U.S. Grain Inspection Service to delegate authority to state departments or agencies to perform official inspection and weighing in accordance with national standards.[89] The *Federal Railroad Safety Act of 1970* similarly permits states to conduct railroad inspections in accordance with national standards.[90] The *Age Discrimination in Employment Amendments of 1986,* a total preemption statute, authorizes the Equal Employment Opportunity Commission to sign cooperative enforcement agreements with state or local government fair-employment agencies.[91]

The Agreement States Program of the Nuclear Regulatory Commission, authorized by a 1959 congressional act, allows states to assume certain regulatory responsibilities provided they adopt standards at least as high as the national standards, but is unusual in only requiring a state radiation-control program to be compatible with, and not necessarily identical to, the commission's regulatory program.[92]

The *Port and Tanker Safety Act of 1978* appears to be a total preemption statute because the secretary of transportation is authorized to require federally licensed pilots on all domestic and foreign self-propelled vessels "engaged in foreign trade when operating in the navigable waters of the United States in areas and under circumstances where a pilot is not otherwise required by state law."[93] The purpose of the act is to prompt states to require use of pilots in areas where they were not required. The federal preemption is terminated immediately in each such area when the state requires a state-licensed pilot and notifies the secretary.

Partial Preemption

This type of preemption assumes two forms with the first involving congressional enactment of a law assuming complete responsibility for part of a regulatory field. The *Bankruptcy Act of 1898* as amended is unusual in preempting nearly all aspects of bankruptcy regulation.[94] Each state legislature may determine whether a homestead and certain other exemptions should be excluded from seizure in a bankruptcy action.

Abuses have been associated with the authority of a state legislature to establish the value of a homestead exempt from proceedings in the U.S. Bankruptcy Court. So-called "corporate raider" Paul A. Bilzerian's $5 million home in Florida, for example, was sheltered from creditors on two occasions including 2001 when he filed for bankruptcy protection and listed debts of $140 million.[95] Five states—Florida, Iowa, Kansas, South Dakota, and Texas—have an unlimited homestead exemption and serve as magnets for debtors in other states, particularly New York with its $20,000 exemption, desiring to shelter their assets from creditors. Several former top executives of the Enron Corporation, which filed for bankruptcy in 2001, own multi-million dollar homes in Florida and Texas.[96] Only Congress has the authority to solve this interstate problem.

All banks, except the First National Bank of the United States and the Second National Bank of the United States, were chartered by states until 1864 when Congress enacted the *National Banking Act* establishing a dual banking system.[97] Subsequently, Congress enacted other banking acts including the *McFadden Act of 1933* permitting a national bank to open branch banks throughout its home state to the same extent the state permits state chartered banks to establish branches.[98] This act, however, did not allow national and state banks that are members of the Federal Reserve System to establish branches in foreign states. State chartered banks not members of the Federal Reserve System were permitted to establish branches in any state that that permitted such actions.

A congressional preemption statute also may authorize states to continue to exercise their regulatory powers provided they conform to conditions established by Congress. The *Electronic Signatures in Global and National Commerce Act of 2000*, for example contains a section entitled "Exemption to Preemption" that authorizes a state to supersede a section of the act relative to electronic records and signatures in commerce provided the statute or regulation:

> constitutes an enactment or adoption of the Uniform Electronic Transaction Act as approved and recommended for enactment in all the States by the National Conference of Commissioners on Uniform State Laws in 1999,

except that any exception to the scope of such Act enacted by a State under section 3(b)(4) of such Act shall be preempted to the extent such exception is inconsistent with this title or Title II, or would not be permitted under paragraph (2)(A)(ii) of this subsection.[99]

The more important type, in terms of interstate economic relations, is minimum standards preemption based upon a statute either establishing national minimum regulatory standards in a functional field and/or authorizing federal departments and agencies to promulgate rules and regulations establishing such standards. The authorization for departments and agencies to establish standards has had a major impact on interstate relations.

Minimum Standards Preemption. This type of preemption assumes two forms. The first form involves Congress establishing minimum regulatory standards and allowing a state to continue to regulate provided its standards are stricter than the national one. The *Port and Tanker Safety Act of 1978* stipulates with respect to navigable waters "nothing contained in this section, with respect to structures, prohibits a State or political subdivisions thereof from prescribing higher safety equipment requirements or safety standards than those which may be prescribed by regulations hereunder."[100] The *Natural Gas Policy Act of 1978* contains a similar provision stipulating "nothing in this act shall affect the authority of any State to establish or enforce any maximum lawful price for the first sale of natural gas produced in such State which does not exceed the applicable maximum lawful price, if any, under title I of this act."[101] There is no requirement that a state must obtain approval in advance from a federal department or agency to establish higher standards.

The second form may be viewed as "contingent" total preemption threatening a federal department or agency will assume complete regulatory responsibility in a functional area in the event a state fails to submit to the concerned federal department or agency a plan containing standards meeting or exceeding the federal ones and evidence the state possesses the necessary qualified personnel and equipment to enforce the standards. The department or agency in approving a submitted state plan delegates to the state regulatory primacy whose purpose is to ensure only a state agency will enforce the standards, thereby avoiding dual inspections and enforcement actions by federal and state inspectors burdening business firms subject to the standards. This type of preemption allows states a degree of regulatory discretion by permitting the adoption and implementation of standards higher than the federal ones to address problems that may be unique and would not be solved by implementation of the federal standards.

The first minimum standards preemption act is the *Water Quality Act of 1965* (now *Clean Water Act*) that directed each state to adopt "water quality standards applicable to interstate waters or portions thereof within such State" and an implementation and enforcement plan.[102] Congress decided several regional and national problems, environmental ones in particular, could not be solved by offering grants-in-aid to state and local governments to support remedial actions. The conclusion was drawn that in the absence of nationally mandated minimum regulatory standards a state would hesitate to take vigorous actions to solve several types of problems that have spillover costs adversely affecting other states and/or nations for fear high regulatory standards would encourage certain industries to move to states with lower standards and would discourage new industrial firms from locating in the state. Many states favored the congressional establishment of minimum national standards to prevent the development of industrial-haven states that would allow certain types of factories to pollute the environment.

An interviewed Connecticut environmental protection commissioner reported minimum standard preemption afforded his state an option other than filing of an original jurisdiction suit in the U.S. Supreme Court seeking a writ of mandamus directing Massachusetts to remove pollutants from streams flowing into the Connecticut River; i.e., apply pressure on the U.S. Environmental Protection Agency (EPA) to require Massachusetts to initiate remedial action.[103]

A minimum-standards preemption bill generates lobbying in Congress by groups seeking exemptions. The political influence of the farm lobby is revealed by a provision in the *Clean Water Act of 1977* stipulating the EPA administrator "shall not require a permit under this section for discharges composed entirely of return flows from irrigated agriculture, nor shall the administrator directly or indirect require any State to require such a permit."[104]

The other major minimum standards preemption acts are the *Air Quality Act of 1967* (now *Clean Air Act*), *Safe Drinking Water Act of 1974,* and the *Surface Mining Control and Reclamation Act of 1977.*[105] Relative to the latter act, in 1981 the U.S. Supreme Court rejected a constitutional challenge:

> If a State does not wish to submit a proposed permanent program that complies with the Act and implementing regulations, the full regulatory burden will be borned by the federal government. Thus, there can be no suggestion that the act commandeers the legislative process of the States by directly compelling them to enact and enforce a federal regulatory program.[106]

A key question is whether states adopt standards meeting the minimum federal requirements or adopt higher standards. A study, based upon a 1998 Council of State Governments air pollution survey, found twenty-nine percent of the responding thirty-eight states had established one or more ambient air standard(s) higher than the ones required by EPA and concluded "economic pressures have not overwhelmed the states' ability to set their own environmental standards.[107]

The *Natural Gas Policy Act of 1978* contains a similar provision: "Nothing in this act shall affect the authority of any State to establish or enforce any maximum lawful price for the first sale of natural gas produced in such State which does not exceed the applicable maximum lawful price, if any, under title 1 of this act."[108]

A congressional statute simultaneously can contain minimum standards provisions and *Imperium in Imperio* provisions. The *Occupational Safety and Health Act of 1970* utilizes both types of provisions and stipulates "nothing in this act shall prevent any state agency or court from asserting jurisdiction under state law over any occupational safety or health issue with respect to which no standard is in effect under section 6."[109] The Ohio Manufacturers' Association filed a suit against the City of Akron contending its "right-to-know" ordinance was preempted by the act. The U.S. District Court for the Northern District of Ohio rejected the challenge and its decision was upheld in 1986 by the U.S. Court of Appeals for the Sixth Circuit which opined "we cannot accept plaintiff's contention that Congress expressly preempted local regulation by these provisions establishing a national standard. Furthermore, we agree with the trial court to the extent that express preemption, by definition, must be clearly manifested, especially when local health and safety provisions are endangered."[110]

It is important to note state and local government laws and regulations may be preempted in certain instances by a rule promulgated by a federal department or agency acting under authority of a partial preemption statute. State and local governments specifically are authorized by the *Toxic Substances Control Act of 1976* to regulate chemical substances or mixtures until the EPA administrator promulgates a rule or order applicable to a substance or mixture designed to protect public health.[111]

Additionally, this act allows a degree of subnational governmental regulatory flexibility subsequent to the promulgation of a rule or order by authorizing the administrator, upon the application of a state or local government, to promulgate a rule exempting a chemical substance or mixture from the federal standards if the state or local governmental standards provide a higher degree of protection against injury to the environment or public health than the federal requirements and do not "unduly burden interstate commerce."[112]

Preemption Relief

States typically lobby members of Congress not to enact most preemption bills that commonly are promoted by industrial groups. If states are unsuccessful in persuading Congress to reject a preemption bill, they may lobby

Congress to enact an amendment providing relief from one or more burdensome provisions of the statute. Similarly, states may lobby Congress to reverse a decision of the U.S. Supreme Court holding a congressional statute preempts state regulatory authority in the absence of an explicit statutory preemption declaration.

Referring to Congress' use of its interstate commerce power, Chief Justice John Marshall of the United States Supreme Court in *Gibbons v. Ogden* in 1824 opined:

> The wisdom and the discretion of Congress, their identify with the people, and the influence which their constituents possess at elections, are, in this, as in many other instances, as that, for example of declaring war, the sole restraints on which they have relied to secure them from its abuse.[113]

Herbert Wechsler in 1955 drew upon the Marshall thesis to develop the "Political Safeguards of Federalism" theory positing that the political process can be employed by states to protect their reserved powers from congressional encroachment.[114] In 1985, Justice Harry A. Blackmun of the U.S. Supreme Court employed this theory in his opinion in *Garcia v. San Antonio Metropolitan Transit Authority* by writing "the principal and basic limits on the federal commerce power is inherent in all state participation in federal government action."[115] He was responding to the charge that Congress exceeded its delegated powers in enacting a statute applying national minimum wage and overtime-pay provisions to non-supervisory employees of subnational governments, thereby imposing a heavy fiscal burden on these governments.

The Marshall-Wechsler-Blackmun thesis in effect is a restatement of the leadership-feedback model of policy development with Congress providing leadership by enacting a preemption statute to solve a problem and subsequently amending the statute as the result of feedback from state and local government detailing the adverse and possibly unintended consequences of the statute. Ten preemption relief statutes were enacted by Congress during the administration of President Ronald Reagan.[116]

The *Safe Drinking Water Act of 1986* mandated state and local governments supplying public drinking water have to initiate action to ensure the water meets nationally established standards, which increased in each of the subsequent years and resulted with a significant number of small local governments facing a dilemma; i.e., abandon their water-supply function or be forced into bankruptcy by attempts to comply with the standards.[117] Protests by state and local governments persuaded Congress in 1996 to provide relief from many of the most expensive mandated standards, the only post Reagan preemption relief statute.[118]

Promotion of Uniform State Laws

Nonharmonious state laws in an age of interstate commerce and travel cause major problems for business firms and citizens. The framers of the U.S. Constitution apparently assumed Congress would exercise its interstate commerce and other preemption powers to remove the regulatory authority of the states responsible for burdensome diverse laws impeding such commerce. Congress, for a variety of political reasons, has decided not to establish uniform national policies in many regulatory fields.

Congress nevertheless has encouraged and, in some instances, pressured states into enacting uniform or nearly uniform state statutes. Congress, since its enactment of the *Weeks Act of 1911,* has on a number of occasions granted its consent-in-advance to specific interstate compacts, which establish a uniform regulatory policy, to encourage state legislatures to enact these compacts (see chapter 8).[119]

Enactment of uniform state laws has been promoted by congressional grants-in-aid with attached uniform conditions. In 1974 Congress used a more coercive means to encourage the enactment of state uniform laws by utilizing a cross-over sanction that threatened states with a loss of ten percent of their respective highway grant-in-aid for failure to reduce the maximum highway speed limit to fifty-five miles per hour to conserve motor fuels during the Arab oil embargo.[12] Subsequently, Congress enacted other statutes containing a cross-over sanction.

Other methods have been employed by Congress to secure its goal of uniform state regulatory laws. It decided in 1982 to promote interstate cooperation by creating the National Driver Register, which allows each state and the District of Columbia to obtain information on their licensed drivers convicted of major traffic violations in sister states.[121] All states and the district participate in the register by entering information on motor vehicle operators whose applications for a license has been rejected or revoked. As noted, the *Commercial Motor Vehicle Safety Act of 1986* was the result of lobbying by the National Governors Association. Each state is required by the act to check with the Register before the issuance of a commercial driver/operator license.

In 1990 Congress decided to promote the enactment of a uniform law by all state legislatures by a opt-out method, thereby respecting the quasi-sovereignty of the states. The *Department of Transportation Appropriation Act of 1991* directs each state legislature to enact a statute providing for the revocation of a driver's license of a individual convicted of a drug-related crime or to vote to opt out of the requirement by enacting a resolution, concurred in the governor, and sending it to the U.S. secretary of transportation.[122] A state failing to enact such a law or to opt out suffered a ten percent reduction in federal highway aid.

The *Hotel and Motel Fire Safety Act of 1990* pressured states to enact uniform fire safety standards by forbidding traveling federal government employees to stay in a hotel or motel unless it conforms with the standards and attaching the same condition to grants-in-aid to fund state and local government employees attending a conference, meeting, or training seminar in a hotel or motel.[123]

Congress in the same year took another step to encourage interstate cooperation in a region of the nation by establishing an Ozone Transport Commission whose members are representatives of the District of Columbia and twelve northeastern states.[124] At the urging of the commission, in 1994 the U.S. Environmental Protection Agency authorized the district and the concerned states to adopt the California Low Emission Vehicles Program to help.[125] The commission in the same year launched a program to reduce emissions of nitrogen oxide from fossil-fuel burning electrical generating plants and reported in 2000 such emissions had been reduced by fifty percent since 1990.[126]

Responding to lobbying by insurance companies, Congress enacted the *Gramm-Leach-Bliley Financial Reorganization Act of 1999,* which establishes minimum regulatory standards in thirteen areas that states must follow and contains a contingent preemption provision.[127] The latter provision threatened states with the establishment of a federal insurance agent licensing system if twenty-six states failed to implement a uniform licensing system for agents by November 12, 2002 (see chapter 8).

The following year, Congress enacted the *Electronic Signatures in Global and National Commerce Act,* which preempted the regulatory powers of the states, but authorized state legislatures to enact a statute provided it "constitutes an enactment of adoption of the *Uniform Electronic Transportation Act* as approved and recommended for enactment in all the states by the National Conference of Commissioners on Uniform State Laws in 1999."[128]

Summary and Conclusions

The delegation by the U.S. Constitution of broad regulatory powers to Congress enables it to remove totally or partially state and local government laws impeding the free flow of commerce among sister states. To date, Congress generally has been reluctant to fully exercise its delegated interstate commerce and taxation powers to remove interstate-trade barriers and prevent interstate competition for industrial and other business firms, and to eliminate problems that spill over from one state into a sister state(s).

Congress for the first time recognized in 1911 that it could enact a statute to encourage interstate cooperation by granting consent in advance to states to enter into specific interstate compacts. Subsequently, Congress enacted other statutes encouraging state legislatures, by conditional grants-in-aid and cross-over sanctions, to enact uniform state laws. More recently, Congress has enacted statutes containing a contingent preemption provision, a Sword of Damocles, notifying states their regulatory power in a given area will be preempted totally if their state legislatures fail to enact a uniform state law. This new technique has been successful to date in persuading the legislatures to enact uniform state regulatory policies.

Chapter 4 examines the role of the judiciary, the U.S. Supreme Court in particular, in regulating interstate economic relations and the reasons why Congress, by its silence, appears to prefer regulation of such relations by the judiciary.

CHAPTER 4

Judicial Ground Rules

The Articles of Confederation and Perpetual Union created a unicameral Congress with equal representation from each state, but contained no provision for a chief executive or a judiciary. The Philadelphia Convention, called to consider amendment of the articles, debated the question of the need for a national judiciary as did citizens in the various states. Alexander Hamilton described "the want of a judiciary power" as the crowning defect of the confederation established by the articles and noted:

> To avoid the confusion which would unavoidably result from the contrary decisions of a number of independent judicatories, all nations have found it necessary to establish one court paramount to the rest, possessing a general superintendence and authorized to settle and declare in the last resort a uniform rule of civil justice.[1]

Opponents of such a judiciary rejected Hamilton's view and maintained judges in each state could interpret impartially the national Constitution and statutes as well as the state Constitution and statutes. Proponents countered a neutral national judiciary also was needed to resolve two types of controversies—interstate disputes and suits between citizens of sister states—because experience under the articles revealed state courts in adjudicating the latter type of disputes did not always rule impartially.

The convention decided the proposed U.S. Constitution should create only one court—the United States Supreme Court—and delegated power to Congress to create inferior courts as needed.[2] Hamilton devoted four letters to New York City newspapers to defend the convention proposed national judicial system. He sought to convince readers the proposed national judicial branch "is beyond comparison the weakest of the three departments of power" and is essential for the protection of the constitution and rights of citizens, a fixed salary for judges protects their independence, and the constitution limits the national judicial power to appropriate subjects.[3] He also addressed the controversial power of Congress to create inferior national courts by explaining the power "is evidently calculated to obviate the necessity of having recourse to the Supreme Court in every case of federal cognizance."[4]

Hamilton was aware a controversy surrounded the question whether courts could declare statutes unconstitutional. He defended the right of courts to void acts by explaining "[it] is far more rational to suppose the courts were designed to be an intermediate body between the people and the legislature in order . . . to keep the latter within the limits assigned to their authority" and added "the power of the people" is superior to the power of the legislature and the judiciary, and judges should be bound by the will of the people as expressed in the Constitution.[5]

In 1819 the U.S. Supreme Court in *McCulloch v. Maryland* developed the doctrine of implied powers, which greatly expanded the powers of Congress, and invalidated for the first time a state statute.[6] The court examined the question whether Maryland could levy a tax upon notes issued by the Bank of the United States chartered by Congress and answered the question in the negative.

The Constitution is silent relative to the number of U.S. Supreme Court justices and authorizes the president to appoint all national judges subject to the "advice and consent of the Senate."[7] Ratification of the proposed constitution automatically established a dual judicial system composed of national courts and state courts with concurrent jurisdiction over a number of subjects as described in a subsequent section. The latter courts are organized as independent systems in each state and are not dependent upon the national court system. We first examine the national-judicial power by focusing upon key decisions of the U.S. Supreme Court.

The National Judicial Power

The U.S. Constitution defines the judicial power as extending

> to all cases, in law and equity, arising under this constitution, the laws of the United States, and treaties made, or which shall be made, under their authority;—to all cases affecting ambassadors, other public ministers, and consuls;—to all cases of admiralty and maritime jurisdiction;—to controversies to which the United States shall be a party;—to controversies between two or more states; . . . between citizens of different states—between citizens of the same state claiming lands under grants of different states . . .[8]

State courts have exclusive jurisdiction over all other cases. Congress, however, enacted in 1948 a statute stipulating that a U.S. court may grant an injunction to stay proceedings in a state court if "authorized by Act of Congress, or where necessary in aid of its jurisdiction, or to protect or effectuate its judgments."[9]

The Constitution recognizes states as semisovereign units and grants the U.S. Supreme Court nonexclusive original (trial) jurisdiction over interstate disputes (see below). Furthermore, in 1996 Congress amended earlier statutes that assigned exclusive jurisdiction to the U.S. District Court over suits brought by a citizen of one state against a citizen of another state (diversity of citizenship) by increasing the necessary amount in controversy to $75,000 or more in order to evoke the court's jurisdiction.[10]

However, drawing a distinct line between national court jurisdiction and state court jurisdiction is often a difficult task. A citizen of Pennsylvania, who had lost a court suit in Pennsylvania including its Supreme Court, sought to bring his suit in the U.S. District Court and attempted to meet the jurisdictional requirements as to diversity of citizenship by maintaining his rights protected by the federal *Civil Rights Act* had been violated. His suit was rejected in 1963 by the U.S. District Court for the Western District of Pennsylvania, which opined the court "will not act as a court of review simply because a party feels that the state courts have denied him his own predetermined remedy."[11] The U.S. Court of Appeals for the Third District upheld the lower court's ruling and the U.S. Supreme Court affirmed.[12]

The unamended Constitution also extended the judicial power to cases "between a state and citizens of another state . . . and between a state, or the citizens thereof, and foreign states, citizens or subjects." This authorization was repealed by the Eleventh Amendment to the Constitution.

It is important to note that only cases of a justiciable character arising under the constitution, congressional statutes, and treaties fall within the federal judicial power. Executive or legislative questions are political questions beyond the reach of courts. Only Congress, for example, may declare war.

Discretionary Original Jurisdiction

The original jurisdiction over disputes between states conferred on the Supreme Court by the Constitution was nonexclusive. In 1789, Congress enacted a judiciary act which made the jurisdiction exclusive and authorized the Supreme Court to promulgate rules for the conduct of business in all U.S. courts.[13] Although Congress enacted statutes pertaining to the implementation of the constitutional full faith and credit clause and the interstate rendition clause (see chapter 2), no statute has been enacted governing the procedure for the invocation of the original jurisdiction or procedures of the U.S. Supreme Court.

A literal reading of section 2 of Article III of the U.S. Constitution appears to suggest certain types of cases automatically would lead to the Supreme Court exercising its original jurisdiction. The court, however, has opined its exercise of original jurisdiction is discretionary and in 1905 emphasized a suit by a state against a sister state must be of serious magnitude before the court will exercise such jurisdiction.[14] The court in another interstate dispute explained in 1983 it possesses "substantial discretion to make case-by-case judgments as to the practical necessity of an original forum in the court of particular disputes within its constitutional jurisdiction" and nine years latter emphasized its judgments with respect to its case-by-case jurisdiction rest upon prudential and equitable standards.[15]

U.S. Supreme Court rule 17, a gate-keeping one, stipulates a state desiring to sue a sister state(s) must seek the court's expressed permission to file an original jurisdiction suit by filing a motion and a supporting brief. The respondent state(s) also files a brief with the court. Upon receiving a motion, the court usually appoints a special master to collect evidence from the party states and to prepare a report and recommendations relative to facts and law. The court does not always accept all the facts reported by the master.[16]

The court specifically encourages states to settle their disputes through negotiations in order to prevent overburdening the court and has opined original jurisdiction will be invoked sparingly. If the master's report does not produce a negotiated settlement, the party states submit briefs to the court which hears oral arguments to assist it in deciding whether to invoke original jurisdiction. In making its determination, the court investigates the party states to determine whether the complainant state is a nominal party, a justiciable controversy exists, and the case is an appropriate one for the exercise of such jurisdiction.

The Party States. The court will not invoke its original jurisdiction until it determines each state is a genuine party to a dispute. In 1972, the court denied Illinois' motion for leave to file a brief of complaint against the City of Milwaukee, Wisconsin, because the city is not a state.[17] Twelve years later, the court denied Puerto Rico's motion to seek the issuance of a writ of mandamus ordering the rendition of a fugitive from justice to Puerto Rico apparently on the ground the writ would be served upon the governor rather than the state.[18]

In 1983, the court rejected a Oklahoma motion to file a complaint against Arkansas because it was a nominal party and the genuine parties were codefendent municipalities and private corporations which, according to the complaint, were polluting waters flowing into Oklahoma.[19]

The court also makes another determination concerning the complainant state; i.e., does the state have standing to bring a suit in its propriety capacity or as *parens patriae* (father of its people)? In 1900, the court established such a right.[20] The Eleventh Amendment to the U.S. Constitution forbids a citizen of a state to file suit against a sister state unless the latter waives its sovereign immunity. The court in 1971 rejected Pennsylvania's motion to sue New Jersey because the proposed suit was "nothing more than a collectivity of private suits against New Jersey for taxes withheld from private parties."[21] According to the court, a state may sue in its *parens patriae* capacity only if "its sovereign or quasi-sovereign interests are implicated and it is not merely litigating as a volunteer for the personal claims of its citizens."[22]

A most interesting case involving the parties to a interstate dispute originated with the levying by the New Hampshire General Court (state legislature) in 1991 of a statewide ad valorem property tax on the Seabrook Nuclear Power plant and providing for a tax credit against the state's business profits tax. The plaintiff states did not levy a statewide ad valorem property tax on nuclear power plants in their states or offer a tax credit to their respective public utilities against their business profits taxes for property taxes paid on the Seabrook plant.

Twelve electric utility companies, including ones headquartered in sister states, owned the plant. On the surface, a challenge to the constitutionality of the tax should be brought by the utility companies in the U.S. District Court. Nevertheless, Connecticut, Massachusetts, and Rhode Island decided they would seek—in their proprietary capacity as electricity consumers and in their *parens patriae* capacity—to invoke the U.S. Supreme Court's original jurisdiction by contending the property tax and associated tax credit violated (1) the congressional *Tax Reform Act of 1976,* which forbids discriminatory state taxation of electricity, (2) the interstate commerce clause of the U.S. Constitution by imposing an undue burden on interstate commerce, (3) the Fourteenth Amendment to the U.S. Constitution by depriving the plaintiff states and their citizens of equal protection of the laws, and (4) the privileges and immunities clause of the Constitution (Art. IV, §2).[23] The plaintiff states highlighted the fact New Hampshire did not levy a property tax on conventional electric power generating plants.

In its response brief, New Hampshire argued (1) the sister states lacked standing to sue, (2) the suit was premature as consumers had not yet paid the tax, (3) any alleged injury would be minor, (4) relief could be provided by an alternative forum, and (4) the plaintiffs' suit lacked merit.[24] The U.S. Supreme Court turned down New Hampshire's answer by granting the plaintiff states' motion and appointing a special master to collect facts and prepare a report with recommendations. The master issued his report in 1992, which favored the plaintiff states.[25] The newly elected New Hampshire governor did not want his two-year term bogged down with a trial in the U.S. Supreme Court and directed that an out-of-court settlement be sought.

Such a settlement was reached by New Hampshire with the concerned utilities in the plaintiff states in 1993 and allowed New Hampshire to keep the $35 million the statewide property tax had generated provided the General Court amended the law. New Hampshire Senior Assistant Attorney General Harold T. Judd conducted negotiations with attorneys representing the utility companies and reported a representative of an attorney general of one plaintiff state attended a negotiation meeting, but was not an active participant in the negotiations.[26] This evidence suggests the southern New England states were acting as *parens patriae* for their electric utility companies.

A Justiciable Controversy. The second criterion employed by the U.S. Supreme Court to assist it in making a decision whether to invoke its original jurisdiction is the existence of a justiciable controversy requiring adjudication by a law court. The court examines a motion to file suit to determine whether it would raise the possibility of the filing of a large number of suits in equity involving claims that are mutually exclusive. In 1939, the court reviewed the claims of each of four states to levy an estate tax. The estate in question would be exhausted if each state is allowed to levy such a tax. The court decided to exercise its original jurisdiction on the ground the dispute was a justiciable one.[27] A case raising a similar issue reached the court in 1978 in a suit involving the domicile of decedent Howard Hughes and the court held the dispute was not a justiciable interstate controversy and should be adjudicated in each of the involved states.[28] In 1982, however, the court invoked its original jurisdiction as the result of a motion to file a complaint in which the executors of the estate contended adverse California and Texas decisions would result in exhaustion of the estate by inheritance taxes imposed by the states and the federal government.[29] Four justices dissented and maintained the controversy was not ripe because unsatisfied tax judgments had not been collected by the contending states.[30]

The court explained in 1940 "it must appear that the complaining state has suffered a wrong through the action of the other state, furnishing ground for judicial redress, or is asserting a right against the other state which is susceptible of judicial enforcement according to the accepted principles of the common law or equity systems of jurisprudence."[31] Mootness also is a ground for the court to refuse to invoke its original jurisdiction. The court summarily denied in 1981 California's motion to enjoin Texas and four other states from quarantining the former's fruits and vegetables in order to prevent the Mediterranean fruit fly from spreading to their states.[32] The discontinuance of the quarantines mooted the controversy.

Appropriateness. The third criterion employed by the Supreme Court to determine whether it should invoke its original jurisdiction is appropriateness. Faced with a crowded calendar, in 1971 the court decided for the first time to utilize this criterion in a suit filed by Ohio against a corporation and later employed the criterion in three interstate disputes.[33] The court will allow a state's motion to file a complaint against a sister state only if the dispute is an appropriate one for the exercise of original jurisdiction as determined by three factors: parties to the suit, seriousness of the subject matter, and existence of an alternative forum.

The court typically will exercise original jurisdiction if the party states to an interstate disputes are acting in their sovereign capacities and the subject matter, such as boundary and water rights, is a serious one. In 1981, the court decided not to invoke its original jurisdiction to settle a dispute alleging breach of contract with respect to scheduled football games between San Jose State University and West Virginia University because the dispute was a minor one and a state court would be an appropriate alternative forum.[34]

The existence of a more appropriate alternative forum induced the court in 1976 to reject Arizona's motion to file a complaint against New Mexico on the ground Arizona electric utility companies and a Arizona political subdivision already had filed a suit in a New Mexico court raising the same question with respect to the U.S. Constitution.[35] The fact that Louisiana had intervened in a suit involving private parties in a Louisiana court relative to whether a Mississippi River island was in Louisiana or Mississippi, persuaded the court in 1988 to reject Louisiana's motion to file a complaint against Mississippi.[36]

Vincent L. McKusick reviewed motions filed by a state to sue another state and concluded the principal reason the court summarily denied the motions, when an opinion was published, was the existence of an alternative forum in approximately fifty percent of the cases.[37]

Types of Interstate Disputes

The U.S. Supreme Court in 1902 noted it sits as an international tribunal in adjudicating interstate disputes and applies "federal law, state law, and international law, as the exigencies of the particular case may demand."[38] In 1907, the court reiterated its earlier opinion by noting interstate relations are governed by international law.[39] The court, however, has not explicated its reference to international law or its application to interstate suits. The court, in 1934, however, explained its interpretation of an interstate compact provision necessitates the use of treaty construction, including diplomatic correspondence but not verbal statements made by negotiators of a treaty.[40] In effect, the court has fashioned an interstate common law combining elements of the common law and international law.

McKusick reviewed interstate suits adjudicated by the U.S. Supreme Court between October 1, 1961, and April 25, 1993, and reported there were twenty-two boundary cases, sixteen right-to-water cases, two water abatement cases, three state escheat of unclaimed property cases, three state tax cases, eight state regulation case, and four miscellaneous cases.[41] Many of these cases are of great economic importance.

Boundary Disputes

State statutes delineate the boundaries of a state, but a bordering state is not required to recognize such boundaries. The boundary disputes arising after the Declaration of Independence are attributable to vague land grants by the crown and surveyors' errors. An example is the dispute over what today is the State of Vermont. New Hampshire interpreted the Mason Grant of 1629 as conferring title to the state of land west of the Connecticut River claimed by New York. The dispute was settled in 1791 when Congress admitted Vermont as the fourteenth state.

In 1799 the U.S. Supreme Court settled the first boundary dispute in *New York v. Connecticut* and in 1927 resolved a similar dispute between New Mexico and Texas on the basis of a condition imposed by Congress for the admission of the New Mexico Territory to the Union as a state.[42] An 1850 congressional statute established the boundary line between the two states and made acceptance of the boundary a requirement for admission of the Territory, which accepted the boundary by incorporating it into the state constitution.

Not surprisingly, rivers often serve as state boundaries. A dispute occasionally arises because a river changes its course and the concerned states can not agree on the boundary. The court in *Louisiana v. Mississippi* in 1984 held the live thalweg in the Mississippi River's navigable channel was the boundary line.[43] The thalweg in international law posits the original flow of a stream continues to be the boundary between nation states when the river in question changes its course.

The court noted in this case the definition of thalweg is not precise and the court had viewed the term as "the middle or deepest or most navigable channel in 1906."[44] The deepest channel and the most navigable channel are not necessarily the same. The party states agreed the boundary is determined by the thalweg and river traffic defines the thalweg. The court's task was to determine the normal course of vessel traffic. This rule, as developed by the court, is part of the interstate common law developed to establish state boundary lines. The court in 1995 agreed to hear a special master's finding that the thalweg had shifted, as river currents had eroded parts of an island and built it up elsewhere, thereby merging the island into the Louisiana river bank.[45]

The doctrine of acquiescence also is employed by the court to settle boundary disputes. In 1980, the Court's decision favored California because Nevada had not objected to the boundary line for a century.[46] In a similar case—*Illinois v. Kentucky*—in 1991 the court ruled Kentucky, in order to justify its boundary claim on the basis of acquiescence, "would need to show by a preponderance of the evidence . . . a long and continuous possession of, and assertion of sovereignty over, the territory . . ."[47] Kentucky failed to provide the needed evidence.

The states involved in an original jurisdiction suit in the U.S. Supreme Court may continue negotiations to reach an out-of-court agreement to' settle a boundary dispute. New Hampshire and Maine were involved for many years in what the media termed a "Lobster War" involving a disputed boundary line in the Atlantic Ocean. Maine's lobster regulatory laws are stricter than those of New Hampshire. New Hampshire in 1973 brought an original action against Maine in the court, but continued to negotiate with Maine. In 1976, upon reaching an agreement, the two states sought and received the Supreme Court's approval for the agreement, thereby terminating the suit.[48]

An interstate compact consented to by Congress is another method of settling an interstate boundary dispute (see chapter 8). The North Carolina General Assembly and South Carolina General Assembly each enacted an interstate compact to settle their boundary dispute and Congress granted its consent to the compact in 1981.[49] Similarly, the Missouri General Assembly and the Nebraska State Legislature each enacted an interstate compact establishing the border between them and Congress in 1999 granted its consent.[50] And Oklahoma and Texas in 2000 received the consent of Congress for an interstate compact settling their boundary dispute.[51]

A boundary dispute may generate another interstate dispute. The Portsmouth Naval Shipyard is located on an island in the middle of the Piscataqua River, which is the boundary line between New Hampshire and Maine. The boundary dispute between the two states generated an interstate tax dispute because Maine levies a personal income tax and New Hampshire does not. Maine claimed the island and levied its income tax on all shipyard workers. New Hampshire protested and maintained Maine lacked jurisdiction to levy the income tax on New Hampshire residents. In 1990, the U.S. Department of Justice advised the U.S. Navy not to withhold the Maine income tax from New Hampshire workers until the U.S. Supreme Court settles the boundary dispute.[52]

Water Disputes

Interstate suits involving allocation of water and water pollution are of great economic importance to the disputants. The former disputes were historically settled according to the doctrine of riparian rights or the doctrine of prior apportionment. The first doctrine determines priority to the use of water by ownership of adjoining property. The second doctrine assigns priority to the first user of the water.

The U.S. Supreme Court developed in 1907 the doctrine of equitable apportionment to settle water allocation disputes by providing for the sharing of interstate waters.[53] Disputes often have involved the Colorado River, which originates in the Rocky Mountains in Colorado and flows through

Utah to form the Arizona boundary line with California and Nevada. Water diverted from this large river made the economic development of southern California possible.

In 1952, Arizona sued California in the U.S. Supreme Court alleging southern California was drawing more Colorado River water than the six other states with access to the water combined. This dispute involved a 1922 interstate water allocation compact. In 1963, the court supported, in general, Arizona's claims during periods when there is normal water flow, but authorized the U.S. Secretary of the Interior to allocate river water whenever the flow drops below normal.[54] This suit was the fifth one involving the allocation of the river's water.

Disputes over Colorado River waters continue. California is required to reduce its consumption of such waters over a fifteen-year period and had to demonstrate by December 31, 2002, how the state would reduce consumption or face the threat of an immediate reduction in the volume of river waters imposed by the U.S. Department of the Interior. The department on August 30, 2002, approved the state's plan to reduce its dependence on the river's waters by constructing a one billion dollar facility to pump water under private land in the Mojave Desert and store the water.[55]

A key component of the state's plan is termed the San Diego Plan and involves water boards in San Diego County purchasing water rights to the Colorado River owned by farmers in the Imperial Valley for $130 million.[56]

The North Platte River was the source of a similar controversy involving the respective water-rights claims of Colorado, Nebraska, and Wyoming. In 1945, the court issued a decree establishing interstate priorities on the waters of the river and apportioning the flow of a portion of the river during the irrigation season.[57] In 1986, Nebraska sought the issuance by the court of an order for enforcement of the decree and injunctive relief. In 1987, the court appointed a special master who supervised pretrial proceedings and discovery, and filed a report in 1992 with the court. The latter, in *Nebraska v. Wyoming*, in 1993 ruled that the decree did not grant Nebraska rights to excess water of the Laramie River that empty into the North Platte River, and to the extent Nebraska sought to modify the decree and not to enforce it, a higher standard of proof revealing substantial injury was required.[58]

This court decision did not end the dispute. In 1995, the court agreed to exercise its original jurisdiction over Nebraska's challenge to actions by Wyoming involving a tributary of the North Platte River, and denied Wyoming's request for leave to file a counter claim and a cross claim for relief under the 1945 decree.[59] The court opined: "simply put, Wyoming seeks to replace a simple apportionment scheme with one in which Nebraska's share would be capped at the volume of probably beneficial use, presumably to Wyoming's advantage."[60]

The New York State Legislature authorized New York City to acquire land and construct large reservoirs in the Catskill Mountains, which are the headwaters of the Delaware River whose waters also flow through New Jersey, Pennsylvania, and Delaware. The city's rapid population growth resulted in increasing diversion of waters from the river. New Jersey sued New York for allowing the city to withdraw an excess amount of water from the river and the U.S. Supreme Court in 1931 decreed the city could divert no more than 440,000,000 gallons of water daily from the river or its tributaries and required construction of a treatment plant in Port Jervis, New York, prior to the discharge of treated sewage into the Delaware and Neversink Rivers.[61] In response to a petition to amend the decree to permit the city to divert additional waters from the Delaware River, the court in 1954 adopted the report of its special master, suspended the 1931 decree, and authorized additional water diversion subsequent to completion of a new reservoir on the East Branch of the river and a further diversion of water upon completion of the Cannonsville Reservoir.[62] These court decisions did not settle the water disputes, but led to the enactment of the first federal-interstate compact—Delaware River Basin Compact—which generally has achieved its goals including water allocation (see chapter 8).[63]

In 1987, the court settled an allocation dispute under the Pecos River Compact without specifying the amount of water to be delivered by New Mexico annually to Texas.[64] Article III(a) of the compact stipulates "New Mexico shall not deplete by man's activities the flow of the Pecos River at the New Mexico-Texas state line below an amount which will give to Texas a quantity of water equivalent to that available to Texas under the 1947 condition."

Texas, prior to filing an original action in the court in 1974, engaged in fruitless negotiations with New Mexico for many years. The court in 1980 adopted the report of the special master containing a new inflow-outflow methodology for determining the amount of water that Texas should receive.[65] The methodology received the court's imprimatur in 1984, but both states raised objections.[66] New Mexico, in particular, maintained it was not obligated to deliver water that she was under no obligation to refrain from using. The court ruled in favor of Texas and opined its remedy was not limited to prospective relief and could provide monetary relief.[67]

A complicated interstate water dispute erupted in 2002 and involved the question of whether the U.S. Army Corps of Engineers could release water from the Fort Peck Reservoir. The specific issue in question pits maintaining reservoir water levels to protect fisheries against ensuring adequate water in the Missouri River to float barges in the downriver states.[68] Montana sought and obtained an order from the U.S. District Court in Billings preventing the release of the reservoir water and a second U.S. District Court judge in South Dakota issued a similar order against the release of water from the Lake Oahe and Lake Francis Case reservoirs. Nebraska and other Missouri River states filed a lawsuit to obtain a court order requiring the Corps of Engineers to release more water from the Fort Peck Reservoir.

The Oklahoma Water Resources Board in 2002 threatened to take Texas to court because Texas allegedly was wrongfully storing approximately two billion gallons of Canadian River water annually that belongs to Oklahoma.[69] The board specifically maintains Texas violated an interstate river compact by constructing a large reservoir that does not serve municipalities as required under the compact.

Water disputes also have an international dimension. In 1944, the United States entered into a treaty with Mexico stipulating the latter must permit water from six tributary rivers to flow into the Rio Grande River. One-third of this water was allocated to south Texas and the remaining water to Mexican farmers in bordering states. Since 1992, Mexico has failed to deliver the required 430 million cubic meters of waters annually to south Texas.[70] President Vincente Fox of Mexico reached an agreement with the Mexican states—Coahulla, Chichuahua, and Tamaulipsa—bordering the river to improve conservation of waters and provide the required amount to south Texas. On July 4, 2002,[71] the United States and the Mexican government signed an agreement designed to settle the water problem by spending $210 million on water conservation and irrigation programs in the Mexican states and Texas.[72] Mexico will discharge more water into the Rio Grande and invest $40 million in programs to improve water use efficiency in the bordering states. The 1944 treaty also provided for a specified amount of Colorado River water to be delivered to Mexicali.

Tax Disputes

Interstate-tax disputes are relatively common and are examined in more detail in chapter 6. Although the U.S. Supreme Court has upheld the constitutionality of state imposed mineral extractive taxes, it struck down Louisiana's "first use tax" levied on natural gas extracted from wells in the Gulf of Mexico and processed in the state.[73] The ground for invalidation of the tax was the fact it was imposed on gas extracted from areas that belong to all United States citizens and was passed on to consumers in sister states.

Wyoming brought a novel suit, on interstate commerce clause grounds, challenging the constitutionality of an Oklahoma law requiring coal-fired electric-generating plants in the state to burn a mixture of coal whose contents include a minimum of ten percent coal mined in the state. The court invalidated the tax by agreeing with Wyoming's objection that the tax caused a decline in state's revenues from a severance tax on coal as Oklahoma utilities no longer could burn only Wyoming low sulfur coal.[74] Justice Clarence

Thomas dissented and raised the question of *parens patriae* by opining the dispute is not an interstate one, but rather is a dispute between Wyoming coal-mining companies and Oklahoma.[75] He explained the court's ruling will allow any state direct access to the court if it can demonstrate any tax revenue loss, even a de minimis one, is caused by the action of a sister state.

Bona Vacantia Suits

An escheats or unclaimed property law has been enacted by every state providing that dividends, interest, real property, securities, and wages not claimed after a stipulated time period are deemed to be abandoned and title to the assets reverts to the state.[76]

The U.S. Supreme Court in 1965 in *Texas v. New Jersey* established rules a state must follow in order to take title to unclaimed property.[77] The primary rule stipulates that "fairness among the states requires that the right and power to escheat the debt should be accorded to the state of the creditor's last known address as shown by the debtor's books and records."[78] The secondary rule, which awards the right to claim abandoned property to the debtor state, accords recognition to the inadequacy of the primary rule in certain cases because there may be no record of the owner's address or last known address. In other words, the secondary rule awards the right to escheat to the debtor's state subject to a claim by a state with a superior right to escheat under the primary rule.

The court in 1972 adjudicated the competing claims of New York and Pennsylvania for money order proceeds of the Western Union Company resulting from its inability to locate the payees or to refund the money to the senders because the company did not record their addresses. The primary rule generally does not apply to such funds since the addresses of the payees were not known. Several states contended application of the secondary rule would result in the company's domicile state receiving a much larger share of the unclaimed funds. These states recommended a rule authorizing the state of the place of purchase of money orders to escheat under the primary rule. The court, however, adhered to its secondary rule contained in the court's 1965 opinion and rejected the recommendation.[79]

The court resolved a Delaware and New York dispute over unclaimed securities in 1993. Delaware contended $360 million in unclaimed dividends, interests, and other securities were escheated wrongfully by New York. The court appointed a special master who recommended the right to escheat should be awarded to the state in which the principal executive officers of the issuers of securities are located. The two states registered their objections to this recommendation.

The court explained its 1965 precedent required the court to determine that the state in which the intermediary holding the securities is located has the right to escheat funds belonging to individuals who cannot be located.[80] The case was remanded to the special master with the notation "if New York can establish by reference to debtors' records that the creditors who were owed particular securities distributions had last known addresses in New York," its right to escheat under the primary rule will supersede Delaware's right under the secondary rule.[81] Failure of the two states to reach an agreement would result in the special master deciding how much money New York owes to Delaware.

In 1995, the two states reach an agreement providing New York would pay Delaware $200 million in funds escheated over several years and $35 million annually for an indefinite period.[82] In addition, the two states reached an agreement to share approximately $182 million with the other forty-eight states, who sued the two states, over ten years to settle a dispute over unclaimed dividend and bond interest payments.

The Silence of Congress

The constitutional delegation of exclusive power to Congress "to regulate commerce with foreign nations, and among the several States, and with the Indian tribes" (Art. I, §8) suggests state statutes based upon economic provincialism would conflict with congressional statutes and, under the supremacy of the laws clause, the state statutes would be invalid. Congress, as noted in chapter 3, was slow to exercise this delegated power and courts were called upon to determine the constitutionality of state statutes imposing barriers to the free flow of commerce. Only five cases involving the commerce clause reached the U.S. Supreme Court prior to 1840, but the number increased to twenty by 1860, thirty by 1880, seventy-seven by 1890, 148 by 1890, and 213 by 1898 in reflection of the great growth of commerce and industry.[83] Subsequently, the number of such cases sky-rocketed.

A controversy involving a New York statute that granted a monopoly to Robert Fulton and Robert R. Livingston with respect to the operation of steamboats in the state was brought to the U.S. Supreme Court on appeal. Thomas Gibbons challenged the monopoly on the basis of the dormant or unexercised interstate commerce clause and a coasting license issued under provisions of a 1793 congressional statute.[84] New York maintained it possessed authority to regulate the coasting trade adjacent to the state's shores as a concurrent power since the constitutional grant of authority to regulate interstate commerce was not exclusive and states were not forbidden to regulate such commerce.

In 1824, the U.S. Supreme Court in *Gibbons v. Ogden* for the first time invalidated a state statute creating an interstate trade barrier on the ground it violated the dormant interstate-commerce clause.[85] Chief Justice John Marshall rejected the argument of the counsel for Ogden that commerce encompasses only traffic defined as buying and selling by holding "[c]ommerce undoubtedly is traffic, but it something more; it is intercourse. . . ."[86] He explained U.S. intercourse in foreign commerce includes all aspects of commerce and such intercourse applies to interstate commerce. He utilized the dispute to develop the doctrine of the continuous journey, which holds Congress possesses plenary power to regulate a steamship traveling only in New York State because some of the goods and passengers carried, after unloading and disembarking in the state, will continue their journey by other means to sister states. He specifically opined: "Commerce among the States cannot stop at the external boundary line of each state, but may be introduced into the interior."[87] Under the dormant interstate-commerce clause doctrine, the clause, even though unexercised by Congress, limits the powers of states and the court will determine the limits.

As explained in chapter 3, Congress in enacting regulatory statutes does not always include an explicit preemption statement or savings clause, and courts are called upon to determine whether the statutes are preemptive in nature. Congress' failure to include such a statement in some acts may be the result of a number of members, who favor a bill, indicating to the bill sponsor(s) or leaders of their respective house that politically these members could not vote to approve the bills containing an explicit preemption clause for fear of retribution at the polls.

Courts also are faced with the problem of determining whether a state or local government law or regulation is constitutional when Congress has been silent on the subject matter. The U.S. Supreme Court developed two doctrines—"Original Package" and "Silence of Congress"—to determine when goods moving in foreign and interstate commerce lose their constitutional protection against state regulation and taxation. The first doctrine is traceable to *Brown v. Maryland* in which the court in 1827 rejected the state's claim federal jurisdiction terminated upon payment of import duties and ruled a Maryland license tax on importers and wholesalers of foreign goods constituted an import tax levied without the required constitutional permission of Congress (Art. I, §10) and conflicted directly with tariff acts enacted by Congress.[88] The court specifically noted imported goods at a given point lose their constitutional protection against state regulation or taxation, but retain such protection while they are in their original packages in the importer's warehouse. Chief Justice Marshall added he assumed "the principles laid down in this case to apply equally to importation from a sister State."[89]

In 1829, Marshall wrote the opinion in another major case—*Willson v. The Blackbird Creek Marsh Company*—upholding a Delaware statute authorizing construction of a dam on a navigable creek, entirely within the state, that flows into the Delaware River in the absence of a congressional statute on the subject.[90] He opined:

> We do not think that the act empowering the Blackbird Creek Marsh Company to place a dam across the creek can, under all the circumstances of the case, be considered as repugnant to the power to regulate commerce in its dormant state, or as being in conflict with any law passed on the subject.[91]

This decision appears to be at variance with the *Gibbons* and *Brown* decisions holding Congress has exclusive power to regulate interstate commerce. Marshall apparently considered the Delaware statute to be purely a police power regulation designed to promote public health by reclaiming marshes adjacent to the creek.[92]

Roger B. Taney replaced Marshall as chief justice in 1835. Taney's views on interpretation of the U.S. Constitution differed sharply from Marshall's. In 1847, the court acknowledged Congress has plenary power to regulate interstate and foreign commerce, yet unanimously upheld the constitutional validity of the liquor dealers' license laws of New Hampshire, Massachusetts, and Rhode Island on the basis of the court's "Original Package" doctrine.[93] Speaking for the court, Taney held:

> . . . the mere grant of power to the general government cannot, upon any just principles of construction, be construed to be an absolute prohibition to the exercise of any power over the same subject by the States. The controlling and supreme power over commerce with foreign nations and the several States is undoubtedly conferred upon Congress. Yet . . . the State may nevertheless, for the safety or convenience of trade or for the protection of the health of its citizens, make regulations of commerce for its own ports and harbours, and for its own territory; and such regulations are valid unless they come in conflict with a law of Congress.[94]

The Taney Court in *Cooley v. The Board of Wardens* in 1851 opined there were details of commerce subject to state regulation until supplanted by an act of Congress.[95] The decision focused upon a Pennsylvania requirement that all ships entering a harbor must take on a state licensed pilot paid at a fixed rate to ensure the safety of the ships. The court over the next two decades issued similar decisions, but subsequently came to rely less on the 1851 doctrine.

Felix Frankfurter in 1937 noted Taney challenged the dormant interstate commerce clause doctrine holding the clause limits the powers of states and the court would determine the limits on state powers.[96] Frankfurter summarized Taney's views as follows:

He flatly denied that the mere grant of the commerce power operated to limit state power. The commerce clause was what it pretended to be, an authority for Congress to act. Finally, the Court's function was to determine the existence of a conflict between state and federal legislation purporting to regulate commerce, whenever it became necessary to the disposition of a particular litigation, and then to override the state statute only if an indubitable conflict with the act of Congress was found to exist.[97]

Taney served as chief justice for close to three decades and never voted to hold a state statute to be unconstitutional on the ground it offended the dormant interstate commerce clause.

Salmon P. Chase, who succeeded Taney as chief justice, did not play a major role in developing this doctrine although the court in 1872 commenced to invalidate state statutes allegedly interfering with the unexercised constitutionally delegated exclusive power "to regulate commerce with foreign nations, and among the several States, and with the Indian Tribes . . ." (Art. I, §8).[98]

In 1874, Chief Justice Morrison R. Waite replaced Chase at a time when the due process of the law clause of the Fourteenth Amendment became an additional source of limitation on the powers of states.[99] In 1875, the court invalidated a Missouri license tax imposed on peddlers of goods produced in sister states and opined: "It is sufficient to hold now that the commerce power continues until the commodity has ceased to be the subject of discrimination by reason of its foreign character."[100]

The constitutionality of an Illinois statute regulating the rates charged by grain storage firms was challenged on the grounds the statute intruded upon the delegated power of Congress to regulate interstate commerce and violated the equal protection of the laws clause and the due process of the law clause of the Fourteenth Amendment.[101] Chief Justice Waite in *Munn v. Illinois* in 1876 delivered the court's opinion rejecting these arguments and sustaining the statute.[102] Waite also rejected the argument, based upon the due process of law clause, that only courts could determine what is reasonable compensation for utility services. He wrote:

> In countries where the common law prevails, it has been customary from time immemorial for the legislature to declare what shall be a reasonable compensation under such circumstances . . . the controlling fact is the power to regulate at all. If that exists, the right to establish the maximum charge, as one of the means of regulation, is implied.[103]

Referring to the silence of Congress, the court in 1885 upheld the constitutionality of a nondiscriminatory Louisiana property tax levied upon coal imported in barges from Pennsylvania:

> When Congress shall see fit to make a regulation on the subject of property
> transported from one State to another, which may have the effect to give it
> a temporary exemption from taxation in the State to which it is transported,
> it will be time enough to consider any conflict that may arise between such
> regulation and the general taxing laws of the State.[104]

Two years later, the court invalidated a county tax levied upon salesmen who
sold products by sample on the ground a tax can not be levied on offers to sell
them before the products have been shipped to the state.[105] The court
announced its decisions had established a doctrine relative to the exclusive
regulatory power of Congress holding its failure "to make express regulations
indicates its will that the subject be left free from any restrictions or imposi-
tions; and regulation of the subject by the States, except in matters of local
concern only ... is repugnant to such freedom."[106] In 1890, the Supreme Court
struck down a Minnesota law requiring the inspection of cattle, hogs, and
sheep twenty-four hours prior to their slaughter for food because the law discriminated against animals slaughtered in sister states.[107]

More recently, the U.S. Supreme ruled in 1975 the constitutional prohibition of levying of "imposts or duties on imports" by states without the
consent of Congress does not prohibit the levying of a property tax on
imported products.[108]

Justice Robert H. Jackson of the U.S. Supreme Court summed up the
commerce clause in the following terms:

> The commerce clause is one of the most prolific sources of national power and
> an equally prolific source of conflict with legislation of the State. While the
> Constitution vests in Congress the power to regulate commerce among the
> States, it does not say what the States may or may not do in the absence of con-
> gressional action, nor how to draw the line between what is and what is not
> commerce among the States. Perhaps even more than by interpretation of its
> written word, this Court has advanced the solidarity and prosperity of this
> Nation by the meaning it has given to these great silences of the Constitution.[109]

Preemption Criteria

A number of congressional statutes contain a clause stipulating "this act is
intended to supersede any law of any State or political subdivision thereof
inconsistent with its provisions," but most statutes held to be preemptive do
not contain such a clause.[110]

In 1942, attorney George B. Braden explained a rule stipulating state
laws would remain in force unless specifically prohibited by federal law "would
be intolerable. Congress could not be asked to anticipate all possible legisla-

tive conflicts, nor could it really solve the problem by blanket prohibition. In some instances a tag end proviso nullifying all statutes 'conflicting with this act' would only restate the problem. Some leeway must be left."[111] The consequence is courts are called upon often to decide whether a congressional statute preempts a state statute or local government ordinance.

The U.S. Supreme Court emphasized in several opinions there are no precise criteria by which it can determine the intent of Congress in the absence of an explicit statement in a law of an intention to preempt. The court in 1941 explained each challenge of a state law on the ground of inconsistency with a federal statute requires a determination on the basis of the particular facts of the case.

> There is not—and from the very nature of the problem—there can not be any rigid formula or rule which can be used to determine the meaning and purpose of every act of Congress. This Court, in considering the validity of state laws in the light of treaties o federal laws touching on the same subject, has made use of the following expressions: Conflicting; contrary to; occupying the field; repugnance; difference; irreconcilability; violation; curtailment; and interference. But none of these expressions provides an infallible constitutional test or an exclusive constitutional yardstick. In the final analysis, there can be no one crystal clear distinctly marked formula. Our primary function is to determine whether, under the circumstances of this particular case, Pennsylvania's law stands as an obstacle to the accomplishment and execution of the full purposes and objectives of Congress.[112]

Two tests of congressional preemption were explicated by the court in 1947: (1) "[T]he question in each case is what the purpose of Congress was" and (2) does the federal law involve "a field in which the federal interest is so dominant that the federal system will be assumed to preclude enforcement of state laws on the same subject?"[113] In interpreting the *Noise Control Act of 1972*, the court opined:

> Our prior cases on preemption are not precise guidelines in the present controversy, for each case turns on the peculiarities and special features of the federal regulatory scheme in question. . . . Control of noise is of course deep-seated in the police power of the States. Yet the pervasive control vested in EPA [Environmental Protection Agency] and FAA [Federal Aviation Administration] under the 1972 Act seems to use to leave no room for local curfews or other local controls.[114]

The court in 1979 held a congressional statute granting federal courts jurisdiction over allegations of violations of constitutional rights does not cover a suit based simply on the fact a state law conflicts with the national Social Security Act.[115] The court conceded the state law by conflicting with the act facially violated the supremacy of the law clause of the U.S. Constitution (Art. VI), but the violation was not of the type that confers jurisdiction upon federal courts.

On occasion, the court voids only part of a state statute or local ordinance on preemption grounds. In 1978, the court validated the first section—requiring oil tankers to be guided by state-licensed pilots—of a three section Washington statute pertaining to Puget Sound and struck down the other two sections containing specified designed standards for oil tankers and banning tankers over 125,000 deadweight tons from the Sound.[116]

The court in *Hodel v. Virginia Surface Mining and Reclamation Association* in 1981 built upon its 1976 reasoning in *National League of Cities v. Usery,* by enunciating three tests for determining whether the *Surface Mining Control and Reclamation Act of 1977* preempted state law.[117] "First, there must be a showing that the challenged statutes regulates the 'States as States.' . . . Second, the federal regulation must address matters that are indisputably 'attributes of state sovereignty.' . . . And, third, it must be apparent that the States' compliance with the federal law would directly impair their ability 'to structure integral operations in areas of traditional functions.'"[118]

In the court's opinion, the plaintiffs failed to demonstrate the federal statute regulated states as states and the states are not mandated to enforce the standards contained in the statute because failure of a state to submit a proposed regulatory program complying with the federal law to the U.S. Department of the Interior results in the federal government assuming "the full regulatory burden."[119] The court emphasized "there can be no suggestion that the Act commandeers the legislative processes of the States by directly compelling them to enact and enforce a federal regulatory program."[120]

The court's five to four majority upholding the preemption powers of Congress changed in 1992 when the court, by a similar vote, ruled in *New York v. United States* Congress does not possess authority to require a state to accept ownership of low-level radioactive wastes or regulate such waste in conformance with national standards on the ground the statute encroached upon the powers reserved to the states by the Tenth Amendment to the U.S. Constitution.[121]

Concurrent State Judicial Jurisdiction

The U.S. dual- or parallel court system offers litigants an option in many types of cases to file a suit in a U.S. court or in a state court. As noted, exclusive federal court jurisdiction is restricted to cases involving interstate disputes, the United States or another nation as a party, and admiralty. In 1789, Congress created the U.S. District Court and the U.S. Circuit Court, but respected the semi-sovereignty of states by restricting the jurisdiction of these courts.[122] The U.S. District Court, for example, originally had jurisdiction over diversity of citizenship cases only if a suit involved $500 or more. This threshold amount periodically has been increased, and currently is $75,000.[123] State courts hear suits involving lesser amounts and had exclusive jurisdiction over suits involving federal questions until 1875 when Congress granted the U.S. District Court original jurisdiction over federal questions.[124] The jurisdiction of federal courts subsequently increased greatly as the result of congressional acts expanding the rights of citizens and preempting certain regulatory powers of states. Federal courts can enjoin state court proceedings through issuance of injunctions or declaratory judgments, but state courts may not enjoin federal court proceedings.[125]

Writing in 1974, John W. Winkle, III explained the "imprecise residency requirements for diversity plaintiffs have permitted large corporations, foreign entrepreneurs, and even commuters more flexibility in their selections."[126] Litigants generally select state courts and may do so to gain a tactical advantage in a trial. In 1991, attorney Morris Dees stated he decided to bring his civil law suit against white supremacist Tom Metzger in an Oregon court rather than the U.S. Supreme Court:

> We chose state court because Oregon discovery rules are quite different than the federal rules. You can do trial by ambush in Oregon. You have no interrogatories, no production of evidence; you don't have to give the names of witnesses or give the other side your documents.[127]

Concern state courts may reflect local prejudice has induced a number of litigants to file suit in the allegedly more impartial U.S. District Court. A defendant in a state court suit may be able to have a case removed to the U.S. District Court under the *Removal of Causes Act of 1920* on the ground a state court may be partial to the plaintiff.[128] The Supreme Court in recent years has rendered several decisions clarifying the act.

In 1996, the U.S. Supreme Court opined a U.S. District Court decision in a case removed from state court improperly because of lack of subject-matter jurisdiction may be entered provided the defect is remedied prior to the issuance of the final judgment.[129] And in 1998, the court held a case may be removed from a state court to the U.S. District Court when one or more claims are subject to Eleventh Amendment immunity.[130]

Summary

Establishment of a dual-judicial system by the U.S. Constitution immediately raised the question of the dividing line between national jurisdiction and state jurisdiction. The system, depending upon the issue in contention, often allows a litigant a choice of a state or a U.S. forum and also allows the losing party in the highest court in a state to petition the U.S. Supreme Court for the issuance of a writ of certiorari if a federal question is involved. The court rejects most such petitions because of its crowded calendar. The bulk of the cases adjudicated by the court are the result of appeals of lower federal court decisions and not appeals of the decisions of the highest state courts. Furthermore, the *Removal of Causes Act of 1920* allows a case to be removed to the U.S. District Court, which may adjudicate the controversy or remand the case back to the state court.

The U.S. Supreme Court exercises its original jurisdiction to settle interstate suits based upon the criteria of (1) genuine party states not representing a nominal party, (2) a justiciable controversy involving a state suffering a wrong, and (3) appropriateness with respect to whether there is an alternative forum. The most common dispute involves state boundary lines and is followed by regulatory disputes and tax disputes.

The silence of Congress in enacting regulatory statutes to ensure the free flow of commerce among the several states led to the court developing its dormant interstate commerce clause doctrine holding a state statute or regulation will be invalidated if it offends the clause in the absence of a congressional statute on the subject. The court also is called upon to determine whether a congressional statute preempts state regulatory authority in the absence of an explicit preemption provision.

Chapters 5 and 6 examine interstate trade barriers and discriminatory state taxation, respectively, and methods of removing barriers and discriminatory taxes.

CHAPTER 5

Interstate Trade Barriers

The Treaty of Paris of 1783 ending the war between the United Kingdom and its former colonies in North America was followed within one year by the outbreak of interstate trade warfare as tariffs were erected by each of the five New England states and most of the middle Atlantic states. Connecticut levied discriminatory duties on goods imported from Massachusetts and Pennsylvania levied similar duties on Delaware merchandise. New York levied fees on boats containing vegetables that were rowed across the Hudson River and also imposed clearance fees on coastal ships. Each of these actions invited retaliation by sister states.

The Federalists explained the proposed U.S. Constitution would eliminate such barriers by its grant of authority to Congress "[t]o regulate commerce with foreign nations, and among the several States, and with the Indian tribes . . ."[1] Alexander Hamilton in advocating adoption of the proposed fundamental law painted a black picture of each state adopting a commercial intercourse policy that "would occasion distinctions, preferences, and exclusions, which would beget discontent . . ." and "the infraction of these regulations, on one side, the efforts to prevent and repel them, on the other, would naturally lead to outrages and these to reprisals and wars."[2]

James Madison identified the lack of authority for Congress to regulate commerce among sister states as a major defect of the Articles of Confederation and Perpetual Union and cited the burden placed on states "which import and export through other States" which would "load the articles of import and export, during the passage through their jurisdiction, with duties which would fall on the makers of the latter and the consumers of the former."[3] Madison contended "a superintending authority" over interstate and foreign commerce was essential and the Congress under the proposed constitution would be such an authority.

The U.S. Constitution contains five provisions designed to promote free trade:

1. Congress is granted authority to regulate commerce with foreign nations, the Indian tribes, and among the several states (Art. I, §8).
2. Congress is forbidden to levy export duties (Art. I, §9).
3. Congress may not give preference to the ports of one state over the ports of any other state (Art. I, §9).

4. A state may not levy an import or export duty without the consent of Congress, which may revise or abolish the duty, and a duty can be levied only to raise funds to finance the state's inspection laws with any surplus revenue dedicated to the U. S. Treasury (Art. I, §10).

5. A state may not deny any of its privileges and immunities to citizens of other states (Art. 4, §2).[4]

Interstate Trade Barriers

States as semisovereign governments utilize their license, police, proprietary and tax powers on a daily basis for legitimate purposes. Exercise of the reserved license power and police power in particular are essential if the health, safety, welfare, convenience, and morals of the public are to be protected. The power to tax, of course, is essential for raising funds to finance state functions. The proprietary power affords the state legislature the option of deciding whether the state should engage in business activities such as electric power generation.

These state powers can be employed deliberately or inadvertently to create trade barriers among sister states. As one would suspect, powerful economic interest groups occasionally pressure the state legislature to enact statutes or heads of departments to promulgate regulations offering the groups protection against interstate and foreign competition. Courts, however, do not always invalidate economic protection statutes or administrative rules and regulations as explained below.

A more subtle form of economic mercantilism is illustrated by the Vermont Department of Agriculture's "seal of quality" program under which farmers producing products meeting the state's standards are allowed to affix the state's seal of quality to packages containing their products. The quality seal may generate additional sales and higher prices for the state's farmers.[5]

Police Power Barriers

State economic and social regulation based upon the police power is definable only in the broadest of terms as the authority of a state to regulate persons and property in order to protect and promote public health, safety, welfare, morals, and convenience. Justice Oliver Wendell Holmes of the U.S. Supreme Court in 1911 opined "the police power extends to all great public needs. It may be put forth in aid of what is sanctioned by usage, or held by the prevailing morality or strong and preponderant opinion to be greatly and immediately necessary to the public welfare."[6]

Most commonly, the police power is exercised by the enactment and enforcement of a statute, but the power may be exercised summarily by a state or local government officer in response to an emergency situation including collapse of buildings, infectious diseases, fires, neglected children, and riots. General-purpose local governments exercise the police power as instrumentalities of the state.

Meat products from sister states also have been subject to improper use of the police power. The Minnesota State Legislature in 1889, for example, enacted a statute prohibiting the sale of dressed meat within any municipal subdivision unless the animals were inspected there within twenty-four hours prior to slaughter and declaring a violation of the statute to be a misdemeanor.[7] The ostensible purpose of the statute was to protect the health of Minnesota citizens. Writing for the U.S. Supreme Court in 1890, Justice John M. Harlan explained the animal inspection statute would be a valid exercise of the state's police power if the purpose is to ensure meats are safe for human consumption, but invalidated the statute as protectionist and violative of the dormant interstate commerce clause of the U.S. Constitution because citizens of other states could not comply with the statute's terms.[8] More recently, the 1973 Kansas State Legislature approved a bill requiring all beef and other red meats from sister states sold in the state to be labeled "Imported," but the governor vetoed the bill.

Florida avocado growers brought suit in the U.S. District Court for the Northern District of California seeking to enjoin a California law determining the maturity of avocados by oil content on the ground the law conflicted with a U.S. Department of Agriculture regulation promulgated by the U.S. secretary of agriculture and violated the equal protection of the laws clause of the Fourteenth Amendment. The court in 1961 rejected the contentions of the plaintiffs and the decision was appealed.[9] Writing for the U.S. Supreme Court in 1963, Justice William Brennan opined the law neither violates the supremacy of the law clause of the U.S. Constitution nor denies avocado growers equal protection of the laws.[10] Brennan observed

> the maturity of avocados is a subject matter of the kind this Court has traditionally regarded as properly with the scope of state superintendence . . . and it would be unreasonable to infer that Congress delegated to the growers in a particular region the authority to deprive the States of their traditional power to enforce otherwise valid regulations designed for the protection of consumers.[11]

The term quarantine refers to a period of forty-days confinement and initially was imposed on ship passengers arriving in a port who had been exposed to an infectious disease. States and the U.S. government each possess the power to impose quarantines. Congress in 1796 enacted a statute prohibiting the interstate shipment of goods in violation of state health and quarantine laws.[12] In 1884, Congress enacted the *Cattle Contagious Disease Act,* and in 1912, enacted the *Plant Quarantine Act.*[13]

The Mediterranean fruit fly can cause serious crop damage. To prevent its spread, Alabama, Florida, Mississippi, South Carolina, and Texas in 1981 imposed quarantines on all fruits from California.[14] New York took similar action in 1983 by imposing a quarantine on importation of poultry products from four Pennsylvania counties because of the outbreak of avian influenza, caused by a virus, on ninety poultry farms where subsequently federal and Pennsylvania officers ordered the slaughter of approximately three million chickens to prevent the spread of the virus.[15] And California and Texas in 1988 banned the importation of Florida citrus fruit in an attempt to keep a bacterial plant disease, canker, from entering their states.[16] A state imposed quarantine often is challenge in court as violating the dormant interstate commerce clause, but the challenge typically is rejected by the court if there is evidence the quarantine is essential to prevent the spread of a disease or insect.

No one objects to a state utilizing its police power to inspect food to ensure its freshness and to eliminate adulteration and fraud or to impose quarantines to prevent the spread of animal diseases and insect pests. During the great depression of the 1930s, California utilized its motor vehicle regulations and quarantine powers as subterfuges to deter the immigration of poor people, especially those from Oklahoma. Many states during the same decade erected barriers to sister state farm products generally and to dairy products in particular. A 1939 special report to the U.S. secretary of agriculture urged action against "a very small group of quarantines that seem to be used not so much to prevent the spread of diseases or pests as to afford protection to growers within the State."[17]

Such barriers continued after World War II and in 1959, Florida required eggs imported from sister states to be labeled "Imported" by shippers of eggs.[18] A different approach was employed by New Jersey, which permitted only eggs laid within the state to be certified under the state's consumer labeling system.[19] Arizona, Florida, and Georgia at one time permitted only eggs laid within the state to be labeled "fresh eggs."

Milk has been subjected to discriminatory trade barriers within a specified milkshed for more than 125 years ostensibly to ensure the milk is fresh. As noted, states legislatures delegated to general-purpose local governments the police power and it occasionally is utilized to erect intrastate and interstate trade barriers. Madison, Wisconsin, for example, enacted an ordinance prohibiting the sale of milk unless it was pasteurized within five miles of the city's center. The city maintained the ordinance was designed to protect the health of its citizens, but the U.S. Supreme Court in 1951 invalidated the ordinance and explained the city could send its milk inspectors to dairies located more than five miles from the city's center.[20]

More recently, New York in 1994 forbade Vermont Milk Producers, Incorporated to sell milk in the state because the seller advertised its milk as free of synthetic hormones. New York alleged the labels on milk cartons violated the federal Food and Drug Administration's (FDA) recommendations for milk produced without the synthetic hormone recominant bovine somatropin.[21] New York maintained that the FDA considers the hormone safe and the Vermont milk labels suggested other milk was inferior to its milk. After conferring with FDA officers, New York lifted its ban on the milk.

North Carolina in the 1970s utilized a statute allowing only federal grading systems to be employed in labeling apples in order to protect the state's apple farmers against competition from apple growers in the State of Washington who advertised nationally that their apples were graded by state standards. North Carolina alleged the statute was designed to prevent the misleading of consumers by various labeling systems. The U.S. Supreme Court in 1977 invalidated the state statute because it was restricted to closed cartons of apples and consequently consumers usually do not see the apples in such cartons.[22]

Citing its authority under the Twenty-first Amendment to the U.S. Constitution, the 1984 New York State Legislature enacted a law permitting grocery stores to sell a diluted wine if it was made from grapes grown in the state. The U.S. District Court in 1985 struck down the law because it "is plain and simple economic protectionism of New York–grown grapes, at the expense of out-of-state grapes, and a violation of the interstate commerce clause of the most simple kind."[23]

It is important to note Congress has assisted states since 1796 in many instances when the police power is employed. The 1796 statute prohibits shipment of goods in interstate commerce in violation of state health and quarantine laws.[24] A second example is the federal *Contagious Disease Act of 1903* which authorizes the secretary of agriculture to cooperate with states in the suppression of dangerous livestock diseases and forbids states to interfere with the interstate shipment of animals if they have been certified by a federal inspector they are free of disease and have not been exposed to a disease.[25] To help state to prevent the spread of plant diseases, the *Terminal Inspection Act of 1915* directs postmasters, upon receipt of packages containing plants on a list prepared by the secretary of agriculture, to transport the packages to state terminal inspection stations where the plants are inspected for diseases.[26]

Proprietary Powers Barriers

Semisovereign states are proprietors of their respective public domain and in their corporate capacity employ millions of officers and staff, and spend revenues to execute their reserved powers. Chapter 2 explained the U.S.

Constitution (Art. IV, §2) forbids states to deny privileges and immunities to citizens of other states, but the U.S. Supreme Court has upheld statutes enacted by state legislatures in their proprietary capacity that discriminate against foreign corporations and nonresidents. Courts, however, on other grounds may invalidate statutes upheld on interstate commerce grounds.

Proprietary powers were utilized by New York in 1889 to make aliens ineligible for state employment, by California in 1897 to grant preference to building materials and institutional supplies produced in the state, by New Hampshire in 1901 to favor printing firms owned by residents, and by Maine in 1909 to give preference to in-state contractors.[27] Forty-seven of the forty-eight states by 1940 had at least one statute favoring in-state products.[28] State and local governments today typically restrict public employment, with the exception of specified positions, to their residents.

These governments purchase huge quantities of finished goods and materials, and may give preference in entering into construction contracts and purchasing building materials, public school textbooks, and other supplies to in-state firms. Eleven states grant preference to in-state bidders in purchasing products, fourteen states favor products, including building stone and coal, extracted in their respective state, and thirteen states grant preference to in-state firms relative to printing contracts. A number of state statutes grant a limited preference to in-state bidders if their prices are not more than three to five percent above the prices of bidders in sister states. Interstate comity prevails relative to the preference laws of twenty-two states that contain a reciprocity provision for the wavier of preference. New York, for example, negotiates with states that impose a penalty on New York firms bidding on contracts. In 1995, New York and Ohio signed administrative agreements with Indiana and Ohio to end the five percent penalty each state had been imposing on the other state's firms bidding on contracts.[29]

State governments are market participants as well as market regulators. The South Dakota Cement Commission, acting as a market participant, restricted the sale of cement produced at its plant to its residents during a period of cement shortage. Such a policy facially appears to violate the dormant commerce clause. A Wyoming concrete distributor filed a suit against the commission, but the U.S. Supreme Court in 1980 affirmed the commission's right to restrict the sale of cement and explained a distinction must be made between the roles of a state as a market regulator and as a market participant.[30]

Licensing and Taxing Powers Barriers

State and local governments require licenses for individuals and firms desiring to engage in a wide variety of professions and activities. Discriminatory licensing requirements can protect individuals engaged in a specific profession in a state against competition by their counterparts in other states. Many states have entered into reciprocity agreements with sister states eliminating barriers to the interstate movement of professionals.

Itinerant vendors commonly must obtain a license issued by a local government prior to offering products for sale within its jurisdiction. Foreign corporations (chartered in sister states) and alien corporations (chartered in a foreign nation) commonly must pay a license fee for the privilege of conducting business within a state. Several state legislatures in the 1920s, acting upon complaints of small merchants, levied graduated licenses taxes on chain stores based upon the number of stores in the state. The U.S. Supreme Court in 1931 upheld the constitutionality of the Indiana chain store license tax.[31]

Dairying was a little changed component of general agriculture until 1851 when the first cheese factory was established and by 1870 there were thousands of such factories in the United States.[32] The invention of the mechanical centrifugal separator, that removed fat from milk, sharply reduced the time required to make butter and ensured better quality. These developments, combined with the large growth in population, led to the development of dairying as a major industry. Major potential competition in the form of a new product, however, surfaced.

Oleomargarine, a substitute for butter, was developed in France in the early years of the nineteenth century, but the first factory to manufacture oleomargarine in the United States was not established until 1874. Although the two products are each produced in factories, political pressures emerged to protect dairying and proponents discovered such protection could take the form of state laws against adulteration of products and fraudulent sale of oleomargarine as butter. In 1878, the New York State Legislature and the Pennsylvania General Assembly enacted such laws. Subsequently, in 1885, the latter enacted a statute prohibiting the manufacture and sale of oleomargarine.[33] The U. S. Supreme Court in 1888 upheld the constitutionality of this statute as a valid exercise of a state's police power.[34]

Dairy states pressured their U.S. representatives and senators to persuade Congress to enact a statute reducing the competitive threat of oleomargarine to butter. In 1886, Congress responded to the pressure and enacted a statute defining butter and levying a tax upon and regulating the manufacture and sale of oleomargarine.[35] Oleomargarine manufacturers convicted of violating the 1885 Pennsylvania statute appealed to the U.S. Supreme Court, which in 1898 examined the congressional and Pennsylvania statutes, reversed the convictions, and opined: "A state has power to regulate the introduction of any article, including a food product, so as to insure purity of the article imported, but such police power does not include the total exclusion even of an article of food."[36] This decision, however, did not prevent states from using their licensing powers to regulate oleomargarine. The state legislature in Oregon and Washington in 1923 ignored the 1898 court decision and enacted statutes prohibiting the manufacture and sale of the product, but the statutes were repealed as voters employed the protest referendum.[37]

The dairy industry continued to pressure Congress and it enacted the *Grout Act of 1902* imposing a tax of ten cents per pound on colored oleomargarine and a one-fourth cent tax per pound on uncolored oleomargarine.[38] Dairy interests continued to concentrated their attack on oleomargarine in Congress, which responded with the *Brigham-Townsend Act of 1931* holding oleomargarine "to be yellow when it has a tint or shade containing more than 1.6 degrees of yellow, or of yellow and red collectively, but with an excess of yellow over red, measured in terms of the Lovibund Tintometer or its equivalent."[39] These interests also pressured state legislatures to enact statutes levying a tax of five to fifteen cents per pound on oleomargarine, and by 1935 nine states had such statutes.

Several state legislatures in the late 1930s enacted laws exempting from taxation oleomargarine containing "domestic ingredients" instead of imported ingredients or, in the case of cattle-producing states, containing a large percentage of animal fats.[40] Restrictive state laws penalizing the use of cottonseed oil by imposition of an excise tax on oleomargarine containing such oil resulted in threats of retaliation by states, such as Alabama and Louisiana.[41]

State legislatures, acting under the Twenty-first Amendment to the U.S. Constitution, also commonly discriminate against beers and wines produced in other states by imposing a lower tax on beers and wines made with domestic ingredients. Such laws invite retaliation as illustrated by a Missouri law in the 1930s barring the sale of liquors imported from a state with laws designed to protect its liquor producers and Michigan and Pennsylvania retaliatory actions barring importation of beer from the other state.[42]

The 1990 Florida State Legislature took another approach and imposed a $295 "impact fee" on motor vehicles purchased or titled in other states and subsequently registered in Florida allegedly to recover the cost of highway construction and maintenance.[43] In 1994, the Florida Supreme Court struck down the fee by opining it violated the interstate commerce clause of the U.S. Constitution.[44]

The City of Virginia Beach, Virginia, in 1993 employed an innovative approach to raising revenue by imposing a personal property tax on three satellite transponders used by International Family Entertainment, a subsidiary of the Walt Disney Company, to transmit the Family Channel's programs. The transponders are located on communications satellites circling the Earth. The tax was challenged and Judge Thomas S. Shadrick of the Virginia Beach Circuit Court held the city lacked statutory authority to levy a tax on the transponders and ordered the city to repay the revenue collected.[45] The city appealed the decision in 2002, and the Virginia Supreme Court affirmed the decision and noted the state statute relied upon by the city "does not contain any rules for the determination of a situs for transponders or the satellites to which the transponders are affixed."[46]

One type of interstate trade barrier is the product of the *McCarran-Ferguson Act of 1945* under which Congress exempted the insurance industry from the interstate commerce clause of the U.S. Constitution.[47] State legislatures are allowed to enact statutes discriminating against foreign insurance corporations. MetLife, for example, has to obtain the approval of fifty states and U.S. territories for a new form and "it takes forever to get a new form approved."[48] The U.S. Supreme Court in 1985, however, opined the act does not exempt the industry from the protection of the equal protection of the laws clause of the Fourteenth Amendment to the U.S. Constitution.[49]

The insurance industry lobbied Congress for relief and achieved a degree of success with the enactment in 1999 of a comprehensive financial institution act establishing minimum standards in thirteen regulatory areas and threatening imposition of a federal insurance agent licensing system if twenty-six states do not adopt a uniform licensing system by November 12, 2002 (see chapter 8).[50]

State legislatures over the decades enacted a large number of statutes levying taxes that facially violate the dormant interstate commerce clause. Nevertheless, the U.S. Supreme Court has validated a significant number of these statutes, including ones levying use taxes on products purchased outside the state (see judicial decisions below).

Removal of Trade Barriers

Reciprocal state laws, congressional preemption, and judicial decisions have been employed to remove interstate trade barriers. Preemption statutes increasingly have been enacted by Congress removing regulatory power partially or totally from states in order to promote the free flow of commerce in the United States. The U.S. Supreme Court's broad interpretation of the interstate commerce clause has given Congress nearly free reign to regulate commerce among sister states if it so chooses. As noted, the court employs its dormant commerce clause doctrine to strike down state statutes and local government ordinances placing an undue burden on interstate commerce.

Reciprocity

Interstate reciprocity is based upon comity and has proven to be an effective mechanism for the prevention of the erection of interstate trade barriers and removal of existing ones. Reciprocity may be incorporated in a statute or inter-state administrative agreement. State income tax statutes typically include reciprocal provisions or authorize tax credits to prevent a citizen of one state being taxed by sister states.

Congressional consent is not required for reciprocity statutes or agreements since they are noncontractual in nature. Chief Justice Charles E. Hughes of the U.S. Supreme Court in 1939 explained:

> Each state has the unfettered right at any time to repeal its legislation. Each state is competent to construe and apply its legislation in cases that arise within its jurisdiction. If it be assumed that the statutes of the two states have been enacted with a view to reciprocity in operation, nothing is shown which can be taken to alter their essential character as mere legislation and to create an obligation which either state is entitled to enforce as against the other in a court of justice.[51]

The court ruled the *Missouri Death Tax Act*'s reciprocity clause did not give rise to a controversy between Massachusetts and Missouri conferring original jurisdiction on the court.

The invention of the motor vehicle and its subsequent widespread use for interstate travel and transportation of goods promoted the reciprocity movement during the second and third decades of the twentieth century. The first conference dedicated to motor vehicle reciprocity was held in 1931 in French Lick, Indiana.[52] An Interstate Bus and Truck Conference was held in Harrisburg, Pennsylvania, in 1933 and a follow-up conference was held in Salt Lake City the next year to promote bus and truck registration reciprocity. The Council of State Governments and the State Commissions on Interstate Cooperation sponsored in 1939 the first National Conference on Interstate Trade Barriers in Chicago.[53]

Currently, each state and each Canadian province, based upon comity, recognize the vehicle registrations of other states and other provinces. Similarly, the states and provinces recognize operator licenses issued by other states and provinces with certain exceptions involving primarily the age of the operator. Reciprocity agreements contain a provision authorizing a vehicle to be operated in another state or province for a stipulated period of time. If the operator wishes to continue to drive in another state or province beyond the reciprocity period, he/she must register the vehicle and obtain a operator license in the other state or province.

Motor vehicle reciprocity statutes or administrative agreements also provide a operator convicted of a motor vehicle violation in a sister state or province may have his/her operator's license suspended or revoked by the home state or province because of convictions in other jurisdictions. Thirty-

six states and the District of Columbia treat out-of-state motor vehicle convictions in the same manner as in-state convictions.[54] In addition, several foreign nations notify states when their drivers have had their licenses suspended
or revoked.[55]

State statutes relating to specified occupations and professions typically
have reciprocity provisions. By 1930, only Connecticut, Florida, Massachusetts, and Rhode Island did not have medical license reciprocity agreements.[56]
Today, a small number of states, including New York, have a single body
responsible for licensing and disciplining persons in most professions. The
New York State Department of Education, for example, has jurisdiction over
thirty-nine professions and the judiciary has jurisdiction over lawyers.[57] The
department is not authorized by law to provide for licensing reciprocity, but
does endorse a sister state professional license subject to the individual meeting New York State requirements. Other New York reciprocity statutes relate
to milk, interstate transportation of dependent and indigent persons, and
interstate transportation of patients with tuberculosis.[58]

Interstate compacts (examined in chapter 8) could be used to remove
trade barriers, but have not been used for this purpose.

Preemption Laws

Congress has employed its delegated authority to regulate interstate commerce, backed by the supremacy of the law clause, to enact preemption laws
invalidating state statutes and administrative rules and regulations burdening
commerce among the several states.[59] As noted in chapter 3, Congress has not
exercised its preemption powers fully and did not exercise certain delegated
powers for decades. Congress, for example enacted minor bankruptcies acts in
1800, 1843, and 1867, but subsequently repealed them, thereby leaving bankruptcy regulation to the states. Their bankruptcy laws were very divergent by
1898 and were impeding interstate commerce. In consequence, Congress preempted state authority to regulate bankruptcy with the exception of determining the homestead amount to be excluded from bankruptcy proceedings.[60]
Problems with state regulation of railroad safety similarly induced Congress
to enact statutes providing for uniform railroad safety standards.[61] State commissions regulating railroad rates in the first two decades of the twentieth century tended to engage in local protectionism and Congress in the *Transportation Act of 1920* authorized the Interstate Commerce Commission to
determine intrastate rates if there was evidence of undue preference or prejudice between interstate and intrastate commerce.[62]

Numerous preemption acts subsequently were enacted, including ones
described in chapter 4, when the general silence of Congress ended. The
Wool Products Labeling Act of 1940 and the *Fur Products Labeling Act of 1951*

established national labeling systems.[63] Complaints from citizens relative to pricing of new motor vehicles induced Congress to enact the *Automotive Information Disclosure Act of 1958*.[64] The lack of uniformity in the labeling of grain caused problems for exporters and Congress responded by enacting the *Grain Standards Act of 1968* totally preempting responsibility for establishing standards and conducting inspections.[65] Other preemption statutes providing for national uniformity and removal of interstate trade barriers include the *Egg Products Inspection Act of 1970* and the *Nutrition Labeling and Education Act of 1990*.[66]

Deregulation of certain industries was a prominent characteristic of congressional decision making in the late 1970s and early 1980s as illustrated by the *Airline Deregulation Act of 1978, Motor Carrier Act of 1980*, and *Bus Regulatory Reform Act of 1982*.[67] Historically, railroad companies had great influence in state legislatures and reacted in the 1920s to diversion of freight to the growing motor trucking industry by using their influence to persuade legislatures to enact statutes reducing its competitive advantage in servicing certain markets. Size and weight restrictions were placed on motor trucks and justified on the grounds that large trucks cause major damage to highways, thereby requiring repairs financed with taxpayer funds. Trucking companies directed their complaints at the nonuniformity of size and weight limits in the various states increasing shipping costs to the disadvantage of consumers. Firms operating tandem and "triple rigs" were faced with the legal necessity of decoupling one or two trailers in order to enter and travel within certain states.

Trucking companies took their complaints to Congress and argued for nationally uniform truck size and weight limits to lower shipping costs, thereby reducing the rate of inflation. The companies were supported by the National Governors Association (NGA) whose 1980–81 policy positions expressed concerned with the increased costs imposed on trucking firms by nonuniform size and weight limits and recommended "that Congress immediate enact legislation establishing national standards for weight (80,000 gross; 20,000 per single axles, 34,000 for tandem) and length (60 ft.)."[68] In 1982, Congress responded affirmatively to the trucking industry complaints and NGA's recommendations by enacting the *Surface Transportation Assistance Act* totally preempting state size and weights limits relative to trucks traveling on interstate highways and on sections of the national-aid highway system as determined by the U.S. secretary of transportation.[69]

The act achieved its purpose of eliminating state nonuniform truck size and weight limits, but unfortunately was responsible for creating safety problems on many state highways not designed to accommodate large trucks. State complaints prompted Congress to enact two statutes in 1984—*Motor Carrier Safety Act* and *Tandem Truck Safety Act*—authorizing state and local governments to impose reasonable safety restrictions on the operation of truck trac-tor–semitrailer combinations and directing the secretary of transportation to promulgate minimum commercial motor vehicle safety standards.[70]

Although the trucking industry achieved major success in terms of the 1982 act, the industry argued two other state requirements were impediments to the free flow of interstate commerce. The first impediment required a truck operating in more than one state on a regular basis must be registered in that state. Once again Congress proved to be responsive to the trucking industry and enacted the *Surface Transportation Efficiency Act of 1991* whose title IV is termed the *Motor Carrier Act of 1991* and effectively pressured all states to participate in the International Registration Plan (see chapter 8).[71] States failing to participate in the plan may not enforce an alternative commercial registration plan.

The second impediment was state truck fuel tax reporting requirements. The *Motor Carrier Act* also effectively requires all states to participate in the International Fuel Agreement by stipulating a state legislature may not enact a statute and a state administrator may not promulgate a regulation mandat-ing a trucking company to pay a fuel tax "unless such law or regulation is in conformity with the International Fuel Agreement with respect to collection of such a tax by a single base state and proportional sharing of such taxes charged among the states where a commercial vehicle is registered."[72]

Congress is free to devolve its regulatory powers to states and has done so. In some instances, states have enacted statutes based upon congression-ally devolved powers to create interstate trade barriers. In 1945, for example, Congress enacted the *McCarran-Ferguson Act* devolving authority to states to regulate the insurance industry and a number of states enacted statutes favor-ing domestic insurance companies (see chapter 8).[73] In addition, Congress has enacted statutes designed to strengthen the enforcement of the states' police power. Statutes enacted in 1796 and 1797 prohibit the shipment in interstate commerce of goods in violation of the health or quarantine laws of a state and the *Plant Quarantine Act of 1912* authorizes states to establish a quarantine against shipment of diseased or infested plants not subject to a federal quarantine.[74]

Decentralized banking, reflecting a fear of centralized economic power, was a characteristic of the United States until 1927 when Congress enacted the *McFadden Act* authorizing a nationally chartered bank to establish branch banks subject to state laws allowing them and approval of the comptroller of the currency.[75] The act was the congressional response to a 1924 decision of the U.S. Supreme Court holding that national banks could not establish branches, but state banks could do so if authorized by state law.[76] This act allows a bank to establish branches in its home state and/or other states by incorporating a bank holding company to control separate banks that legally were not branches. In 1956, Congress enacted a statute providing for national regulation of bank holding companies by making their acquisition of other banks subject to approval of the board of governors of the Federal Reserve System.[77] A savings clause in the act, however, allows states to continue to regulate banks and bank holding companies and their subsidiaries.[78]

The 1982 New York State Legislature enacted a statute permitting bank holding companies incorporated in other states to acquire a bank in New York provided reciprocity was extended by the other concerned states. By 1994, all states with the exception of Hawaii enacted similar statutes. It should be noted a regional approach was adopted by New England and southeastern states based upon reciprocity by sister states in their respective region. This approach produced so-called super regional banks and was designed to exclude large banks chartered in California and New York. Although a regional trade barrier was created, the U.S. Supreme Court in 1985 upheld the constitutionality of the New England regional approach.[79]

It is apparent the bank holding company device burdens the free flow of interstate commerce by increasing the cost of bank operations and restricting the potential benefits to consumers of branch banking services. Customers of a branch bank located in Connecticut near the New York border, for example, generally were not allow to deposit funds at the New York branches of the same bank holding company.

The *Interstate Banking and Branching Efficiency Act of 1994* removed the remaining legal restraints on branch banking.[80] This act may promote conflicts in state laws as state usury laws are not uniform. In 1978, the U.S. Supreme Court in a case involving an interstate loan held the laws of the state where the bank's headquarters is located, and not the laws of the borrower's state, determine the rate of interest a bank may charge.[81]

The 1994 act allows a bank to be located in more than one state with respect to state usury laws and raises an important question. Does a New York bank which purchases branches in Connecticut, for example, have the legal right to collect New York–loan charges in Connecticut? The question also can be phrased in terms of whether a bank is able to export interest rates from its home state to branches in other states?

Judicial Decisions

Individuals and companies affected adversely by interstate trade barriers have turned to the courts since the early decades of the nineteenth century for remedies, particularly in the absence of congressional action to remove the barriers. Plaintiffs alleging the unconstitutionality of burdens placed by states upon the free flow of commerce between sister states rely upon the interstate commerce clause, privileges and immunities clause, and/or equal protection of the laws clause of the U.S. Constitution.

Early Court Decisions. The lack of debates over the interstate commerce at the 1787 constitutional convention suggests the delegates assumed state legislatures would be reluctant to place burdens on the free flow of commerce in the newly created economic union in view of the fact Congress was delegated authority to regulate such commerce and would strike down any state imposed impediments to free trade. Congress, however, failed to exercise this delegated power except on a limited basis and those adversely affected by trade barriers came to rely upon the dormant commerce clause doctrine, developed by the U.S. Supreme Court, to invalidate barriers.

Courts typically start with the presumptive validity of a state statute alleged to burden interstate commerce. It was not until 1824 that the U.S. Supreme Court ruled on the constitutionality of an alleged interstate trade barrier. The question at issue was the constitutionality of a New York State statute granting a monopoly on the operation of steamboats in the state to Robert Fulton and Robert R. Livingston. Writing for the court in *Gibbons v. Ogden,* Chief Justice John Marshall developed the doctrine of the continuous journey holding Congress possessed the authority to regulate a steamship traveling only on New York State waters because a number of passengers carried on the ship after disembarking were transported to other states as was some of the merchandise carried on the ship.[82]

Thomas Gibbons challenged the monopoly as violating the interstate commerce clause and a coasting license issued under provisions of a 1793 congressional statute. Marshall, in effect, developed the dormant commerce clause doctrine, which holds the clause, in the absence of a congressional statute based on the clause, places a limit on the powers of states and the limit would be determined by the court.

Building upon this decision, the Marshall court in *Brown v. Maryland* in 1827 declared invalid a Maryland statute imposing a discriminatory license tax of fifty dollars on importers on the ground the tax interfered with foreign commerce in the same manner as "a tax directly on imports."[83] The decision directly pertained to foreign commerce, yet the court majority noted "the principles laid down in this case . . . apply equally to importations from a sister state."[84]

A change in interpretation of certain provisions of the U.S. Constitution occurred with the accession of Roger B. Taney to the chief justiceship in 1835. His 1847 opinion in license cases took notice of the plenary power of Congress to regulate interstate and foreign commerce, but explained a "State may nevertheless, for the safety or convenience of trade, or for the protection of the health of its citizens, make regulations of commerce for its own ports and harbors, and for its own territory; and such regulations are valid unless they come in conflict with a law of Congress."[85]

The Taney Court in *Cooley v. The Board of Wardens* in 1851 explicitly opined certain details of interstate commerce could be subject to state regulations until supplanted by a congressional statute.[86] At issue was a Pennsylvania statute designed to enhance harbor safety by requiring all vessels entering a harbor in the state must be under the control of a pilot paid at a fixed rate. This opinion was the forerunner of other decisions stipulating states could regulate interstate commerce if their regulations did not impose an undue burden or have an impermissible indirect effect on such commerce. States continued to be allowed by Congress to regulate harbor pilots and anchorage rules, harbor buoys and lights, and erection of docks, piers, and wharves. States also are permitted to construct bridges and dams over navigable waters.

In 1869, the U.S. Supreme court upheld as constitutional a facially discriminatory Alabama tax of fifty cents per gallon levied on dealers importing liquors into the state by developing the doctrine of complementary extraction holding, in the case at issue, that other sections of Alabama statutes imposed an identical fifty-cent tax on brandy and whiskey produced in the state.[87]

The court does not always uphold the constitutionality of a facially discriminatory tax under its doctrine of complementary extraction. An example involves a Michigan statute levying a $300 fee on individuals selling or soliciting for sale of liquors to be shipped into the state that was struck down by the court in 1886.[88] Michigan argued the state also imposed a more burdensome tax, $400 annually, on firms manufacturing and selling liquors in the state. In rejecting this argument, the court explained the two taxes affected difference classes of parties since one tax was levied on the principal party and the other tax was levied on agents of the principal who sold or were soliciting orders on behalf of the principal. The court concluded the different natures of the two taxes provided "an immense advantage to the product manufactured in Michigan, and to the manufacturers and dealers" in the state.[89]

Writing for the U.S. Supreme Court in 1890, Justice John M. Harlan explained animal inspection laws seeking to ensure meat is fit for human consumption were valid exercises of the police power in spite of their impact on interstate commerce, but were invalid if they served to prevent importation of meats of animals slaughtered in sister states.[90]

Decisions Post 1900. The U.S. Supreme Court continued to uphold a number of facially discriminatory state taxes during the early decades of the twentieth century, including a 1926 decision declaring constitutional a Louisiana tax of twenty-five mills on the rolling stock of foreign railroad corporations lacking a domicile in the state.[91] Payers of this tax were exempted by the state constitution from local taxes and there was only a four mill differential between the state tax and the average local tax.[92] The court concluded the state tax did not amount to significant discrimination in view of the lack of evidence it was intended to discriminate against nonresidents.[93]

Six year later, a South Carolina six-cent per gallon license tax imposed on individual importing petroleum products for consumption in the state was ruled constitutional on the ground the tax was a complementary one because another state law imposed an identical per gallon license tax on petroleum product dealers selling such products in the state.[94] The court noted the state Constitution does not mandate that all requirements be incorporated in a single statute.

The court in 1933 upheld as constitutional an animal quarantine order of the New York Commissioner of Agriculture and Markets prohibiting the importation into the state of cattle unless they were from herds certified as free of Bang's disease after three tests within one year.[95] The order, a Great Depression action, was designed to protect the state's farmers from out-of-state competition and achieved its goal of preventing the importation of cattle.

On the other hand, the court in 1935 struck down the *New York Milk Control Act,* a type of economic provincialism, because it was designed to increase the price of milk and to shield the state's dairy farmers from competition by out-of-state low price milk.[96] Michael E. Smith viewed this decision as

a major step in the movement away from the older, special doctrines based on subject matter toward the present pervasive distinction between discriminatory and nondiscriminatory regulations. The decision also initiated the abandonment of other older doctrines, such as the conceptual distinction between interstate and intrastate commerce and between direct and indirect impacts on interstate commerce.[97]

Writing for a unanimous court, Justice Harlan F. Stone opined in 1938 states may regulate the weight and width of trucks provided there is a rational basis for the regulations in the absence of a congressional regulatory statute.[98] Rejecting the argument South Carolina's regulations were unconstitutional, he emphasized "the fact that many states have adopted a different standard is not persuasive. The conditions under which highways must be built in the several states, their construction, and the demands made upon them are not uniform."[99] The *Surface Transportation Assistance Act of 1982,* as noted, preempts state authority to regulate the size and width of trucks operating on interstate highways and sections of the national-aid highway system as determined by the secretary of transportation.

Later in 1938, Justice Stone extended his earlier 1938 opinion by explaining the interstate commerce clause was not designed to exempt individuals and firms "from their just share of state tax burdens even though it increases the costs" of operations.[100] In 1939, he added the court's function "is only to determine whether it is possible to say that the legislative decision is without rational basis.[101]

U.S. Solicitor General Robert H. Jackson in 1940 commented on the impact of a state regulation:

> The menace consists in its perversion. The purpose to discriminate may not appear on the face of the most burdensome measure. It often appears only in its administration and application, and this is usually not susceptible of proof. The question before the court in most instances is not whether state control is better than no control at all. Unable to solve the problem in any practicable manner, the Supreme Court must be slow to condemn laws which do not clearly discriminate against interstate commerce.[102]

The *McCarran-Ferguson Act of 1945*, as explained above, devolved to states authority to regulate the insurance industry. The U.S. Supreme Court in 1946 interpreted the act as validating a South Carolina gross receipts tax levied on foreign insurance companies and rejected an interstate commerce clause challenge of the constitutionality of the tax.[103] Writing in 1981, U.S. Supreme Court Justice William Brennan in *Western & Southern Life Insurance Company v. State Board of Equalization* identified three provisions of the U.S. Constitution "under which a taxpayer may challenge an allegedly discriminatory state tax: the commerce clause, the privileges and immunities clause; and the equal protection clause."[104] The case involved a challenge by an Ohio insurance company of a California retaliatory tax authorized by a 1964 state constitutional amendment.[105] The court rejected the privileges and immunities challenge because, as explained in chapter 2, corporations are not entitled to the protection of the privileges and immunities clause. In addition, the court explained under the *McCarran-Ferguson Act* an interstate commerce clause challenge and an equal protection of the laws clause challenge were inapplicable because the California State Legislature defined the retaliatory tax as a privilege tax.

In 1985, however, the court, however, opined the *McCarran-Ferguson Act* does not protect a state tax discriminating against a foreign insurance company from an equal protection of the laws challenge and invalidated an Alabama statute levying a substantially higher gross premiums tax rate on foreign insurance companies than the rate levied on domestic insurance companies.[106]

Justice Robert H. Jackson of the U.S. Supreme Court explained in 1949

> this court consistently has rebuffed attempts of states to advance their own commercial interests by curtailing the movement of article of commerce . . . while generally supporting their right to impose even burdensome regulations in the interest of local health and safety.[107]

Ten years later, the court struck down an Alaskan four percent license tax on freezer ships and floating cold storage units based on the value of the raw fish caught in the waters of the state.[109] Artic Maid maintained the tax was discriminatory and violated the interstate commerce clause because the tax exempted fish caught and frozen in Alaska prior to canning in the state. Alaska argued the tax was a complementary one since a six percent tax on the value of salmon was levied on Alaskan canneries; the court accepted this argument.[109]

The court similarly upheld in 1969 an Alabama business license tax of five dollars per week levied on traveling photographers for each local government in which they operated.[110] Noting the state imposed a twenty-five dollar annual tax on photographers with fixed locations in the state, the court opined a disproportionate burden was not placed on traveling photographers since the tax they were required to pay was less than the tax paid by fixed location photographers.[112]

In 1976, the court rejected an interstate commerce clause challenge to a Maryland statute granting subsidies to in-state derelict motor vehicle firms to encourage proper disposal of such vehicles.[112] In 1980, the court rejected a challenge to a South Dakota statute giving preference to resident purchasers of cement produced by a state-owned factory.[113] Can a city give preference to its residents with respect to employment in city-financed construction projects? The court in 1983 answered in the affirmative.[114]

The court rendered an important decision in *Maryland v. Louisiana* in 1981 by rejecting the latter's claim its "First Use" tax within the state of natural gas not subject to a severance tax levied by Louisiana or another state was valid as a complementary tax.[115] Facts established in the trial court revealed the tax had as its target natural gas from the outer continental shelf (OCS). Opining the tax was not similar to a use tax that serves as a complement to a sales tax, the court stressed "Louisiana has no sovereign interest in being compensated for the severance of resources from the federally owned OCS land."[116]

In 1984, the court in *Armco, Incorporated v. Hardesty* reviewed a West Virginia business and occupation tax levied upon the privilege of engaging in business with the amount of the tax determined by each firm's gross receipts. Every business activity, including manufacturing and wholesaling, was subject to the tax, and a single firm engaged in more than one activity was subject to being taxed multiple times. One exception was contained in the tax law; i.e., a firm engaged in manufacturing is exempt from the tax if the firm also is engaged in wholesaling. The court invalidated the statute and noted: "The fact that the manufacturing tax is not reduced when part of the manufacturing takes place out of state, makes clear that the manufacturing tax is just that, and not in part a proxy for the gross receipts tax imposed on Armco and other sellers in other states."[117]

Justice John Paul Stevens in 1987 took cognizance of the varying responses of the U.S. Supreme Court to interstate commerce clause challenges of state taxes and highlighted, relative to a Pennsylvania axle tax and registration marker fee, "the difficulties of reconciling unrestricted access to the national market with each state's authority to collect its fair share of revenues from interstate commercial activity."[118] The concerned statute was struck down because flat taxes failed the court's internal consistency, which holds a permissible tax is one that would not result in interference with the free flow of commerce if levied by every jurisdiction. Flat taxes discriminate against foreign truckers since they on average travel only one-fifth as many miles annually in a given state as state truckers travel.

The following year, the U.S. Supreme Court invalidated a tax credit authorized by the Ohio General Assembly in an attempt to promote the production of ethanol (ethyl alcohol) by domestic firms.[119] The court observed the tax credit violates the interstate commerce clause because the credit is denied to producers of ethanol in other states and explained the court's decisions "leave open the possibility that a state may validate a statute that discriminates against interstate commerce by showing that it advances a legitimate local purpose that cannot be adequately served by reasonable nondiscriminatory alternatives."[120] The court specifically noted that direct subsidization of domestic firms in general does not violate the interstate commerce clause.[121]

A 1937 New York milk licensing statute stipulates applications for licenses to distribute milk in the state are subject to the approval of the commissioner of agriculture and markets who is not authorized to issue a license if the entrance of a new distributor into the market would cause destructive competition. The commissioner denied a New Jersey dairy's request for an extension of its license. The refusal was challenged and the U.S. District Court for the Eastern District of New York in 1987 reversed the decision of the commissioner on the ground it discriminated against interstate commerce.[122]

Section 2 of the Twenty-first Amendment to the U.S. Constitution provides "the transportation of importation into any state, territory, or possession of the United States for delivery or use therein of intoxicating liquors, in violation of the laws thereof, is hereby prohibited." Although states are granted broad powers to regulate the sale and/or use of such liquors, their regulations and tax laws can clash with the interstate commerce clause. In 1984, the U.S. Supreme Court in *Bacchus Imports Limited v. Dias* struck down as violative of the dormant interstate commerce clause a Hawaii twenty percent excise tax on the sale of wholesale liquor with the exception of Hawaiian-produced alcoholic beverages.[123]

Two years later, the court held unconstitutional a section of the New York Alcoholic Beverage Control Law forbidding a distiller licensed to conduct business in the state to sell beverages to wholesalers except in accordance with a monthly price schedule previously filed with the state liquor authority and an affirmation the schedule prices are not higher than the lowest prices the distiller charges wholesalers in sister states during the month.[124]

The Connecticut General Assembly enacted a similar statute to prevent the loss of alcoholic beverages sales to sister states with lower prices and to ensure residents could purchase such beverages at prices that do not exceed prices in bordering states. This statute differed from the New York one by allowing out-of-state shippers to change their prices after the posting of the price schedule and filing of the required affirmation. The court in 1989 found the statute had an impermissible extraterritorial effect and emphasized "the interstate commerce clause dictates that no state may force an out-of-state merchant to seek regulatory approval in one state before undertaking a transaction in another."[125] Chief Justice William Rehnquist wrote a strong dissent, joined by Justice John Paul Stevens and Justice Sandra Day O'Connor, maintaining the Connecticut statute differed markedly from the New York one and "Connecticut has no motive to favor local brewers over out-of-state brewers, because there are no local brewers."[126] The dissent concluded:

> The result reached by the Court in this case can only be described as perverse. A proper view of the Twenty-first Amendment would require that States have greater latitude under the commerce clause to regulate producers of alcoholic beverages than they do producers of milk. But the Court extends to beer producers a degree of commerce clause protection that our cases have never extended to milk producers.[127]

The following year the court invalidated a Florida excise tax favoring beverages made from the state's agricultural products as violative of the same clause.[128]

State tax departments seek to maximize state revenues, but face a difficult problem when attempting to collect taxes from mail-order firms headquartered in a sister state. The departments must demonstrate the firms have a nexus to the state. In 1976, the U.S. Supreme Court in *National Bellas Hess, Incorporated v. Department of Revenue of Illinois* struck down a Illinois tax law requiring a firm, which had no office or salespersons in the state, to collect the state use tax on goods purchased by Illinois residents on the grounds an undue burden was placed on commerce among the several states and the due process of law clause of the Fourteenth Amendment was violated.[129]

A similar case reached the court in 1992 and involved a mail order firm that had no office or salespersons in North Dakota. In *Quill Corporation v. North Dakota,* the court announced it was superseding its earlier due process of law clause decisions requiring a physical presence in a state before it could impose a duty on a firm to collect a use tax.[130] The court's opinion distinguished between the clause's requirement of "minimum contacts" with a state and the physical presence or "substantial nexus" with the state required by the interstate commerce clause before a state could require a firm to collect the use tax. Concluding the corporation lacked a "substantial nexus" or a physical presence in the state, the court ruled North Dakota could not require the corporation to collect the tax and in *obiter dictum* held "the underlying issue is not only one that Congress may be better qualified to resolve, but also one that Congress has the ultimate power to resolve."[131] The U.S. Advisory Commission on Intergovernmental Relations estimated mail order sales escaping state use taxes in 1994 totaled $3.3 billion.[132]

The court addressed another aspect of the use tax in 1994. A Missouri 1.5 percent use tax on the privilege of consuming, storing, or using within the state articles of personal property purchased in other states was disallowed by the court in local governments where the tax exceeded the sales tax.[133] In its decision, the court noted the interstate commerce clause contained "a negative command forbidding the States to discriminate against interstate trade" and "the burdens imposed on interstate and intrastate commerce must be equal" if a tax system is to qualify as a constitutional "compensatory" one.[134]

Another contentious issue requiring the attention of the U.S. Supreme Court is the interstate shipment of wastes. Not surprisingly, several state legislatures enacted statutes in attempts to inhibit the importation of such wastes. In 1978, the court held a New Jersey law prohibiting importation of most liquid and solid wastes from sister states has not been preempted by a congressional statute, yet was unconstitutional because the state law violated the dormant interstate commerce clause.[135] A note to the decision explained it did not address the question whether a state legislature could limit use of facilities in the state to residents under the "market participant exception" to the clause involving a state as a market participant rather than a market regulator.

In 1992, the court opined it was unconstitutional for the Michigan State Legislature to evade the dormant interstate commerce clause's prohibition of interstate trade barriers by allowing the governing bodies of counties to decide whether to prohibit private landfill operators in their respective counties to accept wastes generated outside their borders.[136] A second decision, based also on the dormant clause, in the same year invalidated a facially discriminatory Alabama special fee levied on disposal of hazardous wastes generated outside its borders, but did not address the question whether a differential fee based on the cost of disposing of waste would be constitutionally valid.[137]

In 1992, the U.S. District Court for the District of Minnesota invalidated ordinances, enacted by Faribault and Martin Counties in Minnesota, mandating all compostable solid waste generated within the two counties be delivered to the Praireland Solid Waste Composting Facility.[138] The U.S. Court of Appeals for the Eighth Circuit upheld this decision in 1993 and opined:

> We find that the Counties Ordinances discriminated against interstate commerce and are economic protectionist measures that violate the commerce clause. We sympathize with the Counties' efforts to establish a system of waste management. However, we must decide in accord with the principles of the dormant commerce clause.[139]

Two years later, an Oregon $2.50 per ton surcharge on waste generated in other states was held to be discriminatory by the court since a surcharge of only $0.85 per ton was levied on the disposal of waste generated in the state.[140] The state did not assert the disposal of out-of-state waste imposed a higher cost upon the state than in-state generated waste, but contended the surcharge was a "compensatory tax" requiring waste shippers in other states to pay their fair share of the costs imposed on Oregon by the disposal of their wastes. In its opinion, the court expressed reluctance "to recognize new categories of compensatory taxes" and, referring to its *Armco* decision involving a West Virginia gross receipts tax, explained "earning income and disposal of waste at Oregon landfills are even less equivalent than manufacturing and wholesaling."[141]

A Town of Clarkstown, New York, ordinance requiring solid wastes processed or handled within the town be processed or handled only at the town's transfer station was struck down by the U.S. Supreme Court in 1994 on the ground ". . . the flow control ordinance drives up the cost of out-of-state interests to dispose of their solid waste. Furthermore, the ordinance prevents anyone except the favored local operator from performing the initial processing step."[142]

The U.S. Supreme Court in the same year addressed the question of the constitutionality of a pricing order issued by the Massachusetts commissioner of food and agriculture imposing an assessment on all fluid mild sold by dealers to Massachusetts retailers with the funds collected distributed only to Massachusetts dairy farmers in spite of the fact approximately two-thirds of the milk is imported from sister states. The court found the pricing order to discriminate against interstate commerce and therefore was unconstitutional.[143]

Congress is free to delegate powers to states and has done so on occasions as noted above. In 1978, Congress enacted the *Interstate Horseracing Act* authorizing states to preempt the congressional prohibition of interstate off-track wagering.[144] The act stipulates interstate simulcasts of horse races require the consent of state agencies and a horsemen's association. The U.S. Court of Appeals for the Sixth Circuit in 1994 overturned a U.S. District

Court opinion declaring the act invalid because it restricts commercial free speech guaranteed by the First Amendment to the U.S. Constitution.[145]

State courts also are forums where alleged state restraints of the free flow of commerce can be adjudicated. The New Hampshire Supreme Court in 1986 opined a state statute levying taxes on motor carriers registered in sister states facially discriminated against interstate commerce.[146] The Maine Supreme Judicial Court in the same year invalidated a 1984 state statute levying a reciprocal tax on motor vehicles registered in sister states that impose a tax or fee on the same class of motor vehicles registered in Maine.[147] The law had applied to only thirteen states that imposed a tax on Maine registered vehicles, but was ruled discriminatory since the statute did not levy a similar tax on Maine registered trucks. The court advised Maine truck owners affected by the taxes levied by the thirteen sister states to challenge the constitutionality of these taxes.

Summary

State erected trade barriers assume many forms including subtle ones that facially appear to be nondiscriminatory. The oldest and most common form of barrier is a tax discriminating against residents and firms in sister states. The police power of the states may be used for important and legitimate purposes such as protecting the public's health and safety, but also can be utilized to erect barriers to protect a state's business firms from competition by foreign firms. The proprietary powers of a state have been increasingly utilized since the turn of the twentieth century to favor the state's business firms in terms of state contracts for printing and purchases of goods and raw materials, and preferential hiring practices. As noted above, protectionist policies invite retaliatory actions by other state legislatures.

Reciprocity has been a common method of removing interstate trade barriers and has been most successful in terms of motor vehicle operators' licenses and registrations. Congress, if it so chose, could eliminate all barriers to commerce among sister states by preempting the regulatory authority of states. Such preemption became more common in the latter decades of the twentieth century, yet Congress remains reluctant to utilize its delegated powers fully to promote a more perfect economic union even when the U.S. Supreme Court explains the political branch is better qualified to deal with barriers to interstate commerce than the courts.

The principal guarantor of the free flow of commerce in the United States has been the judiciary (see chapter 4) with both state and national courts, when called upon, not hesitating to invalidate discriminatory state and local government laws and regulations. Particular credit must be given to the

U.S. Supreme Court's dormant interstate commerce clause doctrine for helping to ensure the free movement of raw materials and products among the several states.

Economic protectionism is only one important facet of interstate economic relations. A second important facet is competition by states for tax revenues in the form of tax exportation. Not surprisingly, courts are called upon to superintend the competition, a subject examined in chapter 6.

CHAPTER 6

Interstate Tax Revenue Competition

A federal system makes it possible for states to export taxes, but the ability of individual states to do so varies considerably. Most state legislators seek to promote their prospects for reelection by voting for programs and projects strongly desired by their respective constituents, and seek to minimize the accompanying resident taxpayer costs by shifting them in part, whenever possible, to business firms and individuals in other states. One method of achieving the latter goal is tax exportation in the form of innovative taxes and fees paid to the state by nonresident citizens and business firms. A second method is state operation of a lottery whose ticket sales include nonresidents. Lotteries are operated in thirty-seven states and produce net proceeds in excess of $12 billion annually (see chapter 7).[1]

The state legislature of a tourist state may find it advantageous to levy taxes upon persons renting motor vehicles, staying in hotels and motels, and eating in restaurants.[2] New Hampshire, a leader in innovative taxation, levies such taxes and additionally imposes a small excise tax on alcoholic spirits sold legally only by state-operated stores whose lower prices attract residents of nearby states. The state's large sales of such beverages to nonresidents enable it to command volume discounts from suppliers, thereby helping the state to keep its beverage prices low.[3]

Price differentials in the retail price of cigarettes, attributable to low state excise taxes, similarly encourage their purchases by nonresidents. To curtail underage smoking and to raise additional revenues, many state legislatures increased the cigarette excise tax significantly in recent years. Organized crime is involved deeply in the smuggling of alcoholic beverages, tobacco products, and motor fuels wherever there is a significant retail price differential for these products between states attributable to excise tax differentials. The Tax Foundation estimated a smuggler makes a profit of $100,000 or more per truckload of smuggled cigarettes.[4]

Tax differentials, which encourage smuggling by individuals and organized crime, also are created by the fact five states do not levy a sales tax and a use tax—Alaska, Delaware, Montana, New Hampshire, and Oregon—and the differential in rates of such taxes in other states. Chief Executive L. Dennis Kozlowski of Tyco International Limited, an art collector, was indicted in New York in 2002 on the charge he evaded payment of more than one million dollars in sales tax on expensive works of art through a scheme to avoid the combined New York State and City 8.25 percent sales tax.[5] One evasion involved the removal of a $425,000 painting from his Manhattan apartment and its shipment to Tyco's United States operational base in Exeter, New Hampshire, the signing of a receipt for the painting in Exeter by a company employee, and the immediate return of the painting to Kozlowski's Manhattan apartment. A second evasion involved a $3.95 million Monet painting with the art dealer drafting an invoice indicating the painting was being shipped to Exeter, New Hampshire, and not to Kozlowski's apartment.

New York launched a counter-attack against the loss of sales tax revenue to New Jersey subsequent to its decision to allow retailers in sections of Elizabeth, Kearny, and Orange near New York City, to collect a three percent sales tax on purchases in place of the state's six percent sales tax. New York sent tax department employees across the Hudson River to write down the license plate numbers of New York vehicles in parking lots.[6] Owners of the vehicles received letters informing them they owed a New York use tax equivalent to the difference between the sales tax rates in the two states. New York also sent its tax employees to parking lots in Pennsylvania near the state boundary line and since 1990 has been examining U.S. Customs Service records to identify state residents who purchased goods in foreign nations and failed to pay the state use tax. It also is important to note the U.S. Supreme Court has ruled states may not require mail order firms to collect the sales tax for a state on purchases made by its residents unless the firms have a nexus to the state (see chapter 5). Similarly, Congress in 1998 enacted a statute forbidding state and local governments to impose taxes on Internet access for three years and in 2001 extended the prohibition to November 1, 2003.[7] Uncollected state sales taxes on Internet commerce is estimated to have totaled approximately $26 billion in 2000.[8] Congress, if it so wishes, can employ its interstate commerce power to reverse the U.S. Supreme Court's decision on mail orders and authorize states to require mail order firms and Internet order firms to collect applicable sales taxes.

Resource rich states are in an advantageous position, as explained below, to impose a tax on extractive firms and harvesters of marine resources with most of the tax exported to business firms and residents of other states consuming the exported resources. Such taxes are justified on the ground of the environmental damages associated with the extractions and harvesting and the loss of an irreplaceable mineral resources.

Documentary taxes are levied by many states on mortgages, real estate transfers, and/or securities transfer. Relative to the latter, approximately eighty percent of the value of such transfers occurs in New York City and results in the state exporting much of its stock transfer tax to nonresidents.[9]

Mandatory state motor vehicle insurance coverage also encourages residents in states with high premiums to use a "mattress" address in a sister state with low premiums to register their vehicles. New Hampshire has relatively low motor vehicle insurance premiums in comparison with premiums in nearby Massachusetts. Police in the latter state, commencing in 1995, placed an orange sticker on each parked New Hampshire registered vehicle explaining the Commonwealth's registration requirements.[10] If a police officer spots the identical vehicle a second time, he/she logs it by location, license plate number, and time. The vehicle owner receives a notification within thirty days to report to the Registry of Motor Vehicles for a hearing on whether the owner is a bona fide resident of Massachusetts.

The U.S. Constitution grants Congress only a few exclusive powers by forbidding state legislatures to employ the same powers. The power to regulate interstate commerce is one of the most important delegated powers not exercised fully by Congress, apparently because it prefers to allow courts to adjudicate certain types of disputes. The reader should be aware that the Constitution does not forbid state regulation of such commerce, although the supremacy of the laws clause (Art. 6) provides for the negation of a state constitutional provision, statute, or administrative regulation conflicting directly with a congressional statute. Nevertheless, courts do not always invalidate a state statute or administrative regulation facially conflicting with a congressional statute.

Congress did not enact a major regulatory statute based on its interstate commerce power until 1887 and did not enact a statute regulating state taxation of interstate commerce until 1959.[11] This statute is a narrow one and was prompted by a U.S. Supreme Court opinion that a state legislature could tax the apportioned net income of a firm engaged only in interstate business within the state.[12] The statute specifically exempts a seller from a state income tax if the seller only solicits orders for the sale of tangible goods; service industries are excluded from the exemption. Congress later enacted several statutes restricting the authority of state legislatures to levy taxes on federal savings and loan associations, generation of transportation of electricity, national banks, stock transfers, and transportation industries to prevent discrimination against foreign (chartered in sister states) firms.

Individuals and business firms turn to the courts to seek relief from discriminatory taxation in the absence of congressional statutes prohibiting or restricting the authority of state legislatures to impose such taxes upon interstate commerce (see chapter 4). Somewhat surprisingly, the U.S. Supreme Court did not strike down a state tax as violative of the interstate commerce clause until 1872 when a Pennsylvania tax of two cents per ton levied on the transportation of goods was invalidated.[13] The court opined the tax was based on tonnage, the distance the freight moved did not affect the tax, and hence it was "not proportioned to the business done in transportation."[14]

Although the Twenty-first Amendment to the U.S. Constitution delegates to states broad authority to regulate intoxicating liquors including the prohibition of the sale and consumption of such liquors, state alcoholic beverages taxes can be challenged in court on the ground they violate the interstate commerce clause of the Constitution (see chapter 5).

The following sections describe and analyze methods of state revenue enhancement by taxing professional athletes and by exportation of excise taxes, severance taxes, corporate taxes, and commuter income taxes.

Taxation of Nonresident Professional Athletes

Taxation of professional athletes who play in several states is a particularly difficult problem in a federal system lacking uniformity in state taxation. Typically, the tax is imposed regardless of whether a player performs on the field. The origin of the so-called jock tax is traceable to Michael Jordan and his Chicago Bulls teammates defeating the Los Angeles Lakers in the 1991 National Basketball Association's World Championship game.[15] The California State Legislature decided to extend its state income tax to the Bulls and the Illinois General Assembly retaliated by levying a similar tax on nonresident professional athletes who are residents of a state levying a similar tax.

Twenty states with professional sports teams levied such taxes in 2002 on players in the National Basketball Association, American and National Baseball Leagues, National Football League, and National Hockey Association (see Figure 6.1). A similar income tax is levied upon rock stars and their associates. Certain cities also levy an income tax on nonresident professional athletes. New York State, for example, levies its personal income tax on a visiting athlete based upon his income and the number of games played, whereas other states determine the amount of the income tax due on the basis of the athlete's income and the number of preseason training days, practice days, and game days.[16]

Politically, taxing nonresident professional athletes is popular because of the extremely high salaries many receive and ease of enforcement because of their inability to flee to tax havens. The Tax Foundation describes the tax as "poor tax policy" because it also is imposed on the staff of teams, "is arbitrary because it targets a specific occupation," requires each athlete to file income tax returns in a number of states, and "the incidence of the jock tax is not aligned with the location of economic activity that gives rise to it, a misalignment that creates inefficiencies."[17]

Although often termed double taxation, the jock tax is not double taxation because the home state of each professional athlete allows a credit for income taxes paid in sister states. In view of the fact state income taxes are

FIGURE 6.1
State Income Taxation of Nonresident Professional Athletes

(Top Income Tax Rate Shown for Each State)

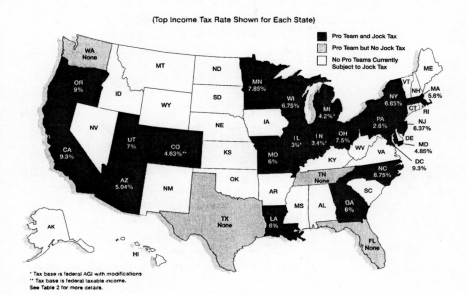

* Tax base is federal AGI with modifications
** Tax base is federal taxable income.
See Table 2 for more details.

Source: Special Report, No. 115 (Washington, DC: Tax Foundation, July 2002), p. 4.
Reprinted with permission of the Tax Foundation.

graduated, a professional athlete pays less in extra income taxes if his home
state has a high income tax rate structure. It is apparent the athletes paying the
highest jock tax are those who officially reside in states lacking an income tax
on earned income: Alaska, Florida, Nevada, New Hampshire, South Dakota,
Tennessee, and Texas since they are not entitled to a credit for income taxes
paid to other states.

Excise Tax Differentials

Retail prices of alcoholic beverages and tobacco products vary widely between
states because of their freedom to determine excise tax rates and whether to
levy a sales tax. Sales tax states attempt to prevent the loss of tax revenue by
levying a use tax, at the same rate as the sales tax, upon residents who made
out-of-state purchases and brought the products to their homes. The use tax,
however, is generally ineffective because it depends upon self-reporting of

out-of-state purchases and tax payment.[18] The tax is effective with respect to out-of-state purchases of motor vehicles because a sales tax state will not allow the registration of such vehicles without evidence the use tax has been paid. Several sales tax states have signed reciprocal cooperating agreements allowing each state to audit the books of stores selling products to nonresidents and send a use tax bill to their residents who made out-of-state purchases.

Case Studies

Alcoholic beverages and tobacco excise taxes are important sources of revenues and states initiate actions to preserve these sources. Smuggling of these products between states was not a major problem prior to states imposing sales taxes and sharply increasing excise taxes. The importance of the excise tax revenues gained from the sale of alcoholic beverages and cigarettes to non-residents was highlighted in a 1992 American Legislative Exchange Council report revealing New Hampshire received substantial tax revenues from the sale of these products to nonresidents.[19] In 1993, the council published a similar report on cross-border sales in the southeastern United States noting "North Carolina has had relatively low excise tax rates on cigarettes, and experienced substantial cross-border benefits."[20]

Bootlegging. Congress is free to exempt state regulatory laws from the interstate commerce clause and did so commencing with the *Wilson Act of 1890* in order to assist dry states to enforce their laws prohibiting the sale and consumption of alcoholic beverages.[21] This act stipulates such beverages upon entering a state become subject to its police power, but was weakened by judicial interpretation enabling a mail order firm to ship liquor to a consignee for personal consumption in a dry state. Congress responded to the judicial interpretation by enacting the *Webb-Kenyon Act of 1913* making illegal the receipt and resale of alcoholic beverages contravening a state law.[22]

The Twenty-first Amendment to the U.S. Constitution, which repealed national prohibition in 1933, generally incorporates the provisions of these two acts. All state legislatures have enacted so-called direct shipment statutes, enacted to protect state merchants, regulating interstate shipment of alcoholic beverages to some extent. These statutes may be placed in three categories:

1. Direct shipment of beverages to persons twenty-one and over for personal consumption from sister states is allowed by fifteen states if they accord reciprocity,
2. limited amounts may be shipped to residents,
3. no direct shipments are permitted by seven states.[23]

The U.S. Supreme Court has not addressed the question of whether these statutes violate the interstate commerce clause of the U.S. Constitution or are a valid exercise of power authorized by the Twenty-first Amendment to the Constitution.

Courts continue to be called upon to resolve clashes between the amendment and the interstate commerce clause. In 1936, the U.S. Supreme Court upheld the constitutionality of a California law imposing a $500 license fee on importers of out-of-state beer against an interstate commerce clause challenge, but the 1937 California State Legislature repealed the law.[24] More recently, the U.S. Supreme Court in 1984 invalidated an excise tax levied by the Hawaii State Legislature on the sale of liquor at wholesale because the statute exempted several Hawaii produced beverages (see chapter 5).[25]

State legislatures have established two alcoholic beverages control systems. Currently, eighteen states directly control the retail and wholesale sale of alcoholic beverages and the remaining thirty-two states utilize licensing systems to control sales.[26] New Hampshire utilizes the former system and locates many of its state liquor stores near the boundaries of sister states and its state liquor commission expends approximately eighty percent of its advertising appropriations in other states.[27] The state has no beverage bottle tax law and when Massachusetts adopted such a law the price of a case of beer increased by nearly three dollars and encourages its residents to shop in New Hampshire (see Figure 6.2). In addition, Massachusetts blue laws closed all but essential stores on Sundays until 1983, thereby diverting customers to New Hampshire. Maine also reported a major loss of excise tax revenue attributable to its residents purchasing the beverages in New Hampshire. Residents of nearby states who purchase alcoholic beverages also shop for other products in New Hampshire to avoid paying a sales tax.[28]

New York tax officers in the 1960s utilized roadblocks to deter smuggling of alcoholic beverages between the city of Plattsburgh and Vermont where prices were lower, and between Staten Island and New Jersey which had lower prices.[29] States with high excise taxes commonly engage in border surveillance as illustrated by Massachusetts Tax Commissioner Henry F. Long in the 1950s stationing enforcement officers near New Hampshire liquor stores in the period preceding major holidays who made note of Massachusetts license plate numbers of vehicles parked near the stores. A bill for the use tax on one case of liquor was sent to the owners of the vehicles. New York similarly stationed its agents near the parking lot of a state liquor store in Bennington, Vermont, in 1976 who wrote down the license plate numbers of New York vehicles whose owners received a tax bill from the state for $3.25 plus a fifty-percent penalty for every gallon of alcoholic beverages purchased in Vermont.[30]

The Warren County, New Jersey, prosecutor in 1965 signed expulsion orders against Pennsylvania tax officers who were recording registration

FIGURE 6.2
Net Interstate Cross-Border Sales As a Percentage
of Total Packaged Beer Sales by State, 1997

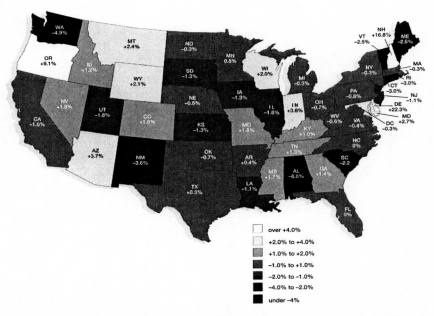

Source: Patrick Fleenor, *How Excise Tax Differentials Affect Cross-Border Sales of Beer in the United States* (Washington, DC: Tax Foundation, May 1999), p. 7. Reprinted with permission of the Tax Foundations.

numbers of Pennsylvania vehicles parked in the vicinity of liquor stores in Phillipsburg, New Jersey.[31] The District of Columbia and several Indiana and Kentucky cities have made it illegal for neighboring state tax agents to record vehicle registration numbers in liquor store parking lots.[32]

Vermont tax agents visit nearby New Hampshire state liquor stores parking lots, record the license plate numbers of parked vehicles, and notify their State Police who stop any of these vehicles subsequently entering Vermont. This technique has been successful in seizing contraband alcoholic beverages transported by upstate New York smugglers because the Vermont state excise tax had not been paid. Pennsylvania has posted its tax officers outside Maryland liquor stores and Maryland has objected even though its agents engage in the same practice relative to Maryland vehicles parked near District of Columbia liquor stores.[33]

Interstate cooperation in curtailing smuggling is illustrated by New York State police who in 1994 arrested two Canadian citizens for transporting cases of liquor after their truck and automobile were followed by police officers in two states from a discount liquor store in Maryland through Pennsylvania to New York.[34]

The effectiveness of border surveillance in protecting a state's alcoholic beverages excise tax revenues is questionable. According to the director of the New York Miscellaneous Tax Bureau, "border patrols can't really make a dent in 'liquor runs.' The patrols are sporadic, expensive, and enforcement is almost impossible even after the letters are sent."[35] He also reported approximately forty percent of letter recipients paid the tax.[36]

The 1993 New York State Legislature decided to utilize a more effective method to reduce smuggling of alcoholic beverages from New Jersey by bars and restaurants in New York City. A tax law amendment mandates shippers of such beverages to obtain a license from the New York State Department of Taxation and Finance, and to maintain a manifest for each shipment.[37] The law also provides for forfeiture of any seized liquors. Enforcement agents discovered large shipments of alcoholic beverages from southern states to upstate New York warehouses and subsequent smuggling of liquors into Canada through the Mohawk Indian reservation that spans parts of New York and Canada.[38]

Buttlegging. Cigarette smuggling has a long history and Congress for the first time took action to assist state and local governments to collect tobacco excise taxes by enacting the *Jenkins Act of 1949* prohibiting the use of postal service to evade payment of such taxes.[39] A 1955 amendment to the act requires shippers of cigarettes into a state to file a monthly memorandum with the state tax administrator listing each shipment during the previous month and the name of the recipient.[40] The amendment was challenged on the ground it allegedly violates the Fifth Amendment's constitutional privilege against selfincrimination. The challenge was rejected and the amendment was upheld as constitutional by the U.S. District Court for the Southern District of New York in 1971.[41] The U.S. General Accounting Office reported in 2002 Internet cigarette vendors were flouting the act and one Web site informed potential purchasers "we do not report to tax authorities in ANY state. One hundred percent guaranteed."[42] Smuggling, however, generally was not viewed as a major source of lost tax revenues until the mid-1960s when New York and several other states increased their excise tax on cigarettes from five to ten cents a package. Organized crime saw the opportunity for vast profits and the almost immediate subsequent sharp increase in smuggling persuaded New York Governor Nelson A. Rockefeller to convene in 1967 a cigarette tax enforcement conference attended by officers from thirteen states, members of Congress, and the Federal Bureau of Investigations. North Carolina, the largest tobacco producer, was the only state at the time that did not have a tobacco products excise tax and the source of most illegal cigarettes transported by motor vehicles, private airplanes, ships, and trucks. Malcolm L. Fleisher of the Retail Tobacco Dealers of America estimated the tax differential was responsible for retailers in New York City losing approximately twenty-five percent of their cigarette sales and millions of dollars in related sales.[43] In appointing a task force to develop recommendations to curtail cigarette smuggling, Governor Rockefeller in 1973 maintained it "is making the ordinary citizen an unthinking partner of organized crime" and "is unwittingly financing other enterprises of organized crime, including narcotics, the corruption of public officials, and loan-sharking."[44]

The New York State commission of investigations estimated more than 100,000 illegal cigarette cartons were sold in the state every day in 1975.[45] In the same year, the U.S. advisory commission on intergovernmental relations reported state and local governments were losing approximately $400 million in cigarette excise tax revenues annually due to smuggling.[46] The following year, New York State Senator Roy M. Goodman held a news conference, attributed more one-half of all cigarette sales in New York City to buttleggers, and reported they made profits of one million dollars weekly.[47] Five black-hooded executives of tobacco companies attended the conference and stated their firms had been targets of hijackers who burglarized their warehouses and safes containing tax indicia (decals or meter impressions). The New York Department of Taxation and Finance reported in the same year that more than 100,000 cartons of untaxed cigarettes were seized in 1976.[48]

One solution for the tax differential problem is the repeal of all state cigarette excise taxes and the simultaneous increase in the federal excise tax to produce additional revenues to be distributed to states as compensation for revenue losses resulting from the repeal of their respective excise taxes. New York State Commissioner of Finance and Taxation James H. Tully Jr. proposed this solution in 1977 and indicated his state would save in excess of $100 million annually in administrative and enforcement costs and gain more than $400 million in revenues lost to buttleggers.[49] In this year, the excise tax differential ranged from two cents per package in North Carolina to twenty-three cents in New York City and allowed buttleggers to make a profit of $2.10 on each package sold in the city.[50]

Pressure on Congress to address the problem of interstate smuggling of cigarettes increased and Congress responded by enacting the *Contraband Cigarette Act of 1978* making it a federal crime to distribute, possess, purchase, receive, ship, or transport more than 60,000 cigarettes lacking the tax indicia of the state where they were found.[51] The act stipulates primary enforcement responsibility for collection of the excise tax is retained by states and the federal government will assist only enforcement beyond the jurisdictional reach of a state. Congress gently suggested improved interstate cooperation as a remedy by noting the act "shall not be construed to inhibit or otherwise affect any coordinated effort by a number of states, through interstate compact or otherwise, to provide for the administration of state tax laws. . . ."[52] The act apparently has deterred smuggling to a limited degree and the U.S. Advisory Commission on Intergovernmental Relations in 1985 noted "a relatively small percentage of those persons arrested for cigarette smuggling were convicted and very few were sent to jail."[53]

The commission also reported large numbers of tobacco retailers and wholesalers in high excise tax states closed their businesses as the result of but-tlegging and counterfeiting of state cigarette tax indicia was a major problems. Smugglers in low tax states offer wholesalers a premium price if they supply cigarettes without tax indicia and the cigarettes are stamped with counterfeit stamps to facilitate their sale. Smuggling is a serious problem in several states and accounts for 26.7 percent and 22.7 percent of cigarettes consumed in Hawaii and Michigan in 1997, respectively (see Table 6.1).

The excise tax differential increased greatly in the 1990s as states sought to increase revenues and to persuade smokers to reduce or stop smok-ing to improve their health and resulted in increased cigarette sales in states with lower excise taxes.[54] In 1992, Massachusetts' voters increased the tax from twenty-six to fifty-one cents per package effective on January 1, 1993, to coincide with a federal excise tax increase of four cents per package. New Hampshire tax officers were pleased with the ninety cents differential in the price of cigarettes in the two states.[55] In 1993, Vermont tax officers projected their cigarette excise tax revenues would increase substantially as the result of the 1993 New York State Legislature increasing the tax from thirty-nine to fifty-six cents per package.[56] The tax differential decreased two years later when the Vermont State Legislature increased its excise tax from twenty to forty-four cents.

The downturn in the U.S. economy in 2001 created financial problems for most states and their state legislatures turned to the cigarette excise tax as a source of additional revenue. The Connecticut State Legislature facing a projected $350 million fiscal deficit, for example, increased its excise tax in 2002 by sixty-five cents to $1.11 a package, the first increase in seven years.[57] The tax is estimated to produce an additional $170 millions over the next biennium. Several other states quickly followed Connecticut's lead. The 2002 New York State Legislature increased the state excise tax on cigarettes from $1.11 to $1.50 per package and authorized New York City to increase its excise tax on a package of cigarettes from 8 cents to $1.50, thereby producing combined excise taxes of $7.00 in the city.[58] The excise tax increases in the city are projected to result in a decrease of approximately fifty percent in the sales

TABLE 6.1
State Cigarette Consumption by Supply Source, Fiscal Year, 1997

| | Taxable Sales | Smuggling | Cross-Border Activity | | | | | Memo: Weighted Per Pack State & Local Cigarette Tax ($FY 97) |
			Cross-Border Shopping	Military Sales	Native American Sales	Mexican Sales	
United States	86.7%	7.8%	3.6%	0.6%	0.8%	0.5%	34.9¢
Alabama	94.8%	4.8%	-0.7%	0.0%	0.5%	0.0%	21.9¢
Alaska	91.5	2.6	0.0	0.8	5.1	0.0	40.6
Arizona	88.7	3.8	0.4	1.7	3.0	2.4	58.0
Arkansas	84.8	8.2	6.8	0.2	0.0	0.0	31.5
California	86.1	9.3	0.0	0.8	1.1	2.7	37.0
Colorado	95.2%	4.0%	0.0%	0.3%	0.5%	0.0%	20.0¢
Connecticut	87.2	11.7	-18.3	0.7	0.4	0.0	50.0
Delaware	94.9	4.8	-19.2	0.3	0.0	0.0	24.0
Florida	88.9	8.5	1.4	0.8	0.4	0.0	33.9
Georgia	97.6	1.7	-1.2	0.5	0.1	0.0	12.0
Hawaii	62.0%	26.7%	0.0%	11.3%	0.0%	0.0%	60.0¢
Idaho	62.0	26.7	0.0	11.3	0.0	0.0	60.0
Illinois	83.2	6.2	10.5	0.0	0.0	0.0	50.0
Indiana	97.2	2.8	-40.1	0.0	0.0	0.0	15.5
Iowa	90.2	9.4	-1.2	0.0	0.4	0.0	36.0

State						
Kansas	91.8%	5.3%	1.5%	0.4%	0.9%	0.0%	24.0¢
Kentucky	99.9	0.0	-9.3	0.1	0.0	0.0	3.0
Louisiana	95.3	4.2	-2.9	0.1	0.4	0.0	20.0
Maine	86.5	9.7	2.4	0.5	0.9	0.0	37.0
Maryland	78.0	8.1	13.2	0.6	0.0	0.0	36.0
Massachusetts	71.3%	10.2%	17.9%	0.3%	0.3%	0.0%	69.7¢
Michigan	69.7	22.7	5.4	0.1	2.1	0.0	75.0
Minnesota	95.7	2.6	1.0	0.1	0.5	0.0	48.0
Mississippi	95.0	3.9	0.3	0.4	0.4	0.0	18.0
Missouri	95.8	4.1	-7.3	0.1	0.0	0.0	20.1
Montana	92.2%	3.9%	-0.7%	0.0%	4.0%	0.0%	18.0¢
Nebraska	88.0	8.5	1.1	1.2	1.3	0.0	34.0
Nevada	86.5	8.9	-0.6	2.2	2.4	0.0	35.0
New Hampshire	94.4	5.2	-143.8	0.4	0.0	0.0	25.0
New Jersey	90.5	9.0	-24.9	0.2	0.3	0.0	40.0
New Mexico	82.8%	4.8%	-2.1%	0.6%	9.1%	2.7%	21.0¢
New York	64.4	15.7	18.4	0.6	0.9	0.0	58.9
North Carolina	99.0	0.1	-1.6	0.5	0.4	0.0	5.0
North Dakota	95.0	2.5	-0.4	0.6	1.9	0.0	44.0
Ohio	93.4	5.2	1.4	0.0	0.0	0.0	24.5
Oklahoma	89.0%	5.3%	-3.7%	0.9%	4.8%	0.0%	23.0¢
Oregon	82.9	14.1	-2.6	0.5	2.5	0.0	50.3
Pennsylvania	92.9	7.1	-6.4	0.0	0.0	0.0	31.0
Rhode Island	95.8	3.6	-9.1	0.4	0.2	0.0	61.0
South Carolina	99.0	0.6	-0.2	0.3	0.1	0.0	7.0

(continued on next page)

TABLE 6.1 (continued)

	Taxable Sales	Cross-Border Activity					Memo: Weighted Per Pack State & Local Cigarette Tax ($FY 97)
		Smuggling	Cross-Border Shopping	Military Sales	Native American Sales	Mexican Sales	
South Dakota	90.5%	4.2%	-1.0%	0.1%	5.2%	0.0%	33.0¢
Tennessee	96.9	2.1	0.9	0.1	0.0	0.0	13.0
Texas	83.0	10.3	1.6	1.8	0.7	2.6	41.0
Utah	81.8	13.4	-2.6	1.2	3.5	0.0	26.5
Vermont	88.2	11.8	-19.0	0.0	0.0	0.0	44.0
Virginia	98.4%	0.6%	6.3%	0.8%	0.1%	0.0%	7.3¢
Washington	66.2	22.5	2.7	3.2	5.4	0.0	82.5
West Virginia	96.5	3.5	-8.7	0.0	0.0	0.0	17.0
Wisconsin	86.7	11.7	-2.9	0.0	1.6	0.0	44.0
Wyoming	97.0	2.1	-3.8	0.0	0.9	0.0	12.0
District of Columbia	61.8%	16.4%	19.3%	2.5%	0.0%	0.0%	65.0¢

Source: Tax Foundation Tax Features 42, August 1998, p. 3. Reprinted with permission of the Tax Foundation.

of cigarette while raising revenues by approximately $249 million annually. The state would lose approximately $247 million in excise tax revenues in the city that may be offset in part by increased sales in the state outside the city. Smokers could save approximately $35.00 per carton by making their purchases on an Indian reservation or via the Internet.

The principal sources of smuggled cigarettes are Virginia with its 2.0 cents excise tax per pack and Kentucky with its 3.0 cents excise tax. Congress cooperates with states by enacting statutes to assist them in their efforts to curb evasion of their laws.[59] The *Jenkins Act of 1949*, as noted, makes it a federal crime for a person or firm to use the postal service to evade payments of state and local government excise taxes.[60] Other modes of transportation are not covered by this act and a violation is only a misdemeanor. Federal prosecutors, in consequence, rely upon the *Mail Fraud Act of 1909* to prosecute buttleggers since a violation of the act is a felony.[61]

Buttlegging also is a major problem in Canada where excise taxes are approximate five times higher than United States and state taxes. The cost of a carton sold legally is more than forty-five dollars compared to approximately twenty dollars in neighboring states. Smugglers typically charge thirty dollars per carton and smuggle cigarettes through the Akwesasne Reserve, the home of approximately 12,000 Mohawk Indians who live on both sides of the international boundary line. The Jay Treaty of 1794 between the U.S. Government and the United Kingdom guarantees Mohawk Indians free passage throughout their reservation and the right to conduct commerce across the international boundary line without payment of a duty or tax. The Royal Canadian Mounted Police, Ontario Police, and Cornwall Police operate a joint task force that has seized large quantities of contraband cigarettes.[62] Canada has similar problems with the smuggling of alcoholic beverages, clothing, jewelry, and perfume because of high taxes. In recent years, smugglers have branched out into bringing firearms, illegal immigrants, and firearms into Canada.[63]

Indian Reservation and Military Post Sales. Seven states reported in 1985 their largest loss of excise tax revenues from the untaxed sale of cigarettes was attributable to military post exchanges and eight states were convinced the sale of cigarettes on Indian reservations was the most important or second most important reason for lower state excise tax revenues. Table 6.1 reveals Native American reservations were the source of 0.8 percent of sales in the United States, but 9.1 percent of sales in New Mexico. The sharp increase in state excise taxes on cigarettes has increased dramatically cigarette sales on many reservations.[64]

There is a similar loss of state excise tax revenues due to the sale of alcoholic beverages and motor fuels on reservations. Off reservation and military post business firms selling such products place pressure on the governor and the state legislature to prevent or restrict excise tax-free sales. A number of states with reservations have negotiated agreements with one or more of their tribes providing for the collection of state excise taxes on reservation sales in exchange for state conferral of specified benefits on the Indian tribes. It also should be noted state excise tax revenue also is lost because Congress allows tourists returning from a foreign nation to bring one quart of alcoholic spirits and a stated number of cigarettes free of tax.

The *Indian Trade and Intercourse Act of 1790* and the *Indian Trader Act of 1876* govern commerce on Indian reservations and various treaties between Indian tribes and the United States recognize the tribes as sovereign nations.[65] In consequence, states generally have been deprived of regulatory authority over Indian tribes and suffer the loss of millions of dollars in excise tax revenue due to tax-exempt sales of alcoholic beverages, cigarettes, and motor fuels sold to nonresidents on reservations.

The U.S. Supreme Court is called upon periodically to determine whether state and local governments may tax sales on Indian reservations. In *Moe v. Confederated Slaish and Kootenal Tribes of Flathead Reservations,* the U.S. Supreme Court in 1976 opined a state may not levy an excise tax on the purchase of cigarettes by an Indian resident of a reservation, but sales to nonresidents could be taxed.[66] In 1980, the court in *Washington v. Confederated Colville Tribes* held the state could levy an excise tax on cigarettes purchased on reservations by nonmembers of the Indian tribe and tribal sellers could be required to purchase and affix state tax stamps on cigarettes sold to nonmembers.[67] This opinion also allows the state to seize unstamped cigarettes shipped to the reservation from other states in the event the tribes fails to assist in collecting the state tax. The court did not rule on the state's contention it has the power to seize cigarettes on reservations intended for sale to nonmembers.

The New York State Department of Taxation and Finance in 1989 promulgated regulations placing a limit on the number of tax-free cigarettes wholesalers may sell to retailers on Indian reservations. The number is determined by multiplying the number of members of a tribe by per capita consumption of cigarettes in the state. Wholesalers selling more than the limit must pay in advance to the state a fifty-six cents excise tax per package. The Appellate Division of the New York Supreme Court invalidated the regulations, the New York Court of Appeals upheld the lower court decision, and the state appealed the decisions to the U.S. Supreme Court.[68] In 1994, the latter court reversed the lower courts' decision and held the *Indian Trader Act of 1876* did not preempt the authority of a state to promulgate reasonable regulations to assess and collected a tax, and the New York tax regulations did not impose an excessive burden on Indian traders.[69]

Deliberate Tax Exportation

The interstate commerce clause of the U.S. Constitution is designed to promote the free flow of interstate commerce, but does not necessary protect taxpayers in one state from taxes levied by sister states. States endowed with valuable resources, minerals and timber in particular, levy severance taxes on firms exporting most of their products to other states and the firms pass the taxes along to their customers. New Hampshire, as explained in chapter 4, used an ingenious tax, similar to a severance tax, to export ninety percent of its incidence to business firms and residents in Connecticut, Massachusetts, and Rhode Island by levying a state property tax on the state's single nuclear power station owned by twelve public utilities including eleven in the southern New England states.

A second method of exporting taxes is employment of tax apportionment formulas placing a heavier tax burden on foreign corporations. A third method is the offer of tax credits to domestic firms only. A fourth method is the levying by a state legislature of a so-called commuter income tax. A fifth method, described in detail above, is the deliberate state policy of keeping excise taxes on alcoholic beverages and cigarettes low to encourage residents of sister states to travel to the state to purchase these products.

Severance Taxes

Michigan in 1846 apparently was the first state to levy a severance tax and its low rate did not generate complaints by other states. Thirty-three states were levying such taxes by 1981.[70] Subsequently, several states substantially raised the severance tax rates and triggered a strong protest by eastern states that are major importers of minerals and timber. Nine states levy severance taxes on coal, natural gas, and oil that are major sources of revenue. Texas does not levy a state income tax in part because approximately one-quarter of its revenue is derived from natural gas and oil severance taxes. The rates of such taxes vary from 4.5 percent on oil extracted in Oklahoma to 30.5 percent on coal mined in Montana.

Commencing in the 1920s, the U.S. Supreme Court rendered decisions relating to natural resources taxation. The "Heisler Triology" of decisions held severances of resources were similar to manufacturing in preceding the flow of interstate commerce and consequently were "local" activities exempt from interstate commerce clause challenges.[71] In its *Heisler* decision, the court feared the nationalization of all industries could be a consequence of a decision holding the clause encompasses articles to be exported from a state.[72] In 1932, the court developed a corollary to the local activity doctrine positing a state could levy a tax on "local incidents" of an interstate business activity such as electrical power generation.[73] The corollary was an exception to the broader court holding a state could not tax the privilege of conducting interstate business. Elaborating on its local activity doctrine in 1970, the court explained "the extent of the burden that will be tolerated will . . . depend on the nature of the local interest involved, and on whether it could be promoted as well with a lesser impact on interstate activities."[74]

A change in the interpretation of the interstate commerce clause commenced in *Complete Auto Transit Incorporated v. Brady* in 1977 when the court replaced the privilege doctrine with "a standard of permissibility of state taxation based upon its effect rather than its legal terminology."[75] The decision involved the constitutionality of a Mississippi privilege tax. The court opined a state tax is valid provided it "is applied to an activity with a substantial nexus with the taxing state, is fairly apportioned, does not discriminate against interstate commerce, and is fairly related to the services provided by the state."[76]

Approximately forty percent of U.S. coal reserves, including sixty-eight percent of low-sulfur coal, are located in Montana and Wyoming. Montana exports ninety percent of its mined coal to other states and in 1921 levied a small severance tax. In 1975, the Montana Legislative Assembly increased the tax to 30.5 percent on each pound of coal with a heating value of 7,000 British Thermal Units (BTU).[77] The Wyoming State Legislature in the same year increased the severance tax from 2.0 percent to 17.5 per cent.

Four Montana coal and eleven electric utility companies in sister states in 1978 sought to have the tax declared unconstitutional on the ground it imposed an undue burden on interstate commerce and justified their contention in part by citing the report of a legislative conference committee stating the impact of the tax would be extraterritorial. The Montana Supreme Court in 1980 upheld the constitutionality of the tax and the U.S. Supreme Court affirmed the decision the following year.[78] The latter court rejected a preemption challenge by holding the *Federal Mineral Lands Leasing Act of 1920* and the *Federal Coal Leasing Amendments of 1975* did not prevent the Montana Legislative Assembly from levying the tax and also abandoned the *Heisler* "local activities" exceptions.[79]

The taxpayers, according to the court, had nexus to Montana, there was no apportionment question and hence no multiple taxation, the tax was uniform regardless of the place of mining, and a firm with a nexus can be required to support general governmental services and not simply services benefiting the firm's activities. Walter Hellerstein, a leading state tax expert, is convinced "the court is an institutionally incapable and politically inappropriate body for determining the appropriate level of a tax."[80]

In 1982, the U.S. Supreme Court delivered a decision holding Indian tribes could levy mineral severance taxes, but did not include within its decision whether the taxes could be levied on minerals extracted from fee lands in a reservation owned by non-Indians or whether the taxes could be imposed outside a reservation in territory termed "Indian Country."[81]

Tax Apportionment Formula

The proliferation of multistate and multinational corporations has made it difficult for each state to ensure corporations pay their fair shares of taxes in a nondiscriminatory manner. States utilize three methods—separate accounting, specific allocation, and formula apportionment—to determine the taxable amount of income of a multistate or multinational corporation. The first method suffers from the difficulty of separating income earned in a state from income derived elsewhere. Specific allocation also has limited applicability because it provides specific types of income, interest is an example, must be allocated entirely to one state.

States rely primarily upon a three-factor apportionment formula—payroll, property, and sales—to calculate the ratio between the income of a corporation earned in the state in relation to its multistate or multinational income. The formulas employed by states are not uniform and result in the definition of taxable income differing from state to state and possibly extraterritorial taxation. State legislatures commonly employ apportionment formulas and conditional tax credits to reduce taxation of their citizens and firms, and increase extraterritorial taxation. Such formulas and credits increase the complexity of their tax systems and impose significant compliance costs on foreign firms and generate court challenges as noted in a subsequent section.

The U.S. Supreme Court has been called upon since 1891 to review interstate apportionment of corporate taxes when the court examined a Pennsylvania tax on nondomiciliary scheduled railroad rolling stock. The court upheld the validity of the tax on the ground the tax was apportioned according to track mileage in Pennsylvania relative to the total track mileage used by the rolling stock.[82] In 1905, however, the court struck down a Kentucky tax levied on an entire fleet of rolling stock as violative of the due process of law clause of the U.S. Constitution because many cars were based outside the state and could be subject to taxation by a sister state.[83]

The following year, the court viewed favorably a New York tax on the entire rolling stock of a domestic railroad corporation which owned a substantial number of rail cars that seldom were in the state and found no violation of due process of law clause because there was no evidence presented the rolling stock could be taxed by a nondomiciliary state.[84] The court in 1944 extended this decision to airlines by upholding a Minnesota personal property tax levied on the entire fleet of a domestic airline corporation in spite of the fact the aircraft were flying continuously in interstate commerce with the exceptions of time periods when they were loading or unloading passengers and cargo or were undergoing maintenance.[85] The rationale for the decision was the same as in 1906; Justice Felix Frankfurter reported evidence was lacking that "a defined part of the domiciliary corpus . . . acquired a permanent location; i.e., a taxing situs elsewhere."[86] In 1954, however, the court applied its railroad rolling stock decisions to airlines by finding valid a nondomiciliary apportioned Nebraska state property tax levied on airplanes owned by an interstate airline with regularly scheduled stops in the state.[87]

The court in 1948 reviewed the apportionment of New York's gross receipts tax on transportation relative to the Greyhound Bus Corporation whose buses also traveled extensively in New Jersey and Pennsylvania, and held the tax was invalid because it was not apportioned on the basis of the number of miles the concerned buses traveled though various states.[88]

Until 1949, the court had ruled consistently that only the domiciliary state could tax vessels. The court in that year upheld the validity of an ad valorem property tax apportioned on the basis of the number of miles of inland water traversed by foreign corporation vessels.[89]

The court rendered an important decision in 1978 relative to the single-factor formula for apportioning net income between states. The court reviewed the Iowa single-factor gross receipts tax that an Illinois plaintiff alleged resulted in taxation by several states since most use the three-factor formula. The plaintiff company argued the latter formula would allocate twelve percent of the firm's 1972 net income to Iowa whereas the single-factor formula produced an allocation of eighteen percent. In its ruling, the court explained a nationally uniform apportionment formula is not required and a successful challenge of the Iowa formula would be dependent upon the company proving that part of its income allocated to Iowa was generated in other states.[90]

Proration of a Florida fuel tax levied on common carriers had been based on mileage traveled in the state until 1983 when the state legislature replaced the prorating tax on fuel sold to airlines with a five-percent tax on a state-determined price of $1.148 a gallon.[91] The tax had to be paid by all airlines even if their primary operations were outside the state. WardAir Canada, Incorporated challenged the tax on the grounds it violated a non-scheduled air service agreement entered into by Canada and the United States in 1974 and the Federal Aviation Act preempted the tax. In 1986, the U.S. Supreme Court rejected the plaintiff's arguments and specifically opined the tax was not preempted and does not violate the dormant interstate commerce clause.[92]

The Pennsylvania General Assembly imposed third-structure taxes—axle tax and marker fee—on non-Pennsylvania residents operating trucks based in sister states. The tax and fee were challenged on the grounds flat taxes subjected foreign trucking firms to a higher charge per miles traveled in the Commonwealth compared to domestic trucks and did not approximate the cost of the use of the highways. The court in *American Trucking Associations v. Scheiner* in 1987 agreed by opining flat taxes fail the court's internal consistency test requiring that a tax levied by every state could not place an impermissible burden on interstate commerce (see chapter 5).[93] Justice John Paul Stevens delivered the court's opinion and noted the complexities of the court's task by observing "the uneven course of decisions in this field reflects the difficulties of reconciling unrestricted access to the national market with each state's authority to collect its fair share of revenues from interstate commercial activities."[94]

Two years later, the court reviewed a 1985 Illinois five percent tax on telecommunications originating or terminating in the state charged to an Illinois service address regardless of whether each call was an interstate or an intrastate one. The Illinois General Assembly authorized a tax credit to any taxpayer offering proof a tax had been paid on the same call in another state. Although the court admitted an interstate telephone call could be subject to double taxation, the court ruled this possibility is an insufficient basis to strike down the tax.[95] Justice Thurgood Marshall explained the concerned tax differed from the third-structure taxes Pennsylvania levied on trucks because these taxes burdened foreign trucking firms in contrast to the Illinois tax whose burden fell on a resident "who presumably is able to complain about and change the tax through the Illinois political process."[96] The justice emphasized the interstate commerce clause was not intended to protect the residents of a state from taxes imposed by their own state legislature. He further noted the precise path of electronic telephone signals can not be determined in contrast to the number of miles domestic and foreign trucks travel on Pennsylvania's highways.

New Jersey employed the unitary tax system to assess the Bendix Corporation (now Allied-Signal Incorporated) for taxes on income including a gain from its sale of stock it owned in another corporation. The U.S. Supreme Court in 1992 endorsed the unitary tax system, but ordered New Jersey to refund the tax on the gain on the ground a state may not tax a nondomiciliary corporation's income derived from a unrelated business activity including the sale of stock.[97]

Another case involving the alleged failure of a state to apportion a tax fairly came to the court in 1995. By a seven to two vote, an Oklahoma sales tax on the price of interstate bus tickets sold in the state was upheld on the ground the tax did not violate the dormant interstate commerce clause.[98] This decision was distinguished from the court's 1948 decision invalidating New York's gross receipts tax on transportation services on the ground multiple taxation could occur under the New York tax since each state might levy a gross receipts tax on the same transportation services. In contrast, the Oklahoma tax was levied on the purchase of a ticket and no other state could levy a similar tax on the ticket.

Congress enacted the *Natural Gas Policy Act of 1978* to initiate the process of deregulation of the natural gas industry.[99] The Federal Energy Regulatory Commission in 1992 completed the transition of the industry to deregulation. This act had major tax consequences for New York as large industrial purchasers of gas previously could not buy gas directly from the suppliers and had to purchase gas from public utilities. Under the act, the large industrial uses of gas could by-pass the public utilities.

Anticipating the commission's action, the 1991 New York State Legislature enacted the *Natural Gas Import Tax Act* to recapture the revenue from the corporate franchise tax and tax on the gross income of firms selling gas for "ultimate consumption or use" that would be lost when deregulation became effective.[100] The act levied a 4.25 percent tax on the price paid for the privilege of importing gas through pipes or mains or causing gas services to be imported for consumption in this state.

An audit by the New York State Department of Taxation and Finance discovered the Tennessee Gas Pipeline Company had imported gas, but paid the privilege tax to the state only between 1991 and 1996, and consequently owed $1.6 million in taxes plus interest and penalties. The company contended and the state attorney general conceded the tax discriminates against interstate commerce. Citing U.S. Supreme Court decisions, the New York Court of Appeals in 2001 explained a facially discriminatory tax may not violate the interstate commerce clause of the U.S. Constitution if the tax "advances a legitimate local purpose that cannot adequately be served by reasonable nondiscriminatory alternatives."[101] In invalidating the tax, the court agreed with the company's contention the tax violated the internal consistency test by failing to provide a credit for taxes assessed on the out-of-state purchase of the gas (see chapter 5).[102]

Unitary Business-Formula Apportionment

California's use of a unitary business-formula apportionment to determine the amount of the state's franchise tax a multinational corporation must pay has resulted in diplomatic protests by the governments of Japan, United Kingdom, and other nations.[103] California determines the total earnings of such a corporation and develops an allocation fraction for the corporation by calculating an unweighted average of three ratios—California payroll to worldwide payroll, California property value to total worldwide property value, and California sales to worldwide sales. The taxable income of a corporation allocable to California is determined by multiplying the corporation's allocation fraction by the total income of the unitary firm.

The constitutionality of the California unitary tax was challenged by Alcan Aluminum Limited, a Canadian corporation, and Imperial Chemical Industries, PLC, a British firm. The U.S. District Court rejected the suit, but the U.S. Court of Appeals for the Seventh Circuit in 1988 reversed the decision.[104] Two years later, the U.S. Supreme Court heard an appeal by California and opined the firms had standing to bring suit under Article III of the U.S. Constitution, but the *Tax Injunction Act of 1937* barred this type of suit.[105]

California's unitary tax system also was challenged on the ground it violated the interstate commerce clause and due process clause of the U.S. Constitution. Barclays Bank, a British corporation, argued the system places a distinct tax burden on a foreign-based multinational company and produces double international taxation. In delivering the U.S. Supreme Court's decision in 1994, Justice Ruth B. Ginsburg explained there was no evidence Congress intended to prohibit the unitary system and "the history of Senate action on a United States/United Kingdom tax treaty . . . reinforces our conclusion that Congress implicitly has permitted the states to use the worldwide combined reporting method."[106] If the bank had been successful in its suit, California would have been required to repay in excess of $2.1 billion to approximately 2,000 multinational corporations in the form of tax refunds and abatements of pending assessments.[107]

Tax Credits

State legislatures authorize tax credits for a variety of purposes. California allows a corporation income tax credit of eight to twelve percent for the cost of research and a ten percent credit for the cost of a solar energy system installed in commercial buildings.[108] Virginia offers a ten percent tax credit for the cost of equipment used in the state for processing recycled personal property and Illinois grants a tax credit for employment of workers in enterprise zones.[109] These incentives encourage firms to local or expand facilities within the states offering the incentives, but may discriminate against interstate commerce.

New Mexico levied a tax on electrical energy generation at a rate of approximately two percent of the retail charge per net kilowatt-hour. In 1997, the U.S. Supreme Court struck down the tax on the ground the associated tax credit could be used only to offset the gross receipts tax on local electricity sales and the credit could not be used by firms selling electricity to sister states.[110] The court in its opinion made specific reference to the *Tax Reform Act of 1976* prohibition of discriminatory taxation against consumers in sister states in the generation of electricity.[111]

The 1968 New York State Legislature amended its tax law with respect to the transfer tax on securities by authorizing a fifty percent lower tax rate for transactions by nonresidents if the sales are made in New York and establishing

$350 as the maximum tax imposed on a resident or nonresident taxpayer if the sales take place in the state.[112] The U.S. Supreme Court in 1977 found the provisions to be unconstitutional on the ground they favored "local enterprises at the expense of out-of-state business" and noted the decision does not prohibit a state from competing with other states for interstate commerce as "such competition lies at the heart of a free trade policy."[113]

A New York state franchise tax was imposed on corporations that included the income of their subsidiaries engaged in the export of goods subject to a partial offsetting credit for income generated from exports shipped from a place of business in the state. The tax was challenged and the U.S. Supreme Court in 1984 dismissed New York's argument the credit simply forgave "a portion of the tax that New York had jurisdiction to levy" under a fairly apportioned tax formula on the ground the credit violates the interstate commerce clause by discriminating against foreign firms in an attempt to persuade them to conduct more of their business in the state.[114]

The court in 1984 was called upon to decide whether a West Virginia 0.27 percent gross receipts tax on the business of selling tangible property at wholesale violated the interstate commerce clause because West Virginia manufacturers were exempted from the tax. The state legislature additionally levied a 0.88 percent tax on the value of products manufactured in the state. Under this tax system, a West Virginia manufacturer has a larger tax burden. Nevertheless, the court held the tax to be invalid on the ground "a state may not tax a transaction or incident more heavily when it crosses state lines than when it occurs entirely within the state."[115]

The Alabama State Legislature levied a substantially lower gross premiums tax on domestic insurance companies compared to foreign ones that were allowed to reduce but not eliminate the tax rate differential by investing in Alabama assets and securities. In its decision, the U.S. Supreme Court noted the *McCarran-Ferguson Act of 1945* exempts the insurance industry from the interstate commerce clause, but nevertheless invalidated the tax as violating the equal protection of the laws clause of the U.S. Constitution.[116]

A different tax scheme was employed by the Washington State Legislature to discriminate against interstate commerce; i.e., a manufacturer who sold produces and paid the wholesale tax was not subject to the manufacturing tax. The Supreme Court in 1987 held the tax violated the interstate commerce clause and dismissed the state's argument the imposition of the manufacturing tax on goods manufactured in the state and sold in sister states was valid as a compensating tax for failure of the state to identify the burden that would be compensated for by the tax.[117]

In 1993, the U.S. Court of Appeals for the Second Circuit decided a complex case involving the Vermont motor vehicle use tax granting a credit against the tax for any sales tax paid to the state. The credit obviates the requirement for most Vermont residents to pay the use tax. A court challenged arose when a nonresident who purchased an automobile in a sister state moved to Vermont and discovered he was not entitled to a tax credit in Vermont or in his former state of residence where he purchased the automobile. The U.S. District Court for the District of Vermont opined the tax did not violate the interstate commerce clause and an appeal was made to the Court of Appeals.[118]

The tax had been examined earlier by the U.S. Supreme Court and struck down as violating the equal protection of the laws clause without addressing the interstate commerce clause objection raised by the plaintiff.[119] In its decision, the court explained it "again put to one side the question whether a state must in all circumstances credit sales or use taxes paid to another state against its own use tax."[120]

Vermont responded to this decision by promulgating a new rule narrowing the scope of the tax by stipulating the tax credit is not available to a Vermont resident who purchases and registers an automobile in a sister state prior to its registration in Vermont.[121] The U.S. District Court for the District of Vermont upheld the modified tax rule, but the U.S. Court of Appeals for the Second Circuit invalidated the rule on the ground it failed to meet the internal consistency test and consequently was not apportioned fairly, thereby violating the interstate commerce clause by imposing "a greater tax burden on vehicles transported into Vermont from other states than it does on Vermont-based vehicles not so transported."[122]

Commuter Income Taxes

Does state taxation of the income of nonresidents earned in the state constitute taxation without representation, a major complaint against the British crown incorporated in the Declaration of Independence in 1776? The U.S. Supreme Court answered this question in the negative relative to business firms in 1920 by upholding an Oklahoma tax on the net income of a nonresident derived from sources within the state and rejected arguments the tax imposed an undue burden on interstate commerce, denied plaintiffs due process of law and equal protection of the laws, and privileges and immunities.[123] The court specifically opined:

> The practical burden of a tax imposed upon the net income derived by a nonresident from a business carried on within the state certainly is no greater than that of a tax upon the conduct of a business, and this the State has the lawful power to impose.[124]

The court in the same year in *Travis v. Yale & Towne Manufacturing Company* rendered a similar decision opining a state may tax nonresident business firms and may limit their deductions to ones related to the production of the income subject to the state tax.[125] It also is important to note that Philadelphia' lead in levying a municipal income tax in 1939 has been followed by more than 3,500 municipalities and these taxes also apply to suburbanites who work in the taxing municipalities regardless of whether they are citizens of the state.[126]

The levying by two or more states of a personal and/or corporate income tax may result in double taxation. A number states levying such taxes have signed reciprocal income tax agreements with other states exempting nonresidents from the tax. Several states also have lessened the tax burden placed on their residents by allowing them a credit for income taxes paid to other states.

Nonresidential income taxation must conform with the equal protection of the laws clause of the Fourteenth Amendment to the U. S. Constitution. The New Hampshire General Court (state legislature) in 1970 imposed an income tax on residents and nonresidents, but included provisions that excluded residents from paying the tax.[127] In 1975, the U.S. Supreme Court invalidated the tax as violative of the equal protection of the laws clause because the tax applied only to nonresidents.[128] The court would have upheld the constitutionality of the tax had it applied equally to residents and nonresidents.

The so-called "spousal tax" refers to provisions in statutes of approximately one-half of the states levying a graduated income tax upon a nonresident deriving income within the state and basing the tax rate upon the combined income of the taxpayer and his/her spouse. Maine, for example, levies a graduated income tax on Maine and New Hampshire workers at the Portsmouth Naval Shipyard located near the state border. New Hampshire workers object to Maine's policy of determining the tax rate on the basis of the total income of a worker and his/her spouse, even though only the income earned in Maine is taxed, because the policy places a taxpayer in a higher tax bracket.[129]

In 1992, the New York Court of Appeals addressed the issue of the state's spousal tax and rejected a privileges and immunities challenge. The court opined:

> Plaintiffs would have us compare them to New York residents with a total income equivalent to plaintiffs' New York income alone. Plaintiffs would urge, for example, that a nonresident earning $20,000 in New York, but with reported income of $410,000 should be taxed at the same rate as a resident with an income of $20,000. But plaintiff's hypothetical taxpayers are not similarly situated in terms of ability to pay.[130]

The court concluded the plaintiff's complaint is directed at the graduated income tax. Judge Stewart F. Hancock dissented, criticized the court for relying upon two decisions of the U.S. Supreme Court involving a state inheritance tax and a state chain store tax, respectively, and opined a state may not tax income earned beyond its borders by a nonresident.[131] He added: "It seems to me that when property outside the State is taken into account for the purposes of increasing the tax upon property within it, the property outside is taxed in effect."[132]

The New York Court of Appeals in 2000 unanimously upheld the state legislature's repeal of New York City's commuter income tax of 0.45 percent for state residents, effective in July 1999, and opined the tax must be repealed for nonresident commuters.[133] Approximately 800,000 commuters who work in the city received refunds, including approximately 340,000 Connecticut and New Jersey residents whose refunds totaled $115 million. The court specifically found the repeal statute violated the interstate commerce clause and the privileges and immunity clause of the U.S. Constitution.[134]

Summary and Conclusions

State tax revenue competition is an inherent feature of the U.S. federal system. A state legislature constitutionally may levy specified taxes whose burden falls primarily upon nonresidents and foreign and alien corporations. Extraterritorial taxation varies considerably among the several states and includes taxes levied on hotel and motel occupancy, restaurant meals, and severance of natural resources. A few states purposely impose low excise taxes on cigarettes and alcoholic beverages to encourage sales of such products to residents of nearby states.

Certain states, epitomized by California and New York, are aggressive in seeking to enhance their tax revenues and their tax laws and administrative rules are subjected often to court challenges. It is most surprising that Congress did not utilize its interstate commerce power until 1959 to restrict state taxation powers or subsequently use this power more frequently to cover a broader range of state tax policies. The U.S. Supreme Court has been the most important defender of taxpayers against unfair interstate tax revenue competition and it and other courts fill the void in congressional tax policy regulation. In 1991, the court explained it serves "as a defense against state taxes, which, whether by design or inadvertence, either give rise to serious concerns of double taxation, or attempt to capture tax revenues that, under the theory of the tax, belong of right to other jurisdictions."[135] The court on a number of occasions has included in its decision a call for Congress to regulate state taxation on the ground Congress is better equipped to so regulate. The court, however, refuses to encroach upon the powers of legislative bodies by mandating a "single constitutionally mandated method of taxation."[136]

The ingenuity of state legislators and tax administrators in designing a complex tax scheme to enhance state revenues are revealed in the court decisions examined in this chapter. Courts have opined a state may not tax a business firm engaged in interstate commerce unless the firm has a nexus to the state and a firm with such a nexus can be taxed only in a nondiscriminatory manner to raise revenues to cover the firm's fair share of state expenses. A court examining a tax law or regulation has to balance the need of a state for revenue against the burden placed on interstate commerce.

Severance taxes on minerals and timber resources generated relatively little legal controversy until the 1970s when several mineral and timber rich states increased sharply their severance taxes and exported most of the tax burden to firms and residents of other states. Although the constitutionality of such taxes has been challenged, the U.S. Supreme Court has upheld them.

A particularly difficult area of taxation involves multistate and multinational corporations and the use of the unitary taxation system has generated a significant number of major law-suits against states. Tax officers admit it is difficult to devise a equitable method to tax the income of nondomiciliary corporations engaged in interstate commerce that ensures each such corporation contributes its fair share of taxes to a state. Particular controversy involves the tax apportionment formulas applied by the various states and such formulas have been protest by foreign nations registering diplomatic protests with the U. S. government.

The competitive nature of the federal system ensures state legislators and administrative rule makers will continue to devise taxes whose incidence can be exported to consumers and business firms in sister states with the expectation each new law or administrative rule may be invalidated by a court. When such invalidation occurs, the state legislature and/or tax administrators return to the drawing board to develop a new tax scheme to achieve the purpose of revenue enhancement.

Tax revenue competition is not the only form of interstate competition. Chapter 7 examines competition for business firms utilizing tax and other incentives, gamblers, sports franchises, and tourists.

CHAPTER 7

Competition for Business Firms, Sports Franchises, Tourists, and Gamblers

A federal system encourages states to generate revenues and create employment opportunities by attracting business firms, major league sport franchises, tourists, and gamblers. State recruitment efforts are supported in many instances by cities. Subnational governments also offer incentives to business firms to expand their operations and other incentives to persuade them not to relocate to another state or local government. Southern states in the late 1940s and 1950s were successful in luring many New England textile companies because of lower labor costs.

Competition for industry primarily was interstate in nature until the 1960s when such competition became international as the result of numerous nation states offering grants and other assistance to foreign business firms to construct facilities in their countries.[1] Developing nations with low labor costs have been especially successful in attracting labor-intensive U.S. firms, including ones that initially moved from New England to southern states. A newer development involves corporations with factories in the United States reincorporating in Bermuda or another nation without an income tax or low taxes to avoid federal and state taxes. A *New York Times* editorial in 2002 explained how Stanley Works, based in New Britain, Connecticut, could avoid paying taxes in the United States by implementing its announced plan to reincorporated in Bermuda:

> This becomes possible under a popular tax-avoidance scheme being peddled by major accounting and law firms that involves, in addition to reincorporating in Bermuda, establishing corporate residence in a second sunny offshore jurisdiction, Barbados. Under the terms of a favorable tax treaty, corporate profits earned in the United States can be shipped there and essentially laundered into deductible expenses.[2]

Corporate reincorporations of this nature deprive states of a substantial amount of tax revenue. Furthermore, there is evidence the chief beneficiaries of such a reincorporation may be corporate officers because their salary and bonuses typically are based in part on the firm's profitability and/or its stock price that could increase as taxes decline.[3] John Trani of Stanley Works reportedly "stands to pocket an amount equal to 58 cents of each dollar the company allegedly would save in corporate income taxes in the first year after its proposed move to Bermuda."[4] The company on August 1, 2002, decided not to reincorporate apparently because of public criticism and two bills progressing through Congress denying tax benefits to companies reincorporating offshore after March 20, 2002.[5]

States and large cities have competed often to attract a major league sports team or retain one since the Brooklyn Dodgers were induced to move to Los Angeles in 1947. Cities that are homes to such a team have come under increasing pressure from franchise holders to construct a new stadium or expand and renovate the existing one under the threat the franchise will be moved to another city which has offered to construct a new stadium. In effect, a number of franchise owners have played one city off against another city and blackmailed the city where the franchise is located into an agreement providing for a new or renovated stadium.

State government efforts to attract tourists are supported by local governments in recreational and scenic areas in particular, which band together to encourage tourists to visit their respective area. In recent years, a number of states have competed to attract gamblers by legalizing casinos subject to state regulation and operating lotteries selling tickets to nonresidents.

An interesting development is the creation in 1997 of the Arizona Office of Senior Living to promote the retirement industry.[6] Individuals fifty-five years of age and older are estimated to spend more than $14 billion in the state annually and their incomes generally are not affected by down turns in the economy. These individuals typically impose a light burden on the state's social welfare system because they have ample income and private health insurance, and many volunteer their services to help the less fortunate by raising funds for charities and tutoring school children. Furthermore, spending by retirees boosts the economy of small rural towns lacking an industrial base.

Interstate competition for tourists generates little criticism, but financial incentives offered by state and local governments to attract industrial firms have been subjected to major criticisms including charges they cause locational distortions, are costly, often provide no net benefits, and are part of a zero sum game because many of the firms had decided to relocate or construct a new factory in the absence of incentives.

Opponents of such incentives cite the example of Kentucky's successful effort to induce a Canadian steel company to construct a mill in the state by providing a tax incentive totaling approximately $350,000 for each new employee.[7] This incentive and other similar large incentives, such as Alabama's $300 million package to attract Mercedes-Benz, led to calls for Congress to curtail such competition under its delegated power to regulate commerce between the states and its taxation power by removing the tax exempt status of state and local government bonds, known as municipal bonds, if utilized to subsidize industrial firms locating in their respective jurisdiction.[8] Critics maintain there is a lack of accountability associated with the incentive programs and "the benefit to a state are difficult to measure."[9]

The foci of this chapter are interstate competition for business firms, sports franchises, tourists, and gamblers with primary attention devoted to the industrial promotion policies of the various states. The relative locational importance of state and local government taxes, regulatory policies, and labor costs are assessed.

It is important to note states also engage in economic cooperation, including economic development, by means of interstate compacts and administrative agreements (see chapter 8).

Competition for Industry

Early in the nineteenth century, state governments recognized the potential of canals as magnets for industry and shortly thereafter the even greater importance of railroads. In consequence, state legislatures initially promoted the development of canal systems and subsequently railroad systems by authorizing canal and railroad companies to acquire needed rights-of-way by means of eminent domain and state financing of canal building that often could be described only as reckless. The result was serious financial problems for several states. The New York State Legislature, for example, was forced to levy a special state property tax to raise needed revenues and voters reacted by demanding that the state legislature propose constitutional amendments to prevent such reckless financing in the future. A new Constitution, drafted by a convention and ratified by voters in 1846, among other things, forbids the state legislature to give or loan money to any private corporation.[10] Constitutional prohibitions, however, often prompted state legislatures to seek methods of avoiding the prohibitions. One evasion method is the creation by the state legislature of public authorities which are not subject to a constitutional requirement, such as voter approval of issuance of full faith and credit bonds, because the authorities are quasi-governmental bodies.[11]

Early in the nineteenth century, states did not directly encourage specific business firms to locate in their respective states, but relied upon canal companies initially and later railroad companies to attract industrial firms to construct factories near canal and/or rail facilities. Currently, firms specializing in developing facilities for industrial firms work in conjunction with the concerned state department.

Industrial development bonds became a favorite tool of states seeking to attract firms because they allow states to borrow funds at below market–interest rates and their holders to receive interest exempt from state and U.S. income taxes. Bond proceeds are used to construct facilities subsequently sold at low prices or rented to industrial firms. The intense competition between northern and southern states by 1963 led the Federal Reserve Bank of Boston to publish in its quarterly review an article entitled "New War Between the States" highlighting the subsidization of industrial firms agreeing to construct a factory in their respective state.[12]

The article identified the northern states "weapons" as privately financed business development corporations (BDC) and state government financing of industrial buildings by direct loans and/or insurance. The southern states "weapons" were exemption of newly located industrial firms from state and/or local government taxation, and issuance of municipal bonds to raise funds for private industrial development.

The 1949 Maine State Legislature chartered the first BDC and authorized it to issue stocks to raise funds to facilitate the borrowing of larger amounts of funds from commercial lending institutions to be used to promote economic development. State chartered commercial banks are exempted from state-lending regulations if funds are loaned to a BDC. The latter typically loans funds to small firms unable to obtain long-term financing from financial institutions. In consequence, BCDs have a higher loss rate than commercial banks.

Another favorite device is the creation by state legislatures of state industrial building authorities to insure commercial lenders' loans to a company to construct a factory typically for up to ninety percent of the value of the land and buildings. The borrower pays the cost of the insurance in the form of a charge of 0.5 to 1.0 percent of the outstanding loan balance. This device enables a state such as New York, which constitutionally has been forbidden since 1846 to loan funds to a private firm, to assist such firms.[13]

Today, the state legislature in most states has granted authority to municipalities to raise funds for economic development purposes by issuance of bonds supported by revenues generated by leases of industrial facilities. These bonds have been criticized on the grounds a firm in many instances would have located in a given municipality without a subsidy and tax-exempt bonds issued to finance facilities constitute an indirect federal tax subsidy to a private firm since interest received by bond holders is not subject to the U.S. personal or corporate income tax. Local governments also subsidize these firms by exempting totally the facilities from the property tax or allowing a partial or full tax abatement for a specified number of years. Extensive use of tax exemptions or abatement shifts the incidence of the property tax burden to other taxpayers including preexisting industrial firms.

The U.S. Advisory Commission on Intergovernmental Relations (ACIR) examined recruitment of business firms and identified "competition in the areas of education, public welfare, and public works infrastructure . . . and right-to-work laws and laws regulating workers' compensation insurance."[14] Creation of free ports by state legislatures, commencing in the 1960s, has been another method of attracting business firms. They have proven to be particularly attractive to firms desiring to construct and operate major distribution centers because products in the free port prepared for interstate shipment are exempt from the general property tax.

A study by the Council of State Government (CSG) discovered the variety of assistance provided by forty-four states offering "tax breaks to businesses for equipment and machinery, goods in transition, manufacturers' inventories, raw materials in manufacturing, and job creation."[15] The study also reported the number of states offering tax incentives for job creation increased from twenty-seven to forty-four between 1984 and 1993 and southern states were most active in offering incentives. The high percentage of women employed today convinced a number of state legislatures to offer tax credits for the cost of day care.

States offer general and customized tailored incentives to address the requirements and wishes of a firm being recruited. The CSG study revealed particularized incentives were offered to

> the service industry (Sears, Roebuck & Company, $240 in Illinois); Chase Manhattan Bank in New York City, $235 million; NBC, $150 million, (New York City); manufacturing companies (Canada's Dogasco and Co-Steel, $140 million to Gallatin County, Ky.); aviation (Northwestern Airlines maintenance facility, $350 million, to Duluth, Minn.); and domestic and foreign automobile companies (General Motors, $70 million, to Spring Hill, Tenn.; Toyota, $147 million, to Georgetown, Ky.).[16]

Incentives totaling $130 million interested BMW in South Carolina as the location for a factory, but the only site the firm would consider contained 140 middle class homes. This fact did not prove to be an obstacle as the state and Spartanburg purchased all the homes for $36.6 million.[17] The Scott Paper Company in 1993 moved its corporate headquarters from Philadelphia to Boca Raton, Florida, in part because Palm Beach County provided a $280,000 grant and the state offered tax credits and state-financed job training for company employees.[18] Mississippi not only offered the Nissan Motor Company $295 million in incentives to construct and operate a truck plant in the state, but also employed its eminent domain power to acquire land from African American farmers who refused to sell their land, thereby triggering a major controversy.[19]

Business firms, in common with owners of major league sports franchises, often are successful in playing one state off against another state in bidding wars with the principal winner being the firms. CSG offered the following advice to state economic development officers considering the offer of customized incentives to a commercial, financial, or industrial firm:

- seek additional information when offering customized incentive packages and refrain from offering such incentives packages to lure businesses from other states;
- require more thorough analyses to evaluate information on the economic impact of a customized incentive package, and examine policy alternatives;
- establish clear and consistent policies on business incentives, with enforceable contract provisions applicable to recipient firms as a condition of the customized incentive award;
- be aware of the potential ethical problems that can be associated with recruiting large businesses from other states.[20]

Alabama took an unusual approach to economic development in 2002 when its pension fund invested $240 million in financially troubled US Airways to gain a 37.5 percent ownership share after the airline exits the jurisdiction of the U.S. Bankruptcy Court in 2003.[21] Fund Director David G. Bronner indicated the investment may result in additional US Airways flights to the larger cities in the state and/or the transfer of some of the airline's back-office operations to the state.

Business Climate

The decision of a business firm to locate, expand, or close a facility has been influenced by the local government physical infrastructure, labor force, quality of public services, and perception of whether the tax and regulatory policies of a state government are friendly, neutral, or hostile to the business community. New York for years had a poor business climate in the eyes of many national and international firms such as General Electric, and experienced great difficulty in attracting major firms to construct factories in the state. More recently, business firms have been including an educated and skilled work force as a business climate factor.

How important are state and local taxes in affecting a business firm's plant or headquarters location decisions? Firms not surprisingly prefer low taxes that do not have a major negative impact on their profits and nonburdensome flexible regulations. Chief Executive Victor J. Riley Jr. of KeyCorp explained in 1994 the move of the bank's headquarters from Albany, New York, to Cleveland was prompted in part by New York's tax law providing that financial holding companies are taxed on forty percent of the dividends they receive from foreign subsidiaries (chartered in other states) in contrast to Ohio which taxes only in-state income.[22] In 2002, CSX Corporation Chief Executive Jack Snow stated local government property taxes in New York were "killing our growth opportunities up here" and the corporation is reluctant to upgrade its tracks for use by high-speed trains and will remove tracks from unused lines to reduce its property tax bill.[23]

ACIR reported in 1967 plant location studies conducted since the 1960s indicate the taxation level in states in a region is not considered to be a major factor by most firms in deciding upon a region of the nation.[24] Firms pay closer attention to taxation differential between states and their locational advantages after selecting a region of the nation for the construction of a new facility.

A firm making a plant locational decision investigates the total tax burden within a state. State taxes may be low, but local government taxes may constitute a major burden and encourage a firm to consider a site in a nearby state with low combined state and local government taxes. States levying a sales tax and relatively high excise taxes often are viewed as business friendly because less state revenue will need to be raised from business firms. High state corporate and personal income taxes tend to be viewed negatively by business firms with the result other important locational factors must be relied upon to attract firms such as a skilled labor force, excellent air and ground transportation facilities, and/or a central market location. Deregulation or regulatory reform reducing business compliance costs and a tax system minimizing compliance costs also are significant locational factors.

ACIR reported once a state has gained a reputation as a high tax state "it is difficult to erase the image" and that "for many firms the particular state or local levy which appears to have the greatest influence on managerial decisions is the general property tax. In jurisdictions where this tax is levied upon business inventories it is possible to discern a clear interrelationship between the property tax costs and decisions made by management."[25]

The commission reported a textile company with plants in North Carolina and South Carolina could minimize taxes by keeping inventories in the latter state where most inventories are tax exempt.[26] Similarly, the Burroughs Corporation had been paying a $6,615 inventory tax on each $150,000 computer stored in California, but avoided the tax beginning in 1964 by storing all warehouse merchandise destined for California in Reno, Nevada, where there is no inventory tax.[27]

A second commission report on plant location, published in 1981, presented evidence supporting its 1967 conclusions. The report revealed the typical manufacturer's labor costs are several times larger than all state and local government taxes, and consequently a small wage differential is of greater importance than a small tax differential to the firm.[28] Interstate and interregional movements of large manufacturing firms are not common. The Great Lakes and Mideast regions, however, experienced the loss of more firms to another region, the Southeast, than to their regional sister states.[29] The commission explained:

> It is noteworthy that several high-tax states and several low-tax states do not show the level of manufacturing firm births that might be expected if the association between taxes and firm births were casual. The high-tax states are Massachusetts, Arizona, Wyoming, California, and Hawaii. Wyoming can be dismissed as an aberration because (1) it is remote; (2) it is relatively sparsely settled; and (3) its high taxes originated in natural resource exploitation where the burden is passed on to the users of the resources, only a few of whom reside in Wyoming. Aside from Wyoming, the experience in other high-tax states cannot be explained easily. Despite above-average taxes per $1,000 of personal income, four states show above-average birthrates of single establishment manufacturing firms.[30]

The high tax reputation of Massachusetts no doubt resulted in a number of firms disregarding the commonwealth as a site for a new facility. Nevertheless, Massachusetts had a higher new manufacturing firm growth rate in the period subsequent to 1969 than its 1969 percentage of major manufacturing firms in New England.[31] In 1993, the Massachusetts General Court (state legislature) took a step to improve its tax image by increasing its corporation income tax investment credit from one to three percent.[32] High-tax states offering such a tax incentive in most instances restrict it to new firms.

The tax climate of a state clearly impacts the locational decision-making of many firms chartered by one of the fifty states. State and local government taxes, however, generally do not affect the locational decisions of certain alien corporations (chartered in another nation) because their respective nation grants corporation tax credits against a firm's tax liability for corporation income taxes paid in the United States.[33]

Business firms make rational plant locational decisions to maximize their profits by generally selecting a state where total production costs including taxes will be lowest. The optimal location for a new facility varies by industry. A higher production cost location, for example, may be selected if distribution and marketing costs are important decisional factors. Similarly, a firm contemplating constructing an aluminum factory that will consume large quantities of electrical energy will give a high weight to energy cost as a decisional factor.

The importance of a highly skilled work force has been demonstrated by national and international companies constructing factories in relatively close proximity to the Massachusetts Institute of Technology to facilitate recruitment of its graduates who prefer to reside in the Greater Boston area and to draw upon the Institute's professors as consultants. Various states have increased sharply spending on public education, including higher education, in recent years in recognition of the importance of an educated work force in attracting and retaining business firms. The shortage of qualified public school teachers has resulted in competition to recruit teachers from foreign nations to teach mathematics and science.[34]

Other important locational factors are the availability at a reasonable price of a large parcel of land serviced by sewer and water facilities; relatively close proximity to excellent air, ground, and/or water transportation facilities; raw materials; adequate low-cost electrical power; and favorable subnational governmental taxes and regulatory climate. Automobile companies in the 1980s, for example, "liked the absence of many unions and the lower average wage" in southern states.[35]

Occasionally, the movement of a company to a new location is not related directly to the factors listed above. Candy makers, including Hershey Foods Corporation, and Tootsie Roll Industries Incorporated, have opened plants in Mexico where the cost of sugar is one-half of the federally supported price in the United States and labor costs are a fraction of such costs in the United States.[36] Kraft Foods Incorporated purchased the Life Savers Company of Holland, Michigan, and announced it would close the plant in 2003 and transfer its operations to a plant near Montreal.[37] A company spokesman attributed the plant closing decision to the underutilized plant in Quebec and the lower cost of Canadian sugar and corrugated paper. The Coalition for Sugar Reform reported in 2002 the wholesale price per pound of sugar is approximately sixteen cents in Canada and twenty-seven cents in the United States, thereby allowing Kraft Foods Incorporated to make sugar cost savings of approximately $9 million annually by moving Life Savers production to Canada.[38]

New Jersey successfully employed various types of incentives to attract New York firms, but discovered in 2002 many of its firms had been lured in part by tax incentives and job-training grants to Pennsylvania's Lehigh valley where real estate is less costly and taxes are lower.[39] New Jersey reported it enticed 116 firms, similar to the ones loss to the Lehigh valley, to the state in 1998, including 17 from Pennsylvania and 50 from New York.

The importance of the regulatory climate of a state should not be underestimated. Many state have established a maximum interest rate limit on credit card debt in order to protect their residents. Should a state legislature decrease the allowable maximum interest rate charge on such debt, banks will transfer their credit card operations to a state, such as Delaware or South Dakota, which have deregulated interest rates. Banks also will threaten to transfer their credit card operations to another state should the state legislature enact a statute ending interest rate deregulation.[40] Similarly, a industrial company may not be interested in constructing a new plant emitting air and/or water pollutants in a state with air and water quality standards higher than the minimum standards established by Congress and the U.S. Environmental Protection Agency.[41]

Assessing Tax and Other Incentives

Advocates identify six major advantages of financial incentives to attract a business firm to locate a facility in a state.

1. A new firm immediately benefits from lower total production costs.
2. Incentives negate to a degree any adverse locational factors such as higher transportation costs.
3. Incentives can give a state an advantage over other states when a firm is in the process of making a final location decision restricted to a short list of sites in two or three states.
4. Existing firms can be encouraged by fiscal incentives to expand within the state.
5. The new firm may produce spillover benefits by helping to attract other firms.
6. The perceived business climate of the state is improved.

Critics identify six disadvantages of fiscal incentives.

1. They typically are available only to new plants and consequently discriminate against existing state's firms unless they invest in a new plant.
2. The amount of state and local government revenue available for use to achieve other important policy objectives is reduced. Particular objections were raise after Alabama provided incentives of approximately $300 million to attract a Mercedes-Benz plant in view of a court order requiring the state to spend hundreds of millions of additional dollars to upgrade its public school system.[42]
3. Incentives often do not achieve their goals because they are insufficient to negate other adverse locational factors.
4. The value of incentives is reduced to the point where they have little positive effect in attracting firms because of the deductibility of state and local government taxes from a corporation's gross income allowed by the U.S. Internal Revenue Code.
5. Total regional employment and production may not be increased if incentives simply encourage firms to relocate facilities within a region.
6. Experience reveals a number of factories benefiting from fiscal incentives failed to provide the number of new jobs promised.

Pennsylvania, for example, spent $70 million to attract a Volkswagen factory, yet it only provided employment for approximately 6,000 persons instead of the promised 20,000 and closed within a decade.[43] Dick Netzer, an economist, concluded "the empirical evidence on what works in economic development is thin or unpersuasive."[44]

Border Wars

Efforts by various states to attract business firms from sister states in a region have resulted in bad interstate relations which may make states less willing to cooperate with each other in a joint effort to achieve regional goals. New Jersey and New York often are competitors seeking to attract industrial firms. New York Governor George E. Pataki in 1995 rejected a proposed contract under which the state-owned New York Power Authority would supply low-cost electric power to New Jersey Transit."[45] The governor explained "the power authority 'made a deal to provide low cost economic development power to the State of New Jersey. We took a look at that and said 'My God, what is going on?'"[46] Pataki failed to note the power would be supplied to New Jersey Transit for use only by its trains after they entered New York City with commuters and tourists.

Connecticut, New York City, and New Jersey agreed in 1991 they would not compete for each other's business firms by means of advertisements or aggressive recruiting. Nevertheless, New Jersey within a few months violated the agreement by utilizing revenues from the World Trade Center, owned by the Port Authority of New York and New Jersey, to establish an industrial recruitment fund.[47]

In 1994, Swiss Bank was persuaded to move from New York City in response to Connecticut tax incentives totaling over $130 million over the following ten years.[48] A furious Mayor Rudolph W. Giuliani of New York City immediately arranged for the purchase of advertisements in Connecticut newspapers explaining competitive bidding to attract firms will prove injurious to both states and contending "Connecticut taxpayers will pay $60,000 for each job, an unbelievable amount."[49] In response, Connecticut state officers alleged the 1991 agreement was broken by New York City and explained Swiss Bank had approached the state seeking a new location. They also estimated $300 million in new tax revenues will be generated by the bank and the $120 million tax inducements were reasonable in the light of the new tax revenues and employment generated.[50] Mayor Giuliani almost immediately announced the city no longer would abide by the agreement with Connecticut, but would honor a similar 1991 agreement with New Jersey.[51]

In 1994, the New York Mercantile Exchange announced plans to move to New Jersey, but was persuaded by a $184 million state and city subsidy, amounting to $22,700 for each of the Exchange's employees, to construct a new building in Battery Park City.[52] The following year, the Coffee, Sugar, and Cocoa Exchange and the Cotton Exchange cancelled plans to accept New Jersey incentives and move from Manhattan to the state upon the offer of $91 million in subsidies by the State of New York and New York City.[53]

The New York Stock Exchange considered moving to New Jersey, but New York State and New York City officers in 1998 negotiated a $1 billion incentive agreement with the exchange for its construction of a new tower and trading complex near its present location.[54] A securities firm in 1997 moved employees from Jersey City to the World Trade Center in response to incentives worth millions of dollars, but decided to return to Jersey City with the aid of at least $8.3 million in New Jersey incentives after its offices were destroyed on September 11, 2001.[55] A second financial firm with offices in the center announced it was considering moving to New Jersey, but "real estate brokers familiar with the company's plans said Euro Brokers planned to move to 199 Water Street in Manhattan and was merely using the Jersey card as leverage."[56]

A case study of two firms, one moving to and the other located in Keene, New Hampshire, reveals more clearly the motivations of certain relocating firms. New Hampshire and Vermont in 2001–2002 engaged in competition to be the new corporate headquarters for C&S Wholesale Grocers, Incorporated of Brattleboro, Vermont—the third largest such wholesaler in the nation.[57] The firm has sales of more than $9.5 billion annually and received an offer of $1.9 million in tax credit incentives from the State of Vermont that combined with other incentives could total $6 million.[58] New Hampshire did not offer such incentives. The firm, however, selected Keene, New Hampshire, eighteen miles east of Brattleboro. Company president Richard Cohen stated: "The Keene location proved to be the best choice for C&S primarily because the larger 44 acre site provided us with a more physically attractive and flexible setting for our new corporate headquarters campus."[59] The other expressed reasons were the Keene airport, hangar location of the company's corporate jet; many corporate executives reside in Keene; and availability of housing. There may be an unstated reason for the move; i.e., New Hampshire does not levy an income tax except on intangible income and does not levy a sales tax. Approximately 300 executives will be transferred to Keene, but the warehouse will remain in Brattleboro.

Three days prior to the announcement by C&S Wholesale Grocers, Incorporated, the National Grange Mutual Insurance Company of Keene announced it would move its seventeen top executives to a new corporate headquarters in Jacksonville Florida. The company explained: "The ability to attract high-level professional, managerial, and executive talent, will be a key factor in our future success, and issues such as housing availability and limited job opportunities for relocating spouses in the Keene area have been a concern for us in recent years."[60]

Undesirable border wars involving competition for business firms would not occur if all states follow the 1994 guidelines developed by the National Governors Association calling for:

- using individual state development objectives, identified criteria, and a calculated rate of return to offer public subsidies that will be available to and benefit all businesses;
- assisting projects that otherwise would not occur, rather than just influencing the location;
- encouraging joint ventures between government and businesses;
- investing in people and in communities as foundations of a healthy economic environment, instead of concentrating resources in the fortunes of one company or project;
- providing special assistance to encourage investment in distressed areas or to bring jobs to populations experiencing high unemployment; and
- developing provisions to recoup subsidies if the business community fails to deliver promised benefits in return for state subsidies.[61]

The association recommended employment of cost-benefit analysis by state government officers prior to offering fiscal and tax incentives to a firm because "the use of development subsidies to foster and sustain economic growth remains much more an 'art' than a science."[62] Explaining permanent economic growth is not based upon "one-time investments," the association urged states to calculate the rate of return on development subsidies to determine their ability to generate resources that can be invested in the future.[63]

Border wars do not always involve competition for specific business firms. The New York Independent System Operator, a nonprofit organization supervising the state's grid and power markets, announced in 2002 it would seek the approval of the Federal Energy Commission to merge with the New England Independent System operator.[64] Such a merger would save New York electricity consumers an estimated $282 million over a three year period, and is opposed by Connecticut and Massachusetts because of the fear the merger would result in higher electricity rates in their states.

Similarly, a twenty-four mile Cross-Sound Cable between Connecticut and Long Island has been a source of dispute between Connecticut and New York. Chairman Richard M. Kessel of the Long Island Power Authority, a state authority, on August 14, 2002, requested U.S. Secretary of Energy Spencer Abraham to order Connecticut to activate the cable.[65] On August 17, 2002, Abraham declared an electric power emergency and ordered the activation of the cable.[66]

Cluster Development

Observers noticed in the post World War II period that firms in certain industries tended to locate manufacturing plants and research facilities in close proximity to each other, suggesting individual location decisions were based upon the same criteria. Electronic firms were attracted to the greater Boston area in the 1950s and 1960s, and the circumferential Route 128 became known popularly as the electronic highway. In this instance, the magnet was the Massachusetts Institute of Technology. More recently, California's silicon valley became the home to numerous telecommunications firms and the greater Boston area became a center for biomedical research.[67]

Arizona took note of these clusters and developed in 1992 its Strategic Development Plan for Economic Development based upon ten development clusters: food, fiber, and natural products; high technology; mining and minerals; transportation; health and biomedical technology; tourism; optics; software; environmental technologies; and business services.[68] The clusters encourage suppliers of raw materials and parts to locate near manufacturing plants, provide a larger pool of workers, and encourage cluster firms to organize strategic alliances.

Sports Franchises

Competition for sports franchise generates bidding wars among states and cities, and threats of retaliation. The major sports leagues—baseball, basketball, football, ice hockey, and soccer—operate in a monopolistic manner by determining the number of teams, their ownership, and locations, yet only major league baseball is exempted from the *Sherman Antitrust Act*.[69] In 1922, Justice Oliver Wendell Holmes of the U.S. Supreme Court delivered its unanimous decision holding baseball does not fall within the meaning of interstate commerce.[70] Describing the business of baseball as giving exhibitions, he opined:

> [t]he fact that in order to give exhibitions the Leagues must induce free persons to cross state lines and must arrange and pay for their doing so is not enough to change the character of the business . . . the transport is a mere incident, not the essential thing. That to which it is incident, the exhibition, although made for money would not be called trade of commerce in the commonly accepted use of those words. That which in its consummation is not commerce does not become commerce among the States because the transportation that we have mentioned takes place.[71]

Present day owners of major league baseball, basketball, football, and ice hockey franchises, in contrast to early owners, are experts at persuading cities and/or states to finance the reconstruction of existing stadiums or to construct new ones by threatening to move their franchises to other cities offering to construct new stadiums. Approximately one-half of the 115 major professional franchises had requested or were beneficiaries of new or reconstructed stadiums by 1997.[72] States and cities constructed six major league baseball stadiums in the period 1990–1998 with the franchise owners paying only thirteen percent of the costs.[73]

Most stadiums today are publicly owned and critics term franchise owners welfare recipients. The first publicly owned facility is the Memorial Coliseum constructed in Los Angeles as part of its successful bid to be the venue for the Olympic games. Whereas the early stadiums were located in large cities and readily accessible by the subway or trolley, the stadiums constructed in the mid-1950s and 1960s often were located in the suburbs, were accessible only by motor vehicles, and in consequence had large paved parking lots. By the 1990s, there was a counter trend involving locating new stadiums in the central city, illustrated by the opening in 1992 of Oriole Park at Camden Yards in Baltimore, as part of central city redevelopment projects.[74] Another explanation for the trend are luxury boxes generate "tens of millions of dollars" that do not "have to be shared with the league or other teams."[75]

The first two of the following three case studies highlight the nature of the interstate and intercity sports franchise competition, and the third case describes how a city unsuccessful in obtaining a state legislative appropriations to help finance an arena found an unusual source of needed revenue.

Hubert Humphrey Metrodome

The Minnesota Twins baseball team and the Minnesota Vikings football team had been playing in the relatively small Metropolitan Stadium, constructed in 1955, in Bloomington and owned by the Metropolitan Sports Area Commission. The teams increasingly became dissatisfied with the stadium and the Vikings threatened to depart the area after their lease expired in 1975.[76] The Minneapolis city council as early as 1971 expressed interest in construction of a new sports facility. Various stadium proposals were advanced and debated in the period 1973 to 1977 when a bill was enacted by the Minnesota State Legislature and signed into law by Governor Rudy Perpich providing for the appointment of a commission to select the stadium design and site.

Four alternatives, including no new stadium, were considered and a decision was made, by a four to three vote, on December 1, 1978, to construct a domed stadium in Minneapolis. Bonds backed by a two percent tax on liquor in the metropolitan area were to be issued to finance construction, but bills were introduced in the 1979 state legislature to repeal the tax and were supported by a group composed primarily of bar owners. The Senate approved the repeal bill and the new governor, Albert H. Quie, indicated he would sign the bill if it reached his desk. The Vikings threatened to depart the area. To prevent the departure, a new bill was introduced in the state legislature authorizing construction of a domed stadium with costs limited to $46 million and imposing a motel-hotel tax and a liquor tax to serve as backing for the bond issue. The bill was debated in both houses, compromise provisions were approved, and the bill became law. Subsequently, the newly created Metropolitan Sports Facilities Commission engaged in extensive but successful lease negotiations with the Twins and the Vikings leading to the signing of a contract providing for thirty-year leases and an escape clause for the Twins allowing them to terminate the lease if they failed to sell 1.4 million tickets annually for three seasons. The multipurpose Metrodome became operational in 1982.

Carl Pohlad became the new owner of the Twins in 1984 and by 1994 was burdened by a heavy debt load and a $10 million assessment as part of a $280 million major league collusion settlement.[77] In contrast to the National Football League franchise owners who share radio and television network revenues, baseball owners shared little revenue. Negotiations were carried on by Pohlad's sons with a small number of key political and business leaders, including the chairman of the sports commission, for construction of a retractable roof domed stadium. A complicated tentative agreement was reached and announced at a news conference on January 9, 1997.

The owner indicated he would give the state a 49 percent ownership of the team and contribute $82.5 million to the state to assist in funding the new stadium, but after a stipulated period of time the state would be obligated to repay the funds and pay the owner for his ownership share estimated to be worth approximately $85 million. Under the tentative agreement, the state in theory later could sell its ownership share to the new majority owner and recoup more than $85 million provided the value of the franchise continued to increase.

The news media reported the franchise owner would give $157.8 million to help finance the new stadium. Investigative reporter Jay Weiner concluded:

> That $157.8 million included $82.5 million that was guaranteed to come back to the Pohlads. It included $25 million that would be raised by such items as naming rights and concessionaire fees; this was $25 million that was not Pohlad money at all. And finally, the last estimated $50 million piece was the value ascribed to 49 percent of the team that Carl Pohlad would give to the state and attempt to receive significant tax benefits.[78]

It soon became apparent the 1997 state legislature would not enact a stadium bill the owner wanted. The franchise was sold in 1998 to Red McCombs for $246 million and in 2002 he was contemplating moving the franchise because the state legislature has not appropriated funds for a new stadium.[79]

New York Yankees

Yankee Stadium in the Bronx was built entirely with private money, but was an aging facility by 1990 in spite of renovations financed in part by the city over the decades. Team owner George Steinbrenner sought city financed renovations or a new publicly constructed stadium. The New York Giants and the New York Jets already had been enticed by incentives to move to New Jersey.

Governor Mario M. Cuomo of New York feared similar enticements would result in the Yankees moving across the Hudson River. In consequence, he threatened in 1993 to seek legalization of casino gambling in New York if New Jersey, which has casinos in Atlantic City, offered incentives to the Yankees to relocate in the state.[80] New Jersey in 1995 reportedly offered to construct a $350 million stadium in the Meadowlands for the Yankees and Steinbrenner in the same year conferred with city officers relative to a renovation of Yankee Stadium with additional parking and a theme park estimated to cost $600 million.[81] He continued to press for a new stadium in New York City and had the support of Mayor Rudolph W. Giuliani (1995–2001) who was interested in the construction of new stadiums for the Yankees, New York Mets, and possibly New York Jets.

The September 11, 2001, terrorists attack on the World Trade Center made it financially impossible to build such stadiums. The mayor, however, continued to work on an agreement with the Mets and the Yankees, and reached a tentative one on December 28, 2001, providing for stadiums estimated to cost $1.8 billion.[82] Municipal bonds would be issued to raise approximately $800 million, each team would make in lieu of taxes payments of $23 million each year for the first twenty of the thirty-five year leases after which the payments would increase each year, and the state would make infrastructure improvements including roadways.[83] The mayor later amended the agreement to allow the Yankees to leave the city upon sixty days notice if the city does not arrange for the construction of the stadium and cancelled the obligation of the Mets to turn over advertising revenues to the city.[84] Newly inaugurated Mayor Michael R. Bloomberg announced on January 7, 2002, the city lacked the funds to proceed with the construction of the stadiums.[85]

In late spring 2002, the mayor devised a plan for a $1 billion entertainment and sports complex, including a stadium for the Jets, over the rail yards on the west side of Manhattan that would be part of the city's offer to host the summer Olympic games in 2012; the city's bid will not be considered without to evidence of progress on the site by 2005.[86]

Although the Yankees remain in New York City, their farm club—Albany-Colonie Yankees—was unable to secure improvements to its stadium and received the permission of the Eastern League to move the team to Norwich, Connecticut, at the conclusion of the 1994 season.[87] The city of Norwich and its Community Development Association offered to construct a $1.4 million stadium and the team owners agreed to contribute $400,000 to finance it.[88] Governor Cuomo sent a letter to George Steinbrenner requesting that the team be kept in Albany and the latter rescinded the approval for the team to move and agreed to contact other league owners to have the move cancelled.[89] Nevertheless, the team moved to Norwich.

Newark Sports Arena

The city of Newark, New Jersey, with the support of Governor James B. McGreevey, has sought without success on three occasions an appropriation by the state legislature to assist in the construction of a sports arena in the downtown area for the New Jersey Nets and Devils. The latest rejection occurred in June 2002 during a special session of the state legislature.

In late August 2002, it appeared the city had found a way to construct the arena without a state appropriation. The city has a long-standing disagreement over the rent the Port Authority of New York and New Jersey pays for the lease of the city-owned Newark International Airport. The city and the authority reached an agreement settling in part the rent dispute and providing the city with $265 million.[90] The owners of the two sports franchises will contribute $125 million and the city and Essex County will appropriate $50 million to supplement the funds received from the authority.

Competition for Tourists and Gamblers

Tourism provides employment for a state's residents and also is a source of revenue for a state levying taxes on sales, meals, and hotel and motel occupancy, thereby reducing the tax burden of resident taxpayers. Gambling increasingly is relied upon by states to generate additional revenues without levying a tax on the general citizenry or classes of citizens.

Tourism

States recognize the importance of advertising to attract tourists and spend hundreds of millions of dollars on advertising. The state of New York's $34 billion tourism industry generates employment for approximately 767,000 individuals and is the second largest industry after agriculture.[91] The state's tourism advertising budget is approximately $11 million annually and is supplemented by an additional $6 million distributed to county and regional tourism programs providing matching funds. Targeting audiences, such as those interested in culture and heritage, is part of the state's strategy to increase the number of tourists. The state also is encouraging New York City and Niagara Falls visitors to travel elsewhere in the state. Acknowledging the importance of foreign tourists, in 2001, the state employed a London consultant to promote upstate New York to tour operators in Europe.

New Hampshire similarly targets two primary groups—childless couples and families.[92] Advertisements emphasizing bed and breakfast facilities and cultural attractions are aimed at the former group, and ones highlighting mountain biking, rock climbing, swimming holes, and other outdoor activities are featured to attract the second group. The state seeks to attract English visitors by featuring advertisements with the following tagline: "We kicked you out in 1776. Now we've changed our minds."

Madison Avenue advertising firms are employed by states to develop sophisticated print, radio, and television advertisements, and focus groups are utilized to determine the image a state wishes to project. New York developed a catchy slogan—I Love New York—in 1977 that has been imitated by numerous governments and organizations and launched a new age in tourism promotion. New York state introduced the slogan by spending four-million dollars on television advertisements featuring a song donated by Steve Karmen and dancers from the Broadway show *A Chorus Line* at a time when New York City was experiencing serious financial difficulties. The slogan has been imprinted on bumper stickers, coffee mugs, and T-shirts, and became even more popular after the terrorists' attack on the World Trade Center in 2001. "Even soldiers in Afghanistan wore buttons with the iconic symbol."[93]

Other states have attempted to develop a similar slogan, but only "Virginia Is for Lovers" has been highly successful and long-lived. States also used their motor vehicle license plates as mobile advertising—Maine uses "Vacationland" and New Hampshire employs the revolutionary war slogan "Live Free or Die" along with the outline of the "Old Man of the Mountains." The latter state receives a considerable amount of free advertising by holding the first presidential primary election in the nation every four years since 1952.

State tourist slogans are not always successful and are abandoned. Wisconsin state officers discontinued the slogan "Escape to Wisconsin" when they discovered "some residents were removing the word 'to' from the bumper sticker so that it read 'Escape Wisconsin.'"[94] Charles Mahtesian in 1994 explained "Florida's latest slogan . . . could be read in Spanish as 'Florida Is Two-Faced.'"[95] Advertising firms engaged by states draw upon U.S. Census Bureau data to tailor marketing programs for specific audiences and exercise caution to ensure the programs do not contain a negative image of the state.

Tourist states and cities need to readjust their advertising programs in the light of changing tourists' preferences, and national and international developments. Tourism is the second largest New Hampshire industry and the state in 2001 was planning to advertise more heavily in more distant locations, but discovered after the September 11, 2001, terrorists' attack on the World Trade Center that tourists preferred to stay closer to their homes.[96] The state benefits from the fact approximately eighty-five percent of its tourists travel by motor vehicle.

The New Hampshire General Court (state legislature) in 2002 increased by $2.0 million to $5.6 million the appropriation for the state department of travel and tourism development, yet the state is being outspent by other states.[97] The department is seeking to increase the number of overnight and return visitors, and mid-week and off-season visitors. Advertisements include four-color inserts in major newspapers, such as *The New York Times,* and French language inserts in newspapers in neighboring Quebec. Also launched is a "Discover New Hampshire: Vacation in Your Own Backyard" campaign in cooperation with five radio stations and aimed at the state's residents.

Local governments, such as New York City and Niagara Falls, are often major television advertisers in other states and generally link their advertising programs to their respective state programs. New Orleans is famous for its Mardi Gras, but the city's reputation as the murder capital of the United States no doubt deters many potential tourists from visiting the city.

Although New York City is a major tourist magnet, the city is losing convention business because of the lack of an adequate center.[98] The Jacob K. Javits Center was described as "the eighth wonder of the world" when it was constructed, but its 814,000 square feet of space places it as the thirteenth largest center in the nation. It is estimated the city loses sixty-five major conventions annually because of the lack of convention space that is compounded by the absence of a major hotel connected to the center.

The famous Eire Canal, now part of the 524–mile long New York State Barge Canal, was constructed with state financial assistance to connect the Hudson River with the state's interior lakes, including the Great Lakes. Initially successful, the fortunes of the canal declined with the development of the railroad and later the motor truck. Neglected for decades, the fortunes of the canal system changed when it was transferred by the state legislature to the New York Thruway Authority in 1992.[99] The authority was authorized to levy tolls for vessels passing through locks and lift bridges, and created a subsidiary corporation—New York State Canal Corporation—with the Thruway Authority board of directors serving as the ex officio board of directors of the Canal Corporation. A "Canal Recreationway Plan" was adopted in 1995 and called for $146 million in revitalization projects over fifteen years, but later was reduced to $32.3 million over five years.[100]

The plan was completed in 2002 and focused on improving seven harbors, fifty-seven locks, sixteen lift bridges, and related facilities, and construction of amphitheaters, biking and walking trails, parks, and visitors' centers.[101]

These improvements have been a boon for tourism and for residents who live in the vicinity of the canal system. The number of pleasure boats passing through locks increased thirteen percent in the period 1996–2002.

Sponsorship of a major event, such as a beauty contest or boxing match, is an effective technique to attract tourists. The event organizer, however, may engage in a bidding war similar to one initiated by a major sports team owner announcing potential plans to move the franchise unless the state and/or city provides incentives for the team to remain. The Miss America pageant, held in Atlantic City, New Jersey, since 1921, is one of the best-known annual events in the United States. Pageant President Robert M. Renneisen Jr. in 2001 sought the assistance of the Atlantic City Convention and Visitors Authority, a unit of the New Jersey Sports and Exposition Authority, in reducing the cost of staging the pageant projected to have a $500,000 loss in 2002.[102] He reported the Mohegan Sun Casino in Connecticut would provide a better deal and result in a profit of $1 million instead of a loss. Mayor James Whelan in 2001 stated the city has many needs for funds and at some point the city may conclude it would be best if the pageant found a new location.

The highly profitable Walt Disney Company in 1994 decided to construct a new theme park thirty-five miles southwest of Washington, D.C., in Haymarket, Virginia, provided the commonwealth's General Assembly appropriates more than $163 million for highway improvements, tax credits, tourism promotion, and employee training, and the county government provides $40 million.[103] The 1995 General Assembly authorized issuance of twenty-year bonds whose total cost to the commonwealth would be approximately $250 million including interest.

Gambling

Many states and cities seek to bolster their revenues and provide employment for their citizens by attracting gamblers. Gambling in 1992 was the thirteenth largest source of Rhode Island state revenue, but rose to the third largest source in 2002.[104] Atlantic City, New Jersey, and Las Vegas, Nevada, are examples of cities heavily reliant upon gambling and its associated activities for tax revenues. Gambling assumes numerous forms including pari-mutuel and off-track betting on dog and horse races, and electronic slot machines in bars first authorized by Montana in 1985.[105]

The following sections focus on the two principal forms—lotteries and casinos—of legalized gambling.

Lotteries. Lotteries were a source of colonial revenue for public and private purposes, including improving ivy-league colleges and generating state revenues until the last one, operated by Louisiana, was terminated in 1894. Lotteries were abandoned because they generally were viewed as involving fraud and causing social problems such as poverty induced by compulsive gamblers.[106] Congress enacted a 1890 statute banning lottery materials from the U.S. Mail and a 1895 statute excluding such materials from interstate commerce.[107]

The New Hampshire General Court in 1964 inaugurated a state lottery because members were aware most of the revenue would come from residents of neighboring states and its lead has been followed by thirty-eight states, the District of Columbia, Puerto Rico, Virgin Islands, and five Canadian provinces. In addition to citing the need for state revenues for essential functions, supporters in certain states argue a lottery competes with illegal gambling controlled by organized crime and thereby achieves a desirable social purpose. The early lotteries were a gambling monopoly as no other form of gambling was allowed. Today, legal alternatives to lotteries are available in a number of states and include casinos and pari-mutuel betting on greyhound and horse racing.

State competition to increase lottery revenues has resulted in one or two daily drawings, weekly drawings, and multi-state lotteries offering exceptional large jackpots. Scratch-off tickets have become exceptionally popular and accounted for forty percent of New York lottery tickets sold in fiscal year 2001–2002.[108] The effects of lotteries, in economist terms, are regressive as the burden is placed primarily upon lower income individuals and inefficient because administrative and pay out costs are high. To offset their negative social effects, supporters of lotteries agreed all or part of the proceeds should be dedicated to support desirable public programs such as education and environmental protection.

Experience reveals there is a positive correlation between the size of the lottery jackpot and the sale of tickets. Maine, for example, complained in 1984 its lottery sales were suffering from the illegal sale of Massachusetts Megabucks lottery tickets.[109] Groups of states decided to form large jackpots multistate lotteries with longer odds and lobbied Congress to repeal the 1890 and 1895 statutes. Congress amended the ban by exempting lottery tickets and authorizing a state legislature to out-out of the prohibition of interstate transportation of gaming devices.[110]

Currently, three multistate lotteries were established by interstate administrative agreements and the Tri-State Megabucks Lottery was established by an interstate compact enacted by the Maine, New Hampshire, and Vermont state legislatures. Twenty states and the District of Columbia participate in the Multistate Powerball Lottery, ten states operate Mega Millions (formerly the Big Game Lottery), and three states participate in Lotto South. The $366 million Big Game jackpot of May 10, 2000, is the largest one to date.[111] These lotteries draw many individuals from out-of-state. The $280 million Powerball jackpot resulted in town officers in Bryam, Cos Cob, Old

Greenwich sections of Greenwich, and Riverside, Connecticut, receiving permission from the Connecticut Lottery Corporation to suspend lottery ticket sales on August 24, 2001, because the influx of New York motorists seeking to purchase tickets had caused numerous traffic accidents, blocked emergency vehicles, and resulted in children being locked in vehicles while their parents waited in long lines to purchase tickets.[112]

John K. Mikesell reviewed state lotteries in 2001 and made the following findings among others:

• Lottery sales have grown substantially since the mid-1980s but have not kept pace with the growth of other forms of commercial gambling . . .
• Lottery net proceeds exceed $1 billion in two states (New York and Texas) . . .
• Lottery proceeds are an insignificant component of the state revenue portfolio . . .
• The cost of administering the lottery is high, averaging 41.4¢ required to produce $1 of lottery net proceeds . . .
• The performance of individual state lotteries varies widely . . .[113]

He concluded privatization of state lotteries would improve their performance.[114]

Casinos. Casino gambling was legal only in Nevada and New Jersey until Congress enacted the *Indian Gaming Regulatory Act of 1988* placing gambling on Indian reservations in three classes.[115] Class I games are defined as social ones conducted for minimal value prizes that are engaged in as part of tribal celebrations and ceremonies. Class II games include bingo and lotto and are regulated by each tribal government with oversight by the National Indian Gaming Commission, an agency of the U.S. government. Class III games are regulated jointly by the concerned state government and the tribal government under provisions of a state-tribal agreement similar to an interstate agreement. Only the governor is authorized to negotiate on behalf of the state. The act does not allow a tribal government to conduct a specified game, but does authorize the government to allow the same types of gambling as conducted by other organizations in the state. In 1992, the Kansas Supreme Court opined the governor lacks authority to bind the state to a state-tribal contract on the basis of the 1988 congressional act.[116]

The downturn in the national economic, accentuated by the terrorists' attack on the World Trade Center, induced many states to expand legalize gambling as a revenue source. For example, the New York State Legislature enacted and Governor George E. Pataki signed in 2001 a bill authorizing installation of video gambling devices at five horse racing tracks and the governor to negotiate with Native American tribes to operate three new casinos in the western part of the state and three in the Catskill Mountains.[117] Donald J. Trump, who operates

Atlantic City casinos, donated large sums of money to an obscure Utica, New York, organization to finance a major statewide advertising campaign against the establishment of new casinos. A coalition opposed to the gambling expansion in 2002 filed suit in the state supreme court, a general trial court, alleging the expansion violated the state constitution's prohibition of gambling other than lotteries and pari-mutuel betting.[118]

Promoters of off-reservation casinos may have found a mechanism to skirt the New York constitutional ban. A Las Vegas casino operator, Park Place Entertainment, in 2000 became a consultant to the St. Regis Mohawk Indian Nation and shortly thereafter purchased a sixty-six acre site in the Catskill Mountains with an option to purchase the remainder of the available 1,416–acres for $50 million.[119] In March 2001, Park Place Entertainment transferred the sixty-six acres to the U.S. Bureau of Indian Affairs to be held in trust for the St. Regis Mohawk Indian Nation, and also entered into an agreement with the nation to manage the proposed casino.

Indian nations highly value a state-tribal compact authorizing them to operate casinos as illustrated by the New York Oneida Indian Nation offering in 1995 to share gaming profits with the State of New York if Governor Pataki would sign a state-tribal agreement authorizing the Oneida Indian Nation to operate a casino in Monticello, twenty-nine miles north of New York City and 100 miles south of the Nation's reservation.[120] The Indian Gaming Regulatory Act permits an Indian tribe to operate a casino beyond its reservation boundaries only with the consent of the governor of the concerned state and the U.S. Secretary of the Interior. In 2002, Governor Jane Hull of Arizona approved a twenty-three year compact with seventeen Indian Nations allowing additional forms of gambling and expansion of casinos near Phoenix and Tucson but restricting gaming to reservation lands.[121]

The second major casino development occurred in 1991 when the Iowa General Assembly legalized riverboat casino gambling. The state legislatures in Illinois, Louisiana, and Mississippi quickly followed suit by legalizing such gambling. The Louisiana State Legislature in 1991 authorized riverboat casino gambling in many parishes (counties) and in 1992 one casino in downtown New Orleans.[122] Although the city was scheduled to have casino gambling on five riverboats, only two boats in 1997 were operating and the land-based casino, operated by Harrah's, closed in 1995 after operating only a few months. A study conducted jointly by six universities in New Orleans estimated in 1997 that the "[c]riminal justice costs related to Harrah's, both while it was open and after it closed, totaled $3,278,608."[123]

There has been an explosion in the number of casinos in the Midwest with a total of eighty-six commercial ones and eighty-seven Indian ones operating in 2002.[124] The casinos replaced many manufacturing firms as employers in small towns. According to the Missouri Riverboat Gaming Association, approximately one-fourth of its employees were formerly welfare recipients and sixteen percent were unemployed. Furthermore, some local businessmen in small towns, such as Boonville, Missouri, are indirectly benefiting economically from casino gambling.

Opponents continue to their efforts to have state legislatures enact laws ending or restricting greatly legalized gambling. Robert Goodman in 1995 highlighted the perverse effects of gambling:

> Politicians and local business leaders, desperate for almost any form of economic growth, turned to what had once been a criminalized activity—closely regulated and policed by the FBI and state and local police forces. What had been feared for its potential for moral corruption, its corrosive impact on the work ethic, and its potential devastation of family savings was suddenly transformed into a leading candidate to reverse the fortunes of communities across America.[125]

The gaming interests, commercial and Indian Nation, have become major contributors to candidates for elective office and opponents fear the corrupting influence of such funds. Initial legislative approval for casinos often contain restrictions and with the passage of times the casinos press for their removal. Goodman reported that Iowa's restrictions on riverboat casinos limiting "stakes to $5 per bet and total losses of any player to $200 per cruise" were dropped when Illinois, Louisiana, and Mississippi authorized such gambling with no restrictions.[126] Gaming opponents also stress the social consequences flowing from the estimated two and one-half million pathological gamblers.[127]

The Role of Congress

Congress is granted plenary power by the U.S. Constitution to regulate interstate and foreign commerce. Nevertheless, Congress has not used its authority to limit or regulate interstate competition to recruit business firms in spite of the fact congressional tax policy fuels in part the competition by allowing state and local governments to issue municipal bonds whose purchasers are exempt from paying the federal income tax on the interest received.

The U.S. Constitution does not address the question whether Congress or a state may tax each other or one of its instrumentalities. The question of intergovernmental tax immunity reached the U.S. Supreme Court in *McCulloch v. Maryland* when the U.S. Supreme ruled Maryland could not tax a federal instrumentality—the Bank of the United States.[128] Intergovernmental tax immunity was made reciprocal by the court in *Collector v. Day* in 1871 when the court opined the salary of a state officer could not be taxed by Congress.[129]

In 1895, the court in *Pollock v. Farmers Loan & Trust Company* struck down an income tax enacted by Congress because the tax was not apportioned on the basis of population among the states as required by the U.S. Constitution and the interest received by holders of state and local government bonds was taxable.[130] Ratification of the Sixteenth Amendment to the U.S. Constitution in 1913, by the requisite three-fourths of the states, reversed this court decision by authorizing Congress "to lay and collect taxes on incomes, from whatever source derived, without apportionment among the several States, and without regard to any census or enumeration." The phrase "from whatever source derived" authorizes Congress to tax the interest received by holders of municipal bonds.

Such interest was exempted from the federal income tax by the *Internal Revenue Act of 1913*.[131] Justice William Brennan of the U.S. Supreme Court in 1988 in *South Carolina v. Baker* noted:

> We see no constitutional reason for treating persons who receive interest on government bonds differently than persons who receive income from other types of contracts with the government, and no tenable rationale for distinguishing the costs imposed on states by a tax on state bond interest from the costs imposed by a tax on the income from any other state contract.[132]

He stressed that "states must find their protection from congressional regulation through the national political process, not through judicially defined spheres of unregulable state activity."[133] This view echoes the 1985 opinion of Justice Harry A. Blackmun in *Garcia v. San Antonio Metropolitan Transit Authority* that "the principal and basic limits on the federal commerce power are inherent in all state participation in federal government action."[134] Justice Brennan, of course, was writing from the perspective of constitutional law and not from a political perspective. Congressional exemption of municipal bond interest from the U.S. income tax is a political decision to provide fiscal assistance to state and local governments by allowing them to borrow funds at a lower rate of interest.

Congress enacted the *Tax Reform Act of 1986* containing a provision requiring subnational governments which reinvested borrowed funds in private securities must remit any arbitrage profit to the U.S. Treasury.[135] South Carolina challenged the requirement and the U.S. Supreme Court opined "that subsequent case law has overruled the holding in *Pollock* that state bond interest is immune from a nondiscriminatory federal tax."[136] In consequence, Congress is free to restrict the issuance of municipal bonds for economic development purposes by subjecting the interest received from such bonds to the federal income tax. The *Revenue and Expenditure Control Act of 1986* was the first statute limiting the use of municipal bond issue proceeds by providing the interest on industrial development bonds is taxable with the exceptions of exempt purposes—airports, air and water pollution control facilities, convention and sports facilities, public transit facilities, sewage and solid waste disposal facilities, and wharves.[137] Congress enacted other statutes relating to tax-exempt municipal bonds in 1969, 1971, 1978, 1980, 1984, and 1986.[138] The latter act eliminated the exemption for convention, parking, private pollution control, and sports facilities.[139]

Concerned with the loss of revenues from tax exemptions, Congress in 1984 enacted a statute establishing a volume limit on several types of industrial bonds first issued by Mississippi in 1913.[140] The *Tax Reform Act of 1986* established for each state a dollar volume maximum amount of tax-exempt bonds—$50 per capita or $150 million—used to finance private business activities.[141] Dennis Zimmerman concluded that "attacking the growth problem with a fairly comprehensive volume limit accomplishes two goals simultaneously. First, it accommodates the diversity with which state and local governments divide responsibility between the public and private sectors. . . . Second, it enables the federal government to control its revenue loss."[142]

Critics of tax exemption for private activity municipal bonds have not been satisfied with the changes enacted by Congress. Dick Netzer in 1991 maintained there is no justification for "small-issue industrial development bonds" and concluded "they are so widely used that they must largely cancel out the locational effects" and result in federal revenue losses that are "large relative to user benefits."[143] Two years later, the U.S. General Accounting Office issued a report containing a similar conclusion and specifically noting the revenues of the federal government "were decreased by more than two billions dollars as the result of the tax-exempt status of interest on industrial development bonds."[144] The report also concluded there was no evidence tax-exempt municipal bond financed projects aided economically depressed areas, assisted start-up firms, created new jobs, or persuaded firms not to move operations to foreign nations.[145] A particularly important finding was that sixty percent of interviewed developers in Indiana, New Jersey, and Ohio reported they would have moved forward with the identical project or a reduced version of the project if tax-exempt industrial development bond funds were not provided.[146]

Does Congress specifically possess authority to regulate directly interstate competition for business firms including owners of sports franchises by prohibiting the use of subsidies? Could Congress attach a cross-over sanction to grant-in-aid statutes threatening states and local governments with the loss of grant funds if they use fiscal incentives to attract business firms and sports franchises?

Relative to the first question, professor Philip P. Frickey of the University of Minnesota Law School in 1996 was convinced that Congress should regulate such interstate competition, on the basis of the interstate commerce clause, and would have to justify such regulation by producing a legislative record clearing indicating "the subsidies are a problem of federalism, rather than virtue of it. . . ."[147] In the same year, Professor Walter Hellerstein of the University of Georgia Law School reviewed four U.S. Supreme Court decisions relative to tax incentives and concluded the court struck down these incentives because each incentive favored in-state firms and "the coercive power of the state gave the tax incentive its bite."[148] Tax incentives offered only to out-of-state business firms clearly do not favor in-state firms.

The second question is easier to answer. The U.S. Supreme Court in *Massachusetts v. Mellon 1923* upheld conditional federal grants-in-aid and in *South Dakota v. Dole* in 1987 sanctioned a cross-over sanction reducing federal highway grants-in-aid to states failing to raise the minimum alcoholic beverage purchase age to twenty-one.[149]

Summary and Conclusions

Experience reveals tax and other state-local governmental incentives can be effective in attracting business firms, sports franchises, tourists, and gamblers from sister states and in some instances from foreign nations. A state industrial development program, based upon incentives, can have major benefits— additional jobs, extra business for domestic firms, increased tax revenues after expiration of tax exemptions, and improved infrastructure if part of the strategy to attract firms.

Domestic companies seldom register complaints about discrimination in terms of tax expenditures, perhaps because they receive indirect benefits from a successful program including lower state unemployment compensation taxes, increased sales, and reduced tax burdens upon expiration of the tax exemptions for new firms. Offers of fiscal incentives to firms in other states and nations, however, may have an adverse effect on domestic firms which may threaten to cancel expansion plans or to leave the state if they are not offered similar incentives. New York City, for example, made economic concessions after the ABC, CBS, and NBC television networks threatened to move their facilities to New Jersey.

Several major disadvantages may be associated with a state's industrial development strategy employing fiscal and other tax incentives. The tax incidence is shifted to other taxpayers during the tax exemption period and opportunity costs are imposed by depriving the state of tax revenues needed to solve other state problems such as educational and environmental ones. Furthermore, incentives are not always successful in the long run, as illustrated by the closure of the Volkswagen plant in Pennsylvania, and may produce a regional zero sum game if the firms recruited come only from sister states in the region, and may generate bad relations between sister states.

The problems generated by interstate competition for business firms have been recognized by the National Governors Association, which developed sensible guidelines for the use of tax and other incentives by states. The success of these guidelines is dependent upon voluntary compliance by all states. Congress is the only body with authority to regulate interstate competition for business firms, but unfortunately has demonstrated little interest in such regulatory action other than establishment of the cap on the volume of tax-exempt municipal bonds that may be employed to financially assist private business activities (see chapter 9).

Competition for sports franchises does not have the national impact of interstate competition for business firms. Nevertheless, such competition is undesirable because it permits the owner of a franchise to blackmail a city and/or state to utilize public funds to construct a new stadium or improve an existing one under the threat the franchise will be moved to a city offering to construct a new stadium.

State competition for tourists is very similar to competitive business firms advertising their products and little objection can be raised against this type of interstate competition. We can not draw the same conclusion relative to interstate competition for gamblers. State-sponsored gambling or legalized gambling can not be justified as an alternative to taxation because the revenues produced are a minor component of total state revenues. The undesirable consequences of gambling, including organized crime activities and the poverty induced for compulsive gamblers and their families, are well-documented.

Chapter 8 focuses on the converse of interstate economic competition; that is interstate economic cooperation by entrance into interstate compacts and interstate administrative agreements including economic development ones.

CHAPTER 8

Interstate Economic Cooperation

Interstate competition for resources and interstate disputes suggest the U.S. federal system is a disharmonious one in need of major constitutional reforms to achieve a more perfect economic union. The competition and the disputes, however, should not overshadow widespread economic and non-economic interstate cooperation that has helped the United States to become the leading economic nation in the world. Interstate comity assumes the forms of interstate compacts, reciprocity statutes, uniform laws, and written and verbal interstate administrative agreements.

The American Bar Association in 1889 recognized the problems created by nonuniform state laws on a wide variety of subjects and decided to promote the enactment of uniform state laws by state legislatures. The 1890 New York State Legislature enacted a law granting the governor authority to appoint three commissioners charged with studying laws relating to marriage and divorce, notarial certificates, insolvency, and other problems, and recommending measures to encourage all state legislatures to enact uniform laws.[1] In 1892, commissioners on uniform laws from seven states attended their first conference and drafted uniform laws relating to acknowledgements on written instruments, validation of wills, and weights and measures. Thirty-one states and two territories appointed such commissioners by 1900 and today all states, the District of Columbia, Puerto Rico, and the U.S. Virgin Islands appoint commissioners. Numerous uniform laws have been drafted and enacted by all or some states. The number of enactments varies greatly between the states with midwestern and northwestern states having the highest propensity and southern states having the lowest propensity to enact such laws.[2] The computer age is recognized by two uniform state laws drafted in 2000 by the National Conference of Commissioners on Uniform State Laws: Uniform Electronic Transactions Act and the Uniform Computer Information Transactions Act.

The foci of this chapter are interstate compacts and administrative agreements promoting the achievement of common economic goals. As explained in chapter 1, Congress, on occasion, encourages sister states to engage in interstate economic cooperation.

Interstate Economic Compacts

States enter into formal concordats for a wide variety of economic and noneconomic purposes relating to allocation of river water, children, civil defense, construction and operation of public facilities, corrections, crime control, detainers, economic development, educational programs, emergency management, energy, environmental protection, flood control, fisheries, forest fires, health, Indian casinos, insect and plant pests, interpleader, libraries, lotteries, low-level radioactive waste, mental health, milk pricing, motor vehicles, multi-state planning, oil and gas, solid waste disposal, supervision of paroles and probationers, taxation, and water quality. Many compacts are economic in nature and other compacts have a different primary purpose and an indirect economic impact. It is important to note an interstate compact consented to by Congress is protected the U.S. Constitution's contract clause (Art. I, §10) forbidding a state legislature to enact a "law impairing the obligation of contracts."

Interstate compacts date to 1785 and many have achieved their declared goals.[3] The process of negotiating a compact on a major subject, however, can be a long and tedious one and may end in failure. Furthermore, success in negotiating the wording of a proposed compact does not ensure that all concerned state legislatures will enact the proposal. And Congress on a number of occasions has been slow in granting its consent to a compact and occasionally has refused to grant consent as illustrated by the Southern Regional Education Compact.

Section 10 of Article I of the U.S. Constitution authorizes states to enter into compacts with the consent of Congress, but contains no required procedures. In contrast to the full faith and credit clause of Article IV, Congress has not enacted a statute specifying the procedure for entrance into a compact that, in common with a treaty, supersedes conflicting state laws.

Whereas the president of the United States is authorized by the U.S. Constitution (Art. II, §1) to negotiate a treaty with a foreign nation, a state governor does not participate directly in drafting a proposed interstate compact. The governor, however, appoints commissioners to draft a compact on a specified subject in conjunction with commissioners of other proposed compact states. Joint commissioners negotiated all compacts until 1930, but this method has been supplemented by other methods in more recent years. The interstate commission on crime drafted the Interstate Compact on Parolees and Probationers, and the southern governors drafted the Southern Regional Education Compact. In addition, federal officers occasionally have been invited by the concerned states to participate in compact negotiations.

The number of potential member states and the subject matter of a compact determine in large measure the degree of difficulty commissioners will experience in reaching an agreement on the wording of a proposed compact. A small number of states usually can reach agreement in a shorter period of time than a large number of states depending on the subject matter. Higher education compacts have been noncontroversial and have been drafted with relative ease. Proposed regional water allocation compacts, on the other hand, affect vital economic interests of the concerned states and prolong negotiations have been required to prepare an acceptable draft compact.

A proposed compact must be submitted to each concerned state legislature where many of the issues debated by the commissioners are reexamined. Legislative fiscal committees closely examine any proposed compact involving major state financial commitments and the legislature may direct the state's commissioners to renegotiate specified compact provisions. Furthermore, one or both legislative houses may insist provisions for legislative and/or gubernatorial oversight must be included in the compact. Should the legislature of a key state fail to enact the compact, the other states may stop their efforts to form a compact. Delays in enactment have been common with one or more legislature not enacting the compact for five or more years. Similarly, a delay may be the result of a legislature making its enactment contingent upon specified legislatures enacting the compact or Congress initiating specified actions.

State legislative enactment of a compact is not the final hurdle that proponents must overcome. Each governor may veto a compact if unsatisfied with its provisions. Delay also may be introduced in the absence of a gubernatorial veto if the compact requires execution by the governor of each member state and a governor refuses to implement the compact as illustrated by the refusal of Governor Herbert H. Lehman of New York to execute the Interstate Compact for the Supervisions of Parolees and Probationers.

Consent of Congress and Amendment

Article VI of the Articles of Confederation and Perpetual Union required the consent of the unicameral Congress for an interstate compact to become effective. This provision was incorporated into the U.S. Constitution in order to protect the national government and the states which are not members of a compact. If states implement a compact without congressional consent, opponents can file a court suit challenging the constitutionality of the compact.

The U.S. Constitution is silent with respect to the procedure for granting consent or its duration or whether consent can be granted in advance of states enacting a compact. A challenge to the constitutionality of a compact can be filed in a state court as well as the U.S. District Court. In 1845, the New Hampshire Supreme Court rejected a challenge contending a 1819 New Hampshire law and a 1821 Maine law providing for the construction of a bridge over the Piscataqua River required congressional consent by opining there is no provision in the U.S. Constitution prohibiting each of two state legislatures to authorize erection of a bridge to the middle of the river.[4] It is noteworthy that the U.S. Supreme Court in 1854 ruled a boundary compact enacted by two state legislatures would be invalid in the absence of congressional consent.[5]

The U.S. Supreme Court rendered a most important decision in *Virginia v. Tennessee* in 1893 by ruling the consent of Congress is required only if a compact tends to increase "the political power or influence" of the states party to the compact and to encroach "upon the full and free exercise of federal authority."[6] Although Congress had not granted consent for a compact between the two states, the court opined congressional reliance upon the compact's terms for judicial and revenue purposes implied the grant of consent. In 1978, the Court rejected a challenge to the Multistate Tax Compact on the ground of lack of congressional consent by noting the compact does not "authorize the member states to exercise any powers they could not exercise in its absence."[7] It has been relatively common for states to submit nonpolitical compacts to Congress for its consent since 1921 when the Port of New York Authority Compact was submitted on the advice of bond counsels who suggested consent would make proposed authority bond issues more appealing to conservative investors. States continue to submit economic development compacts to Congress, which in 1996 gave its consent for a Illinois–Missouri Compact creating the Bi-State Development Agency subject to the requirement that powers subsequently conferred on the agency are subject to the approval of Congress.[8] The following year, Congress granted its consent to the Chickasaw Trail Economic Development Compact enacted by the Mississippi State Legislature and the Tennessee General Assembly.[9]

The Northeastern Interstate Forest Fire Compact, consented to by Congress in 1949, is the first one to authorize a contiguous Canadian province to become a member of the compact with the consent of Congress.[10] Subsequently, a number of other interstate compacts were enacted by state legislatures containing provisions allowing Canadian provinces and/or Mexican states to join the compacts.

Congress may grant consent in-advance for specified compacts or blanket consent in-advance for all compacts on a specified subject. Consent in-advance first was granted in 1911 for compacts designed to promote forest conservation and water supply.[11] Congress occasionally includes in its consent resolution authorization for additional states to become compact members by enacting it. A different approach was employed by Congress in 1951 when it authorized states to enter into interstate civil defense compacts by stipulating they must be filed with the U.S. House of Representatives and the Senate and are deemed to have been consented to unless a concurrent resolution within sixty days disapproves them.[12]

Congress placed a time limit on its consent for several compacts including the Interstate Oil and Gas Compact and the Atlantic States Marine Fisheries Compact, and subsequently made the consent permanent. The ten low-level radioactive waste compacts currently are subject to a five-year time limit. Congress in granting consent typically reserves the right to "alter, amend, or repeal" its consent and reserves all its authority over navigable waters.

Consent Effects

The U.S. Supreme Court has changed its view on the question of whether congressional consent to a compact converts it into federal law. In 1938, the court opined such consent does not convert a compact into the equivalent of a federal statute or United States treaty, but overruled this decision in 1981 in *Cuyler v. Adams*.[13] The latter decision permitted the court to interpret the Pennsylvania statute in question and disregard its interpretation by the Pennsylvania Supreme Court.

Does the Eleventh Amendment to the U.S. Constitution cloak a public authority created by a compact with sovereign immunity from suit in a U.S. court? In 1994, the U.S. Supreme Court opined the Port Authority Trans-Hudson Corporation is self-financing body and subjecting it to suit does not place a potential burden upon the state of New Jersey or the state of New York.[14]

The grant of congressional consent to a compact neutralizes federal statutes containing provisions inconsistent with a compact. A new congressional statute containing inconsistent provisions, however, would repeal provisions of a compact that has received consent with one exception; vested rights are protected by the Fifth Amendment to the U.S. Constitution.

Amendment

Proposed amendments to a compact must follow the compact approval process by securing enactment by each party state legislature, approval of each state governor, consent of Congress and signature of the president if the compact initially received such consent. A member of Congress from a compact state may delay the grant of congressional consent if opposed to the compact or its administration and Congress is free to amend a compact.

Only interstate boundary compacts that have received congressional consent can not be terminated. Several compacts, including the Colorado River Compact, require agreement by all party states for termination. Other compacts allow a state to withdraw from membership provided its governor gives notice to the other party governors of its intention one year in advance.

The Delaware River Basin Compact and the Susquehanna River Basin Compact are unusual in specifying the compact has a 100 years' duration and may be renewed for additional periods of 100 years.

Compact Types and Administration

Membership in a compact may be bilateral, multilateral, sectional, or national. Twenty-five compacts entered into with congressional consent between 1789 and 1920 were bilateral ones establishing boundary lines.[15] Subsequently, there was a marked decrease in the number of boundary compacts and a sharp increase in environmental, river basin, and transportation compacts.[16] The more frequent exercise of Congress's preemption power is responsible for the decline in the number of new regulatory compacts since 1965.[17]

Currently, there are twenty-seven types of compacts classified by subject matter: advisory, agricultural, boundary, civil defense, crime control and corrections, cultural, education, emergency management, energy, facilities, fisheries, flood control, health, lottery, low level radioactive waste, marketing and development, metropolitan problems, military, motor vehicle, natural resources, parks and recreation, pest control, regulatory, river basin, service, tax, and federal-interstate. Boundary compacts are the only ones not in need of administration on a daily basis. Other compacts either are administered by a commission or by departments and agencies of member states.

Compact Commissions

A compact may name the appointing officer(s) or authorize the appointment of commissioners as provided by the law of the state they will represent. Commission members may be placed in three categories: appointees of the governor of each party state, ex officio members who serve as commissioners by virtue of specified state offices held, and representatives of the federal government. Not all compacts contain a provision relative to the suspension or removal of a commissioner.

Commission members usually are authorized to elect a chairman and a vice chairman among their membership and may be authorized to elect other officers. The chairmanship and the vice chairmanship typically are rotated among members from the party states. Authorization for the adoption of bylaws promotes organizational flexibility by allowing the commission to readily assign or reassign the duties of officers. Commission meetings vary from one annually to monthly ones.

The commission is the governing body of a multistate public authority that is not subject to most of the usual financial and personnel controls imposed upon state departments. In consequence, the commission possesses considerably more discretion in carrying out its duties and responsibilities. Many commissions are authorized to levy tolls and fees for use of their facilities and to borrow funds for capital construction projects. A number of compacts, such as the Port Authority of New York and New Jersey Compact (Art. VII), authorize the legislature of a party state to delegate additional powers to the compact commission if the other party states concur.

Powers delegated to commissions vary greatly in importance. Several commissions are advisory bodies; others, particularly water apportionment commissions, are responsible for ensuring member states comply with the compact's restrictions on water that may be diverted or stored; still others are granted broad powers to construct, maintain, and operate various types of facilities; and only a small number possess regulatory and enforcement powers.

Compacts Without Commissions

No compact created a commission until 1921 when the Port of New York Authority Compact was enacted by the New Jersey State Legislature and the New York State Legislature, and received the consent of Congress. Thirty-four compacts currently lack a commission, are administered by state departments and agencies, and relate to children corrections, detainers, emergency management, motor vehicles, mental health, and parole and probation. Although state departments and agencies could administer regional facility and regulatory compacts, a political decision was made that such compacts would be administered by commissions composed chiefly of regional residents and, in some instances, supplemented with ex officio state officers.

Select Economic Compacts

This section reviews the most important commission administered economic compacts. Interstate water compacts are of great significance as reflected in membership by the State of New York in six such compacts. Bridge, economic development, port, and tunnel compacts have major economic benefits for party states and several other compacts, particularly higher education ones, have indirect economic effects. The review commences with the first compact created for the express purpose of promoting economic development.

Port of New York and New Jersey

New Jersey and New York were engaged in disputes over the Hudson River and Bay of New York following the War of Independence until 1834 when an agreement was signed outlining the obligations and rights of the two states to such waters. The states, however, failed to join in cooperative efforts to improve the Port of New York until World War I demonstrated the inability of the port to move efficiently millions of soldiers and vast amounts of supplies to France. In 1917, the governors of the two states established the New York–New Jersey Port Development Commission and charged it with reviewing the 1834 agreement and preparing a port improvement plan.

The commission's recommendations were incorporated into an interstate compact that was enacted by the two state legislatures in 1921 and received the consent of Congress. The compact created the Port of New York Authority (renamed the Port Authority of New York and New Jersey in 1972) charged with developing and operating marine transportation and terminal facilities in area radiating twenty-five miles from the Statute of Liberty in New York harbor.[18]

The authority experienced financial problems in the 1920s, but conditions improved in 1930 when the two states transferred to the authority the newly completed Holland Tunnel under the Hudson River. Toll revenues from this tunnel subsequently were supplemented by tolls from the Lincoln Tunnel and four interstate bridges. The authority also owns and operates six container ports and marine terminals handling more than two million containers each year, three industrial parks, the Port Authority Trans-Hudson (PATH) rapid transit system, the world's busiest bus terminal with more than fifty-seven million passengers annually, and the world's first teleport (satellite communication center). The authority in 1948 leased LaGuardia Airport and Idlewild (now Kennedy International) Airport from New York City and Newark Airport, and also operates Teteboro Airport and the Downtown Manhattan and West 30th Street Heliports.

The authority, praised for the high quality of its management during its early decades, commenced to receive criticism in the 1960s for failure to solve the economic problem created by the lack of a rail freight tunnel under the Hudson River that necessitates trains from the south and west traveling approximately 120 miles to the north to cross the river and travel south to New York City. A new criticism surfaced in 1996 when economist Dick Netzer denied the authority operated as an independent entity and maintained it is controlled by the governors of the two states who in large measure were responsible for "the blunders of the past 20 years. . . ."[19] He explained most authority projects are subsidized by bridge and tunnel tolls and recommended transfer of the PATH system to the New Jersey Transit System, divestiture of its airports, and privatization of the marine terminals.[20] In his judgment, the responsibilities of the authority should be limited to bridges, bus terminals, regional transportation planning, and tunnels.

The authority was characterized in the period 1972–2000 by "drift, patronage, and favoritism, and the search for new goals," according to Jameson W. Doig who agreed with Netzer the governors were issuing the marching orders for the authority.[21] While acknowledging this criticism, Executive Director Robert Yaro of the Regional Plan Association in 2001 indicated the authority has returned to the proper track and is more focused than it has been for four decades.[22]

Education Compacts

The Southern Regional Education Compact of 1949 served as the model for similar compacts enacted by state legislatures in the Midwest, New England, and the West. The initial focus of compact was the sharing the resources of expensive professional schools—dentistry, medical, nursing, pharmacy, and veterinary—on a regional basis. When the New England compact was enacted, for example, only the University of Vermont operated a state medical school and the compact provided a stipulated number of students from each of the other New England states would be admitted to the school upon payment of a reduced tuition fee. Today, the regional higher education compacts operate a variety of programs including an electronic campus, environmental education, technology education partnership, and development of curriculum guidelines. These compacts clearly have produced major economic benefits for participating states.

The New Hampshire General Court and the Vermont General Assembly enacted two interstate compacts creating interstate school districts with the consent of Congress. The Dresden Interstate School District, established in 1961, operates in the towns of Hanover, New Hampshire, and Norwich, Vermont. The Rivendell Interstate School District, established in 1998, operates in the town of Orford, New Hampshire, and three Vermont towns—Fairlee, Vershire, and West Fairlee. It is surprising that no other interstate school district has been formed to pool the fiscal resources of small school districts on either side of a state boundary line to ensure students receive a quality education including work skills.

Water Compacts

These compacts have been formed for the purposes of allocating waters of a major river, fisheries, flood control and prevention, and managing all resources of river basins.

Water Allocation. Interstate disputes over the allocation of the waters of the Colorado River raged in the early decades of the twentieth century and led to the enactment by concerned state legislatures of the Colorado River Compact and congressional consent in 1928.[23] The compact did not create a commission, but requires each party state to cooperate with other party states relative to the compact's water deliver provisions. Should a dispute occur, the compact (Art. VI) directs governors of the member states to appoint commissioners authorized to settle the dispute subject to the approval of the legislatures of the party states. The compact also allows the use of any other dispute resolution mechanism. And, of course, a dispute over the allocation of the river's water can be brought by states to the U.S. Supreme Court for resolution; five such suits have been filed to date.

In 1948, the Arizona, Colorado, New Mexico, Utah, and Wyoming state legislatures enacted the Upper Colorado River Basin Compact establishing a commission with responsibility for dividing the basin's share of water among members; Congress granted consent in 1949.[24] The Arizona State Legislature enacted the compact, but it does not authorize the state to appoint a commission member. The president of the United States is authorized to appoint a member who serves as chairman with voting rights. This concordat is a detailed one specifying the obligation of party states relative to maintaining water flows at Lee Ferry of 7.5 million-acre feet (quantity of water covering an acre to a depth of one foot) annually to ensure the basin's obligations under the earlier Colorado River Compact are met.

Would a single compact commission be preferable to the existing two compacts for the entire Colorado River basin? The U.S. General Accounting Office in 1979 answered the question in the affirmative and recommended congressional establishment of a task force—federal offices, state officers, and water users—to determine the best organizational structure ensuring the needs of the basin are met in the most effective manner and the rights of all parties are protected.[25] The two compacts, however, have not been replaced by a consolidated one.

Chesapeake Bay Compact. The general assembly in Maryland, Pennsylvania, and Virginia each enacted this compact in 1980 to protect and improve the bay environment. Five legislators from each state, governors represented by the head of each state's natural resources department, and three citizens constitute the commission membership. Although the compact established only an advisory body, its 1983 draft Chesapeake Bay Agreement led to the governors, U.S. Environmental Protection Agency (EPA) administrator, and mayor of Washington, D.C., signing in 1987 an interstate administrative agreement setting bay cleanup goals.[26]

More recently, the commission in 1996 created a Bi-State Blue Crab Advisory Committee charged with developing crab-harvesting recommendations for the Potomac River Fisheries Commission, Maryland, and Virginia. In 1999, the Commission released a "Chesapeake 2000" agreement, establishing strategies for achieving the goals of the 1987 agreement, which was signed by representatives of the three states, the EPA administrator, and the mayor of Washington, D.C. The new agreement is designed to promote a tenfold increase in the number of oysters, identify exotic species harming the aquatic economic system, imposition of age and size limits on crabs, and sound land use among other goals.

Interstate Environmental Compact. Increasing water pollution in the greater New York City area generated pressures in the 1920s for the creation of the Tri-State Treaty Commission whose report recommended creation of an interstate public authority charged with abating and eliminating such pollution. The New Jersey State Legislature and the New York State Legislature each enacted the Interstate Sanitation Compact in 1935 and Congress granted its consent in the same year.[27] This compact created the Interstate Sanitation Commission (renamed the Interstate Environmental Compact in 2000), which is unique in specifying numerical water quality standards for two classes of water. The Connecticut General Assembly enacted the compact in 1941. Subsequently, the three state legislatures took advantage of compact Article III authorizing the delegation of additional powers to the commission by enacting statutes permitting the commission to monitor but not regulate air pollution.[28]

The commission initially focused on construction and upgrading wastewater treatment facilities and considerable progress was achieved. In 1986, the commission commenced to enforce its water quality regulations more aggressively and generated conflicts with the three state environmental departments. The latter also possess water pollution regulatory authority and maintained the commission's role should be limited to monitoring pollution. The New York State Legislative Commission on Expenditure Review (LCER) was directed to study the commission and issued a report in 1990. LCER confirmed the commission-departmental friction, conducted a survey of commission members, and reported members representing environmental and health departments were opposed to the commission taking enforcement actions.[29] The report recommended

1. the New York State Legislature should designate the state commissioner of health as an ex officio commission member,
2. the commission should establish a policy detailing appropriate actions that may be taken by its executive committee,
3. staffs of the commission and the state department of environmental conservation should share in advance their plans for discharge inspections and coordinate them, and
4. the New York State Legislature should consider convening a conference of all interested parties to clarify the commission's air and water pollution roles.[30]

No actions were taken on these recommendations, but relations between the New York State Department of Environmental Conservation and the commission improved with the inauguration of Republican Rudolph W. Giuliani as mayor of New York City in 1993 and Republican George E. Pataki as governor in 1994. They decided to end the commission's regulatory role. Currently, there are excellent relations between the commission and the state department of environmental conservation. In particular, the commission is viewed as supplementing the programs of the states and serving as a forum for discussion of water pollution problems.[31]

New England Water Pollution Control Compact. This compact dates to meetings of New England state sanitary engineers prior to World War II whose efforts resulted in Congress granting consent-in-advance to the compact in 1947 and its enactment by each of the six state legislatures.[32] The commission is composed of five members from each state and its primary role has been coordination of water quality programs of member states. Its other activities include training professionals, informing the citizenry of water quality problems, review of proposed state laws and administrative regulations, and organizing workgroups to facilitate exchange of information and develop a cooperative approach to solving problems. Relations between the commission and party states are excellent.[33]

Ohio River Valley Water Sanitation Compact. This compact was enacted by six state legislatures, received the consent of Congress in 1940, and has been remarkably successful in cleaning up one of the most polluted rivers—the Ohio River—in the United States in 1930. Not surprisingly, the river became more polluted during World War II because of increased industrial activity. The postwar period witnessed dramatic improvements in water quality and by 1998 all industrial and municipal wastewater discharges were treated, numerous river events were held, and the river is full of commercial and sports fish species.[34]

Federal-State Compacts

The constitutional provision authorizing states to enter into an interstate compact with the consent of Congress is silent with respect to whether Congress can enact the compact into federal law and become a compact member. Felix Frankfurter and James Landis in 1925 foresaw the possibility of federal-state compacts: "the combined legislative powers of Congress and of the several states permit a wide range of permutations and combinations for governmental actions.[35] Although no federal-state compact emerged until 1961, the 1948 Ohio River Valley Water Sanitation Compact authorizes the president to appoint three members of the compact commission.[36]

Five federal-state compacts have been enacted into law by Congress and the concerned state legislatures: Delaware River Basin Compact, Susquehanna River Basin Compact, Appalachian Regional Compact, Alabama-Coosa-Tallapoosa River Basin Compact, and the Apalachicola-Chattahoochee-Flint River Basin Compact. The first two compacts contain essentially identical wording.

Delaware River Basin Compact. The Delaware River is a major water source for four states—Delaware, New Jersey, New York, and Pennsylvania—which had been engaged in contentious disputes pertaining to the amount of water to be discharged into the river from the large New York City reservoirs in the Catskill Mountains.

In the absence of an interstate compact or congressional allocation of water, disputing states turn to the U.S. Supreme Court to determine a fair allocation of available waters. The court in 1931 issued a decree allowing New York City to divert a maximum of 440,000,000 gallons of water daily from the Delaware River and its tributaries, and requiring construction of a sewage treatment plant in Port Jervis, New York.[37] The U.S. Supreme Court, in response to a petition, in 1954 amended the earlier degree to allow New York City to divert additional water upon completion of a reservoir on the East Branch of the Delaware River and a further diversion upon completion of the Cannonsville Reservoir.[38]

Efforts to form an interstate compact in the 1920s and the early 1950s failed. In 1955, however, the governors of the states and the mayors of New York City and Philadelphia created the Delaware River Advisory Committee to prepare recommendations for solving the water problems in the river basin. The committee played a key role in establishing the Water Resources Foundation for the Delaware River Basin, the recipient of a subsequent Ford Foundation Grant to study the problem. The Maxwell Graduate School of Syracuse University was retained to conduct the study.

The Maxwell Graduate School's report was completed in 1959, published as a book in 1960, and suggested a transitional agency—Delaware River Agency for Water—should be established while negotiations continued for a federal-state compact.[39] The advisory committee decided to proceed immediately to persuade the concerned state legislatures and Congress to enact a federal-state compact. This compact, effective in 1961, was enacted by Congress and the state legislatures of Delaware, New Jersey, New York, and Pennsylvania for an initial period of 100 years and created the Delaware River Basin Commission (DRBC) composed of representatives of the federal government and the states.[40]

Jerome C. Muys conducted research for the National Water Commission and concluded in 1973 "the Delaware River Basin Commission has compiled an impressive record of accomplishments over the past decade, much of which this observer believes would not have resulted but for the existence and efforts of the DRBC."[41] Jeffrey P. Featherstone conducted an in-depth study of the compact and opined in 1999 it has achieved most of its goals.[42] He reported the compact had abated water pollution, conserved water, facilitated intergovernmental coordination, improved stream flows, provided more reliable water supplies, reduced ground water overdrafts, and removed the need for the U.S. Supreme Court to resolve water allocation disputes in the basin.[43]

Northeast Dairy Compact

Widely fluctuating milk prices and the sharp decline in the number of New England dairy farms convinced farmers, the governors, and the state legislatures an interstate dairy compact with regulatory powers was essential to improve the health of the industry. A compact was drafted and enacted by each of the six state legislatures, and received the consent of Congress in 1996 for a period of three years.[44] Consent was extended for two years in 1999, but Congress failed to extend its consent in 2001. Approximately twenty-five other states have enacted similar compacts, but none received the required consent of Congress.

The commission regulated the farm price of Class I fluid milk and processors were required to pay monthly to the commission the difference between the federal market-order price and the commission's over-order price based upon the volume of their respective sales. The funds were utilized to finance commission activities and to make payments to farmers on the basis of the quantity of milk produced.

The compact was a controversial one, described as a cartel, and held responsible for the increase in the price of milk paid by consumers. Debate in Congress on extension of the consent exposed regional divisions with midwestern states united against northeastern and southern states. The compact's termination had no immediate effect on milk prices because the federally regulated milk prices were high and the Commission was not making payments to dairy farmers.

Energy Compacts

Congressional authorization in 1954 for the civilian use of atomic energy led to the state legislative enactment of two compacts designed to promote economic development by promoting the use of such energy. The Southern Interstate Nuclear Compact (renamed Southern States Energy Compact in 1978) was enacted by the concerned state legislatures in 1960 and received congressional consent in 1962.[45] Article I of the compact charges the Southern States Energy Board with promoting energy conservation, industrialization, and development of a balanced economy. The board is the manager of the Southeastern Regional Biomass Energy Program, operates the Southern Water Supply Roundtable with the University of Tennessee, sponsors the Southern States Waste Management Coalition, and has a Task Force on Electric Utility Restructuring among other activities.

A similar compact—Western Interstate Energy Compact—received congressional consent in 1970 and subsequently was renamed the Western Interstate Energy Compact.[46] The compact has eleven states as members and three Canadian provinces as associate members, and authorizes the president to appoint an ex officio member. Its objectives are similar to those of the Southern States Energy Compact.

Fisheries Compacts

The economic importance of fisheries as natural resources and the threatened extinction of several fish species induced groups of states to enter into interstate fisheries compacts. The Maryland General Assembly and the Virginia General Assembly in 1785 enacted the first such compact to establish fishing rights and navigation rules on the Chesapeake Bay and the Potomac River. Although this compact achieved a degree of success, disputes over oysters were common from the 1880s until 1958 when the Potomac River Compact in 1962 received congressional consent and created the Potomac River Fisheries Commission.[47] It is delegated broad powers (Art. III, §2) to regulate the type and size of "all species of finfish, crabs, oysters, clams, and other shellfish . . ."

A similar threat of the extinction of a number of fish species led to the enactment by fifteen state legislatures of the Atlantic States Marine Fisheries Compact and receipt of the consent of Congress in 1942.[48] This compact does not grant enforcement powers to the commission, but a 1986 amendment of the *Atlantic Striped Bass Conservation Act* requires states to comply with the commission's fishery management plan or be subject to a striped bass fishing moratorium imposed by the U.S. Fish and Wildlife Service "on waters more than three miles offshore of a non-complying state."[49] The commission works to the rebuild coastal stocks of striped bass and other fish species, but an overfished problem persists. Congress also granted consent in 1947 to the Pacific Marines Fisheries Compact (now Pacific States Marine Fisheries Compact) and the Gulf States Marine Fisheries Compact in 1949.[50]

Efforts also have been launched to restore Atlantic salmon to the Connecticut River basin by means of an interstate compact—enacted by the state legislatures of Connecticut, Massachusetts, New Hampshire, and Vermont—which received the consent of Congress in 1983.[51] The eight-member commission conducts studies on salmon restoration, submits recommendations to the governors of the member states, promulgate regulations governing salmon fishing in the river, and issues a salmon fishing license for a fee.

The commission has achieved a limited degree of success with an annual return of hundreds of sea-run salmon, development of a river-specific egg source, in-stream production of smolts, installation of fish ladders at five dams, and release of more than nine million salmon annually. The restoration of shad to the river has been so successful the commission removed the limit on the number of shad fishermen may catch. A similar program to restore salmon and other fish to the Merrimack River has been initiated by an interstate administrative agreement described below.

Flood Control Compacts

Annual spring floods in many sections of the United States caused major economic damage and made apparent flood control projects were essential. One response to floods was enactment of interstate flood control compacts as illustrated by three New England ones which have been successful in preventing major floods: Connecticut River Flood Control compact in 1953, Merrimack River Flood Control Compact in 1957, and Thames River Flood Control Compact in 1958.[52] Each compact created a commission responsible for determining annually the amount downriver states must reimburse upriver states for property tax losses resulting from the construction of flood control dams.

Low Level Radioactive Waste Compacts

The Atomic Energy Act of 1946 preempted totally regulation of ionizing radiation until Congress enacted a 1959 amendment to the act authorizing the Atomic Energy Commission (now Nuclear Regulatory Authority) to enter into agreements with individual states allowing them to assume specified regulatory responsibilities.[53] By 1979, only three commercial low-level radioactive waste disposal sites were in operation and the host states—Nevada, South Carolina, and Washington—complained they should not be responsible for storing such wastes produced in sister states.

The congressional response was the *Low Level Radioactive Waste Policy Act of 1980* making each state responsible for disposal of such wastes and encouraging them to enter into interstate waste disposal compacts.[54] Forty-four states entered into ten compacts with renewable five-year congressional consent. No compact, however, has developed a disposal facility because of strong opposition by elected officers and the general public.

Motor Vehicle Compacts

The motor vehicle plays an important role in today's national economy. States, commencing in 1908 with Rhode Island, license operators of motor vehicles in order to protect public safety on the highways. Congress in 1986, with the blessing of the states, enacted the *Commercial Motor Vehicle Safety Act of 1986*, a total preemption statute making it a crime for a truck driver to hold more than one commercial operator's license (see chapter 3).[55] With this one exception, states remain responsible for the issuance, revocation, and suspension of operator licenses.

The ease of interstate travel has necessitated interstate cooperation in the enforcement of the motor vehicle laws of the fifty states. Such cooperation has been promoted by the Interstate Driver License Compact that has been enacted by all states except Georgia, Massachusetts, Tennessee, and Wisconsin. This compact facilitates the reporting of the conviction of a driver for a motor vehicle violation in other states to the state which issued the license. All states except Alaska, California, Michigan, Montana, Oregon, and Wisconsin have enacted the Nonresident Violator Compact which is designed to ensure each nonresident driver answers moving violations appearance tickets or summons.

Multistate Tax Compact

This compact was entered by eight states in 1967 and currently has a membership of twenty-one states and the District of Columbia. The United States Steel Corporation challenged the constitutionality of the compact on the ground Congress did not grant its consent to the compact, but the U.S. Supreme Court in 1978 rejected the challenge by explaining the compact does not "authorize the member states to exercise any powers they could not exercise in its absence. . . ."[56]

The *Uniform Division of Income for Tax Purposes Act* is incorporated into Article IV of the compact and serves as a broad taxation framework. The commission issued detailed regulations in 1971, revised in 1973, facilitating the determination of the state and local government tax liability of multistate taxpayers by means of equitable apportionment of tax bases. Subsequently, the commission drafted the Uniform Protest Statute and Uniform Principles Governing State Transactional Taxation of Telecommunications, and Recommendation Formula for the Apportionment and Allocation of Net Income of Finance Institutions. In addition, the commission has drafted model regulations for corporate income tax allocation and apportionment; special rules for airlines, construction contractors, publishing, radio and television broadcasting, railroads, and trucking companies; and record-keeping regulations for sales and use tax purposes.[57] Of particular importance is the alternative dispute resolution program, developed in conjunction with the Committee on State Taxation, providing for a voluntary, cooperative approach to resolving tax controversies among states with their attendant costs and risks.

Oil and Gas Compact

The sharp oil price declines resulting from the discovery of large Oklahoma and Texas oil fields in the late 1920s prompted many oil industry executives to urge Congress to authorize the secretary of the interior to establish minimum oil prices. An alternative was an interstate compact and six states in 1935 enacted the Interstate Oil Compact (now Interstate Oil and Gas Compact) and it received congressional consent initially for only two years subject to extensions; the time limited was removed in 1979.[58]

The commission has three major programs: promoting responsible exploration for and production of oil and gas resources, assisting states to protect the environment, and advocating a national energy strategy based upon use of domestic oil and gas resources.

Pest Control Compact

The more than 10,000 species of insects, plant diseases, weeds, and other organisms cause billions of dollars of damages annual to crops and forests in the United States. To reduce such damage, the Council of State Governments provided the leadership for the enactment by state legislatures of the Interstate Pest Control Compact that became effective in 1968 and currently has thirty-two members.

The governing board has established a one million dollar insurance fund with a one-time contribution by each member state. Should the fund become depleted, each member will be assessed its proportionate share to restore the fund. Each member state may apply to the insurance fund to obtain resources to assist the state's pest eradication program. In exceptional cases, funding is provided to a nonmember state to assist its pest control efforts.

Solid Waste Compact

Congress granted its consent to the New Hampshire–Vermont Interstate Solid Waste Compact in 1982.[59] This compact is a unique one in that it does not create a governing commission, but authorizes one or more municipalities in each of the two states to enter into an administrative agreement with one or more municipalities in the other state for the construction and operation of a resource recovery facility or sanitary landfill or both subject to EPA approval.

A group of Vermont towns in 1981 organized the Southern Windsor–Windham Counties Solid Waste Management District, and the city of Claremont and a group of New Hampshire towns established the Sullivan County Regional Refuse Disposal District. In 1989, the two districts signed a New Hampshire–Vermont Solid Waste Project Cooperative Agreement, approved by EPA, providing the project would be under the control of joint meetings of the two governing bodies.

Vermont towns are pleased with the compact, but Claremont and New Hampshire towns are dissatisfied with the compact whose incinerator and landfill are located in New Hampshire. The project has a contract with the Wheelebrator Claremont Company, the incinerator operator, which will expire in 2007. It appears the interstate agreement will be terminated upon expiration of the contract.

Waterfront Compact

The Port of New York–New Jersey had been plagued for years by corruption. The two state legislatures decided to solve the problem by enacting in 1953 an interstate compact and Congress granted its consent in the same year.[60] The compact created a two-member commission whose annual budget is submitted to the two state legislatures and becomes effective as submitted unless either governor vetoes or reduces an item(s) within a thirty-day period (Art. XIII[2]).

The commission quickly eliminated two corrupt practices. The "shape-up" was a system of employing dockworkers under which a prospective long-shoreman to obtain work frequently borrowed funds from designated loan sharks to pay to a hiring boss or was required to make kickbacks to the boss. The commission decided to register and license dockworkers and to operate employment information centers. Also eliminated was "public loading," the practice requiring truckers to pay designated persons to load or unload cargo even if there was no need for such services.

Today, the commission's detectives work with the New Jersey State Police and New York State Police, U.S. Attorney's Office for the Southern District of New York, Federal Bureau of Investigation, U.S. Custom Service, U.S. Immigration and Naturalization Service, U.S. Postal Inspection Service, and U.S. Labor Department to prevent merchandise thefts and to interdict illegal drugs in the port.

Interstate Economic Administrative Agreements

The U.S. Constitution contains no references to ad hoc and permanent formal and informal interstate administrative agreements entered into by heads of state departments and agencies with their counterparts in sister states on the basis of enabling statutes. Ad hoc agreements are viewed as temporary ones and most are informal verbal ones. In practice, many of these agreements remain in force for a substantial time period and are difficult to distinguish from formal written agreements intended to be permanent ones.

Locating interstate administrative agreements is a difficult task as no state has a repository of the written agreements or a listing of informal agreements. Interstate compact, by way of contrast, may be located readily by consulting the consolidated laws of each state. The interstate administrative agreements described briefly below cover a wide range of topics and it is apparent some agreements contain language identical or nearly identical to the language of interstate compacts on the same subjects.

Agricultural Agreements

These agreements are cooperative interstate efforts to prevent and stop the spread of animal and plant diseases, and insect pests. One example is the 1949 agreement—entered into by New Jersey, New York, and Pennsylvania—establishing the Regional Continuing Committee on Rabies Control. Another example is the Regional Dairy Quality Management Alliance entered into by thirteen states to promote food safety by means of management practices ensuring animal health and improving dairy farm profitability.

Civil Suits

State attorneys general engage in numerous cooperative activities, particularly through the National Association of Attorneys General. Many of their activities involve civil suits against large companies for misleading advertising, fraud, and price fixing. Two such suits have had major economic ramifications.

Forty states and the Puerto Rican attorneys general successfully sued five major tobacco companies and reached an agreement with them for an out-of-court settlement totaling $246 billion to reimburse the states for their Medicaid expenses incurred to treat residents with tobacco-induced illnesses.[61]

Eighteen states and the U.S. Justice Department in 1998 initiated a major suit alleging Microsoft violated antitrust statutes. Nine of the states and the department reached a settlement with the company in late 2001, but nine other states continued their suit seeking to force Microsoft to place in the public domain its Internet Explorer Web browser and "require the company to auction three licenses to translate its MS Office business software to other operating systems like Linux."[62]

Criminal Justice Agreements

State boundary lines do not impede the movement of criminals whose mobility has been increased dramatically by the development of the railroad, motor vehicle, and airplane. States have entered into numerous agreements, primarily intelligence ones, to apprehend criminals. The New York State Attorney

General's organized Crime Task Force, for example, has informal cooperative agreements with other states and concentrates primarily on five New York organized-crime families which also are active in New Jersey.

Currently six regional criminal intelligence programs, based upon interstate administrative agreements, operate in the United States: Organized Crime Information Center in the South, Rocky Mountain Information Network, New England State Police Administrators Conference, Middle Atlantic Great Lakes Organized Crime Law Enforcement Network, Mid States Organized Crime Information Center, and Western States Information Network. Each organization operates a regional information sharing system linked together by a national intelligence network containing information on more than 625,000 persons.

Education, Licensing, and Library Agreements

States license individuals in many professions, including education and medicine, and often have reciprocity agreements under which a person licensed as a professional in one state automatically is licensed in another state if the person decides to relocate. Interstate library agreements also are common and enhanced greatly the ability of individual libraries to obtain books and other materials requested by clients.

Electronic Purchasing

Cooperative electronic purchasing originated in 1998 when Emall, sponsored by Massachusetts, became operational. Emall is an Internet procurement program under which Idaho, Massachusetts, New York, Texas, and Utah pool their purchasing power to negotiate low process from suppliers who place their products in the states' respective Internet catalog. To be eligible to participate in the program, a supplier is required to have a current contract with one or more member states.

Emergency Assistance Agreements

Formal and informal mutual assistance administrative agreements, including interstate ones, to cope with emergencies apparently are the most common type of agreement. The subject matters covered includes civil disorders, fire fighting, and policing. Although many agreements are verbal ones, written agreements are preferable because they can address liability problems associated with personnel injured in the line of duty while serving beyond their home jurisdiction.

Environmental Agreements

Numerous interstate agreements relate to air pollution abatement, fisheries, plant pests, and waste materials. The public health commissioners of the New England States in 1967 established the New England Staff for Coordinated Air Use Management whose name was changed to the Northeastern States for Coordinated Air Use Management after New York and New Jersey became members. Currently, there are four additional similar regional groups formed by interstate administrative agreements: Mid-Atlantic Regional Air Pollution Task Force, Southeastern States Air Resources Managers, Metro-Four (eight southeastern states), and Western States Air Resources.

Congress in 1990 created the Ozone Transport Commission whose members are twelve northeastern states and the District of Columbia.[63] Two years later, representatives of these states and the district signed an interstate administrative cooperation agreement designed to achieve cleaner air.[64] Subsequently, nine memoranda of understanding were signed pertaining to reformulated gasoline, motor vehicle emissions, low emission vehicles, and similar topics. In a related development, the governors of eight northeastern states and the New York City mayor formed the Northeast Advance Vehicle Consortium for the purpose of reducing pollutants emitted by motor vehicles.

Fisheries Agreements

Fresh waters located on the boundary lines between states raise jurisdictional issues relative to licensing of fishermen. To resolve these issues, states have entered into a large number of interstate administrative agreements generally based upon reciprocity. A typical agreement specifies the reciprocity waters and the covered licenses and stamps, and also provides for the transportation of fish across state boundaries.

Congress in 1976 enacted a statute creating eight regional fisheries councils composed of representatives of states, the director of the national fisheries service, and thirteen members appointed by the U.S. secretary of commerce on the nomination of governors. In addition, there are four non-voting members representing the U.S. Fish and Wildlife Service, Coast Guard, State Department, and Atlantic States Marine Fisheries Commission. Each council is dominated by state representatives and has influenced significantly federal fisheries policies.

The Merrimack River Anadromous Fish Restoration Agreement is a most interesting one because it demonstrates identical interstate goals can be achieved by an interstate agreement or an interstate compact. The purpose is to restore the Atlantic salmon, shad, and river herrings to the Merrimack River that arises in New Hampshire and flows through Massachusetts to the

Atlantic Ocean. The restoration program dates to 1969 when representatives of two Massachusetts fisheries divisions, the New Hampshire Fish and Game Department, the U.S. Bureau of Commercial Fisheries (now National Marine Fisheries Service), and the U.S. Bureau of Sports Fisheries and Wildlife signed an administrative agreement. The goals of the agreement are identical to the goals of the Connecticut River Basin Atlantic Salmon Restoration Compact enacted by Connecticut, Massachusetts, New Hampshire, and Vermont, and consented to by Congress in 1983.[65]

Insurance Regulation

Insurance today is an industry of great interstate and international economic importance. Congress was content to allow state legislatures to regulate the industry and the U.S. Supreme Court in 1868 held insurance was not commerce and hence was exempt from congressional regulation.[66] In 1944, however, the court reversed this decision.[67] Concerned with the loss of revenue flowing from this decision, the states successfully lobbied Congress to enact the *McCarran-Ferguson Act of 1945* reversing the decision by specifically authorizing states to regulate the insurance industry.[68] In consequence, nonuniform and often discriminatory state insurance regulatory policies persisted.

Insurance companies continued to challenge discriminatory policies in court and also lobbied Congress for relief. Success was achieved when Congress enacted the *Gramm-Leach-Bliley Financial Reorganization Act of 1999* establishing minimum regulatory standards in thirteen areas that states must follow.[69] The act also contains a contingent preemption provision stipulating a federal insurance agent licensing system will be implemented if twenty-six states do not adopt by November 12, 2002, a uniform licensing system for agents to be determined by the National Association of Insurance Commissioners (NAIC) after consulting state insurance commissioners.[70] On September 10, 2002, NAIC certified thirty-five states had enacted statutes establishing such a system.[71] NAIC also drafted and promoted the enactment by forty-seven state legislatures of a Producer Licensing Model Act providing for interstate reciprocity.[72]

Working through the association, commissioners have been promoting uniform state policies and launched an accreditation program involving an independent team reviewing the policies of each state insurance department to determine its compliance with the standards.[73] The U.S. General Accounting Office in 2002 reported the association "through its accreditation program had made considerable progress in achieving greater uniformity in carrying out their financial solvency oversight responsibilities."[74] NAIC also decided to draft an interstate insurance compact to establish uniform regulatory policies for annuity, disability income life, and long-term health care products.

Lotteries

Thirty-nine states, the District of Columbia, Puerto Rico, Virgin Islands, and five Canadian provinces currently operate lotteries. Experience revealed the sales of lottery tickets varies with jackpot size. In consequence, groups of states by interstate administrative agreements formed multistate lotteries and successfully lobbied Congress to repeal its statute forbidding interstate sale of tickets and transportation of lottery equipment.[75] Three multistate lotteries—Powerball Lottery, Big Game Lottery, and Lotto South—have been organized by administrative agreements and have large ticket sales. The Tri-State Megabucks Lottery (Maine, New Hampshire, and Vermont) was established by an interstate compact.

Plant Pest Agreements

The work of the thirty-two member Interstate Pest Control Compact is supplemented by four regional plant boards—eastern, central, southern, and western—formed by means of interstate administrative agreements and involving all fifty states, Puerto Rico, British Columbia, and the Mexican district of lower California. These regional plant boards also work closely with the U.S. Department of Agriculture and seek to promote uniformity in state enforcement of plant quarantine and plant inspection policies.

Prescription Drugs

High prescription drug prices led to the formation by Maine, New Hampshire, and Vermont in 2000 of a tri-state pool to purchase such drugs whose prices had been increasing by approximately eight percent per year.[76] The plan, the first multistate one, saves the approximately 300,000 enrollees fifteen percent on their prescription drug purchases. Shortly after establishment of the plan, a group of state legislative leaders of eight states organized the Northeast Legislative Association on Prescription Drug Prices based upon the tri-state pool concept.

Taxation

States enter into reciprocal agreements with each other for the exchange of information to curtail tax evasion by business firms and individuals and for cooperative tax administration. These agreements facilitate the conduct of tax audits to ensure compliance with tax statutes and regulations, and to generate additional revenues. An example is an eleven northeastern states and District of Columbia agreement designed to facilitate the detection of individuals residing and employed in one state who claim residency in another state in an effort to pay lower or no state income taxes.[77] Similarly, the Federation of Tax Administrators drafted a Uniform Exchange of Information Agreements that has been signed by forty-four states, the District of Columbia, and New York City. Previously, these jurisdictions relied upon bilateral information exchange agreements.

Chapter 6 describes the promotion by Congress of the International Fuel Agreement and the International Registration Plan designed to simplify taxation and registration of commercial motor vehicles, thereby improving the national economic union. The former agreement provides a carrier's home jurisdiction, a state or Canadian province, issues credentials allowing each licensee to travel in all member jurisdictions and apportions motor fuel tax revenues among member jurisdictions. The International Registration Plan is a cooperative motor carrier registration reciprocity agreements with license fees shared based on the number of fleet miles operated in each jurisdiction.

The Streamlined Sales and Use Tax Agreement dates to 2000 and established uniform definitions within tax bases, simplified exemption administration, rate simplification, and uniform audit procedures and sourcing rules. In 2002, thirty-six states and the District of Columbia were participating in the agreement and an additional three states were nonvoting participants. Participation in the agreement by vendors is voluntary. The first electronic sales tax payments under the agreement were received by the state treasurers' offices in North Carolina, Michigan, and Kansas in 2002.[78]

Transportation Agreements

Numerous interstate transportation administrative agreements are in effect and many address the problem created by motorists who register their vehicles in another state to lower their insurance premiums and/or to avoid payment of a personal property tax on the vehicles. Other agreements, including ones with Canadian provinces, relate to reciprocal recognition of operator licenses and the failure of motorists to pay traffic fines.

The Commercial Vehicle Safety Alliance represents all states, American Samoa, Guam, Canadian provinces and territories, and Mexican states. It has been successful, via a memorandum of understanding, in establishing common inspection procedures by its members and also collaborates with the U.S. Department of Energy in developing uniform inspection standards for drivers and vehicles transporting radioactive fuel and waste.

The E-Z Pass system, a consortium of seven eastern states, has reduced air pollution and congestion at bridge, tunnel, and turnpike toll plazas by means of electronic toll collection. And the I-95 Coalition since 1993 has been operating an intelligent transportation system promoting mobility and safety in all mode of transportation. Of particular importance is the Coalition's ability to notify traffic management centers along the east coast with information on major incidents on the interstate highway and to suggest alternative highway routes.

Waste Management Agreements

The Northeast Recycling Council dates to 1989 when ten states signed an interstate cooperative memorandum of understanding promoting recycling to minimize the quantity of waste materials by supporting state governments and trade associations source reduction programs and encouraging manufacturers to use recycled materials. The council finances its activities by dues paid by member states and grants.

There are three other similar organizations: Southern States Waste Management Coalition, Mid-Atlantic Consortium of Recycling and Economic Development Officials, and the Northeast Waste Management Officials Association. The latter is composed of state directors of hazardous waste, solid waste site cleanup, and pollution programs in eight states. It prepares reports on mercury deposition rates in water and waste flows, promotes state coordination of regulatory policies for used electronic products, and provides technical support to member states, among other activities.

The Southern States Waste Management Coalition, sponsored by the Southern States Energy Board, published in 1996 a report revealing approximately 138,700 individuals were employed in 1995 by firms processing recovered materials or using them in manufacturing processes in the thirteen state area, metals were the most common materials recovered and used in manufacturing, nine tons of recovered paper were processed annually, 979,000 tons of recovered plastic were converted into pellets and 767,000 tons were used to make plastic sheets, and "approximately $18.5 billion of value was added to recyclables in the region through processing and manufacturing."[79]

Summary and Conclusions

The U.S. Constitution (Art. I, §10) recognizes the desirability of interstate cooperation by allowing states to enter into interstate compacts with the consent of Congress designed to ensure they did not encroach upon its delegated powers or discriminate against one or more states. In 1893, the U.S. Supreme Court opined the consent was required only for political compacts. The scope of such compacts has been expanded by congressional consent authorizing Canadian provinces and Mexican states to join specified compacts.

Interstate compacts were utilized solely to settle boundary disputes until 1921 when the New York State Legislature and the New Jersey Legislature each enacted the Port of New York Authority Compact and it received congressional consent. This compact was the first one to establish a public authority governed by a commission composed of representatives appointed by the governor of each state with the advice and consent of the state senate. Officers of state department and agencies of party states administer the thirty-four compacts that do not create a commission. The range of problems addressed by compacts is large and many compacts have been highly successful in solving their assigned problems.

The number of formal and informal interstate administrative agreements has multiplied in recent decades and experience reveals certain public problems can be addressed effectively either by an interstate compact or by an interstate administrative agreement. The latter is a very flexible instrument as there is no need for legislative enactment of an agreement or for congressional consent for its implementation. The sharp increase in the number of agreements is attributable to their promotion by associations of state officers, Congress relative to certain problems, and federal government administrators. Many agreements are direct products of the electronic revolution that has made them possible.

We conclude the economic and political union, established by the U.S. Constitution, has been made more perfect by interstate compacts and interstate administrative agreements. We anticipate there will be a slow growth in the number of compacts in the foreseeable future, but a sharp increase in the number of formal and informal agreements.

Chapter 9 contains recommendations, addressed to the president, Congress, and states, designed to make the economic union still more perfect.

CHAPTER 9

A More Perfect Economic Union

The U.S. Constitution, effective in 1789, instituted a considerably more perfect economic union than the one established by the Articles of Confederation and Perpetual Union. The Constitution specifically assigns responsibility for ensuring internal free trade to Congress by delegating to it authority (Art. I, §8) to regulate interstate commerce reinforced by the supremacy of the laws clause (Art. VI). This delegation of authority has not been fully effective because of congressional reluctance to enact statutes invalidating state erected taxation and trade barriers as explained below.

In theory, the U.S. Constitution established an *Imperium in Imperio* with states regulating intrastate commerce and Congress regulating interstate commerce. In contrast to the exclusive coinage power delegated to Congress, the delegation of the power to regulate interstate commerce is nonexclusive. Congress, of course, can use its delegated powers to preempt partially or totally state regulation of such commerce.

Congress surprisingly did not enact a statute to promote internal free trade until the *Interstate Commerce Act of 1887* and the *Sherman Antitrust Act of 1890* removed certain private corporate barriers to commerce among the states.[1] Although statutes preempting the unexercised regulatory authority of states were enacted as early as 1790, Congress for eleven years did not enact a preemption statute invalidating current state regulatory laws in order to establish a nationally uniform policy in a functional area. The earliest acts preempting state regulatory authority were 1800, 1841 and 1867 limited preemption bankruptcy acts that subsequently were repealed.[2] Furthermore, *An Act to Establish a Uniform System of Bankruptcy of 1898* was a partial-preemption statute and did not establish a completely uniform system throughout the nation.[3]

As explained in chapter 4, the U.S. Supreme Court in *Gibbons v. Ogden* in 1824 stepped forward to become the protector of internal free trade by developing its dormant interstate commerce clause doctrine stipulating a state statute creating an interstate trade barrier conflicting with the clause is unconstitutional.[4] The court also struck down barriers because they violated the U.S. Constitution's privileges and immunities clause (Art. IV, §2) and/or equal protection of the laws clause of the Fourteenth Amendment. Congress, for time and a variety of political reasons, clearly prefers to

199

leave to the courts responsibility for determining the constitutionality of subnational governmental statutes and administrative regulations allegedly burdening interstate commerce.

States, by voluntarily relinquishing some of their quasi-sovereign powers, have achieved a degree of success in making the economic and political unions more perfect. Uniform public policies in various functional areas have been achieved by two methods. First, many state legislatures have enacted uniform state laws, drafted by the National Conference of Commissioners on Uniform State Laws since the last decade of the nineteenth century. Second, a significant number of regulatory interstate and federal-state compacts have been enacted by state legislatures with or without the consent of Congress since 1921. Unfortunately, disharmonious state regulatory and taxation policies continue to hinder the full economic developmental potential of the U.S. federal system and interest groups adversely affected by the policies lobby Congress to exercise its preemption powers to establish nationally uniform standards. The evidence presented in chapter 8 reveals states have failed to take full advantage of the potential of interstate compacts and interstate administrative agreements for the establishment of uniform state regulatory and taxation policies.

State erected trade barriers, described in chapter 5, are not the only state actions weakening the economic union. Chapter 6 is devoted to an examination of the exportation of taxes by states legislatures seeking to maximize their respective state's revenues without increasing the tax burden placed on their respective citizens. State taxes discriminating against foreign and alien business corporations (chartered in a sister state or foreign nation, respectively) and citizens of sister states and other nations impose an unfair tax burden on them in some instances. Such discrimination has a major adverse impact on interstate and international commercial intercourse and invites retaliation.

Chapter 7 documents the undesirable consequences of interstate competition for business firms, sports franchises, tourists, and gamblers from sister states and foreign nations. Each state is analogous to a business firm in a free market characterized by perfect competition in which a second firm offers a lower price on an identical product, thereby pressuring the first firm to lower its price to match the price of its competitor or suffer a decline in sales and revenues. When one state, for example, lowers its business taxes, exempts new firms from specified taxes, or provides other subsidies to new firms, sister states may lose firms to the first state unless they initiate similar policies and the principal beneficiaries may be wealthy national and international corporations.

There are many other interstate problems impacting the economic union. Interstate use of water has been the subject of contentious debates in the southwest for decades and increasingly is a source of interstate tension in states that historically had an adequate supply of water. Interstate compacts can be utilized to resolve certain water disputes, yet it is apparent only Congress and the president can address successfully intractable water allocation problems.

This chapter builds upon the principal interstate economic relations findings and conclusions presented in chapters 4–8 to develop recommendations addressed to Congress, the president, state legislatures, and governors designed to make more perfect the economic union.

Recommendations for an Improved Economic Union

Past experience suggests achieving significant improvements in the economic union, with a few exceptions, will be a slow process. In theory, states by means of interstate concordats and interstate administrative agreements could establish uniform policies in all regulatory areas throughout the United States. In reality, it is difficult for states unanimously to agree to a common policy in a functional field because of the political strength of interest groups in each state committed to preserving policies under which benefits accrue to the groups.

Only on rare occasions will all or most states be willing to surrender any of their quasi-sovereign powers and turn to Congress with a request to enact a total preemption statute to solve a major interstate problem they have been unable to solve. An example of such a problem is the former practice of many truck drivers each obtaining a commercial driver's license from each of several states. A driver whose license was suspended or revoked by one state would use a license issued by another state to continue driving. States finally concluded only a national licensing system could solve the problem and had no objections to the totally preemptive *Commercial Drivers License Act of 1986,* which makes it a federal crime for a driver to have more than one license on which must be recorded convictions for highway violations.[5]

Congress, state legislatures, and governors generally neglect interstate relations unless there is a major multistate problem demanding their attention. On the other hand, state department and agency heads are on the front line of interstate relations and have entered into numerous administrative agreements, within the limits of their legal authority, facilitating the free movement of commerce with their counterparts in other states. Listed below are recommendations to improve the economic union.

Congress

The interstate commerce roles of Congress can be placed in three broad categories: inhibitor, facilitator, and initiator. The first role is a negative role; i.e.,

Congress, for example, fails to grant its consent to an interstate economic compact enacted by two or more state legislatures and signed by governors or refuses to enact a statute, desired by a majority of the states, designed to solve an interstate economic problem.

Congress' facilitator role is illustrated by the granting of consent-in-advance to states to enter into specific interstate compacts. This consent, however, often contains a stipulation that any compact drafted and enacted by state legislatures must be submitted to Congress for its consent.

Congress also has facilitated commercial intercourse across state lines by utilizing its delegated power (Art. IV, §1) to prescribe the manner in which full faith and credit must be given by each state to the acts, records and judicial proceedings of sister states. There appears to be no major need for additional full faith and credit statutes promoting the free flow of interstate commerce.

The initiator role of Congress refers to enactment of a preemption statute removing all regulatory authority in a given functional field from states or establishing minimum regulatory standards for state implementation because disharmonious policies of the states were impeding interstate commercial intercourse. A well-known example of a total preemption statute is the *Surface Transportation Assistance Act of 1982* invalidating state restrictions on the size and weight of trucks permitted to operate on their respective highways.[6] The *Clean Water Act of 1977* is an example of a minimum standards preemption act allowing a state to continue to regulate water quality provided its standards meet or exceed the minimum national standards and the state possesses qualified personnel and the necessary equipment.[7]

Two major actions should be initiated by Congress to speed up the development and implementation of uniform state economic regulatory policies throughout the nation short of the exercise of preemption powers. First, section 10 of Article 1 of the U.S. Constitution grants the national legislature complete control over interstate compacts. In consequence, there is no reason why Congress should not enact a statute granting consent-in-advance to any compact entered into by two or more states. The latter are most unlikely to enter into a compact encroaching upon congressional powers and any such compact could be invalidated by a statute or by a court. Should a new compact hinder the flow of commerce, Congress could invalidate it by statute.

Congress also could take two related actions. First, states could be authorized to enter into compacts on any subject provided copies of each compact are filed with the U.S. House of Representatives and the Senate. A compact would become effective after sixty days if not disapproved by a joint resolution. Second, the same process could be applied to amendments to compacts that have received congressional consent. In fact, it would be desirable for Congress to grant blanket authority to states to amend current compacts with respect to their declared goals without submitting amendments to Congress.

The second major action could be the threat of congressional preemption of state regulatory powers to encourage state legislatures to enact uniform statutes, drafted by the National Conference of Commissioners on Uniform State Laws, designed to eliminate disharmonious state regulatory policies. Varying numbers of state legislatures have enacted each uniform state law drafted by the conference. Forty states and the District of Columbia, for example, have enacted the 1999 Uniform Electronic Transaction Act, but only six states have enacted the 1988 Uniform Securities Act.[8]

The threat of congressional preemption should be employed only with respect to uniform state laws enacted by a relatively large number of states. Such a threat might encourage state legislatures failing to enact a designated uniform state law to reconsider it and/or work with the conference to amend the law to remove or modify an objectionable provision(s).

Similarly, Congress could respect state sovereignty by enacting an opt-out regulatory statute, under its interstate commerce power, requiring each state legislature without a specified uniform state law to vote on the question of its enactment. If the state legislature enacts the law, uniformity is increased. It is reasonable to assume a uniform state law perceived by the citizenry to be desirable would make it politically difficult for state legislators to vote to opt out.

Alternatively, Congress should consider enacting as federal law a uniform state law, drafted by the conference, removing major barriers to interstate commerce if a significant number of states fail to enact the uniform state law. Although state legislatures which have not enacted it may object, Congress can not be accused of trampling upon the sovereign rights of the states in view of the fact the uniform law was drafted by a national association of state officers.

Note should be made of the fact uniform state laws have not been drafted to address a number of major politically sensitive problems caused by nonharmonious state laws, particularly taxation ones. Congress should encourage the conference to draft such uniform or model laws.

A vague threat that Congress will exercise its preemption power if states fail to solve a problem may encourage them collectively to conduct studies designed to fashion a common policy, but produce little in terms of concrete positive action. Enactment of a bill by Congress and signed by the president containing a contingent preemption clause can trigger intense state actions to develop a uniform policy. The *Gramm-Leach-Bliley Financial Reorganization Act of 1999* provided for the establishment of a federal licensing system for insurance agents if twenty-six state legislatures did not enact a uniform licensing system by November 12, 2002.[9] This act stimulated action by the National Association of Insurance Commissioners to ensure the requisite number of state legislatures enact statutes establishing such a system and success was achieved in 2002. In addition, this act encouraged the association to draft an interstate compact providing for uniform regulation of life insurance, annuities, and extended health care policies.

A similar approach could be employed by Congress to encourage state legislatures to enact the model regulations, statutes, and guidelines drafted by the Multistate Tax Commission, established by an interstate compact in 1967, to remove costly tax impediments to interstate commerce.[10]

The great increase in interstate and international commerce has brought to the forefront the question of the fairness of state taxation of multistate and multinational business firms. Chapter 6 explains the unitary tax apportionment system, which was utilized by California, led to diplomatic protests by several foreign nations that their corporations are taxed unfairly and raised the possibility of retaliation by these nations. The Multistate Tax Commission has sought to promote nationally uniform state taxation policies and has achieved a degree of success. Although forty-five states participate in the commission's activities, only twenty-one states have enacted the compact. Five additional states have the full benefits and voting rights of members even though they have not enacted the compact. Sixteen other states are associate members who "wish to participate in meetings with an eye to considering broader participation in commission activities."[11] The commission's experience after more than three decades suggests it will be unable to solve all major interstate taxation problems.

A strong case can be made for congressional enactment of a statute containing state tax jurisdiction standards, income apportionment rules, and tax-base definitions. Such a law would establish a more uniform interstate corporate taxation system, reduce the compliance burden placed on all multistate and multinational corporations, and ensure greater tax equity for these taxpayers. The congressional statute could mandate states to implement the standards, rules, and definitions, or authorize a cross-over sanction under which a state would be threatened with the loss of a percentage of its federal highway grants-in-aid if it fails to implement them. As a minimum, Congress should mandate states to utilize uniform federal apportionment rules for allocating the income of multistate and multinational corporations and partnerships, and employ the deduction and exclusions provisions of the U. S. Internal Revenue Code.

There has been a large increase in the number of total and partial preemption statutes since 1965.[12] At least one total preemption statute has made interstate cooperation in solving a problem impossible. Several state attorneys general in the early 1990s initiated actions to enforce their respective state deceptive practices act against airline companies, but their actions were stopped by a 1992 U.S. Supreme Court decision opining the *Airline Deregulation Act of 1978* totally preempts the regulatory power of the states with respect to airlines.[13] Congress should review all preemption statutes on a continuous basis to identify provisions in need of amendment or repeal because they inhibit interstate cooperation. Consideration also should be given by Congress to the development of a code of restrictions for each preemption statute identifying actions states may not initiate.

The interstate smuggling problems, including organized-crime activities, caused by state excise tax differentials, could be eliminated by a congressional statute preempting state excise taxes, increasing the rate of national excise taxes, and providing for sharing of the additional excise tax revenues by the states. The New York State Commissioner of Finance and Taxation, as noted in chapter 6, stated in 1977 his state would save more than $100 million in administrative and enforcement costs and gain more than $400 million in revenues lost to buttleggers if state excise taxes on cigarettes were replaced with a higher federal excise tax and revenue sharing.

A less dramatic action would be congressional amendment of the *Jenkins Act of 1949* to make it a federal felony for any person or business firm to use any delivery method to evade payments of state and local government excise taxes.[14] Currently, the act applies only to the postal service and a violation is simply a misdemeanor.

Congressional regulation of interstate competition for industrial firms is essential because it distorts the budgetary processes of states, results in the neglect of programs in urgent need of more resources, and benefits chiefly wealthy national and international corporations. In many instances, they have decided upon the locations of new facilities but use the threat of locating facilities in other states to persuade the state of greatest interest to offer economic and other incentives. The cap placed by Congress on the amount of tax-exempt private activity bonds by states has not had a significant impact on interstate competition for business firms. To help solve the unemployment problems in inner cities and rural areas, Congress could make taxable the interest on municipal bonds issued to raise funds to promote industrial development unless the funds are used as incentives for the location of new or expanded facilities in inner cities and rural areas.

Congress has created organizations, composed of state representatives, to encourage interstate cooperation. The National Driver Register and the Ozone Transport Commission are examples of such organizations that have been effective in promoting conjoint state actions to solve particular national and regional problems, respectively. Congress should give serious consideration to the establishment of similar organizations.

The President

The single governmental officer who can command national attention at any time is the president of the United States. Few presidents, however, have devoted special attention to interstate economic relations. Two outstanding examples of presidential initiatives are President Theodore R. Roosevelt convening in 1908 a conference of governors that subsequently became the National Governors Association, and President Herbert C. Hoover requesting in 1929 the creation of the National Committee for Uniform Traffic Laws and Ordinances that has had a major impact in terms of improving interstate economic relations.

The explosion in the number of federal grants-in-aid to state and local governments contributed to the decision by presidents in the latter half of the twentieth century to establish within the executive office of the president of an intergovernmental relations office. For a variety of reasons, the office under various presidents has paid scant attention to interstate problems. It would be highly desirable to include within the office a unit devoted to studying disharmonious state policies impeding the free flow of commerce and developing recommendations the president can transmit to Congress and state legislatures for enactment to promote interstate economic intercourse.

The president should include in his/her annual state of the union message a section on interstate economic relations highlighting problems and outlining approaches to their solution. Similarly, the president's annual economic report to Congress could emphasize these problems and encourage it to enact remedial statutes and state legislatures to enact interstate compacts and uniform state laws.

Furthermore, the president specifically could direct cabinet secretaries, where appropriate, to promote cooperative interstate economic relations and to prepare a report on their implementation actions. There is a history of departmental secretaries taking the lead in solving interstate problems. The secretary of agriculture in 1924 encouraged development of a uniform numbering and marking system for highways by appointing a joint board, composed of state highway engineers, to design such a system. The board recommended that the American Association of State Highway Officials should be responsible for implementing the system and the association continues to be responsible to this day.

The U. S. Environmental Protection Agency (EPA) oversees the implementation of several minimum standards preemption acts, including the delegation to states of regulatory primacy if they have submitted standards and enforcement procedures meeting minimum national standards. EPA in granting regulatory primacy should encourage on a continuing basis states in a region to engage in joint cooperative programs to solve environmental problems. The agency in the past has encouraged states to mobilize their resources to jointly attack a major environmental problem. In 1995, for example, EPA released a comprehensive plan, developed in cooperation with eight states, to restore the health of the Great Lakes.[15]

State Legislatures

Interstate relations tend to be a low priority with state legislatures as evidenced by the fact no state legislature has a major committee devoted to such relations. New York had a famous joint legislative committee on interstate cooperation which performed yeoman tasks for three decades and was responsible for the drafting of several interstate compacts. Today, the New York Assembly lacks an interstate relations committee and the Senate has only a select committee limited primarily to collecting and publishing annually a directory of interstate compacts.

There is a great need for the resurrection by state legislatures of commissions on interstate cooperation in view of the changing nature of the national economy necessitating close interstate regulatory cooperation or congressional preemption of state regulatory authority. The New Jersey State Legislature established the first one in 1935 and forty-two state legislatures followed its lead by 1940. These commissions and the Council of State Governments drafted interstate compacts and focused national attention on the problem of state mercantilism by sponsoring in 1939 the first National Conference on Interstate Trade Barriers. Commissions were effective organizations in the 1940s and 1950s, but legislatures lost interest in them in the 1960s as the sharp rise in federal grants-in-aid shifted legislative focus to national-state relations and the commissions were abolished or not funded. There are twenty-four state inter-governmental relations commissions today, but their focus is exclusively on state-local relations.

No state currently reviews on a periodic basis interstate compacts and interstate administrative agreements to determine their need or effectiveness. State commissions on interstate relations could exercise continuous oversight over compacts and agreements by proposing their termination or amendment; promote the enactment of uniform state laws; review congressional statutes to determine which ones should be enacted into state law; draft interstate compacts; and advise Congress on the need for national assistance to solve multi-state problems. Furthermore, commissions could review state statutes to determine whether they should be amended to grant additional authority to heads of state departments and agencies to enter into administrative agreements with their sister state counterparts.

An additional function could be exploration of the desirability of the enactment of one or more interstate compacts combining the limited economic resources of small local governments, including school districts, located near state boundary lines. Currently, there are only two such compacts and each created an interstate school district involving towns in New Hampshire and Vermont.

Governors

High profile interstate disputes and problems command the attention of governors who historically have played leadership roles in resolving the disputes and problems. Although they continue to play this leadership role, it is apparent they could play a greater role if they assigned additional staff to monitor interstate relations and promote establishment of harmonious interstate economic policies. Governors have advisors on intergovernmental relations, but most focus on national-state and/or state-local relations because they tend to be politically more sensitive than interstate relations.

An enlarged staff would enable the governor to include in his/her annual state of the state address a section on interstate problems including recommended solutions. To highlight such problems, a governor could deliver an annual state of interstate relations message to the legislature. A governor with an interest in the presidency may discover that prominence in solving serious interstate problems could promote his/her candidacy.

Concluding Comments

It is unrealistic to assume Congress, the president, and state legislatures will devote significantly more of their energy and time to the study of interstate economic problems and their resolution by means of interstate cooperation. When Congress and the president conclude national government actions are necessary, they may decide the preferable approach is congressional enactment of total preemption statutes to solve present and emerging interstate problems because of the difficulty of obtaining the cooperation of all states in addressing the problems.

National associations of state officers are acutely aware of the threat of additional congressional preemption, monitor preemption bills closely, and occasionally initiate actions to reduce the threat of preemption. Many associations could play an enlarged role in encouraging state legislatures to enact uniform laws and interstate compacts if they wish to forestall congressional enactment of additional preemption statutes. W. Brooke Graves, a leading expert on intergovernmental relations, in 1938 wrote: "No student of government can reasonably protest the transfer to the federal government of powers which the states are either unable or unwilling to use effectively."[16] This statement remains valid in the first decade of the twenty-first century.

Congressional preemption on the surface appears to be the most desirable mechanism for resolving serious national economic problems flowing from the lack of uniform state laws. The proliferation of various types of total and partial preemption statutes since 1965 raises questions as to their effectiveness and whether some or all of these statutes hinder or make impossible cooperative interstate actions to address multistate problems. As noted, total congressional assumption of airline regulatory authority has prevented state attorneys general from jointly utilizing state deceptive practices laws to protect their citizens. Such preemption also may prevent states from initiating a quick action to solve a state or regional problem or to develop innovative solutions.

The ability of states to function as laboratories of democracies developing new solutions for problems, which can be copied by sister state legislatures and Congress, can be removed or limited by preemption statutes. Furthermore, the possibility of ordinary citizens influencing policy decisions may be diminished if responsibility for a current state function is assigned completely to Washington, D.C.

In sum, Adam Smith's law of comparative advantage still applies and the economic union of the United States can be strengthened most effectively by states engaging in conjoint activities to establish uniform or nearly uniform economic regulatory policies in major functional areas that have not been preempted and cooperative economic development programs. Congress, as recommended above, should play a major facilitative role in encouraging interstate economic cooperation.

Notes

Chapter 1

1. *Constitution of the United States*, preface.
2. *The Federalist Papers* (New York: New American Library, 1961), p. 491.
3. *Gibbons v. Ogden*, 22 U.S. 1 at 204–05, 9 Wheat. 1 at 204–05 (1824).
4. Consult Joseph F. Zimmerman, *Contemporary American Federalism: The Growth of National Power* (Leicester: Leicester University Press, 1992), and Joseph F. Zimmerman, *Interstate Relations: The Neglected Dimension of Federalism* (Westport, CT: Praeger Publishers, 1996).
5. Joseph F. Zimmerman, *Interstate Cooperation: Compacts and Administrative Agreements* (Westport, CT: Praeger Publishers, 2002).
6. R. H. Inglis Palgrave, ed., *Dictionary of Political Economy* (London: Macmillan and Company, Limited, 1896), p. 727.
7. Adam Smith, *An Inquiry into the Nature and Causes of the Wealth of Nations* (New York: The Modern Library, 1937).
8. Ibid., pp. 424 and 625.
9. Henry S. Commager, ed., *Documents of American History to 1898*, 8th ed. (New York: Appleton-Century-Crofts, 1968), vol. 1, p. 120.
10. Ibid., pp. 128–32.
11. Martin Diamond, "What the Framers Meant by Federalism," in Robert A. Goldwin, ed., *A Nation of States: Essays on the American Federal System*, 2nd ed. (Chicago: Rand McNally, 1974), p. 29.
12. *The Federalist Papers*, p. 89.
13. Ibid., pp. 144–45.
14. Frederick H. Cooke, *The Commerce Clause of the Federal Constitution* (New York: Baker, Voorhis & Company, 1908), p. 5.
15. Gaillard Hunt, ed., *The Writings of James Madison* (New York: G.P. Putnam's Sons, 1901), vol. II, p. 362.
16. *The Federalist Papers*, p. 112.
17. Ibid., p. 48.
18. Ibid., p. 71.
19. Gaillard Hunt, ed., *The Writings of James Madison*, vol. II, p. 362.
20. *The Federalist Papers*, pp. 50–51.
21. Ibid., pp. 62–63.

22. Max Farrand, ed., *The Records of the Federal Convention of 1787* (New Haven: Yale University Press, 1966), vol. II, p. 24.

23. Ibid., p. 27.

24. *The Federalist Papers*, p. 246.

25. Ibid., p. 102.

26. Ibid., p. 292.

27. Ibid., p. 118.

28. Ibid., p. 198.

29. Ibid.

30. Ralph Ketcham, ed., *The Anti-Federalist Papers and the Constitutional Convention Debates* (New York: New American Library, 1986).

31. Ibid., p. 281.

32. Ibid., p. 296.

33. Ibid., p. 317.

34. Ibid., p. 319.

35. Ibid., p. 323.

36. See his speeches in Ibid., pp. 327–56.

37. Charles A. Beard, *An Economic Interpretation of the Constitution of the United States* (New York: The Macmillan Company, 1913).

38. Introduction to the 1935 edition of Beard's book, pp. viii–ix.

39. William Bennett Munro, *The Government of the United States* (New York: The Macmillan Company, 1937), pp. 43–44.

40. Robert F. Brown, *Charles Beard and the Constitution* (Princeton: Princeton University Press, 1956).

41. William H. Riker, *Federalism: Origin, Operation, and Significance* (Boston: Little Brown and Company, 1964), pp. 17–20.

42. *McCulloch v. Maryland*, 17 U.S. 316, 4 Wheat. 316 (1819).

43. *U.S. Constitution*, Art. II, §2.

44. *Missouri v. Holland*, 252 U.S. 416 at 433–34, 40 S.Ct. 382 at 383–84 (1920). See also the *Migratory Bird Treaty Act of 1918*, 40 Stat. 755.

45. *Noble State Bank v. Haskell*, 219 U.S. 104 at 111, 31 S.Ct. 186 at 188 (1911).

46. Joseph F. Zimmerman, *State-Local Relations: A Partnership Approach*, 2nd ed. (Westport, CT: Praeger Publishers, 1995).

47. Zimmerman, *Interstate Cooperation: Compacts and Administrative Agreements.*

Chapter 2

1. *Bank of Augusta v. Earle*, 38 U.S. 519, 13 Pet. 519 (1839).

2. *Santa Clara County v. Southern Pacific Railroad Company*, 118 U.S. 394, 6 S.Ct. 1132 (1886).

3. *Gulf, C & S.F. Railway Company v. Ellis*, 165 U.S. 154, 17 S.Ct. 255 (1897).

4. *Sioux City Bridge Company v. Dakota County*, 260 U.S. 441, 43 S.Ct. 190 (1923).

5. *Fire Association of Philadelphia v. New York*, 119 U.S. 110, 7 S.Ct. 108 (1886).

6. *Western & Southern Life Insurance Company v. State Board of Equalization*, 451 U.S. 648, 101 S.Ct. 2070 (1981). See also *McCarran-Ferguson Act of 1945*, 59 Stat. 33, 15 U.S.C. §1011.

7. Kurt H. Nadelmann, "Full Faith and Credit to Judgments and Public Acts," *Michigan Law Review* 56, 1957–58, pp. 37–41.

8. *The Federalist Papers* (New York: New American Library, 1961), p. 271.

9. Henry J. Friendly, "The Historic Basis of Diversity Jurisdiction," *Harvard Law Review* 41, March 1928, pp. 496–97.

10. Ibid., p. 493.

11. *Hampton v. McConnell*, 16 U.S. 234, 3 Wheat. 234 (1818).

12. 1 Stat. 122 (1790).

13. 2 Stat. 298 (1804). This act and the 1790 act are codified as 28 U.S.C. §1738.

14. *Parental Kidnapping Prevention Act of 1980*, 94 Stat. 3569, 28 U.S.C. §1738A.

15. *Full Faith and Credit for Child Support Orders Act of 1994*, 108 Stat. 4063, 28 U.S.C. §1738B.

16. *Defense of Marriage Act of 1996*, 110 Stat. 2419, 1 U.S.C. §1 note.

17. *Violence Against Women Act of 2000*, 114 Stat. 1492, 42 U.S.C. §3796hh.

18. *Mills v. Duryee*, 11 U.S. 481 at 485, 7 Cranch 481 at 485 (1813).

19. *Green v. Van Buskirk*, 72 U.S. 307, 5 Wall. 307 (1866).

20. *Allgeyer v. Louisiana*, 165 U.S. 578, 17 S.Ct. 427 (1897).

21. *Alaska Packers Association v. Industrial Accident Commission*, 294 U.S. 532 at 547, 55 S.Ct. 518 at 523 (1935).

22. *Pacific Employers Insurance Company v. Industrial Accident Commission*, 306 U.S. 493 at 501, 59 S.Ct. 629 at 633 (1939).

23. *Hughes v. Fetter*, 341 U.S. 609, 71 S.Ct. 980 (1951).

24. James R. Pielemeir, "Why We Should Worry About Full Faith and Credit to Laws?" *Southern California Law Review* 60, nos. 4–5, 1987, pp. 1307–308.

25. *Heath v. Arizona*, 474 U.S. 82, 106 S.Ct. 433 (1985).

26. *Gillis v. State*, 333 MD 69, 633 A2d 888 (1993).

27. 63 Stat. 171 (1949).

28. Consult Joseph F. Zimmerman, *Interstate Cooperation: Compacts and Administrative Agreements* (Westport, CT: Praeger Publishers, 2002).

29. *The Federalist Papers*, p. 283.

30. *Virginia v. Tennessee*, 148 U.S. 503 at 520, 13 S.Ct. 728 at 735–36 (1893).

31. *Dixie Wholesale Grocery, Incorporated v. Martin*, 278 KY 705, 129 S.W. 2d 181 (1939) and 308 U.S. 609, 60 S.Ct. 173 (1939).

32. *United States Steel Corporation v. Multistate Tax Commission*, 434 U.S. 452 at 473, 98 S.Ct. 799 at 812–813 (1978).

33. *Weeks Act of 1911*, 36 Stat. 69.

34. *Resource Conservation and Recovery Act of 1976*, 90 Stat. 2801, 42 U.S.C. §6904(B).

35. *Murdoch v. City of Memphis*, 87 U.S. 590, 20 Wall. 90 (1874).

36. *Cuyler v. Adams*, 449 U.S. 433, 101 S.Ct. 703 (1981).

37. *The Federalist Papers*, pp. 143–44.

38. *The Act to Regulate Commerce of 1887*, 24 Stat. 379, 49 U.S.C. §1.

39. *Rendition Act of 1793*, 1 Stat. 302, 18 U.S. §3182. See also *Prigg v. Pennsylvania*, 41 U.S. 539, 17 Pet. 539 (1842).

40. *Ex parte Reggel*, 114 U.S. 642 at 651, 5 S.Ct. 1148 at 1153 (1885), and *Lascelles v. Georgia*, 148 U.S. 537, 13 S.Ct. 68 (1893).

41. *Fugitive Felon and Witness Act of 1934*, 48 Stat. 782, 18 U.S.C. §3182.

42. *Kentucky v. Dennison*, 65 U.S. 66, 24 How. 66 (1861).

43. Ibid., 65 U.S. at 103, 24 How. at 103.

44. Ibid., 65 U.S. at 107, 24 How. at 107.

45. *Puerto Rico v. Branstad*, 489 U.S. 219 at 227, 107 S.Ct. 2802 at 2808 (1987).

46. *Judiciary Act of 1789*, 1 Stat. 73 at 80–81.

47. *Missouri v. Illinois*, 200 U.S. 496, 26 S.Ct. 26 (1905).

48. *Arizona v. New Mexico*, 425 U.S. 794, 96 S.Ct. 1846 (1976).

49. *Pennsylvania v. New Jersey*, 426 U.S. 660 at 666, 96 S.Ct. 2333 at 2337 (1976).

50. *Massachusetts v. Missouri*, 308 U.S. 1 at 15, 60 S.Ct. 39 at 42 (1939).

51. *Ohio v. Wyandotte Chemicals Corporation*, 401 U.S. 493 at 499, 91 S.Ct. 1005 at 1010 (1971).

52. *Arizona v. New Mexico*, 425 U.S. 794, 96 S.Ct. 1846 (1976).

53. *Kansas v. Colorado*, 185 U.S. 125 at 146, 22 S.Ct. 552 at 559 (1902).

54. *The Federalist Papers*, p. 478.

55. Ralph Ketcham, ed., *The Anti-Federalist Papers and the Constitutional Convention Debates* (New York: New American Library, 1986), p. 303.

56. *Connor v. Elliot*, 59 U.S. 591 at 593, 18 How. 591 at 593 (1856).

57. *Corfield v. Coryell*, 6 F.Cas. 546 at 551–52 (CCED Pa, 1823).

58. *Paul v. Virginia*, 75 U.S. 168, 8 Wall. 168 (1868).

59. Ibid., 75 U.S. 168 at 180, 8 Wall. 168 at 180.

60. *Toomer v. Witsell*, 334 U.S. 385 at 396, 68 S.Ct. 1156 at 1162 (1948).

61. *Bank of Augusta v. Earle*, 38 U.S. 519, 13 Pet. 519 (1839).

62. *Hempill v. Orloff*, 277 U.S. 537, 48 S.Ct. 577 (1928).

63. *Metropolitan Life Insurance Company v. Ward*, 470 U.S. 869, 105 S.Ct. 1676 (1985).

64. *McCarran-Ferguson Act of 1945*, 59 Stat. 33, 15 U.S.C. § 1011.

64. *Ward v. Maryland*, 79 U.S. 418, 12 Wall. 418 (1870).

66. Ibid., 79 U.S. 418 at 430, 12 Wall. 418 at 430.

67. *Travis v. Yale and Town Manufacturing Company*, 252 U.S. 60, 40 S.Ct. 228 (1920).

68. *Toomer v. Witsell*, 334 U.S. 385 at 396, 68 S.Ct. 1156 at 1162 (1948).

69. *New Hampshire Revised Statutes Annotated*, §77–B:2(II) (1970).

70. Ibid., §77B–B:2(I) (1970).

71. *Austin v. New Hampshire*, 420 U.S. 656 at 666–67, 95 S.Ct. 1191 at 1198–199 (1975).

72. *Corfield v. Coryell*, 6 F.Cas. 546 at 551–52 (CCED Pa, 1823).

73. *McCready v. Commonwealth*, 94 U.S. 391 at 395–96, 4 Otto 391 at 395–96 (1876).

74. *Starns v. Malkerson*, 401 U.S. 985, 91 S.Ct. 1231 (1971) and *Sturgis v. Washington*, 414 U.S. 1057, 94 S.Ct. 563 (1973).

75. *Baldwin v. Montana Fish & Game Commission*, 436 U.S. 371 at 388, 98 S.Ct. 1852 at 1863 (1978).

76. *Blake v. McClung*, 172 U.S. 256, 19 S.Ct. 165 (1898).

77. *Dunn v. Blumstein*, 405 U.S. 330 at 343–44, 92 S.Ct. 995 at 1004 (1972), and *Baldwin v. Montana Fish & Game Commission*, 436 U.S. 371 at 383, 98 S.Ct. 1852 at 1860 (1978).

78. *Foley v. Connelie*, 435 U.S. 291 at 299–300, 98 S.Ct. 1067 at 1073 (1978).

79. *Wilkins v. State*, 113 Ind. 514, 16 N.E. 192 (1887) and *Ex Parte Spinney*, 10 Nev. 232 (1875).

80. *Bradwell v. Illinois*, 83 U.S. 130 at 142, 16 Wall. 130 at 142 (1872).

81. *La Tourette v. McMaster*, 248 U.S. 465, 39 S.Ct. 160 (1919).

82. *Toomer v. Witsell*, 334 U.S. 385 at 396, 68 S.Ct. 1156 at 1162 (1948).

83. *Supreme Court of New Hampshire v. Piper*, 470 U.S. 274, 105 S.Ct. 1272 (1985).

84. Ibid., 470 U.S. 274 at 285, 105 S.Ct. 1272 at 1279.

85. 1 Stat. 191 (1791).

86. 4 Stat. 401 (1796).

87. 72 Stat. 339 (1958).

88. *Coyle v. Smith*, 221 U.S. 559 at 619, 31 S.Ct. 688 at 692 (1911).

89. William H. Taft, "Arizona and New Mexico," *Congressional Record*, August 15, 1911, p. 3964. See also Joseph F. Zimmerman, *The Recall: Tribunal of the People* (Westport, CT: Praeger Publishers, 1997).

Chapter 3

1. *An Act to Regulate Commerce*, 24 Stat. 379, 49 U.S.C. §1, and *Sherman Antitrust Act of 1890*, 26 Stat. 209, 15 U.S.C. §1.

2. *McCulloch v. Maryland*, 17 U.S. 316, 4 Wheat. 316 (1819) and *Gibbons v. Ogden*, 22 U.S. 1, 9 Wheat. 1 (1824).

3. Woodrow Wilson, *Congressional Government: A Study in American Politics* (Boston: Houghton Mifflin Company, 1925), pp. 36–37.

4. Luther Gulick, "Reorganization of the State," *Civil Engineering* 3, August 1933, p. 421.

5. Harold J. Laski, "The Obsolescence of Federalism," *New Republic* 98, May 3, 1939, pp. 362–69 and Harold J. Laski, *The American Democracy* (New York: The Viking Press, 1948), p. 139.

6. Felix Morley, *Freedom and Federalism* (Chicago: Henry Regnery, 1959), p. 209 agreeing with Alexander Hamilton, *The Federalist Papers* (New York: New American Library, 1961), p. 119.

7. D.W. Brogan, *Politics in America* (Garden City: Anchor Books, 1960), p. 228.

8. Consult Joseph F. Zimmerman, "National-State Relations: Cooperative Federalism in the Twentieth Century," *Publius* 31, Spring 2001, pp. 15–30.

9. 1 Stat. 54 (1789).

10. *Shipping Statute of 1983*, 97 Stat. 553, 46 U.S.C. §8501.

11. *Boundary Water Act of 1984*, 98 Stat. 1874, 46 U.S.C. §8501(b).

12. *United States v. Maine*, 469 U.S. 504 at 524, 105 S.Ct. 992 at 1004 (1985).

13. *Opinions of the Attorney General of New York*, formal opinion No. 85–F7, August 22, 1985.

14. *Sweatt v. Florida Board of Pilot Commissioners*, 776 F. Supp. 1538 (MD Fla, 1991), 985 F.2d 578 (11th Cir. 1993).

15. *Interport Pilots Agency, Incorporated v. Board of Commissioners of Pilots*, 774 Fed. Supp. 734 at 741 (1991).

16. *McCarran-Ferguson Act of 1945*, 59 Stat. 33, 15 U.S.C. §1011.

17. *Paul v. Virginia*, 75 U.S. 168, 8 Wall. 168 (1868) and *United States v. South-Eastern Underwriters Association*, 322 U.S. 533, 64 S.Ct. 1162 (1944).

18. *McCarran-Ferguson Act of 1945*, 59 Stat. 33, 15 U.S.C. §1011.

19. *Interstate Horseracing Act of 1978*, 92 Stat. 1813, 15 U.S.C. §3004.

20. *Kentucky Division, Horsemen's Benevolent & Protective Association, Incorporated v. Turfway Park Racing Association*, 2832 F. Supp. 1097 (E.D. Ky, 1993).

21. *Kentucky Division, Horsemen's Benevolent & Protective Association, Incorporated v. Turfway Park Racing Association*, 20 F. 3d 1406 at 1416–417 (6th Cir. 1994).

22. 1 Stat. 474 (1796).

23. 1 Stat. 619 (1799).

24. 20 Stat. 37 (1878).

25. 26 Stat. 465 (1890).

26. *Fargo v. Michigan*, 121 U.S. 230 at 239, 7 S.Ct. 857 at 860 (1887).

27. *An Act to Regulate Commerce*, 24 Stat. 379, 49 U.S.C. §1.

28. *Hepburn Act of 1906*, 34 Stat. 584, 49 U.S.C. app. §1.

29. *Federal Radio Act of 1927*, 44 Stat. 1162.

30. *Federal Communications Act of 1934*, 48 Stat. 1064, 47 U.S.C §154.

31. *Railroad Revitalization and Regulatory Reform Act of 1976*, 90 Stat. 31, 45 U.S.C. §801 note.

32. Ibid., 45 U.S.C. §11503(b).

33. *Constitution of Maryland*, Art. 41.

34. *Sherman Antitrust Act of 1890*, 26 Stat. 209, 15 U.S.C. §1.

35. *Clayton Antitrust Act of 1914*, 38 Stat. 370, 15 U.S.C. §12, and *Federal Trade Commission Act of 1914*, 38 Stat. 717, 15 U.S.C. §41.

36. *Public Utility Holding Company Act of 1935*, 49 Stat. 803, 15 U.S.C. §79.

37. *Hylton v. United States*, 3 U.S. 171, 3 Dall. 171 (1796) and *United States v. Butler*, 197 U.S. 1 at 66, 56 S.Ct. 312 at 319 (1936).

38. *South Dakota v. Dole*, 483 U.S. 203 at 206–08, 107 S.Ct. 2793 at 2795–796 (1987).

39. *Morrill Act of 1862*, 12 Stat. 503, 7 U.S.C. §301.

40. *Hatch Act of 1887*, 24 Stat. 400, 7 U.S.C. §362.

41. *Carey Act of 1894*, 28 Stat. 422, 43 U.S.C. §461.

42. *Weeks Act of 1911*, 36 Stat. 961, 16 U.S.C. §552.

43. *McGee v. Mathias*, 71 U.S. 143, 4 Wall. 143 (1866).

44. *Massachusetts v. Mellon*, 262 U.S. 447, 43 S.Ct. 597 (1923).

45. *Federal Road Aid Act of 1916*, 39 Stat. 358, 23 U.S.C. §48.

46. *Transportation Act of 1920*, 41 Stat. 456.

47. *National Defense and Interstate Highway Act of 1956*, 70 Stat. 374, 23 U.S.C. §101.

48. *Hatch Act of 1939*, 53 Stat. 1147, 5 U.S.C. §118(i).

49. *Emergency Highway Energy Conservation Act of 1974*, 87 Stat. 1046, 23 U.S.C. §101 note.

50. *Energy Policy and Conservation Act of 1975*, 89 Stat. 933, 42 U.S.C. §6201.

51. *Highway Safety Amendments of 1984*, 98 Stat. 437, 23 U.S.C. §158.

52. *South Dakota v. Doyle*, 483 U.S. 203, 107 S.Ct. 2793 (1987).

53. *Transportation Equity Act of 1998*, 112 Stat. 240, 23 U.S.C. §163.

54. *Hotel and Motel Fire Safety Act of 1990*, 104 Stat. 747, 5 U.S.C. §701.

55. *National Driver Register Act of 1982*, 96 Stat. 1740, 23 U.S.C. §401 note.

56. 24 Stat. 209 (1886).

57. *Shollenberger v. Pennsylvania*, 171 U.S. 1, 18 S.Ct. 757 (1898). See also *Pennsylvania Laws of 1885*, Public Law 22 and *Pennsylvania Statutes*, §§844 et seq.

58. *Revenue Act of 1926*, 44 Stat. 9, 48 U.S.C. §845.

59. *Social Security Act of 1935*, 49 Stat. 620, 42 U.S.C. §301.

60. *Tax Equity and Fiscal Responsibility Act of 1982*, 96 Stat. 324, 26 U.S.C. §1.

61. *South Carolina v. Baker*, 485 U.S. 505, 108 S.Ct. 1355 (1988).

62. *Tax Reform Act of 1986*, 100 Stat. 2085, 26 U.S.C. §1.

63. *Copyright Act of 1790*, 1 Stat. 124, 17 U.S.C. §101, and *Patent Act of 1790*, 1 Stat. 109, 35 U.S.C. §1.

64. *Digital Millennium Copyright Act of 1998*, 112 Stat. 2860, 17 U.S.C. §101 note.

65. *Oregon-Washington Railway & Navigation Company v. Washington*, 270 U.S. 87 at 93, 46 S.Ct. 279 at 283 (1926).

66. *Washington Laws of 1921*, chap. 105.

67. *Oregon-Washington Railway & Navigation Company v. Washington*, 270 U.S. 87, 46 S.Ct. 279 (1926). See also 37 Stat. 315 (1912) and 39 Stat. 1165.

68. Joseph F. Zimmerman and Sharon Lawrence, *Federal Statutory Preemption of State and Local Authority: History, Inventory, and Issues* (Washington, DC: U.S. Advisory Commission on Intergovernmental Relations, 1992), pp. 53–59.

69. *Standard Apple Barrel Act of 1912*, 37 Stat. 250; *Grain Standards Act of 1916*, 39 Stat. 453; and *United States Cotton Standards Act of 1923*, 42 Stat. 1517.

70. Joseph F. Zimmerman, *Federal Preemption: The Silent Revolution* (Ames: Iowa State University Press, 1991), pp. 58–61 and 152–58.

71. *New York v. United States*, 505 U.S. 144 at 166, 112 S.Ct. 2408 at 2423. See also *Low Level Radioactive Policy Act of 1980*, 94 Stat. 3347, 42 U.S.C. §2021d.

72. *Surface Transportation Assistance Act of 1982*, 96 Stat. 2097, 23 U.S.C. §101.

73. *Ocean Dumping Ban Act of 1988*, 102 Stat. 4139, 33 U.S.C. §1401A.

74. Jim Yardley, "New York's Sewage Was a Texas Town's Gold," *New York Times*, July 27, 2001, p. A12.

75. *Violent Crime Control and Law Enforcement Act of 1994*, 108 Stat. 2099, 18 U.S.C. §2721 note.

76. *Omnibus Budget Reconciliation Act of 1986*, 100 Stat. 1892.

77. *Policy Positions: 1980–81* (Washington, DC: National Governors' Association, 1980).

78. *Commercial Motor Vehicle Safety Act of 1986*, 100 Stat. 3207, 49 U.S.C. §2701.

79. Zimmerman and Lawrence, *Federal Statutory Preemption of State and Local Authority*, p. 24.

80. *Flammable Fabrics Act*, 81 Stat. 574, 15 U.S.C. §1191.

81. *United States Grain Standards Act* of 1968, 82 Stat. 769, 7 U.S.C. §71.

82. 14 Stat. 81 (1866).

83. 92 Stat. 1444, 49 U.S.C. §11501(g)(1) (1978).

84. Ibid., 49 U.S.C. §11501(g)(2).

85. *Gun Control Act of 1968*, 82 Stat. 1226, 18 U.S.C. §921.

86. *Bankruptcy Act of 1933*, 47 Stat. 1467, 11 U.S.C. §101, and *Clean Air Act Amendments of 1970*, 84 Stat. 1676, 42 U.S.C. §1857.

87. See, for example, *The Bus Regulatory Reform Act of 1980*, 96 Stat. 1104, 49 U.S.C. §10521.

88. *Atomic Energy Act of 1946*, 60 Stat. 755, 42 U.S.C. §2011.

89. *United States Grain Standards Act*, 82 Stat. 769, 7 U.S.C. §71.

90. *Federal Railroad Safety Act of 1970*, 84 Stat. 971, 45 U.S.C. §431.

91. *Age Discrimination in Employment Amendments of 1986*, 100 Stat. 3342, 29 U.S.C. §623.

92. *Atomic Energy Act of 1959*, 73 Stat. 688, 42 U.S.C. §2021.

93. *Port and Tanker Safety Act of 1978*, 92 Stat. 1475–476, 33 U.S.C. §1226.

94. *An Act to Establish a Uniform System of Bankruptcy of 1898*, 30 Stat. 544, 11 U.S.C. §1 and *Bankruptcy Act of 1933*, 47 Stat. 1467, 11 U.S.C. §1.

95. Philip Shenon, "Home Exemptions Snag Bankruptcy Bill," *New York Times*, April 6, 2001, pp. 1, A19.

96. Philip Shenon, "Home As Shield from Creditors Is Under Fire," *New York Times*, April 4, 2002, p. C1.

97. *National Banking Act of 1864*, 13 Stat. 99, 12 U.S.C. §85.

98. *McFadden Act of 1933*, 44 Stat. 1224, 12 U.S.C. §24.

99. *Electronic Signatures in Global and National Commerce Act of 2000*, 114 Stat. 467–68, 15 U.S.C. §7002.

100. *Port and Tanker Safety Act of 1978*, 92 Stat. 1475, 33 U.S.C. §1225.

101. *Natural Gas Policy Act of 1978*, 92 Stat. 3409, 15 U.S.C. §3431.

102. *Water Quality Act of 1965*, 79 Sat. 903, 33 U.S.C. §1131.

103. Interview with Connecticut Commissioner of Environmental Protection Stanley J. Pac, Hartford, CT, November 8, 1985.

104. *Clean Water Act of 1977*, 91 Stat. 1577, 33 U.S.C. §1342.

105. *Air Quality Act of 1967*, 81 Stat. 485, 42 U.S.C. §1857; *Safe Drinking Water Act of 1974*, 88 Stat. 1665, 42 U.S.C. §201; and *Surface Mining Control and Reclamation Act of 1977*; 91 Stat. 445, 30 U.S.C. §1201.

106. *Hodel v. Virginia Surface Mining and Reclamation Association*, 452 U.S. 264 at 287, 101 S.Ct. 2352 at 2366 (1981).

107. Matthew Potoski, "Clean Air Federalism: Do States Race to the Bottom?" *Public Administration Review* 61, May/June 2001, pp. 337, 339.

108. *Natural Gas Policy Act of 1978*, 92 Stat. 3409, 15 U.S.C. §3431.

109. *Occupational Safety and Health Act of 1970*, 84 Stat. 1590, 5 U.S.C. §1508.

110. *Ohio Manufacturers Association v. City of Akron*, 801 F.2d 824 at 831 (6th Cir. 1986), 16 Envtl.L.Rep. 20942. See also *Ohio Manufacturers Association v. City of Akron*, 628 Fed. Supp. 623 (N.D. Oh, 1986).

111. *Toxic Substances Control Act of 1976*, 90 Stat. 2038, 15 U.S.C. §2617.

112. Ibid., 90 Stat. 2039, 14 U.S.C. §2617.

113. *Gibbons v. Ogden*, 22 U.S. 1 at 197, 9 Wheat. 1 at 197 (1824).

114. Herbert Wechsler, "The Political Safeguards of Federalism: The Role of the States in the Composition and Selection of the National Government," in Arthur W. MacMahon, ed., *Federalism: Mature and Emergent* (New York: Columbia University Press, 1955), pp. 97–114.

115. *Garcia v. San Antonio Metropolitan Transit Authority*, 469 U.S. 528 at 556, 105 S.Ct. 1005 at 1020 (1985).

116. Joseph F. Zimmerman, *Contemporary American Federalism: The Growth of National Power* (Leicester: Leicester University Press, 1992), pp. 68–70.

117. *Safe Drinking Water Act Amendments of 1986*, 100 Stat. 651, 42 U.S.C. §300.

118. *Safe Drinking Water Act Amendments of 1996*, 110 Stat. 1613, 42 U.S.C. §201 note.

119. *Weeks Act of 1911*, 36 Stat. 961, 16 U.S.C. §522.

120. *Emergency Highway Energy Conservation Act of 1974*, 87 Stat. 1046, 23 U.S.C. §101 note.

121. *National Driver Register Act of 1982*, 96 Stat. 1740, 23 U.S.C. §401 note.

122. *Department of Transportation Appropriation Act of 1991*, 104 Stat. 2185, 23 U.S.C. §104 note.

123. *Hotel and Motel Fire Safety Act of 1990*, 104 Stat. 747, 5 U.S.C. §701.

124. *Clean Air Act Amendments of 1990*, 104 Stat. 2448, 42 U.S.C. §7511c.

125. Matthew L. Wald, "California Car Rules Set as Model for the East," *New York Times*, December 20, 1994, p. A16.

126. "New Report Shows Success Story in Air Pollution Trading," a news release issued by the Ozone Transport Commission, March 27, 2000.

127. *Gramm-Leach-Bliley Financial Reorganization Act of 1999*, 113 Stat. 1353, 5 U.S.C. §701(d)(2)(A).

128. *Electronic Signatures in Global and National Commerce Act*, 114 Stat. 468, 15 U.S.C. §7002.

Chapter 4

1. *The Federalist Papers* (New York: New American Library, 1961), p. 150.

2. *United States Constitution*, Art. I, §8 and Art. III, §1.

3. *The Federalist Papers*, pp. 467–69 and 472.

4. Ibid., p. 485.

5. Ibid., pp. 467–68.

6. *McCulloch v. Maryland*, 17 U.S. 316, 4 Wheat. 316 (1819).

7. *U.S. Constitution*, Art. II, §2.

8. Ibid., Art. III, §2.

9. 62 Stat. 968, 28 U.S.C. §2283.

10. 110 Stat. 3850, 28 U.S.C. §1332.

11. *Winkler v. Pringle*, 214 F. Supp. 125 at 126 (W.D.Pa 1963).

12. *Winkler v. Pringle*, 324 F.2d 613 (3rd Cir. 1963), and *Winkler v. Pringle*, 377 U.S. 908, 84 S.Ct. 1169 (1964).

13. *Judiciary Act of 1789*, 1 Stat 73 at 80–81. The act also grants the U.S. Supreme Court authority to promulgate necessary rules for the conduct of business in all U.S. courts.

14. *Missouri v. Illinois*, 200 U.S. 496, 26 S.Ct. 268 (1905).

15. *Texas v. New Mexico*, 462 U.S. 554 at 570, 103 S.Ct. 2558 at 2568 (1983) and *Wyoming v. Oklahoma*, 502 U.S. 437 at 451, 112 S.Ct. 789 at 798 (1992).

16. See the dissent of Justice William H. Rehnquist in *Maryland v. Louisiana*, 451 U.S. 725 at 765, 101 S.Ct. 2114 at 2139 (1981).

17. *Illinois v. City of Milwaukee*, 406 U.S. 91, 92 S.Ct 1385 (1972).

18. *Puerto Rico v. Iowa*, 464 U.S. 1034, 104 S.Ct. 692 (1984).

19. *Oklahoma v. Arkansas*, 460 U.S. 1020, 103 S.Ct 1268 (1983).

20. *Louisiana v. Texas*, 176 U.S. 1, 20 S.Ct. 251 (1900).

21. *Pennsylvania v. New Jersey*, 426 U.S. 660 at 666, 96 S.Ct. 2333 at 2336 (1976).

22. Ibid., 426 U.S. 660 at 665, 96 S.Ct. 2333 at 2335.

23. *Tax Reform Act of 1976*, 90 Stat. 1914, 15 U.S.C. §391.

24. *Connecticut et al. v. New Hampshire.* Answer of Defendant State of New Hampshire, March 24, 1992.

25. *Connecticut, Massachusetts, and Rhode Island: Report of the Special Master*, December 30, 1992.

26. Telephone interview with New Hampshire Senior Assistant Attorney General Harold T. Judd, October 22, 1993.

27. *Texas v. Florida*, 306 U.S. 398, 59 S.Ct. 830 (1939).

28. *California v. Texas*, 437 U.S. 601, 98 S.Ct. 3107 (1978).

29. *California v. Texas*, 457 U.S. 164, 102 S.Ct. 2335 (1982).

30. Ibid.

31. *Massachusetts v. Missouri*, 301 U.S. 1 at 15, 60 S.Ct. 39 at 42 (1940).

32. *California v. Texas*, 454 U.S. 886, 102 S.Ct. 378 (1981).

33. *Ohio v. Wyandotte Chemicals Corporation*, 401 U.S. 493 at 499, 91 S.Ct. 1005 at 1010 (1971); *Arizona v. New Mexico*, 425 U.S. 794 at 796–97, 96 S.Ct. 1845 at 1847 (1976); *California v. West Virginia*, 457 U.S. 1027, S.Ct. (1981); and *Louisiana v. Mississippi*, 488 U.S. 990, 109 S.Ct. 551 (1988).

34. *California v. West Virginia*, 454 U.S. 1027, 102 S.Ct. 561 (1981).

35. *Arizona v. New Mexico*, 425 U.S. 794, 96 S.Ct. 1845 (1976).

36. *Louisiana v. Mississippi*, 488 U.S. 990, 109 S.Ct. 551 (1988).

37. Vincent L. McKusick, "Discretionary Gatekeeping: The Supreme Court's Management of Its Original Jurisdiction Docket Since 1961," *Maine Law Review* 45, 1993, p. 202.

38. *Kansas v. Colorado*, 185 U.S. 125 at 146–47, 22 S.Ct. 552 at 560 (1902).

39. *Kansas v. Colorado*, 206 U.S. 46 at 97, 27 S.Ct. 655 at 667 (1907).

40. *Arizona v. California*, 202 U.S. 341 at 359–60, 26 S.Ct. 688 at 689–90 (1934).

41. McKusick, "Discretionary Gatekeeping," pp. 207–15.

42. *New York v. Connecticut*, 4 U.S. 3, 4 Dall. 3 (1799), and *New Mexico v. Texas*, 275 U.S. 279, 48 S.Ct. 126 (1927).

43. *Louisiana v. Mississippi*, 466 U.S. 96, 104 S.Ct. 1645 (1984).

44. *Louisiana v. Mississippi*, 202 U.S. 1 at 49, 26 S.Ct. 408 at 421 (1906).

45. *Louisiana v. Mississippi*, 514 U.S. 1002, 115 S.Ct. 1310 (1995).

46. *California v. Nevada*, 447 U.S. 125, 100 S.Ct. 2064 (1980).

47. *Illinois v. Kentucky*, 500 U.S. 380 at 383, 111 S.Ct. 1887 at 1881 (1991).

48. *New Hampshire v. Maine*, 426 U.S. 363, 96 S.Ct. 2113 (1976). See also "New Hampshire Goes to High Court in Lobster Dispute," *New York Times*, June 7, 1973, p. 43, and "230–Year Border Fight Settled by Maine and New Hampshire," *New York Times*, July 11, 1974, p. 18.

49. 95 Stat. 988 (1981). See also "North Carolina-South Carolina Seaward Boundary Agreement," *Congressional Record*, September 29, 1981, pp. H6667–668.

50. 113 Stat. 1333 (1999).

51. 114 Stat. 919 (2000).

52. "Justice Department Sides with NH Workers at Shipyard . . . If It's Not in Maine," *Union Leader* (Manchester, NH), October 24, 1990, pp. 1, 16.

53. *Kansas v. Colorado*, 206 U.S. 46, 27 S.Ct. 655 (1907).

54. *Arizona v. California*, 373 U.S. 546, 83 S.Ct. 1468 (1963).

55. Douglas Jehl, "U.S. Approves Water Plan in California, but Environmental Opposition Remains," *New York Times*, August 31, 2002, p. A8.

56. Dale Kasler, "San Diego Attempts to Make Water Deal Work," *Sacramento Bee*, August 28, 2002 (Internet edition).

57. *Nebraska v. Wyoming*, 325 U.S. 589, 65 S.Ct. 1332 (1945).

58. *Nebraska v. Wyoming*, 507 U.S. 584, 113 S.Ct. 1689 (1993).

59. *Nebraska v. Wyoming*, 515U.S.1, 115 S.Ct. 1933 (1995).

60. Ibid., 515 U.S. 1 at 11, 115 S.Ct. 1933 at 1939.

61. *New Jersey v. New York*, 283 U.S. 805, 51 S.Ct. 562 (1931).

62. *New Jersey v. New York*, 347 U.S. 995, 74 S.Ct. 842 (1954).

63. Jeffrey P. Featherstone, "An Evaluation of Federal-Interstate Compacts As an Institutional Model for Intergovernmental Coordination and Management: Water Resources for Interstate River Basins in the United States" (Philadelphia: Unpublished Ph. D. Dissertation, Temple University, 1999), p. 84.

64. *Texas v. New Mexico*, 482 U.S. 124, 107 S.Ct. 2279 (1987).

65. *Texas v. New Mexico*, 446 U.S. 540, 100 S.Ct. 2911 (1980).

66. *Texas v. New Mexico*, 467 U.S. 1238, 104 S.Ct. 3505 (1984).

67. *Texas v. New Mexico*, 485 U.S. 388, 108 S.Ct. 1201 (1988)

68. Mark Henckel, "Montana Now Among States Looking to Courts to Maintain Water Levels," *Billings Gazette*, May 13, 2002 (Internet edition).

69. Jack Money, "State Ready to Sue Texas Over Water," *The Oklahoman*, August 26, 2002 (Internet edition).

70. Alexander Hanrath, "For Moves to Take Steam Out of 'Water War,'" *Financial Times*, June 7, 2002, p. 7.

71. Ibid.

72. Tim Weiner, "U.S. Reaches Partial Deal with Mexico Over Water," *New York Times*, July 5, 2002, p. A14.

73. *Maryland v. Louisiana*, 451 U.S. 725, 101 S.Ct. 2114 (1981).

74. *Wyoming v. Oklahoma*, 502 U.S. 437, 112 S.Ct. 789 (1992).

75. Ibid., 502 U.S. 437 at 476, 112 S.Ct. 789 at 811.

76. Consult, for example, *New York Abandoned Property Law*, §511.

77. *Texas v. New Jersey*, 379 U.S. 674, 85 S.Ct. 626 (1972).

78. Ibid., 379 U.S. 674 at 680–81, 85 S.Ct. 626 at 630.

79. *Pennsylvania v. New York*, 407 U.S. 206, 92 S.Ct. 2075 (1972).

80. *Delaware v. New York*, 507 U.S. 490, 113 S.Ct. 1550 (1993).

81. Ibid., 507 U.S. 490 at 508, 113 S.Ct. 1550 at 1561.

82. Theresa Humphrey, "States Agree to Share Unclaimed Payments," *Times Union* (Albany, NY), January 7, 1995, p. B2.

83. E. Parmalee Prentice and John G. Egan, *The Commerce Clause of the Federal Constitution* (Chicago: Callaghan and Company, 1898), p. 14.

84. 1 Stat. 305 (1793).

85. *Gibbons v. Ogden*, 22 U.S. 1, 9 Wheat. 1 (1824).

86. Ibid., 22 U.S. 1 at 189, 9 Wheat. 1 at 189.

87. Ibid., 22 U.S. 1 at 194, 9 Wheat. 1 at 194.

88. *Brown v. Maryland*, 25 U.S. 419, 12 Wheat. 419, (1827).

89. Ibid., 25 U.S. 410 at 449, 12 Wheat. 419 at 449.

90. *Willson v. The Black-Bird Creek Marsh Company*, 27 U.S. 245, 2 Pet. 245 (1829).

91. Ibid., 27 U.S. 245 at 252, 3 Pet. 245 at 252.

92. Prentice and Egan, *The Commerce Clause of the Federal Constitution*, p. 21.

93. *Thurlow v. Massachusetts, Fletcher v. Rhode Island*, and *Peirce v. New Hampshire*, 46 U.S. 504, 5 How. 504 (1847).

94. Ibid., 46 U.S. 504 at 572, 5 How. 504 at 572.

95. *Cooley v. The Board of Wardens*, 53 U.S. 299, 12 How. 299 (1851).

96. Felix Frankfurter, *The Commerce Clause Under Marshall, Taney, and White* (Chapel Hill: University of North Carolina Press, 1937).

97. Ibid., p. 50.

98. *In re State Freight Tax*, 82 U.S. 232, 15 Wall. 232 (1872).

99. Frankfurter, *The Commerce Clause Under Marshall, Taney, and Waite*.

100. *Welton v. Missouri*, 91 U.S. 275, 1 Otto 275 (1875).

101. *Illinois Laws of 1871*, chap. 114.

102. *Munn v. Illinois*, 94 U.S. 113, 1 Otto 113 (1876).

103. Ibid., 94 U.S. 113 at 133–34, 1 Otto 113 at 133–34.

104. *Brown v. Houston*, 114 U.S. 622 at 634, 5 S.Ct. 1091 at 1097 (1885).

105. *Robbins v. Shelby County Taxing District*, 120 U.S 489, 7 S.Ct. 592 (1887).

106. Ibid., 120 U.S. 489 at 492, 7 S.Ct. 592 at 593.

107. *Minnesota v. Barber*, 136 U.S. 313, 10 S.Ct. 862 (1890).

108. *Michelin Tire Corporation v. Wages*, 423 U.S. 276 at 286, 96 S.Ct. 535 at 541 (1976).

109. *H.P. Hood & Sons v. DuMond*, 336 U.S. 525 at 534–35, 69 S.Ct. 657 at 663–64 (1949).

110. See, for example, the *Flammable Fabrics Act of 1967*, 81 Stat. 574, 15 U.S.C. §1191.

111. George B. Braden, "Umpire to the Federal System," *The University of Chicago Law Review* 10, October 1942, p. 45.

112. *Hines v. Davidowitz*, 312 U.S. 52 at 67, 61 S.Ct. 399 at 404 (1941).

113. *Rice v. Santa Fe Elevator*, 331 U.S. 218, 67 S.Ct. 1146 (1947).

114. *City of Burbank v. Lockheed Air Terminal*, 411 U.S. 624 at 632, 93 S.Ct. 1854 at 1859 (1973).

115. *Chapman v. Houston Welfare Rights Organization*, 441 U.S. 600, 99 S.Ct. 1905 (1979).

116. *Ray v. Atlantic Richfield Company*, 435 U.S. 151, 98 S.Ct. 988 (1978).

117. *Hodel v. Virginia Surface Mining and Reclamation Association*, 452 U.S. 264, 101 S.Ct. 2352 (1981), *National League of Cities v. Usery*, 426 U.S. 833, 96 S.Ct. 2465 (1976), and *Surface Mining Control and Reclamation Act of 1977*, 91 Stat. 445, 30 U.S.C. §1201.

118. *Hodel v. Virginia Surface Mining and Reclamation Association*, 452 U.S. 264 at 287, 101 S.Ct. 2352 at 2366.

119. Ibid.

120. Ibid.

121. *New York v. United States*, 505 U.S. 144 at 175, 112 S.Ct. 2408 at 2428 (1992).

122. *Judiciary Act of 1789*, 1 Stat. 73.

123. 110 Stat 3850, 28 U.S.C. §1332.

124. 13 Stat. 470 (1875).

125. 48 Stat. 955, 28 U.S.C. §2283.

126. John W. Winkle III, "Dimensions of Judicial Federalism," *The Annals of the American Academy of Political and Social Science* 416, November 1974, p. 71.

127. "Finding the Forum for a Victory," *National Law Journal* 13, February 11, 1991, pp. S3–S4.

128. *Removal of Causes Act of 1920*, 41 Stat. 554, 28 U.S.C. §1441. See also Georgene M. Vairo, "Removal Update," *National Law Journal* 24, July 15, 2002, p. B11.

129. *Caterpillar Incorporated v. Lewis*, 519 U.S. 61, 117 S.Ct. 467 (1996).

130. *Wisconsin Department of Corrections v. Schacht*, 524 U.S. 381, 118 S.Ct. 2047 (1998).

Chapter 5

1. *U.S. Constitution*, Art. I, §8. See also *The Federalist Papers* (New York: New American Library), pp. 54–58.

2. *The Federalist Papers*, pp. 62–63.

3. Ibid., pp. 267–68.

4. *U.S. Constitution*, Art. I, §§8–10 and Art. IV, §2.

5. "NH Commissioner Critical of Vermont Seal of Quality," *Union Leader* (Manchester, NH), October 6, 1993, p. 14.

6. *Noble State Bank v. Haskell*, 219 U.S. 104 at 111, 31 S.Ct. 186 at 188 (1911).

7. *Minnesota Laws of 1889*, chap. 8.

8. *Minnesota v. Barber*, 136 U.S. 313, 10 S.Ct. 862 (1890).

9. *Florida Lime and Avocado Growers, Incorporated v. Paul*, 197 F. Supp. 780 (N.D. Ca, 1961).

10. *Florida Lime and Avocado Growers, Incorporated v. Paul*, 373 U.S. 132, 83 S.Ct. 1210 (1963).

11. Ibid., 373 U.S. 132 at 146, 150; 83 S.Ct. 1210 at 1217, 1221.

12. 1 Stat. 474 (1796).

13. *Cattle Contagious Diseases Act of 1884*, 23 Stat. 31, and *Plant Quarantine Act of 1912*, 37 Stat. 315.

14. "States Impose Quarantine on California Produce," *The Keene (NH) Sentinel*, July 10, 1981, p. 5.

15. "Sick Chickens Force Quarantine in PA," *Knickerbocker News* (Albany, NY), November 5, 1983, p. 2A, and William Robbins, "3 Million Chickens Destroyed in Bid to Halt Spread of Virus," *New York Times*, November 28, 1983, pp. 1, B11.

16. "U.S. and Florida Fight Texas and California Over Citrus Shipments," *New York Times*, February 16, 1988, p. A13.

17. George R. Taylor, Edgar L. Burtis, and Frederick V. Waugh, *Barriers to Internal Trade in Farm Products* (Washington, DC: U.S. Department of Agriculture, 1939), p. 92.

18. Lester R. Johnson, "No Maine Potatoes in Idaho?" *Congressional Record*, June 15, 1959, p. A5127.

19. Ibid.

20. *Dean Milk Company v. City of Madison*, 340 U.S. 349, 71 S.Ct. 295 (1951).

21. Bill Eager, "Vermont Milk Legal in New York," *Times Union* (Albany, NY), June 11, 1994, p. B2.

22. *Hunt v. Washington Apple Advertising Commission*, 432 U.S. 333, 97 S.Ct. 2434 (1977).

23. "Act Aiding Sale of State Wines Is Struck Down," *New York Times*, January 31, 1985, p. B3.

24. 1 Stat. 474 (1796).

25. *Contagious Disease Act of 1903*, 32 Stat. 301.

26. *Terminal Inspection Act of 1915*, 38 Stat. 1113. See also the 1936 amendments, 49 Stat. 1461.

27. Frederick E. Melder, *State and Local Barriers to Interstate Commerce in the United States* (Orono, Maine: University Press, 1937), p. 14.

28. F. Eugene Melder, "Trade Barriers Between States," *The Annals of the American Academy of Political and Social Science* 207, January 1940, p. 58.

29. "2 States to Allow New York Business," *Times Union* (Albany, NY), October 14, 1995, p. B8.

30. *Reeves Incorporated v. Stake et al.*, 447 U.S. 429, 100 S.Ct. 2271 (1980).

31. *State Board of Tax Commissioners v. Jackson*, 283 U.S. 527, 51 S.Ct. 540 (1931).

32. Information in this and the following three paragraphs are derived in part from W.R. Pabst Jr., *Butter and Oleomargarine: An Analysis of Competing Commodities* (New York: Columbia University Press, 1937).

33. *Pennsylvania Laws of 1885*, Public Law 22.

34. *Powell v. Pennsylvania*, 127 U.S. 678, 8 S.Ct. 992 (1888).

35. 24 Stat. 209 (1886).

36. *Schollenberger v. Pennsylvania* 171 U.S. 1 at 12, 18 S.Ct. 757 at 761 (1898).

37. Joseph F. Zimmerman, *The Referendum: The People Decide Public Policy* (Westport, CT: Praeger Publishers, 2001).

38. *Grout Act of 1902*, 32 Stat. 193.

39. *Brigham-Townsend Act of 1931*, 46 Stat. 1549.

40. George R. Taylor, Edgar L. Burtis, and Frederick V. Waugh, *Barriers to Internal Trade in Farm Products* (Washington, DC: U.S. Government Printing Office, 1939), p. 20.

41. Ibid., p. 28.

42. Ibid., pp. 33–34.

43. *Florida Statutes*, §319.231 (1991).

44. *Department of Revenue v. Kuhnlein*, 646 So. 2d 717 (Fla, 1994).

45. Alan Cooper, "Out-of-This-World Taxes Are Voided: Satellite Devices Levy to Be Refunded," *Richmond Times-Dispatch*, April 22, 2002, p. 1. The decision is available online at www.courts.state.va.us/txtops/1011307.txt.

46. *City of Virginia Beach v. International Family Entertainment, Incorporated*, 263 Va. 501, 561 S.E.2d 696 (Va, 2002).

47. *McCarran-Ferguson Act of 1945*, 59 Stat. 33, 15 U.S.C. §1011.

48. Telephone interview with Steven Maluk, assistant director of policies of the New York State Department of Insurance, Albany, NY, February 5, 2001.

49. *Metropolitan Life Insurance Company v. Ward*, 470 U.S. 869, 105 S.Ct. 1676 (1985).

50. *Gramm-Leach-Bliley Financial Reorganization Act of 1999*, 113 Stat. 1353, 1422; 5 U.S.C. §§6701(d)(2)(A), 6751. See also Paul Hummer and Michael F. Consedine, "Insurance Catches Up to Internet Revolution," *National Law Journal* 22, March 20, 2000, pp. B9, B15.

51. *Massachusetts v. Missouri*, 308 U.S. 1 at 16–17, 60 S.Ct. 39 at 42–43 (1939).

52. W. Brooke Graves, *Uniform State Action: A Possible Substitution for Centralization* (Chapel Hill: The University of North Carolina Press, 1934), pp. 192–93.

53. Ibid., pp. 195–97.

54. *State and Provincial Licensing Systems* (Washington, DC: National Highway Traffic Safety Administration, 1990), p. 123.

55. Ibid., p. 108.

56. Graves, *Uniform State Action*, p. 229.

57. Joseph F. Zimmerman, *Interstate Cooperation: Compacts and Administrative Agreements* (Westport, CT: Praeger Publishers, 2002).

58. Consult *New York Agriculture and Markets Law*, §258–n; *New York Social Services Law*, §32; and *New York Public Health Law*, §2205.

59. Joseph F. Zimmerman, *Federal Preemption: The Silent Revolution* (Ames: Iowa State University Press, 1991).

60. *Bankruptcy Act of 1898*, 30 Stat. 544, 11 U.S.C. §1.

61. *Hours of Service Act of 1907*, 34 Stat. 1415, 45 U.S.C. §22, and *Boiler Inspection Act of 1911*, 36 Stat. 913, 45 U.S.C. §22.

62. *Transportation Act of 1920*, 41 Stat. 484.

63. *Wool Products Labeling Act of 1940*, 54 Stat. 1128, 15 U.S.C. §68 and *Fur Products Labeling Act of 1951*, 65 Stat. 175, 15 U.S.C. §69.

64. *Automotive Information Disclosure Act of 1958*, 72 Stat. 325, 15 U.S.C. §1231.

65. *Grain Standards Act of 1968*, 82 Stat. 769, 7 U.S.C. §71.

66. *Egg Products Inspection Act of 1970*, 84 Stat. 1623, 21 U.S.C. §301, and *Nutrition Labeling and Education Act of 1990*, 104 Stat. 2353, 21 U.S.C. §301 note.

67. *Airline Deregulation Act of 1978*, 92 Stat. 1708, 49 U.S.C. §§1305 and 1371; *Motor Carrier Act of 1980*, 94 Stat. 793, 49 U.S.C. §1101; and *Bus Regulatory Reform Act of 1982*, 96 Stat. 1104, 49 U.S.C. §10521.

68. *Policy Positions: 1980–81* (Washington, DC: National Governors' Association, 1980).

69. *Surface Transportation Assistance Act of 1982*, 96 Stat. 2097, 23 U.S.C. §101. Consult also Seung-Ho Lee, *Federal Preemption of State Truck Size and Weight Laws: New York State's Reaction and Preemption Relief* (Albany: unpublished Ph. D. Dissertation, State University of New York at Albany, 1994).

70. *Motor Carrier Safety Act of 1984*, 98 Stat. 2832, 42 U.S.C. §2501 and *Tandem Truck Safety Act of 1984*, 98 Stat. 2829–830, 42 U.S.C. §2301.

71. *Motor Carrier Safety Act of 1991*, 105 Stat. 2140, 49 U.S.C. App. §2302(b)(1).

72. Ibid.

73. *McCarran-Ferguson Act of 1945*, 59 Stat. 33, 15 U.S.C. §1011.

74. 1 Stat. 474 and 619, and *Plant Quarantine Act of 1912*, 37 Stat. 315, 7 U.S.C. §151.

75. *McFadden Act of 1937*, 44 Stat. 1224, 12 U.S.C. §§36 and 332.

76. *First National Bank in St. Louis v. Missouri*, 263 U.S. 640, 44 S.Ct. 213 (1924).

77. *Bank Holding Compact Act of 1956*, 70 Stat. 133, 12 U.S.C. §1841.

78. Ibid., 70 Stat. 135, 12 U.S.C. §1849(a).

79. *Northeast Bankcorp. v. Board of Governors of the Federal Reserve System*, 472 U.S. 159, 105 S.Ct. 2545 (1985).

80. *Interstate Banking and Branching Efficiency Act of 1994*, 108 Stat. 2339, 12 U.S.C. §159. Also consult Susan McLaughlin, "The Impact of Interstate Banking and Branching Reform: Evidence from the States," *Current Issues in Economics and Finance* 1, May 1995, pp. 1–5.

81. *Marquette National Bank v. First of Omaha Service Corporation*, 439 U.S. 299, 99 S.Ct. 540 (1978).

82. *Gibbons v. Ogden*, 22 U.S. 1, 9 Wheat. 1 (1824).

83. *Brown v. Maryland*, 25 U.S. 419 at 420, 12 Wheat. 419 at 420 (1827).

84. Ibid., 25 U.S. 419 at 449, 12 Wheat. 419 at 449.

85. *Thurlow v. The Commonwealth of Massachusetts* (The License Cases), 46 U.S. 504, 5 How. 504 (1847).

86. *Cooley v. The Board of Wardens of the Port of Philadelphia*, 53 U.S. 299, 12 How. 299 (1851).

87. *Hinson v. Lott*, 75 U.S. 148, 8 Wall. 148 (1868).

88. *Walling v. Michigan*, 116 U.S. 446, 6 S.Ct. 454 (1886).

89. Ibid., 116 U.S. 446 at 459, 6 S.Ct. 454 at 457.

90. *Minnesota v. Barber*, 136 U.S. 313, 10 S.Ct. 862 (1890).

91. *General American Tank Car Corporation v. Day*, 270 U.S. 367, 46 S.Ct. 234 (1926).

92. *Louisiana Constitution of 1921*, Art. 10, §16.

93. *General American Tank Corporation v. Day*, 20 U.S. 367 at 373, 46 S.Ct. 234 at 236 (1926).

94. *Gregg Dyeing Company v. Query*, 286 U.S. 472, 52 S.Ct. 631 (1932).

95. *Mintz et al. v. Baldwin*, 289 U.S. 346, 53 S.Ct. 611 (1933).

96. *Baldwin v. G.A.F. Seelig, Incorporated*, 294 U.S. 511, 55 S.Ct. 497 (1935).

97. Michael E. Smith, "State Discriminations Against Interstate Commerce," *California Law Review* 74, 1986, pp. 1205–206.

98. *South Carolina State Highway Department v. Barnwell Brothers*, 303 U.S. 177, 58 S.Ct. 510 (1938).

99. Ibid., 303 U.S. 177 at 195, 58 S.Ct. 510 at 519.

100. *Western Live Stock v. Bureau of Revenue*, 303 U.S. 250 at 254, 58 S.Ct. 546 at 548 (1938).

101. *Clark v. Paul Gray, Incorporated*, 306 U.S. 583 at 594, 59 S.Ct. 744 at 751 (1939).

102. Robert H. Jackson, "The Supreme Court and Interstate Barriers," *The Annals of the American Academy of Political and Social Science* 207, January 1940, pp. 75–76.

103. *Prudential Insurance Company v. Benjamin*, 328 U.S. 408, 66 S.Ct. 1142 (1946).

104. *Western & Southern Life Insurance Company v. State Board of Equalization*, 451 U.S. 648 at 655–56 101 S.Ct. 2070 at 2076–077 (1981).

105. *Constitution of California*, Art. XIII, §14 4/5(f)(3).

106. *Metropolitan Life Insurance Company v. Ward*, 470 U.S. 869, 105 S.Ct. 1676 (1985).

107. *H.P. Hood & Sons v. Du Mond*, 336 U.S. 525 at 535, 69 S.Ct. 657 at 663 (1949).

108. *Alaska v. Artic Maid*, 366 U.S. 199, 81 S.Ct. 929 (1961).

109. Ibid., 366 U.S. 199 at 204, 81 S.Ct. 929 at 939.

110. *Dunbar-Stanley Studios, Incorporated v. Alabama*, 393 U.S. 537, 89 S.Ct. 757 (1969).

111. Ibid., 393 U.S. 537 at 542, 89 S.Ct. 757 at 761.

112. *Hughes v. Alexandria Scrap Corporation*, 426 U.S. 794 at 808–09, 96 S.Ct. 2488 at 1497–498 (1976).

113. *Reeves Incorporated v. Stake*, 447 U.S. 429 at 436–37, 100 S.Ct. 2271 at 2277 (1980).

114. *White v. Massachusetts Council of Construction Employees*, 460 U.S. 204, 103 S.Ct. 1042 (1983).

115. *Maryland v. Louisiana*, 451 U.S. 725, 101 S.Ct. 2114 (1981).

116. Ibid., 451 U.S. 725 at 758–59, 101 S.Ct. 2114 at 2135–136.

117. *Armco, Incorporated v. Hardesty*, 467 U.S. 638 at 643, 104 S.Ct. 2620 at 2623 (1984).

118. *American Trucking Association v. Scheiner*, 483 U.S. 266 at 269, 107 S.Ct. 2829 at 2833 (1987).

119. *New Energy Co. v. Limbach*, 486 U.S. 269, 108 S.Ct. 1803 (1988).

120. Ibid., 486 U.S. 269 at 278, 108 S.Ct. 1803 at 1810.

121. Ibid.

122. *Farmland Dairies v. Commissioner*, 650 F. Supp. 939 (E.D. NY, 1987). See also Joseph F. Sullivan, "Federal Judge Voids New Jersey Rules Against Out-of-State Milk," *New York Times*, April 19, 1990, pp. B1, B5.

123. *Bacchus Imports Limited v. Dias*, 468 U.S. 263, 104 S.Ct. 3049 (1984).

124. *Brown-Forman Distillers Corporation v. New York State Liquor Authority*, 476 U.S. 573, 106 S.Ct. 2086 (1986).

125. *Healy et al. v. Beer Institute, Incorporated*, 491 U.S. 324 at 337, 109 S.Ct. 2491 at 2499 (1989).

126. Ibid., 491 U.S. 324 at 346, 109 S.Ct. 2491 at 2504.

127. Ibid. 491 U.S. 324 at 349, 109 S.Ct. 2491 at 2506.

128. *McKesson Corporation v. Division of Alcoholic Beverages & Tobacco*, 496 U.S. 18, 110 S.Ct. 2238 (1990).

129. *National Bellas Hess, Incorporated v. Department of Revenue of Illinois*, 386 U.S. 753, 87 S.Ct. 1389 (1967).

130. *Quill Corporation v. North Dakota*, 504 U.S. 298 at 308, 112 S.Ct. 1904 at 1911 (1992).

131. Ibid., 502 U.S. 298 at 308–11 and 318, 112 S.Ct. 1904 at 1911–913 and 1916.

132. *Taxation of Interstate Mail Order Sales: 1994 Revenue Estimates* (Washington, DC: U.S. Advisory Commission on Intergovernmental Relations, 1994), pp. 2–3.

133. *Associated Industries of Missouri v. Lohman,* 511 U.S. 641, 114 S.Ct. 1815 (1994).

134. Ibid., 511 U.S. 641 at 647–48, 114 S.Ct. 1815 at 1820–821.

135. *Philadelphia v. New Jersey,* 437 U.S. 617, 98 S.Ct. 2531 (1978). See also *New Jersey Laws of 1973,* chap. 363.

136. *Fort Gratiot Sanitary Landfill, Incorporated v. Michigan Department of Natural Resources,* 504 U.S. 353, 112 S.Ct. 2019 (1992).

137. *Chemical Waste Management, Incorporated v. Hunt,* 504 U.S. 334, 112 S.Ct. 2009 (1992).

138. *Waste Systems Corporation v. County of Martin and County of Faribault,* 784 F. Supp. 641 (D. Minn, 1992).

139. *Waste Systems Corporation v. County of Martin and County of Faribault, Minnesota,* 985 F.2d 1381 at 1389 (8th cir. 1993).

140. *Oregon Waste Systems, Incorporated v. Department of Environmental Quality,* 511 U.S. 93, 114 S.Ct. 1345 (1994).

141. Ibid., 511 U.S. 93 at 104, 114 S.Ct. 1345 at 1353.

142. *C & A. Carbone, Incorporated v. Town of Clarkstown, New York,* 511 U.S. 383 at 388, 114 S.Ct. 1677 at 1681 (1994).

143. *West Lynn Creamery Incorporated v. Healy,* 512 U.S. 186, 114 S.Ct. 2205 (1994).

144. *Interstate Horseracing Act of 1978,* 92 Stat. 1811, 15 U.S.C. §3004.

145. *Kentucky Division, Horsemen's Benevolent & Protective Association, Incorporated v. Turfway Park Racing Association,* 20 F.3d 1406 (6th Cir. 1994). See also 832 F.Supp. 1097 (1993).

146. *Private Truck Council of America, Incorporated v. New Hampshire,* 128 N.H. 466, 517 A.2d 1150 (N.H. 1986).

147. *Private Truck Council of America, Incorporated v. Secretary of State,* 503 A.2d 214, 54 USLW 2372 (Me, 1986).

Chapter 6

1. John J. Mikesell, "Lotteries in State Revenue Systems: Gauging a Popular Revenue Source after 35 Years," *State and Local Government Review* 33, Spring 2001, p. 86.

2. *Revenue Diversification: State and Local Travel Taxes* (Washington, DC: U.S. Advisory Commission on Intergovernmental Relations, 1994).

3. "Vermont Looks for Way to Keep Liquor-Buyers from Going to N.H.," *Keene (NH) Sentinel,* January 12, 1996, p. 9.

4. "Cigarette Shoppers and Smugglers Hit the Road to Avoid Taxes As Excises

Climb," *Tax Foundation Tax Features* 42, August 1998, p. 2.

5. Mark Maremont and Gary Putra, "Tyco Ex-CEO Is Indicted for Failure to Pay Taxes," *Wall Street Journal Europe,* June 5, 2002, pp. 1, A5.

6. Steven Prokesch, "New York, Seeking Taxes, Follows Shoppers across Hudson," *New York Times,* December 9, 1992, pp. B1, B5.

7. *Internet Tax Freedom Act of 1998,* 112 Stat. 1681, 47 U.S.C. §1100. Consult also 115 Stat. 703 (2001).

8. "Congress Will Allow Ban on Internet Taxes to Expire," *New York Times,* October 19, 2002, C1, C3.

9. *The Intergovernmental Aspects of Documentary Taxes* (Washington, DC: U.S. Advisory Commission on Intergovernmental Relations, 1964).

10. Shelly Murphy, "Drive Free and Lie? Not on His Watch," *Boston Globe,* May 6, 1995, pp. 1, 6.

11. 71 Stat. 555 and 15 U.S.C. §§381–84 (1959).

12. *Northwestern States Portland Cement Company v. Minnesota,* 358 U.S. 1959, 79 S.Ct. 357 (1959).

13. *In re State Freight Tax,* 82 U.S. 232, 15 Wall. 232 (1872).

14. Ibid., 82 U.S. 232 at 273, 15 Wall. 232 at 273.

15. Information in this section is derived primarily from *Special Report No. 115* (Washington, DC: Tax Foundation, July 2002) and "State Pioneers Tax Change for Visiting Athletes," *Times Union* (Albany, NY), August 4, 1994, p. B2.

16. "State Pioneers Tax Change for Visiting Athletes."

17. *Special Report,* No. 115, p. 3.

18. *Hearing on Interstate Use Tax Collection before the Committee on Small Business, United States Senate, April 13, 1994* (Washington, DC: U.S. Government Printing Office, 1994).

19. Price-Waterhouse, "Voting with Their Feet: A Study of Tax Incentives and Economic Consequences of Cross-Border Activity in New England," *The State Factor* 18, August 1992, pp. 1–60.

20. Price-Waterhouse, "Voting with Their Feet II: The Economic Consequences of Cross-Border Activity in the Southeastern U.S.," *The State Factor* 19, August 1993, p. 23.

21. *Wilson Act of 1890,* 26 Stat. 313, 27 U.S.C. §121.

22. *Webb-Kenyon Act of 1913,* 37 Stat. 699, 27 U.S.C. §122.

23. Vijay Shanker, "Alcohol Direct Shipment Laws, the Commerce Clause, and the Twenty-first Amendment," *Virginia Law Review* 45, March 1999, pp. 356–57. See also Ellen Perlman, "Vintage Politics: The Complexities of Shipping Chardonnay across State Lines," *Governing* 9, December 1995, p. 47.

24. *State Board of Equalization of California v. Young's Market Company,* 299 U.S. 59, 57 S.Ct. 77 (1936).

25. *Bacchus Imports Limited v. Dias,* 468 U.S. 263 at 275–76, 104 S.Ct. 3049 at 3058 (1984).

26. *Summary of State Laws & Regulations Relating to Distilled Spirits* (Washington, DC: Distilled Spirits Council of the United States, Incorporated, 2002).

27. Tom Fahey, "Study: Low Alcohol, Cigarette Taxes Attract Spending to NH, VT, and RI," *Union Leader* (Manchester, NH), August 6, 1992, p. 6.

28. Laurence Dwyer, "Border Battle: Bottle Bill Is Driving Bay State Customers to Shop in New Hampshire," *Boston Globe*, February 20, 1983, p. 21.

29. "Roadblocks Used by State to Shut Off Tax-Free Liquor," *Knickerbocker News* (Albany, NY), February 9, 1966, p. 6A.

30. "The Eyes of Taxers: They're Upon You If You Buy VT Booze," *Times Union* (Albany, NY), December 26, 1976, pp. B1, B10.

31. Homer Bigart, "Jersey Routes Pennsylvania Spies in Border War on Whiskey Prices," *New York Times*, March 5, 1965, pp. 1, 26.

32. Stacy MacTaggert, "The Neverending Whiskey Wars," *Governing* 8, October 1994, p. 32.

33. "Two States Clash on Liquor Sales," *New York Times*, December 14, 1969, p. 73. See also Ben A. Franklin, "Christmas Cheer Is Smuggled Out of Washington," *New York Times*, December 24, 1969, pp. 1, 11.

34. Kenneth C. Crowe II, "Pair to Answer Liquor-Smuggling Charges Today," *Times Union* (Albany, NY), June 9, 1994, p. B7.

35. "The Eyes of Taxers," *Times Union* (Albany, NY), December 26, 1976, p. B1.

36. Ibid, p. B10.

37. *New York Laws of 1993*, chap. 508 and *New York Tax Law*, §421.

38. Kenneth C. Crowe II, "State Stockpiling Contraband Liquors," *Times Union* (Albany, NY), December 9, 1993, pp. B1, B11.

39. *Jenkins Act of 1949*, 63 Stat. 884, 15 U.S.C. §375.

40. 69 Stat. 627 (1955).

41. *United States v. E.A. Goodyear, Incorporated*, 334 F.Supp. 1096 (1971).

42. "Web Sale of Tobacco Costing States," *Boston Globe*, August 13, 2002, p. B2.

43. James K. Batten, "Tax, Law Aides to Map Cigarette Bootleg War," *Knickerbocker News* (Albany, NY), August 30, 1967, p. 3B.

44. Press release issued by the Office of Governor Nelson A. Rockefeller, Albany, NY, February 11, 1973, p. 1.

45. Diane Henry, "Interstate Police Force Urged to Combat Cigarette Smuggling," *New York Times*, March 26, 1975, p. 31.

46. *Cigarette Tax Evasion: A Second Look* (Washington, DC: U.S. Advisory Commission on Intergovernmental Relations, 1985), p. 2.

47. Farnsworth Fowle, "Goodman Renews Effort to Lift City's Cigarette Tax," *New York Times*, January 16, 1976, p. 31.

48. John L. Considine, "Cigarette Smuggling Big Business," *Knickerbocker News* (Albany, NY), January 22, 1971, p. 16A.

49. "If the U.S. Collected All Cigarette Taxes," a letter to the editor from James H. Tully Jr., *New York Times*, May 19, 1977, p. A34.

50. Ibid.

51. *Contraband Cigarette Act of 1978*, 53 Stat. 1291, 18 U.S.C. §2341.

52. Ibid.

53. *Cigarette Tax Evasion: A Second Look*, p. 23.

54. KPMG Peat Marwick, *Effects of Cross-Border Sales on Economic Activity and State Revenues: A Case Study of Tobacco Excise Taxes in Massachusetts, New York City, and Surrounding Area* (Washington, DC: Tax Foundation, 1993).

55. "Mass. Tax Is Good News: Cigarette Buyers Pour into N.H.," *Keene (NH) Sentinel*, January 4, 1993, pp. 1, 5.

56. Craig Brandon, "Butt Smugglers," *Times Union* (Albany, NY), June 24, 1993, p. 1.

57. Paul Zielbauer, "In Connecticut, Governor Signs 61–Cent Cigarette Tax Increase," *New York Times*, March 1, 2002, p. B8.

58. Shaila K. Dewan, "Cigarette Tax Would Cost State Millions, Critics Say," *New York Times*, March 2, 2002, p. B6, and "The Mayor Taxes Will Power," *New York Times*, July 2, 2002, p. A20.

59. David Crary, "Cigarette Taxes Help Spawn Illegal Trade," *Keene (NH) Sentinel*, July 14, 2002, p. 1.

60. *Jenkins Act of 1949*, 63 Stat. 884, 69 Stat. 627, 15 U.S.C. §375.

61. *Mail Fraud Act of 1909*, 35 Stat. 1088, 18 U.S.C. §1341.

62. Clyde Farnsworth, "Canada Cuts Cigarette Taxes to Fight Smuggling," *New York Times*, February 9, 1994, p. A3.

63. Colin Nickerson, "Smuggling Surge Rolls Canada," *Boston Globe*, February 16, 1994, p. 14.

64. Hope Reeves, "Read Their Lips: No Taxes. (Period.)," *New York Times*, July 8, 2002, pp. B1, B6.

65. *Indian Trade and Intercourse Act of 1790*, 1 Stat.135, and *Indian Trader Act of 1876*, 19 Stat. 200, 25 U.S.C. §261. Consult also Bureau of Indian Affairs Regulations, 25 CFR 140.1–126.

66. *Moe v. Confederated Slaish and Kootenal Tribes of Flathead Reservations*, 425 U.S. 463, 96 S.Ct. 1634 (1976).

67. *Washington v. Confederated Colville Tribes*, 447 U.S. 134, 100 S.Ct. 2069 (1980).

68. *Milhelm Attea 7 Brothers, Incorporated v. Department of Taxation and Finance*, 164 A.D.2d 300, 564 N.Y.S.2d 491 (N.Y.A.D.3 Dept, 1990), and *Milhelm Attea & Brothers, Incorporated v. Department of Taxation and Finance*, 81 NY2d 417, 615 N.E.2d 994 (1993).

69. *Department of Taxation and Finance v. Milhelm Attea & Brothers, Incorporated*, 512 U.S. 61, 114 S.Ct. 2028 (1994).

70. "Court Holds States Free to Set Resource Taxes," *New York Times*, July 3, 1981, p. B12.

71. *Hope Natural Gas Company v. Hall*, 274 U.S. 284, 47 S.Ct. 639 (1927); *Oliver Iron Mining Company v. Lord*, 262 U.S. 172, 43 S.Ct. 526 (1923); and *Heisler v. Thomas Colliery Company*, 260 U.S. 245, 43 S.Ct. 83 (1922).

72. *Heisler v. Thomas Colliery Company*, 260 U.S. 245 at 259–60, 43 S.Ct. 83 at 86 (1922).

73. *Utah Power & Light Company v. Pfost*, 286 U.S. 165, 52 S.Ct. 548 (1932).

74. *Pike v. Bruce Church, Incorporated*, 397 U.S. 137 at 142, 90 S.Ct. 844 at 847 (1970).

75. *Complete Auto Transit Incorporated v. Brady*, 430 U.S. 274 at 281, 97 S.Ct. 1076 at 1080 (1977).

76. Ibid., 430 U.S. 274 at 279, 97 S.Ct. 1076 at 1079.

77. The justification of the tax increase is included in the "Statement to Accompany the Report of the Free Joint Conference Committees on Coal Taxation" (Helena: Montana Legislative Assembly, April 16, 1975).

78. *Commonwealth Edison Company v. Montana*, 189 Mont. 191, 615 P.2d 847 (1980) and *Commonwealth Edison Company v. Montana*, 453 U.S. 609, 101 S.Ct. 609 (1981).

79. *Mineral Lands Leasing Act of 1920*, 41 Stat. 437, 30 U.S.C. §181, and *Federal Coal Leasing Amendments of 1975*, 90 Stat. 1089, 30 U.S.C. §181.

80. Walter Hellerstein, "Commerce Clause Restraints on State Taxation: Purposeful Economic Protectionism and Beyond," *Michigan Law Review* 85, February 1987, pp. 762–63.

81. *Merrion v. Jicarilla Apache Tribe*, 445 U.S. 130, 102 S.Ct. 894 (1982).

82. *Pullman's Palace Car Company v. Pennsylvania*, 141 U.S. 18, 11 S.Ct. 876 (1891).

83. *Union Refrigerator Transit Company v. Kentucky*, 199 U.S. 194, 26 S.Ct. 36 (1905).

84. *New York ex. Rel. New York Central & Harlem River Rail Road v. Miller*, 202 U.S. 584, 26 S.Ct. 714 (1906).

85. *Northwest Airlines, Incorporated v. Minnesota*, 322 U.S. 292, 64 S.Ct. 950 (1944).

86. Ibid., 322 U.S. 292 at 295, 64 S.Ct. 950 at 952.

87. *Braniff Airways, Incorporated v. Nebraska State Board*, 347 U.S. 590, 74 S.Ct. 757 (1954).

88. *Central Greyhound Lines, Incorporated v. Mealey*, 334 U.S. 653, 68 S.Ct. 1260 (1948).

89. *Ott v. Mississippi Valley Barge Line Company*, 336 U.S. 169, 69 S.Ct. 432 (1949).

90. *Moorman Manufacturing Company v. Iowa*, 437 U.S. 267, 98 S.Ct. 2340 (1978).

91. *Florida Statutes*, §212.08(4)(a)(2) (1983).

92. *WardAir Canada, Incorporated v. Florida*, 477 U.S. 1, 106 S.Ct. 2369 (1986).

93. *American Trucking Associations v. Scheiner*, 483 U.S. 266, 107 S.Ct. 2829 (1987).

94. Ibid., 483 U.S. 266 at 269, 107 S.Ct. 2829 at 2832.

95. *Goldberg v. Sweet*, 488 U.S. 252, 109 S.Ct. 582 (1989).

96. Ibid., 488 U.S. 252 at 266, 109 S.Ct. 582 at 591.

97. *Allied-Signal, Incorporated v. Director, Division of Taxation*, 504 U.S. 768, 112 S.Ct. 2251 (1992).

98. *Oklahoma Tax Commission v. Jefferson Lines, Incorporated*, 514 U.S. 175, 115 S.Ct. 1331 (1995).

99. *Natural Gas Policy Act of 1978*, 103 Stat. 157, 15 U.S.C. §3301.

100. *New York Laws of 1991*, chap. 166, *New York Tax Law*, §189.

101. *Tennessee Gas Pipeline Company v. Urbach*, 96 NY2d 124 at 130, 750 N.E.2d 52 at 56 (2001).

102. Ibid., 96 NY2d 124 at 134, 750 N.E.2d 52 at 59.

103. Rodd Zolkos, "California Tax Still Irritates Great Britain," *City & State* 5, September 26, 1988, pp. 1, 25.

104. *Alcan Aluminum v. Franchise Tax Board of California*, 1987 WL 15386, and *Alcan Aluminum v. Franchise Tax Board of California*, 860 F.2d 688 (7th Cir. 1988).

105. *Franchise Tax Board of California v. Alcan Aluminum*, 493 U.S. 331, 110 S.Ct. 661 (1990), and *Tax Injunction Act of 1937*, 50 Stat. 738, 28 U.S.C. §1341.

106. *Barclays Bank v. Franchise Tax Board of California*, 512 U.S. 298 at 323–24, 114 S.Ct. 2268 at 2283–284 (1994).

107. Dan Freedman, "High Court Upholds Global Tax Scheme," *Times Union* (Albany, NY), June 21, 1994, p. C8.

108. *California Revenue and Tax Code*, §§23601.5 and 23609.

109. *Virginia Laws of 1990*, chap. 709 and *Virginia Code Annotated*, §58.1–445.1, and *Illinois Revised Statutes*, chap.120, par. 2–201 (G).

110. *Arizona Public Service Company v. Snead*, 441 U.S. 141 at 145, 99 S.Ct. 1629 at 1632 (1979).

111. *Tax Reform Act of 1976*, 90 Stat. 1914, 15 U.S.C. §391.

112. *New York Laws of 1968*, chap. 827 and *New York Tax Law*, §270c.

113. *Boston Stock Exchange v. State Tax commission*, 429 U.S. 318 at 336–37, 97 S.Ct. 599 at 610 (1977).

114. *Westinghouse Electric Corporation v. Tully*, 466 U.S. 388, 104 S.Ct. 1856 (1984).

115. *Armco Incorporated v. Hardesty*, 467 U.S. 638 at 642, 104 S.Ct. 2620 at 2622 (1984).

116. *Metropolitan Life Insurance Company v. Ward*, 470 U.S. 869, 105 S.Ct. 1676 (1985).

117. *Tyler Pipe Industries v. Washington Department of Revenue*, 483 U.S. 232 at 243–44, 107 S.Ct. 2810 at 2818 (1987).

118. *Barringer v. Griffes*, 801 F.Supp. 1284 (D.Vt, 1992).

119. *Williams v. Vermont*, 472 U.S. 14, 105 S.Ct. 2465 (1985).

120. Ibid., 472 U.S. 14 at 28, 105 S.Ct. 2465 at 2475.

121. *Vermont Agency of Transportation, Department of Motor Vehicle*, Rule 86.28–E (July 5, 1985).

122. *Barringer v. Griffes*, 801 F.Supp. 1284 (D.Vt, 1992) and *Barringer v. Griffes*, 1 F.3d 1331 at 1338–339 (2nd Cir. 1993).

123. *Shaffer v. Carter*, 252 U.S. 37, 40 S.Ct. 221 (1920). See *Oklahoma Laws of 1915*, chaps. 107, 164.

124. Ibid., 252 U.S. 37 at 55, 40 S.Ct. 221 at 226.

125. *Travis v. Yale & Towne Manufacturing Company*, 252 U.S. 60, 40 S.Ct. 228 (1920).

126. *The Commuter and the Municipal Income Tax* (Washington, DC: U.S. Advisory Commission on Intergovernmental Relations, 1970).

127. *New Hampshire Laws of 1970*, chap. 20, §1, New *Hampshire Statutes Annotated*, §77–B:1 (1970).

128. *Austin v. New Hampshire*, 420 U.S. 656, 95 S.Ct. 1191 (1975).

129. "NH Workers Won't Get Relief from Maine's 'Spousal Tax,'" *Union Leader* (Manchester, NH), June 23, 1993, p. 7.

130. *Brady v. State*, 80 NY2d 596 at 959, 607 N.E.2d 1060 at 1064 (1992).

131. See *Maxwell v. Bugbee*, 150 U.S. 525, 40 S.Ct. 2 (1919) and *Great Atlantic & Pacific Tea Company v. Grosjean*, 301 U.S. 412, 57 S.Ct. 772 at 777 (1937).

132. *Brady v. State*, 80 NY 596 at 608, 607 N.E.2d 1060 at 1067.

133. *City of New York v. State*, 94 NY2d 577, 730 N.E.2d 920 (2000). See also Richard Perez-Pena, "Court Upholds Law to Repeal Commuter Tax," *New York Times*, April 5, 2000, pp. B1, B7.

134. Ibid., 94 NY2d 577 at 596 and 598, 730 N.E.2d 920 at 929 and 931.

135. *Trinova Corporation v. Michigan Department of Treasury*, 498 U.S. 358 at 386, 111 S.Ct. 818 at 836 (1991).

136. Ibid.

Chapter 7

1. Bernard Simon, "In Men's Clothing, More and More of the Labels Say 'Made in Canada,'" *New York Times*, March 23, 2002, pp. C1, C5.

2. "The Bermuda Tax Triangle," *New York Times*, May 13, 2002, p. A16.

3. David C. Johnston, "Officers May Gain More Than Investors in Move to Bermuda," *New York Times*, May 20, 2002, p. 1.

4. Ibid., p. A13.

5. David C. Johnston, "Musical Chairs on Tax Havens: Now It's Ireland," *New York Times*, August 3, 2002, pp. C1, C3.

6. Information in this paragraph is derived from Jerry Nachtigal, "Arizona

Goes all Out to Entice Wealthy Seniors to Retire There," *Keene (NH) Sentinel*, March 9, 1997, p. C6.

7. Gary Enos, "Big Breaks Lure Plant to Ky.," *City & State* 10, June 21, 1993, p. 1.

8. Charles J. Spindler, "Winners and Losers in Industrial Recruitment: Mercedes-Benz and Alabama," *State and Local Government Review* 26, Fall 1994, p. 192.

9. Ibid., pp. 185, 198.

10. *Constitution of New York*, Art. VII, §§9–12 (1846). These provisions are incorporated in the current New York Constitution as Art. VII, §8.

11. Joseph F. Zimmerman, *The Government and Politics of New York State* (New York: New York University Press, 1981), pp. 235–43.

12. "New War Between the States," *New England Business Review*, October 1963, pp. 1–5.

13. *Constitution of the State of New York*, Art. VII, §9 (1846).

14. *Interjurisdictional Tax and Policy Competition: Good or Bad for the Federal System?* (Washington, DC: U.S. Advisory Commission on Intergovernmental Relations, 1991), p. 4. Consult also Daphine A. Kenyon and John Kincaid, eds., *Competition Among States and Local Governments* (Washington, DC: The Urban Institute, 1991).

15. Keon S. Chi, "State Business Incentives: Options for the Future," *State Trends Forecasts*, June 1994, p. 27.

16. Ibid., p. 11.

17. "The Boom Belt," *Business Week*, September 27, 1993, p. 98.

18. "Scott Paper Leaving Philly for Florida," *Times Union* (Albany, NY), March 14, 1995, p. B12.

19. David Firestone, "Black Families Resist Mississippi Land Push," *New York Times* September 10, 2001, p. A20.

20. Chi, "State Business Incentives," pp. 13, 15.

21. Micheline Maynard, "A Pension Fund Chief Bets on US Airways," *New York Times*, October 5, 2002, pp. C1, C3.

22. Dana Scott, "State Taxes Helped Drive Out KeyCorp, Riley Says," *Times Union* (Albany, NY), February 17, 1994, p. C10.

23. Kenneth Aaron, "Railing Against the State Machine," *Times Union* (Albany, NY), April 23, 2002, p. E1.

24. *State-Local Taxation and Industrial Location* (Washington, DC: U.S. Advisory Commission on Intergovernmental Relations, 1967), p. 63.

25. Ibid., pp. 61–62.

26. Ibid., p. 61.

27. Donald Moffitt, "More States Cancel Inventory Tax on Items for Sales Elsewhere," *Wall Street Journal*, January 25, 1964, p. 1.

28. *Regional Growth: Interstate Tax Competition* (Washington, DC: U.S. Advisory Commission on Intergovernmental Relations, 1981), p. 32.

29. Ibid., p. 34.

30. Ibid., p. 37.

31. Ibid., p. 46.

32. Robert Tannenwald, "Massachusetts' Tax Competitiveness," *New England Economic Review*, January/February 1994, p. 31.

33. James B. Hines Jr., "Altered States; Taxes and the Location of Foreign Direct Investment in America," National Bureau of Economic Research, Incorporated, Working Paper No. 4397, July 1993, p. 1.

34. Abby Goodnough, "Interstate Competition for Teachers from Abroad," *New York Times*, July 18, 2001, p. B9.

35. David Firestone, "State Lures Good Jobs, but Companies Worry About Workers," *New York Times*, January 28, 2002, p. A8.

36. Joel Millman, "Visions of Sugar Plums South of the Border," *The Wall Street Journal*, February 13, 2002, pp. 1, A16.

37. James Prichard, "No Rescue for Life Savers Employees," *Times Union* (Albany, NY), April 14, 2002, p. F2.

38. Ibid.

39. Charles V. Bagli, "Known As Poacher, New Jersey Is Faced by Rival to the West," *New York Times*, March 20, 2000, pp. 1, B5.

40. Alan B. Abbey, "Cuomo Intensifies Bank Reform Effort," *Times Union* (Albany, NY), January 9, 1994, pp. B1, B6.

41. Joseph F. Zimmerman, *Federal Preemption: The Silent Revolution* (Ames: Iowa State University Press, 1991), pp. 92–98.

42. Charles Mahtesian, "Romancing the Smokestack," *Governing* 8, November 1994, p. 38.

43. Chris Farrell, "The Economic War Among the States: An Overview," *The Region*, June 1996, p. 5.

44. Dick Netzer, "An Evaluation of Interjurisdictional Competition Through Economic Development Incentives." In Kenyon and Kincaid, eds., *Competition Among State and Local Governments*, p. 234.

45. "State Won't Become N.J.'s Power Broker," *Times Union* (Albany, NY), July 22, 1995, p. B2.

46. Ibid.

47. Mahtesian, "Romancing the Smokestack," p. 38.

48. Thomas J. Lueck, "New York Buys Ads Charging 'Raid' of Company by Connecticut," *New York Times*, October 11, 1994, p. B1.

49. Ibid.

50. Ibid., p. B5.

51. Steven L. Myers, "Giuliani Says Connecticut Broke Truce," *New York Times*, October 14, 1994, pp. B6, B14.

52. Brett Pulley, "New York Makes Staying Put Irresistible to Coffee Exchange," *New York Times*, October 13, 1995, pp. B1, B3.

53. Ibid., p. B1.

54. Winnie Hu, "Stock Exchange May Move Some Operations to New Site," *New York Times*, July 25, 2002, p. B5.

55. Charles V. Bagli, "Playing the 'Jersey Card,' Firms in Manhattan Compare Incentives," *New York Times*, December 28, 2001, p. D1.

56. Ibid., p. D4.

57. Robert E. Koch, "C&S Courting Both Keene and Brattleboro," *Keene (NH) Sentinel*, October 17, 2001, pp. 1–2.

58. Robert E. Koch and Dan Gearino, "Keene Lands C&S Complex," *Keene (NH) Sentinel*, April 1, 2001, pp. 1–2.

59. Robert E. Koch, "Keene 'Best Choice,'" *Keene (NH) Sentinel*, April 2, 2002, p. 2.

60. Dan Gearino, "Insurance Heads Moving South," *Keene (NH) Sentinel*, March 27, 2002, p. 1.

61. Jay Kayne and Molly Shonka, *Rethinking State Development Policies and Programs* (Washington, DC: National Governors' Association, 1994), p. 3.

62. Ibid., p. 14.

63. Ibid.

64. Jayson Blair, "Power Agencies' Plan to Merge Draws Mixed Reviews of States," *New York Times*, August 22, 2002, p. B2.

65. Jayson Blair, "L.I. Power Officials Ask Federal Regulators to Order Activation of Undersea Line," *New York Times*, August 15, 2002, p. B5.

66. Jayson Blair, "Federal Order Activates L.I. Power Line," *New York Times*, August 17, 2002, pp. B1, B5.

67. Jeffrey Krasner, "Drug Research Giant Heads to Cambridge," *Boston Globe*, May 7, 2002, p. 1.

68. Mary J. Waits, "Building an Economic Future," *State Government News* 38, September 1995, p. 7.

69. *Sherman Antitrust Act of 1890*, 26 Stat. 209, 15 U.S.C. §§1–7.

70. *Federal Baseball Club of Baltimore, Incorporated v. National League of Professional Baseball Clubs, Incorporated*, 259 U.S. 200, 42 S.Ct. 465 (1922).

71. Ibid., 259 U.S. 200 at 208–09, 42 S.Ct. 465 at 466.

72. Joanna Cagan and Neil DeMause, *Fields of Schemes: How the Great Stadium Swindle Turns Public Money Into Private Profit*, rev. ed. (Monroe, ME: Common Courage Press, 1998), p. 29.

73. Sol Stern, "No to Sports Stadium Madness," *City Journal* 8, Autumn 1998, p. 78.

74. Tim Chapin, "The Political Economy of Sports Facility Location: An End-of-the-Century Review and Assessment," *Marquette Sports Journal* 10, Spring 2000, p. 372.

75. Ibid., p. 379.

76. Information in this and the following paragraph is derived primarily from Amy Klobuchar, *Uncovering the Dome: Was the Public Interest Served in Minnesota's 10-*

Year Political Brawl Over the Metrodome? (Prospect Heights, Illinois: Waveland Press, Incorporated, 1986).

77. The information in this paragraph and the following two paragraphs is derived from Jay Weiner, *Stadium Games: Fifty Years of Big League Greed and Bush League Boondoggles* (Minneapolis: University of Minnesota Press, 2000).

78. Ibid., p. 302.

79. "Football Team Valuations," *Forbes* 170, September 2, 2002, p. 71.

80. "Cuomo Warns N.J. to Let Yankees Alone," *Times Union* (Albany, NY), October 7, 1993, p. B2.

81. James Ketterer, "It's Outta Here," *Times Union* (Albany, NY), January 29, 1995, p. B1.

82. Jennifer Steinhauer and Richard Sandomir, "Let's Play Two: Giuliani Presents Deal on Stadiums," *New York Times*, December 29, 2001, p. 1.

83. Ibid., p. D6.

84. Jennifer Steinhauer, "Giuliani Loosened Ball Clubs' Leases Days Before Existing," *New York Times*, January 15, 2002), pp. 1, B4.

85. Jennifer Steinhauer, "Mayor Says There's No Money to Build 2 Baseball Stadiums," *New York Times*, January 8, 2002, p. B3.

86. Charles V. Bagli, "West Side Plan Envisions Jets and Olympics," *New York Times*, May 1, 2002, pp. B1, B6.

87. Pete Dougherty, "The Yanks Are Going to Norwich," *Times Union* (Albany, NY), March 15, 1994, p. A7.

88. Ibid.

89. Bill Eager, "Cuomo Comes Out of the Bullpen in Late Pitch to Save A-C Yankees," *Times Union* (Albany, NY), March 20, 1994, p. 1, and Michael McKeon, "Steinbrenner Wants A-C Yankees to Stay Put," *Times Union* (Albany, NY), March 22, 1994, p. 1.

90. Ronald Smothers, "Newark Approves Arena Financing Deal," *New York Times*, August 24, 2002, p. B4. See also Ron Marsico and George E. Jordan, "New Life for Arena in Newark," *The Star Ledger* (Newark, NJ), August 23, 2002 (Internet edition).

91. Information in this paragraph is derived from Paul Post, "I Love NY Again!" *Empire State Report* 27, July/August 2001, p. 37.

92. Information in this paragraph is derived from Stephen Frothingham, "Plenty of Summer for Everyone," *Union Leader* (Manchester, NH), May 1, 2001, p. B1.

93. Michael Hill, "After a Quarter-Century, We Still (Heart) That Ad Slogan," *Times Union* (Albany, NY), May 13, 2002, p. B5.

94. Charles Mahtesian, "How States Get People to Love Them," *Governing* 7, January 1994, p. 46.

95. Ibid., p. 47.

96. Information in this paragraph is derived from Paula Tracy, "NH Businesses Change Market Strategy," *Union Leader* (Manchester, NH), October 30, 2001, p. A3.

97. Information in this paragraph is derived from Jerry Miller, "NH Tourist Office Getting Aggressive," *Union Leader* (Manchester, NH), April 4, 2002 (Internet edition).

98. Information in this paragraph is derived from Lisa Fingeret, "The Big Apple Needs to Grow," *Financial Times*, June 4, 2002, p. 12.

99. *New York Laws of 1992*, chap. 766.

100. *1997–2002 Capital Plan* (Albany, New York State Thruway Authority, 1997), exhibits I–IV.

101. Information in this paragraph is derived from Elizabeth Benjamin, "$32 M Spent to Revitalize State Canals for Tourism," *Times Union* (Albany, NY), March 20, 2002, p. 19.

102. Information in this paragraph is derived from "Miss America: Atlantic City Gets Pageant 1 More Year," *New York Times*, December 28, 2001, p. D5.

103. Peter A. Brown, "Big Business Exploits War Between the States for New Jobs," *Times Union* (Albany, NY), February 6, 1994, p. B3.

104. "Gambling Now Third Largest Source of Revenue for R.I.," *Union Leader* (Manchester, NH), February 18, 2002, p. B3.

105. Robert Goodman, *The Luck Business* (New York: Martin Kessler Books, 1995), p. 5.

106. For a history of lotteries, consult Ronald J. Rychlak, "Lotteries, Revenues, and Social Costs: A Historical Examination of State-Sponsored Gambling," *Boston College Law Review* 34, 1992–1993, pp. 11–81.

107. 26 Stat. 465, 18 U.S.C. §1302 and 28 Stat. 963, 18 U.S.C. §1301.

108. Joel Stashenko, "Instant Games a Boon for Lottery," *Times Union* (Albany, NY), May 1, 2002, p. B6.

109. "Maine Investigates Illegal Resale of Massachusetts Megabucks Tickets," *Keene (NH) Sentinel*, April 10, 1984, p. 14.

110. 15 U.S.C. §1172(a) and 18 U.S.C. §1301.

111. "Siblings Claim Final Share of Powerball," *USA Today*, August 31, 2001, p. 3A.

112. "Powerball Fever Proves too Much for Greenwich," *Union Leader* (Manchester, NH), August 24, 2001, p. A18.

113. John Mikesell, "Lotteries in State Revenue Systems: Gauging a Popular Revenue Source After 35 Years," *State and Local Government Review* 33, Spring 2001, pp. 97–98.

114. Ibid., p. 98.

115. *Indian Gaming Regulation Act of 1988*, 102 Stat. 2467, 25 U.S.C. §2710. Consult also Anne M. McCulloch, "The Politics of Indian Gaming: Tribe/State Relations and American Federalism," *Publius* 24, Summer 1994, pp. 99–112.

116. *State ex rel. Stephan v. Finney*, 836 P.2d 1169 (Kan. 1992).

117. *New York Laws of 2001*, chaps. 94 and 383. See also James C. McKinley Jr., "Gambling Expansion Is Part of Albany Budget Agreement," *New York Times*, October 24, 2001, pp. D1, D5.

118. *Constitution of New York*, Art. I, §9. See also James M. Odato, "Coalition to Sue Over Expansion of Gambling," *Times Union* (Albany, NY), January 29, 2002, p. B3, and Richard Perez-Pena, "Gambling Bill Is Questioned on Constitutional Grounds," *New York Times*, October 26, 2001, p. D6.

119. Robert C. Morais, "New York State of Mind," *Forbes* 169, April 29, 2002, p. 68.

120. James Dao, "Indians Offer State a Share of Monticello Casino Profits," *New York Times*, March 2, 1995, p. B6.

121. Mary J. Pitzl and Tom Zoeliner, "Hull, Tribes OK Gaming Deals," *Arizona Republic*, February 21, 2002 (Internet edition).

122. "The Effects of Land-Based and Riverboat Gaming in New Orleans," *Louisiana Business Survey* 28, Spring 1997, p. 2.

123. Ibid., p. 9.

124. Information in this paragraph is derived from John Wilgoren, "Midwest Towns Feel Gambling Is a Sure Thing," *New York Times*, May 20, 2002, pp. 1, A14.

125. Goodman, *The Luck Business*, p. 4.

126. Ibid., p. 5.

127. Morais, "Casino Junkies," p. 70.

128. *McCulloch v. Maryland*, 17 U.S. 316 at 431, 4 Wheat. 316 at 431 (1819).

129. *Collector v. Day*, 78 U.S. 122, 11 Wall. 113 (1871).

130. *Pollock v. Farmers Loan & Trust Company*, 157 U.S. 492, 15 S.Ct. 673 (1895).

131. *Internal Revenue Act of 1913*, 38 Stat. 166.

132. *South Carolina v. Baker*, 485 U.S. 505 at 524–25, 108 S.Ct. 1355 at 1367 (1988).

133. Ibid., 483 U.S. 505 at 512, 108 S.Ct. 1355 at 1361.

134. *Garcia v. San Antonio Metropolitan Transit Authority*, 469 U.S. 528 at 556, 105 S.Ct. 1005 at 1082 (1985).

135. *Tax Reform Act of 1986*, 98 Stat. 793, 4 U.S.C. §§421–26.

136. *South Carolina v. Baker*, 485 U.S. 505 at 521–23, 108 S.Ct. 1355 at 1366 (1988).

137. *Revenue and Expenditure Control Act of 1968*, 82 Stat. 251, 26 U.S.C. §103.

138. Dennis Zimmerman, *The Private Use of Tax-Exempt Bonds: Controlling Public Subsidy of Private Activity* (Washington, DC: The Urban Institute Press, 1991), pp. 178–351.

139. *Tax Reform Act of 1986*, 98 Stat. 793, 4 U.S.C. §§421–26.

140. *Deficit Reduction Act of 1984*, 98 Stat. 494, 26 U.S.C. §1 note.

141. *Tax Reform Act of 1986*, 98 Stat. 793, 4 U.S.C. §§421–26. See also Dennis Zimmerman, *The Volume Cap for Tax-Exempt Private-Activity Bonds: State and Local Experience in 1989* (Washington, DC: U.S. Advisory Commission on Intergovernmental Relations, 1990).

142. Zimmerman, *The Private Use of Tax-Exempt Bonds*, p. 219.

143. Netzer, "An Evaluation of Interjurisdictional Competition," p. 237.

144. *Industrial Development Bonds: Achievement of Public Benefits is Unclear* (Washington, DC: U.S. General Accounting Office, 1993), p. 10.

145. Ibid., p. 21.

146. Ibid., p. 20.

147. Philip P. Frickey, "The Congressional Process and the Constitutionality of Federal Legislation to End the Economic War Among the States," *The Region*, June 1996, p. 59.

148. Walter Hellerstein, "Commerce Clause Restraints on State Tax Incentives," *The Region*, June 1996, p. 62.

149. *Massachusetts v. Mellon*, 262 U.S. 447, 43 S.Ct. 597 (1923) and *South Dakota v. Dole*, 483 U.S. 203, 107 S.Ct. 2793 (1987).

Chapter 8

1. *New York Laws of 1890*, chap. 203 and *New York Executive Law*, §165.

2. Kim Q. Hill and Patricia A. Hurley, "Uniform State Law Adoptions in the American States: An Explanatory Analysis," *Publius* 18, Winter 1988, pp. 117–26.

3. For an in-depth analysis, consult Joseph F. Zimmerman, *Interstate Cooperation: Compacts and Administrative Agreements* (Westport, CT: Praeger Publishers, 2002).

4. *Dover v. Portsmouth Bridge*, 17 N.H. 200 (1845).

5. *Florida v. Georgia*, 58 U.S. 478, 17 How. 478 (1854).

6. *Virginia v. Tennessee*, 148 U.S. 503 at 520, 13 S.Ct. 728 at 735 (1893).

7. *United States Steel Corporation v. Multistate Tax Commission*, 434 U.S. 452 at 473, 98 S.Ct. 799 at 813 (1978).

8. *Bi-State Development Agency*, 110 Stat. 883 (1996).

9. *Chickasaw Trail Economic Development Compact*, 111 Stat. 2669 (1997).

10. *Northeastern Interstate Forest Fire Protection Compact*, 63 Stat. 272 (1949).

11. *Weeks Act of 1911*, 36 Stat. 961, 16 U.S.C. §552.

12. *Civil Defense Act of 1951*, 64 Stat.1249, 50 U.S.C. App. §2281(g).

13. *Hinderlider v. La Plata River and Cherry Creek Dutch Company*, 204 U.S. 92, 58 S.Ct. 803 (1938) and *Cuyler v. Adams*, 449 U.S. 433, 101 S.Ct. 703 (1981).

14. *Hess v. Port Authority Trans-Hudson Corporation*, 513 U.S. 30, 115 S.Ct. 394 (1994).

15. Felix Frankfurter and James Landis, "The Compact Clause of the Constitution: A Study in Interstate Adjustments," *Yale Law Journal* 34, May 1925, pp. 735–45.

16. Patricia S. Florestano, "Past and Present Utilization of Interstate Compacts in the United States," *Publius* 24, Fall 1994, pp. 19–22.

17. Joseph F. Zimmerman, *Federal Preemption: The Silent Revolution* (Ames: Iowa State University Press, 1991).

18. *New Jersey Laws of 1921*, chap. 151, and *New York Laws of 1921*, chap. 154. See also Jameson W. Doig, *Empire on the Hudson: Entrepreneurial Vision and Political Power at the Port of New York Authority* (New York: Columbia University Press, 2001).

19. Dick Netzer, "Reinventing the Port Authority," *City Journal* 6, Summer 1996, p. 77.

20. Ibid., pp. 84–89.

21. Ronald Smothers, "As It Turns 80, the Port Authority Looks to Its Roots to Find Its Future," *New York Times*, April 30, 2001, p. B5.

22. Ibid.

23. *Boulder Canyon Act of 1928*, 45 Stat. 1057, 43 U.S.C. §617.

24. 63 Stat. 31 (1949).

25. *Colorado River Basin Water Problems: How to Reduce Their Impact* (Washington, DC: U.S. General Accounting Office, 1979), pp. 53–54.

26. B. Drummond Ayres, "Chesapeake Cleanup Pact Is Signed," *New York Times*, December 16, 1987, p. A20.

27. 49 Stat. 932 (1935).

28. *New Jersey Laws of 1961*, chap. 105; *New York Laws of 1960*, chap. 476; and *Connecticut Public Acts of 1969*, Act 5.

29. *Memorandum to the Legislature: Interstate Sanitation Commission* (Albany: New York State Legislative Commission on Expenditure Review, 1990).

30. Ibid., pp. 2–3.

31. Interview with Director N.G. Kaul, Division of Water, New York State Department of Environmental Conservation, Albany, New York, February 8, 2001. Hereinafter referred to as Kaul Interview.

32. 61 Stat. 682 (1947).

34. Kaul Interview.

34. *Annual Report 1998* (Cincinnati: Ohio River Valley Water Sanitation Commission, 1999), pp. 14–15.

35. Frankfurter and Landis, "The Commerce Clause of the Constitution: A Study in Interstate Adjustments," p. 688.

36. 54 Stat. 752 (1948).

37. *New Jersey v. New York*, 283 U.S. 805, 51 S.Ct. 562 (1931).

38. *New Jersey v. New York*, 347 U.S. 995, 74 S.Ct. 842 (1954).

39. Roscoe C. Martin, Guthrie S. Birkhead, Jesse Burkhead, and Frank J. Munger, *River Basin Administration and the Delaware* (Syracuse, NY: Syracuse University Press, 1960), pp. 341–62.

40. 75 Stat. 688 (1961); *Delaware Laws of 1961*, chap. 71; *New Jersey Laws of 1961*, chap. 13; *New York Laws of 1961*, chap. 148; and *Pennsylvania Acts of 1961*, Act 268.

41. Jerome C. Muys, "Interstate Compacts and Regional Water Resources Planning and Management," *Natural Resources Lawyer* 6, Spring 1973, p. 164.

42. Jeffrey P. Featherstone, "An Evaluation of Federal-Interstate Compacts As an Institutional Model for Intergovernmental Coordination and Management: Water Resources for Interstate River Basins in the United States" (Philadelphia: Unpublished Ph. D. dissertation, Temple University, 1999), p. 182.

43. Ibid., pp. 182–85.

44. 110 Stat. 919, 7 U.S.C. §7256.

45. 76 Stat. 249 (1962).

46. 84 Stat. 979 (1970).

47. 76 Stat. 797 (1962).

48. 56 Stat. 267 (1942).

49. *Atlantic Striped Bass Conservation Act Amendment of 1986*, 100 Stat. 989, 16 U.S.C. §1851 note.

50. 61 Stat. 419 (1947) and 63 Stat. 70 (1949).

51. 97 Stat. 866 (1983).

52. 67 Stat. 45 (1953), 71 Stat. 18 (1957), and 72 Stat. 364 (1958).

53. *Atomic Energy Act of 1946*, 60 Stat. 755, 42 U.S.C. §2011, and *Atomic Energy Act of 1959*, 73 Stat. 688, 42 U.S.C. §2021.

54. *Low Level Radioactive Waste Policy Act of 1980*, 94 Stat. 3347, 42 U.S.C. §2021d.

55. *Commercial Motor Vehicle Safety Act of 1986*, 100 Stat. 3207, 49 U.S.C. §2701.

56. *United States Steel Corporation v. Multistate Tax Commission*, 434 U.S. 452 at 473, 98 S.Ct. 799 at 813 (1978).

57. *Model Regulations, Statutes, and Guidelines: Uniformity Recommendations to the States* (Washington, DC: Multistate Tax Commission, 1995), pp. 1–70.

58. 86 Stat. 383 (1979).

59. 96 Stat. 1207 (1982).

60. 67 Stat. 541 (1953).

61. Joseph F. Zimmerman, "Interstate Cooperation: The Roles of the State Attorneys General," *Publius* 28, Winter 1998, pp. 82–85.

62. Amy Harmon, "U.S. Says Dissenting States Can Pursue Microsoft," *New York Times*, April 16, 2002, p. C10.

63. *Clean Air Act Amendments of 1990*, 104 Stat. 2448, 42 U.S.C. §7511(e).

64. Jerry Gray, "States with Acute Smog Problem Sign Ozone Pact," *New York Times*, August 5, 1992, p. A18.

65. 97 Stat. 866 (1983).

66. *Paul v. Virginia*, 75 U.S 168, 8 Wall. 168 (1868).

67. *United State v. South-Eastern Underwriters Association*, 322 U.S. 533, 64 S.Ct. 1162 (1944).

68. *McCarran-Ferguson Act of 1945*, 59 Stat. 33, 15 U.S.C. §1011.

69. *Gramm-Leach-Bliley Financial Reorganization Act of 1999*, 113 Stat. 1353, 5 U.S.C. §6701(d)(2)(A).

70. Ibid., 113 Stat. 1422, 15 U.S.C. §6751.

71. "Members Certify GLBA Reciprocity Requirement Met," a news release issued by the National Association of Insurance Commissioners, September 11, 2002.

72. E-mail message from Associate Counsel John Bauer of the National Association of Insurance Commissioners, August 12, 2002.

73. *Financial Regulation Standards and Accreditation Program* (Kansas City: National Association of Insurance Commissioners, 2000).

74. Richard J. Hillman, *Efforts to Streamline Key Licensing and Approval Processes Face Challenged* (Washington, DC: U.S. General Accounting Office, 2002).

75. 15 U.S.C. §1172(a) and 18 U.S.C. §1301.

76. Tom Fahey, "Northeast States Eye Prescription Buying Pool," *Union Leader* (Manchester, NH), December 15, 2000, p. B3.

77. Richard J. Meislin, "10 States Link Efforts to Hunt Tax Cheaters," *New York Times*, January 17, 1986, p. B1.

78. "A Taxation Milestone," *Government Technology*, June 2002, p. 20.

79. *Economic Benefits of Recycling in the Southern States* (Norcross, GA: Southern States Energy Board, 1996).

Chapter 9

1. *The Act to Regulate Commerce of 1887*, 24 Stat. 379, 49 U.S.C. §1, and *Sherman Antitrust Act of 1890*, 26 Stat. 209, 15 U.S.C. §1.

2. *Bankruptcy Act of 1800*, 2 Stat. 19, *Bankruptcy Act of 1841*, 5 Stat. 440, and *Bankruptcy Act of 1867*, 14 Stat. 517.

3. *An Act to Establish a Uniform System of Bankruptcy of 1898*, 30 Stat. 44, 11 U.S.C. §1.

4. *Gibbons v. Ogden*, 22 U.S. 1, 9 Wheat. 1 (1824).

5. *Commercial Drivers License Act of 1986*, 100 Stat. 3207, 49 U.S.C. §2701.

6. *Surface Transportation Assistance Act of 1982*, 96 Stat. 2097, 23 U.S.C. §101.

7. *Clean Water Act of 1977*, 91 Stat. 1575, 33 U.S.C. §1261.

8. www.nccusl.org (August 14, 2002).

9. *Gramm-Leach-Bliley Financial Reorganization Act of 1999*, 113 Stat. 1353, 5 U.S.C. §6701(d)(2)(A).

10. *Model Regulations, Statutes, and Guidelines: Uniformity Recommendations to the States* (Washington, DC: Multistate Tax Commission, 1995).

11. www.mtc.gov (August 14, 2002).

12. Joseph F. Zimmerman, *Federal Preemption: The Silent Revolution* (Ames: Iowa State University Press, 1991).

13. *Morales v. Trans World Airlines*, 504 U.S. 374, 112 S.Ct. 2031 (1992) and *Airline Deregulation Act of 1978*, 92 Stat. 1708, 49 U.S.C. §§1305 and 1371.

14. *Jenkins Act of 1949*, 61 Stat. 884, 15 U.S.C. §374.

15. "EPA & States to Restore Great Lakes," *EPA Activities Update*, April 17, 1995, p. 1.

16. W. Brooke Graves, "Influence of Congressional Legislation in the States," *Iowa Law Review* 23, May 1938, p. 538.

Bibliography

Books and Reports

Anderson, William. *The Nation and the States: Rivals or Partners*. Minneapolis: University of Minnesota Press, 1953.

Bard, Erwin. *The Port of New York Authority*. New York: Columbia University Press, 1941.

Barton, Weldon V. *Interstate Compacts in the Political Process*. Chapel Hill: University of North Carolina Press, 1967.

Bird, Frederick L. *A Study of the Port of New York Authority*. New York: Dun & Bradstreet, 1948.

Blakely, M. Murphy, ed. *Conservation of Oil & Gas: A Legal History, 1948*. Chicago: Section of Mineral Law, American Bar Association, 1949.

Book of the States, The. Lexington, KY: The Council of State Governments, published annually.

Brace, Paul. *State Government and Economic Performance*. Baltimore: Johns Hopkins University Press, 1993.

Bradshaw, Michael. *The Appalachian Regional Commission*. Lexington: The University Press of Kentucky, 1992.

Break, George F. *Financing Government in a Federal System*. Washington, DC: The Brookings Institution, 1980.

Brogan, D.W. *Politics in America*. Garden City: New American Library 1960.

Brown, David W. *The Commercial Power of Congress Considered in the Light of Its Origin*. New York: G.P. Putnam's Sons, 1910.

Brunori, David. *State Tax Policy: A Political Perspective*. Washington, DC: The Urban Institute Press, 2001.

Burns, Michael E. *Low-Level Radioactive Waste Regulation: Science, Politics, and Fear*. Chelsea, MI: Lewis Publishers, Incorporated, 1988.

Cagan, Joanna and Neil DeMause. *Field of Schemes: How the Great Stadium Swindle Turns Public Money into Private Profits*, rev. ed. Monroe, ME: Common Courage Press, 1998.

Clark, Cal and Robert S. Montjoy. *Globalization's Impact on State-Local Economic Development Policy*. Huntington, NY: Nova Science Publishers, 2001.

Cleary, Edward J. *The Orsanco Story: Water Quality Management in the Ohio Valley Under an Interstate Compact*. Baltimore: Johns Hopkins University Press, 1967.

Cobb, James C. *The Selling of the South: The Southern Crusade for Industrial Development, 1936–1990*. Urbana: University of Illinois Press, 1993.

Commager, Henry S., ed. *Documents of American History to 1898*, 8th ed. New York: Appleton-Century-Crofts, 1968.

Conant, James B. *Shaping Educational Policy*. New York: McGraw-Hill Book Company, 1964.

Cooke, Frederick H. *The Commerce Clause of the Federal Constitution*. New York: Baker, Voorhis & Company, 1908.

Corwin, Edward S. *The Commerce Power versus States Rights*. Princeton: Princeton University Press, 1936.

Cotterill, Ronald W. and Franklin, Andrew W. *The Public Interest and Private Economic Power: A Case Study of the Northeast Dairy Compact*. Storrs: Food Marketing Policy Center, University of Connecticut, 2001.

Danielson, Michael and Jameson W. Doig. *New York: The Politics of Urban Regional Development*. Berkeley: University of California Press, 1982.

Derthick, Martha. *Between State and Nation*. Washington, DC: The Brookings Institution, 1974.

Dimock, Marshall E. and George C.S. Benson. *Can Interstate Compacts Succeed? The Uses and Limitations of Interstate Agreements*. Chicago: University of Chicago Press, 1937.

Doig, Jameson W. *Empire on the Hudson: Entrepreneurial Vision and Political Power at the Port of New York Authority*. New York: Columbia University Press, 2001.

Due, John F. and Mikesell, John L. *Sales Taxation: State and Local Structure and Administration*, 2nd ed. Washington, DC: The Urban Institute Press, 1994.

Duquette, Jerold. *Regulating the National Pastime: Baseball and Antitrust*. Westport, CT: Praeger Publishers, 1999.

Dye, Thomas R. *American Federalism: Competition Among Governments*. Lexington, MA: Lexington Books, 1990.

Eisiner, Peter K. *The Rise of the Entrepreneurial State: State and Local Economic Development Policy in the United States*. Madison: University of Wisconsin Press, 1988.

Elazar, Daniel J. *The American Partnership*. Chicago: University of Chicago Press, 1962.

Farrand, Max. *The Records of the Federal Convention of 1787*. New Haven: Yale University Press, 1966.

The Federalist Papers. New York: New American Library, 1961.

Fesler, James W. *The 50 States and Their Local Governments*. New York: Alfred A. Knopf, Incorporated, 1967.

Fife, Emerson D. *Government by Cooperation*. New York: The Macmillan Company, 1932.

Financial Regulation Standards and Accreditation Program. Kansas City, MO: National Association of Insurance Commissioners, 2000.

Fleenor, Patrick. *How Excise Tax Differentials Affect Cross-Border Sales of Beer in the United States*. Washington, DC: Tax Foundation, 1999.

———. *How Excise Tax Differentials Affect Interstate Smuggling and Cross-Border Sales of Cigarettes in the United States*. Washington, DC: Tax Foundation, 1998.

Fosler, R. Scott, ed. *The New Economic Role of American States*. New York: Oxford University Press, 1988.

Frankfurter, Felix. *The Commerce Clause Under Marshall, Taney, and Waite*. Chapel Hill: University of North Carolina Press, 1937.

Friendly, Henry J. *Federal Jurisdiction: A General View*. New York: Columbia University Press, 1973.

Graves, W. Brooke. *Uniform State Action: A Possible Substitute for Centralization*. Chapel Hill: University of North Carolina Press, 1934.

Goodman, Robert. *The Luck Business: The Devastating Consequences and Broken Promises of America's Gambling Explosion*. New York: The Free Press, 1995.

Green, Thomas S., Jr. *State Discriminations Against Out of State Alcoholic Beverages*. Chicago: The Council of State Governments, 1939.

Grodzins, Morton. *The American System: A New View of Government in the United States*. Chicago: Rand McNally, 1966.

Guide to the Interstate Compact on the Placement of Children. Washington, DC: American Public Human Services Association, 2000.

Haines, Charles G. *The Role of the Supreme Court in American Government and Politics: 1789–1835*. New York: Russell & Russell, 1960.

Haines, Charles G. and Foster H. Sherwood. *The Role of the Supreme Court in American Government and Politics: 1835–1864*. Berkeley: University of California Press, 1957.

Handbook of High-Level Radioactive Waste Transportation. Lombard, IL: The Midwestern Office of the Council of State Governments, 1992.

Handbook of Interstate Crime Control. Lexington, KY: The Council of State Governments, 1978.

Hansen, Susan. *The Politics of Taxation: Revenue without Representation*. New York: Praeger Publishers, 1983.

Hardy, Paul T. *Interstate Compacts: The Ties That Bind*. Athens: Institute of Government, University of Georgia, 1982.

Hogarty, Richard A. *The Delaware River Drought Emergency*. Indianapolis: The Bobbs-Merrill Company, 1970.

Hunt, Gaillard, ed. *The Writings of James Madison*. New York: G.P. Putnam's Sons, 1901.

To Improve Cooperation Among the States. Chicago: The Council of State Governments, 1962.

IFTA Legislation and State Constitutional Provisions Project: Final Report. Denver: National Conference of State Legislatures, 1999.

Interstate Compacts: 1783–1970: A Compilation. Lexington, KY: The Council of State Governments, 1971.

Interstate River Basin Development. Chicago: The Council of State Governments, 1947.

Jackson, Robert H. *Full Faith and Credit: The Lawyer's Clause of the Constitution.* New York: Columbia University Press, 1945.

Just, Richard E. and Sinaia Netanyaghu, eds. *Conflict and Cooperation on TransBoundary Water Issues.* Boston: Kluwer Academic Publishers, 1998.

Kallenbach, Joseph E. *Federal Cooperation with the States Under the Commerce Clause.* Ann Arbor: University of Michigan Press, 1942.

Kayne, Jay and Molly Shonks. *Rethinking State Development Policies and Programs.* Washington, DC: National Governors' Association, 1994.

Kenyon, Daphne and John Kincaid, eds. *Competition among States and Local Governments: Efficiency and Equity in American Federalism.* Washington, DC: The Urban Institute Press, 1991.

Klobuchar, Amy. *Uncovering the Dome: Was the Public Interest Served in Minnesota's 10-Year Political Brawl Over the Metrodome?* Prospect Heights, IL: Waveland Press, Incorporated, 1986.

Kollin, Stanley. *Interstate Sanitation Commission: A Discussion of the Development and Administration of an Interstate Compact.* Syracuse, NY: Syracuse University Press, 1954.

KPMG Peat Marwick Economic Policy Group. *Effects of Cross-Border Sales on Economic Activity and State Revenues: A Case Study of Tobacco Excise Taxes in Massachusetts, New York City, and Surrounding Areas.* Washington, DC: Tax Foundation, 1993.

Lampe, David, ed. *The Massachusetts Miracle: High Technology and Economic Revitalization.* Cambridge: MIT Press, 1988.

Laski, Harold J. *The American Democracy.* New York: The Viking Press, 1948.

Lass, Daniel A. *1996 Costs of Production in the New England Milk Market.* Amherst: Department of Resource Economics, University of Massachusetts, 1999.

Leach, Richard H. *Interstate Relations in Australia.* Lexington: University of Kentucky Press, 1965.

Leach, Richard H. and Redding S. Sugg Jr. *The Administration of Interstate Compacts.* Baton Rouge: Louisiana State University Press, 1959.

Leuchtenburg, William. *Flood Control Politics: The Connecticut River Valley Problem 1927–1950.* Cambridge: Harvard University Press, 1953.

Maass, Arthur. *Muddy Waters: The Army Engineers and the Nation's Rivers.* Cambridge: Harvard University Press, 1953.

Martin, Roscoe E., et al. *River Basin Administration and the Delaware.* Syracuse, NY: Syracuse University Press, 1960.

McClure, Charles E., Jr. *Economic Perspectives on State Taxation of Multijurisdictional Corporations.* Arlington, VA: Tax Analysts, 1986.

McGowan, Richard. *State Lotteries and Legalized Gambling: Painless Revenue or Painful Mirage.* Westport, CT: Praeger Publishers, 1994.

McMahon, Arthur W., ed. *Federalism: Mature and Emergent.* Garden City, NY: Doubleday & Company, Incorporated, 1955.

Melder, Frederick E. *State and Local Barriers to Interstate Commerce in the United States: A Study in Economic Sectionalism.* Orono, ME: University Press, 1937.

Model Regulations, Statutes, and Guidelines: Uniformity Recommendations to the States. Washington, DC: Multistate Tax Commission, 1995.

Morley, Felix. *Freedom and Federalism.* Chicago: Henry Regnery, 1959.

Murphy, Blakely M. *Conservation of Oil & Gas: A Legal History, 1948.* Chicago: Section on Mineral Law, American Bar Association, 1949.

NASBLA Reference Guide to State Boating Laws, 5th ed. Lexington, KY: National Association of State Boating Law Administrators, 1999.

Nice, David C. *Federalism.* New York: St. Martin's Press, 1987.

Nicholson, Charles F., ed. *The Northeast Interstate Dairy Compact: Milk Market Impacts.* Burlington: Agricultural Experiment Station, University of Vermont, 2000.

O'Brien, Sharon. *American Indian Tribal Governments.* Norman: University of Oklahoma Press, 1980.

Pabst, W.R., Jr. *Butter and Oleomargarine: An Analysis of Competing Commodities.* New York: Columbia University Press, 1937.

Palgrave, R.H. Inglis. *Dictionary of Political Economy.* London: Macmillan and Company, Limited, 1896.

Prentice, E. Parmalee and John G. Egan. *The Commerce Clause of the Federal Constitution.* Chicago: Callaghan and Company, 1898.

Quirk, James and Rodney Fort. *Hard Ball: The Abuse of Power in Pro Team Sports.* Princeton, NJ: Princeton University Press, 1999.

Report on Mutual Aid Agreements for Radiological Transportation Emergencies. Lombard, IL: The Midwestern Office of the Council of State Governments, 1993.

Resource Manual. Santa Fe, NM: Association of Juvenile Compact Administrators, 2000.

Richard, Wilbur C., ed. *The Economics and Politics of Sports Facilities.* Westport, CT: Quorum Books, 2000.

Richardson, James D. *A Compilation of the Messages and Papers of the Presidents, 1789–1897.* Washington, DC: United States Government Printing Office, 1898, vol. 2.

Ridgeway, Marian E. *Interstate Compacts: A Question of Federalism.* Carbondale: Southern Illinois University Press, 1971.

Rivlin, Alice M. *Reviving the American Dream: The Economy, the States & the Federal Government.* Washington, DC: The Brookings Institution, 1992.

Rose, Peter S. *Banking Across State Lines: Public and Private Consequences.* Westport, CT: Quorum Books, 1997.

Rosentraub, Mark S. *Major League Losers: The Real Cost of Sports and Who's Paying for It,* rev. ed. New York: Basic Books, 1999.

Roy F. Weston, Incorporated. *Economic Benefits of Recycling in the Southern States.* Norcross, GA: Southern States Energy Board, 1996.

Saxon, John L. *Enforcement and Modification of Out-of-State Child Support Orders.* Chapel Hill: Institute of Government, University of North Carolina, 1994.

Schmenner, Roger W. *Making Business Location Decisions.* Englewood Cliffs, NJ: Prentice-Hall Incorporated, 1982.

Scott, James A. *The Law of Interstate Rendition Erroneously Referred to As Interstate Extradition: A Treatise.* Chicago: Sherman Hight, Publisher, 1917.

Selznick, Philip. *TVA and the Grass Roots.* Berkeley: The University of California Press, 1949.

Shapiro, Daniel. *Federalism in Taxation: The Case for Greater Uniformity.* Washington, DC: The AEI Press, 1993.

Sherk, George W. *Dividing the Waters: The Resolution of Interstate Water Conflicts in the United States.* Boston: Kluwer Law International, 2000.

Smith, Adam. *An Inquiry into the Nature and Causes of the Wealth of Nations.* New York: The Modern Library, 1937.

Snell, Ronald K. *Weight-Distance Taxes and Other Highway User Taxes: An Introduction for Legislators and Legislative Staff.* Denver: National Conference of State Legislatures, 1989.

Spiegel, John, Alan Gart, and Steven Gart. *Banking Redefined.* Chicago: Irwin Professional Publishing, 1996.

Story, Joseph. *Commentaries on the Constitution of the United States.* Boston: Hilliard, Gray, and Company, 1833.

Sugg, Redding S., Jr. and George H. Jones. *The Southern Regional Education Board: Ten Years of Regional Cooperation in Higher Education.* Baton Rouge: Louisiana State University Press, 1960.

Summary of State Laws & Regulations Relating to Distilled Spirits. Washington, DC: Distilled Spirits Council of the United States, 2002.

Thursby, Vincent V. *Interstate Cooperation: A Study of the Interstate Compact.* Washington, DC: Public Affairs Press, 1953.

2003 Interstate Compacts & Activities. Lexington, KY: The Council of State Governments, 2003.

Voigt, William, Jr. *The Susquehanna Compact.* New Brunswick, NJ: Rutgers University Press, 1972.

Voit, Kevin and Gary Nitting. *Interstate Compacts & Agencies 1998.* Lexington, KY: The Council of State Governments, 1998.

Water Wars. Lexington, KY: The Council of State Governments, 2003.

Watson, Douglas J. *The New Civil War: Government Competition for Economic Development.* Westport, CT: Praeger Publishers, 1995.

Weiner, Jay. *Stadium Games: Fifty Years of Big-League Greed and Bush League Boondoggles.* Minneapolis: University of Minnesota Press, 2000.

Wendell, Mitchell. *Relations Between Federal and State Courts.* New York: Columbia University Press, 1949.

Wilson, Woodrow. *Congressional Government: A Study in American Politics*. Boston: Houghton Mifflin Company, 1925.

Zimmerman, Dennis. *The Private Use of Tax-Exempt Bonds: Controlling Public Subsidy of Private Activity*. Washington, DC: The Urban Institute Press, 1991.

Zimmerman, Joseph F. *Contemporary American Federalism: The Growth of National Power*. Leicester: Leicester University Press, 1992.

———. *Federal Preemption: The Silent Revolution*. Ames: Iowa State University Press, 1991.

———. *Interstate Cooperation: Compacts and Administrative Agreements*. Westport, CT: Praeger Publishers, 2002.

———. *Interstate Relations: The Neglected Dimension of Federalism*. Westport, CT: Praeger Publishers, 1996.

———. *The Recall: Tribunal of the People*. Westport, CT: Praeger Publishers, 1997.

———. *State-Local Relations: A Partnership Approach*, 2nd ed. Westport, CT: Praeger Publishers, 1995.

Zimmermann, Erich W. *Conservation in the Production of Petroleum: A Study in Industrial Control*. New Haven: Yale University Press, 1957.

Zimmermann, Frederick L., and Mitchell Wendell. *The Interstate Compact Since 1925*. Chicago: The Council of State Governments, 1951.

———. *The Law and Use of Interstate Compacts*. Lexington, KY: The Council of State Governments, 1976.

Public Documents

ABC's . . . of the Port Authority of New York and New Jersey, The. New York: The Authority, 1991.

Acid Rain Action Plan. Halifax, NS: Conference of New England Governors and Eastern Canadian Premiers, 1998.

Agency Out of Control: A Critical Assessment of the Finances of the Port Authority of New York and New Jersey. Albany: Committee on Corporations, Authorities, and Commissions, New York State Assembly, 1982.

Alternative Institutional Arrangements for Managing River Basin Operations. Washington, DC: Water Resources Council, 1967.

Annual Report. Warner, NH: Northeastern Forest Fire Protection Commission, 2000.

Annual Report 1998. Cincinnati: Ohio River Valley Water Sanitation Commission, 1999.

Annual Report 1998. Lowell, MA: New England Interstate Water Pollution Control Commission, 1998.

Annual Report 1998–1999. New York: The Waterfront Commission of New York Harbor, 1999.

Annual Report 2000. Boston: Northeast Waste Management Officials' Association, 2001.

Annual Report 2000–2001. Schenectady: New York State Lottery, 2001.

Annual Report of the U.S. Atlantic Salmon Assessment Committee. Nashua, NH: The Committee, 2000.

Articles of Agreement for Proposed Rivendell Interstate School District. Orford, NH: The District, 1998.

Barriers to the Development and Expanded Use of Natural Gas Resources. Oklahoma City, OK: Interstate Oil and Gas Compact Commission, 1992.

Boyd, Eugene. *American Federalism, 1776 to 1995: Significant Events.* Washington, DC: Congressional Research Service, 1995.

Briefing Manual. Warner, NH: Northeastern Forest Fire Protection Commission, 2000.

Business Plan 2000 Update. Saratoga Springs, NY: I-95 Corridor Coalition, 2000.

By-Laws of the Northeast Dairy Compact Commission. Montpelier, VT: 2001.

Challenge to Restore and Protect the Largest Body of Fresh Water in the World, The. Washington, DC: International Joint Commission, 2002.

Cigarette Bootlegging: A State and Federal Responsibility. Washington, DC: U.S. Advisory Commission on Intergovernmental Relations, 1977.

Cigarette Tax Evasion: A Second Look. Washington, DC: U.S. Advisory Commission on Intergovernmental Relations, 1985.

Colorado River Basin Water Problems: How to Reduce Their Impact. Washington, DC: U.S. General Accounting Office, 1979.

Combating Cigarette Smuggling. Washington, DC: Law Enforcement Assistance Administration, 1976.

Commuter and the Municipal Income Tax, The. Washington, DC: U.S. Advisory Commission on Intergovernmental Relations, 1970.

Compact on Education, The. Durham, NC: Education Commission of the States, 1965.

Compact's Formative Years: 1931–1935, The. Oklahoma City, OK: Interstate Oil Compact Commission, 1954.

Connecticut River Basin Anadromous Fisheries Restoration: Coordination and Technical Assistance. Federal Aid Progress Report October 1, 1999–September 30, 2000. Sunderland, MA: U.S. Fish and Wildlife Service, 2000.

Coordination of State and Federal Inheritance, Estate, and Gift Taxes. Washington, DC: U.S. Advisory Commission on Intergovernmental Relations, 1961.

Criminal Penalty for Flight to Avoid Payment of Arrearages in Child Support: Hearing Before the Subcommittee on Crime and Criminal Justice, United States House of Representatives. Washington, DC: U.S. Government Printing Office, 1992.

Dairy Industry: Estimated Impacts of Dairy Compacts. Washington, DC: U.S. General Accounting Office, 2001.

Dairy Industry: Information on Milk Prices and Changing Market Structure. Washington, DC: U.S. General Accounting Office, 2001.

Delaware River Basin Compact. Hearings before Subcommittee No. 1, Committee on the Judiciary, House of Representatives, 87th Congress, First Session on H.J. 225. Washington, DC: U.S. Government Printing Office, 1961.

Delaware River Basin Compact: Report to Accompany H.J. 225. Washington, DC: U.S. Senate Committee on the Judiciary, 1961 (Report No. 854).

Department of Agriculture and Markets Annual Report 1992. Albany, NY: 1993.

Directory of Intergovernmental Contacts. Washington, DC: U.S. Advisory Commission on Intergovernmental Relations, 1994.

Economic Benefits of Recycling in the Southern States. Washington, DC: Southern States Energy Board, 1996.

Effectiveness of Enterprise Zones: Hearing before the Committee on Finance, United States Senate. Washington, DC: U.S. Government Printing Office, 1992

Electric Power Industry Competition Legislation: Hearings Before the Committee on Energy and Natural Resources, United States Senate, April 11, 13, and 27, 2000. Washington, DC: U.S. Government Printing Office, 2000.

Electronic Government: Opportunities and Challenges Facing the FirstGovWeb Gateway. Washington, DC: U.S. General Accounting Office, 2000.

Erkan, Dennis E. *Strategic Plan for the Restoration of Atlantic Salmon to the Pawcatuck River.* Providence: Rhode Island Division of Fish and Wildlife, 2000.

Federal-Interstate Compact Commissions: Useful Mechanisms for Planning and Managing River Basin Operations. Washington, DC: U.S. General Accounting Office, 1981.

Finding Common Ground: Conserving the Northern Forest. Concord, NH: Northern Forest Lands Council, 1994.

Florestano, Patricia S. *Interstate Compacts in Maryland.* Annapolis: Maryland Commission on Intergovernmental Cooperation, 1975.

——— . *A Survey of the Interstate Compacts in Which the State of Maryland Currently Has Membership.* Annapolis: Maryland Commission on Intergovernmental Cooperation, 1972.

Flow Control and Interstate Transportation of Solid Waste: Hearing Before the Subcommittee on Superfund, Waste Control, and Risk Assessment of the Committee on Environment and Public Works, United States Senate, March 1, 1995. Washington, DC: U.S Government Printing office, 1995.

Gaming Activities on Indian Reservations and Lands. Hearing Before the Select Committee on Indian Affairs, United States Senate on S. 555, June 18, 1987. Washington, DC: U.S. Government Printing Office, 1987.

Generating Prosperity in the Valley. Knoxville: Tennessee Valley Authority, 1999.

Grade "A" Pasteurized Milk Ordinance. Washington, DC: U.S. Food and Drug Administration, 1993.

"Guide to Federal Participation in Interstate Compacts." *Documents on Use and Control of the Waters of Interstate and International Streams: Compacts, Treaties, and Adjudications.* Washington, DC: U.S. Government Printing Office, 1956: 247–48.

Healing a River: The Potomac: 1940–1990. Rockville, MD: Interstate Commission on the Potomac River Basin Commission, 1990.

Hearing on Interstate Use Tax Collection: Hearing Before the Committee on Small Business, United States Senate, April 13, 1994. Washington, DC: U.S. Government Printing office, 1994.

Highlights of 1999–2000. Denver, CO: Education Commission of the States, 2000.

Hillman, Richard J. *State Insurance Regulation: Efforts to Streamline Key Licensing and Approval Processes Face Challenges.* Washington, DC: U.S. General Accounting Office, 2002.

Impact of State Economic Regulation of Motor Carriage on Intrastate and Interstate Commerce, The. Washington, DC: U.S. Department of Transportation, 1990.

Implementation of the Indian Gaming Regulatory Act. Hearing Before the Select Committee on Indian Affairs, United States Senate, February 5, 1992, Part 1. Washington, DC: U.S. Government Printing Office, 1992.

Implementation of the Indian Gaming Regulatory Act. Hearing Before the Select Committee on Indian Affairs, United States Senate, March 18, 1992, Part 2. Washington, DC: U.S. Government Printing Office, 1992.

Implementation of the Indian Gaming Regulatory Act. Hearing Before the Select Committee on Indian Affairs, United States Senate, May 6, 1992, Part 3. Washington, DC: U.S. Government Printing Office, 1992.

IMS List Sanitation Compliance and Enforcement Ratings of Interstate Milk Shippers. Washington, DC: U.S. Food and Drug Administration, 1993.

Industrial Development Bond Financing. Washington, DC: U.S. Advisory Commission on Intergovernmental Relations, 1963.

Industrial Development Bonds: Achievement of Public Benefit Is Unclear. Washington, DC: U.S. General Accounting Office, 1993.

Insurance Regulation: Assessment of the National Association of Insurance Commissioners. Washington, DC: U.S. General Accounting Office, 1991.

Insurance Regulation: The Financial Regulation Standards and Accreditation Program of the National Association of Insurance Commissioners. Washington, DC: U.S. General Accounting Office, 1992.

Insurance Regulation: The National Association of Insurance Commissioners' Accreditation Program Continues to Exhibit Fundamental Problems. Washington, DC: U.S. General Accounting Office, 1993.

Insurance Regulation: Scandal Highlights Need for Strengthened Regulatory Oversight. Washington, DC: U.S. General Accounting Office, 2000.

Intergovernmental Aspects of Documentary Taxes, The. Washington, DC: U.S. Advisory Commission on Intergovernmental Relations, 1964.

Interjurisdictional Tax and Policy Competition: Good or Bad for the Federal System. Washington, DC: U.S. Advisory Commission on Intergovernmental Relations, 1991.

International Board of Inquiry for the Great Lakes Fisheries: Report and Supplement. Washington, DC: U.S. Government Printing Office, 1943.

International Joint Commission and the Boundary Waters Treaty of 1909, The. Washington, DC: The Commission, 1998.

International Registration Plan. Albany: New York State Department of Motor Vehicles, 2000.

Interstate Banking: Benefits and Risks of Removing Regulatory Restrictions. Washington, DC: U.S. Government Printing Office, 1993.

Interstate Banking: Experiences in Three Western States. Washington, DC: U.S. Government Printing Office, 1994.

Interstate Cooperation: A Directory of New York's Interstate Compacts and Interstate Agencies. Albany: New York State Senate Select Committee on Interstate Cooperation, 2002.

Interstate Sanitation Commission: The Need for Change, The. Albany: New York State Senate Select Committee on Interstate Cooperation, 1981.

Interstate Sanitation Commission 1992 Annual Report. New York: The Commission, 1993.

Interstate Tax Competition. Washington, DC: U.S. Advisory Commission on Intergovernmental Relations, 1981.

IOGCC Environmental Guidelines for State Oil & Gas Regulatory Programs. Oklahoma City, OK: Interstate Oil & Gas Compact Commission, 1994.

Low-Level Radioactive Wastes: States Are Not Developing Disposal Facilities. Washington, DC: U.S. General Accounting Office, 1999.

Making Connections: 1999 Annual Report. Atlanta: Southern Regional Education Board, 1999.

McBride, Janice L. *A Catalog and Guide to Maryland's Interstate Compacts.* Annapolis: Maryland Joint Committee on Federal Relations, 1987.

Memorandum Report to the Legislature: Interstate Sanitation Commission. Albany: New York State Legislative Commission on Expenditure Review, 1990.

Michigan Single Business Tax: A Different Approach to State Business Taxation. Washington, DC: U.S. Advisory Commission on Intergovernmental Relations, 1978.

Multistate Regional Intelligence Projects: Hearings Before a Subcommittee of the Committee on Government Operations, House of Representatives, May 27–28, Washington, DC: U.S. Government Printing Office, 1981.

Multistate Regional Intelligence Projects: Who Will Oversee These Federally Funded Networks? Washington, DC: U.S. General Accounting Office, 1980.

Multistate Regionalism. Washington, DC: U.S. Advisory Commission on Intergovernmental Relations, 1972.

MWBAC Biennial Report 1997–1998. Hudson, WI: Minnesota-Wisconsin Boundary Area Commission, 1998.

NAIC 2000 Annual Report. Kansas City, MO: National Association of Insurance Commissioners, 2001.

National Capital Section, American Water Resources Association. *A 1980's View of Water Management in the Potomac River Basin.* Washington, DC: U.S. Government Printing Office, 1982.

National Plant Board Membership Manual. Washington, DC: 2000.

Nebraska Blue Book, 1998. Lincoln: Nebraska Secretary of State, 1998.

Needs Assessment. Warner, NH: Northeastern Forest Fire Protection Commission, 1999.

New Directions for Regional Planning. New York: The Report of the Governors' Task Force on the Future of the Tri-State Regional Planning Commission, 1981.

New York Power Authority: Management and Operations. Albany: Office of the New York State Comptroller, 2001.

New York State's Competitiveness: A Scorecard for 12 States. New York: Citizens Budget Commission, 2001.

New York's Competitiveness: A Scorecard for 13 U.S. Metropolitan Areas. New York: Citizens Budget Commission, 2001.

1980's View of Water Management in the Potomac River Basin: A Report for the Committee on Governmental Affairs, United States Senate. Washington, DC: U.S. Government Printing Office, 1982.

1986 Annual Report. Albany: New York State Senate Select Committee on Interstate Cooperation, 1986.

1990 Annual Report. Albany: New York State Senate Select Committee on Interstate Cooperation, 1991.

1991–1992 Annual Report. New York: Waterfront Commission of New York Harbor, 1992.

1992 Annual Report. Albany: New York State Senate Select Committee on Interstate Cooperation, 1994.

1993 Annual Report. Albany: New York State Senate Select Committee on Interstate Cooperation, 1995.

1997 Annual Report. Albany: New York State Senate Select Committee on Interstate Cooperation, 1998.

1997–2002 Capital Plan. Albany: New York State Thruway Authority, 1997.

1999 Annual Report. Harrisburg, PA: Susquehanna River Basin Commission, 2001.

1999 Annual Report. New York: Interstate Sanitation Commission, 2000.

1994 Driver License Administration Requirements and Fees. Washington, DC: Federal Highway Administration, 1994.

Northeast Interstate Dairy Compact: Hearings Before the Subcommittee on Administrative Law and Governmental Relations of the Committee on the Judiciary, House of Representatives on H.R. 4560. Washington, DC: U.S. Government Printing Office, 1994.

Norton, Robert. *Study of NESCAUM As a Model of Regional Consortia.* Boston: Northeast States for Coordinated Air Use Management, 1989.

Observations on the FBI's Interstate Identification Index. Washington, DC: U.S. General Accounting Office, 1994.

Outlook for Multistate Regional Intelligence Projects: Twelfth Report by the Committee on Government Operations, U.S. House of Representatives. Washington, DC: U.S. Government Printing Office, 1981.

Oversight and Reauthorization of the Appalachian Regional Commission and the Economic Development Administration: Hearing Before the Subcommittee on Water Resources, Transportation, and Infrastructure, United States Senate on H.R. 2015. Washington, DC: U.S. Government Printing Office, 1990.

Port of New York and New Jersey Comprehensive Annual Financial Report for the Year Ended December 31, 1999. New York: The Authority, 2000.

Port of New York and New Jersey Comprehensive Annual Financial Report for the Year Ended December 31, 1999. New York: The Authority, 2001.

Public Papers of Franklin D. Roosevelt, Forty-Eighth Governor of the State of New York, 1931. Albany: J.B. Lyon Company, 1937.

Purcell, Margaret R. *Interstate Barriers to Truck Transportation.* Washington, DC: U.S. Department of Agriculture, 1950.

Regional Growth: Interstate Tax Competition. Washington, DC: U.S. Advisory Commission on Intergovernmental Relations, 1981.

Regional Information Sharing Systems: The RISS Program: 1998. Tallahassee, FL: Institute for Intergovernmental Research, 1999.

Regulations of the Northeast Dairy Compact Commission. Montpelier, VT: The Commission, 2001.

Regulatory Initiatives of the National Association of Insurance Commissioners. Washington, DC: U.S. General Accounting Office, 2001.

Report of the Joint Legislative Committee on Interstate Cooperation. Albany, NY: 1936.

Report of the Joint Legislative Committee on Interstate Cooperation. Albany, NY: 1962.

Report of the Joint Legislative Committee on Interstate Cooperation to the 1966 Legislature. Albany, NY: 1966.

Report on the Evaluation of the Delaware River Basin Commission Expenditures As They Relate to New York State. Albany: New York State Department of Environmental Conservation, 1980.

Report to Congress: NHTSA's Involvement in the National Driver Register. Washington, DC: National Highway Traffic Safety Administration, 1993.

Report to Congress on Flow Control and Municipal Solid Waste. Washington, DC: U.S. Environmental Protection Agency, 1995.

Resume: Annual Executive Conference. Albany: New York Joint Legislative Committee on Interstate Cooperation, 1950.

Revenue Diversification: State and Local Travel Taxes. Washington, DC: U.S. Advisory Commission on Intergovernmental Relations, 1994.

Review and Evaluation of Port Authority of New York and New Jersey Actions Relative to Expense Account Irregularities. Albany, NY: Office of the State Comptroller, 1978.

Role of the National Guard in Emergency Preparedness and Response. Washington, DC: National Academy of Public Administration, 1997.

Should the Appalachian Regional Commission Be Used As a Model for the Nation? Washington, DC: U.S. General Accounting Office, 1979.

Southern States Energy Board Annual Report 2000. Norcorss, GA: The Board, 2000.

Staff of the Joint Committee on Taxation. *Trends in the Use of Tax-Exempt Bonds to Finance Private Activities, Including a Description of H.R. 1176 and H.R. 1635.* Washington, DC: U.S. Government Printing Office, 1983.

State-Local Taxation and Industrial Location. Washington, DC: U.S. Advisory Commission on Intergovernmental Relations, 1967.

State and Provincial Licensing System. Washington, DC: National Highway Traffic Safety Administration, 1990.

State Severance Taxes. Hearing Before the Subcommittee on Energy and Agricultural Taxation, United States Senate. Washington, DC: U.S. Government Printing Office, 1984.

State Solvency Regulation of Property-Casualty and Life Insurance Companies. Washington, DC: U.S. Advisory Commission on Intergovernmental Relations, 1992.

State Taxation of Interstate Mail Order Sales. Washington, DC: U.S. Advisory Commission on Intergovernmental Relations, 1992.

Strategic Plan Status Review: Anadromous Fish Restoration Program Merrimack River. Nashua, NH: Technical Committee for Anadromous Fishery Management of the Merrimack River Basin, 1997.

Survey of State Criminal History Information Systems 1999. Washington, DC: U.S. Department of Justice, 2000.

Taft, William H. "Arizona and New Mexico." *Congressional Record* (August 15, 1911), 3964.

Tax Policy and Administration: California Taxes on Multinational Corporations and Related Federal Issues. Washington, DC: U.S. General Accounting Office, 1995.

Tax Policy: Internal Revenue Code Provisions Relating to Tax-Exempt Bonds. Washington, DC: U.S. General Accounting Office, 1991.

Taxation of Interstate Mail Order Sales: 1994 Revenue Estimates. Washington, DC: U.S. Advisory Commission on Intergovernmental Relations, 1994.

Taylor, George R., Edgar L. Burtis, and Frederick V. Waugh. *Barriers to Internal Trade in Farm Products.* Washington, DC: U.S. Government Printing Office, 1939.

Toward Quality Water. Boston: New England Interstate Water Pollution Control Commission, 1981.

Tradition of Consumer Protection. Kansas City, MO: National Association of Insurance Commissioners, 1995.

2000 Annual Report. Washington, DC: Interstate Pest Control Compact, 2000.

2000 Annual Report. Albany: New York State Thruway Authority, 2001.

Unitary Tax: Hearing Before the Subcommittee on International Economic Policy of the Committee on Foreign Relations, United States Senate, September 20, 1984. Washington, DC: U.S. Government Printing Office, 1985.

Use of Interstate Compacts and Agreements in Illinois. Springfield, IL: Intergovernmental Cooperation Commission, 1973.

Where Will the Garbage Go? 2001. Albany: New York State Legislative Commission on Solid Waste Management, 2002.

Working in Partnership. Charlestown, NH: Connecticut River Joint Commissions, n.d.

Zimmerman, Dennis. *The Volume Cap for Tax-Exempt Private-Activity Bonds: State and Local Experience in 1989.* Washington, DC: U.S. Advisory Commission on Intergovernmental Relations, 1990.

Zimmerman, Joseph F. *Measuring Local Discretionary Authority.* Washington, DC: U.S. Advisory Commission on Intergovernmental Relations, 1981.

Zimmerman, Joseph F. and Sharon Lawrence. *Federal Statutory Preemption of State and Local Authority: History, Inventory, and Issues.* Washington, DC: U.S. Advisory Commission on Intergovernmental Relations, 1992.

Articles

Aaron, Kenneth. "CSX Corp. Executive Says New York Overtaxes Railroad Property." *Times Union* (Albany, NY), April 23, 2002, pp. E1, E4.

——— . "Garden Way Workers Reach End of Line." *Times Union* (Albany, NY), September 29, 2001, pp. 1, A8.

——— . "Rail Tax Relief Dies in Budget, CSX Ready to Sue." *Times Union* (Albany, NY), May 18, 2002, p. B10.

Abbey, Alan D. "AT&T's Relay Center to Stay in Clifton Park, for Now." *Times Union* (Albany, NY), February 15, 1995, p. B9.

——— . "Subsidies Ensure Business Growth Will Stay in State." *Times Union* (Albany, NY), April 3, 1994, pp. B1, B2.

Abbott, Frank C. "College Compacts Lower Costs for All." *State Government* 63, July–September 1990, pp. 84–86.

Abel, Albert W. "The Commerce Clause in the Constitutional Convention and in Contemporary Comment." *Minnesota Law Review* 25, March 1941, pp. 432–94.

"Act Aiding Sale of State Wines is Struck Down." *New York Times,* January 31, 1985, p. B3.

"Agreement Reached to Restore Long Island Sound." *EPA Activities Update,* October 3, 1994, p. 1.

"Air Pollution: Message from the President of the United States." *Congressional Record,* January 30, 1967, p. H737.

Albertsworth, Edwin F. "Congressional Assent to State Taxation Otherwise Unconstitutional." *American Bar Association Journal* 17, December 1931, pp. 821–26.

Aldrich, Eric. "Vt. Officials: There's Progress on Connecticut River Bridges." *Keene (NH) Sentinel,* March 30, 1993, p. 2.

"Appeal Likely." *Union Leader* (Manchester, NH), August 21, 2001, p. 3.

Applebome, Peter. "States Raise Stakes in Fight for Jobs." *New York Times*, October 4, 1993, p. A12.

Arrandale, Tom. "The Eastern Water Wars." *Governing* 12, August 1999, pp. 30–34.

———. "Truck Stoppers." *Governing* 14, January 2001, p. 1.

"At Cigarette Tax Enforcement Conference, New York City, September 12, 1967." *Public Papers on Nelson A. Rockefeller: 1967*. Albany, NY: Office of the Governor, 1968: 1309–311.

"Attention Keds Purchasers." *Times Union* (Albany, NY), November 8, 1993, p. A5.

"Attorneys: Interstate and Federal Practice." *Harvard Law Journal* 80, March 1967, pp. 711–29.

Avril, Tom. "Pa. Still Tops in Imports of Garbage." *The Philadelphia Inquirer*, May 21, 2002, p. B1.

Ayres, B. Drummond. "Chesapeake Cleaning Pact Is Signed." *New York Times*, December 16, 1987, p. A20.

Baade, Robert A. "Professional Sports and Economic Impact: The View of the United States Judiciary." *Proceedings of the 90th Annual Conference on Taxation 1997*. Washington, DC: National Tax Association, 1998, pp. 189–203.

Bagli, Charles V. "Big Board Reconsidering New Tower Downtown." *New York Times*, November 9, 2001, p. D5.

———. "Deal to Build New Complex Eludes Mayor and Wall Street." *New York Times*, January 1, 2001, p. B5.

———. "Deal Is Signed to Take Over Trade Center." *New York Times*, April 27, 2001, pp. B1, B8.

———. "Known As Poacher, New Jersey Is Faced by Rival to the West." *New York Times*, March 20, 2000, pp. B1, B5.

———. "Playing the 'Jersey Card,' Firms in Manhattan Compare Incentives." *New York Times*, December 28, 2001, pp. D1, D4.

———. "West Side Plan Envisions Jets and Olympics." *New York Times*, May 1, 2002, pp. 1, B6.

Baglole, Joel and Christopher J. Chipello. "Free Trade, Not Free Sailing: Canada Is Finding Some Fault with NAFTA." *Wall Street Journal Europe*, June 5, 2002, p. A2.

Baird, Denise C. "Mineral Severance Taxes in Idaho: Considerations for the Legislature." *Idaho Law Review* 19, Summer 1983, pp. 607–31.

Baldo, Anthony. "Going to the Highest Bidder: Forget a Mercedes Backlash. States and Cities Will Keep the Incentives Coming for Corporations." *Financial World's Corporate Finance* 8, Spring 1994, pp. 34–38.

Bang-Jensen, Lise. "Vt. Sales Tax 'End Run' Blocked." *Knickerbocker News* (Albany, NY), December 9, 1980, p. 1.

Bania, N. and L.N. Calkins. "Interstate Differentials in State and Local Business Taxation, 1971–86." *Environment and Planning C: Government and Policy* 10, 1992, pp. 147–58.

Bannard, Henry C. "The Oleomargarine Law: A Study of Congressional Politics." *Political Science Quarterly* 2, December 1887, pp. 545–57.

Barber, Mary B. "Is California Driving Business out of the State?" *California Journal* 24, May 1992, pp. 9–14.

Barboza, David. "Chicago, Offering Big Incentives, Will Be Boeing's New Home." *New York Times*, May 11, 2001, p. C3.

Barnes, Brooks and Alexandra Peers. "U.S. Sales-Tax Probe Throws Harsh Light on Art World." *The Wall Street Journal Europe*, June 6, 2002, p. A10.

Barrett, Katherine and Richard Greene, "The New War Between the States." *Financial World* 16, September 3, 1991, pp. 34–41.

Barry, Dan, "Reviving Tradition of Betting Leaders to Division in Saratoga." *New York Times*, February 18, 2002, pp. 1, B5.

Bartik, Timothy J. "Eight Issues for Policy Toward Economic Development Incentives." *The Region*, June 1996, pp. 43–46.

———. "Jobs, Productivity, and Economic Development: What Implications Does Economic Research Have for the Role of Government." *National Tax Journal* 47, December 1994, pp. 947–61.

Batten, James K. "Tax, Law Aides to Map Cigarette Bootleg War." *Knickerbocker News* (Albany, NY), August 30, 1967, p. 3B.

Benjamin, Elizabeth. "$32M Spent to Revitalize State's Canals for Tourism." *Times Union* (Albany, NY), March 16, 2002, p. 19.

Bennett, Julie. "States Look to Share Data, Collect More Taxes." *City & State* 10, May 24, 1993, p. 13.

Benson, Bruce L. "Interstate Tax Competition, Incentives to Collude, and Federal Influences." *The Cato Journal* 10, Spring–Summer 1990, pp. 75–90.

"The Bermuda Tax Triangle." *New York Times*, May 13, 2002, p. A16.

Bernstein, Melvin. "New England's Higher Education Compact Has Stood the Test of Time." *Connection* 16, Summer 2001, pp. 48–50.

Berry, Frances S. "State Regulation of Occupations and Professions." *The Book of the States: 1986–87*. Lexington, KY: The Council of State Governments, 1986, 379–83.

Berry, Frances S. and Pamela L. Brinegar. "State Regulation of Occupations and Professions." *The Book of the States: 1990–91*. Lexington, KY: The Council of State Governments, 1990, 465–70.

Beyle, Thad L. "New Directions in Interstate Relations." *The Annals of the American Academy of Political and Social Science* 416, November 1974, pp. 108–19.

Biemer, John. "Maryland Joins VT, Other States Supporting Air Quality Regulations." *Rutland Herald*, July 12, 2002 (Internet edition).

Bigart, Homer. "Jersey Routs Pennsylvania Spies in Border War on Whiskey Prices." *New York Times*, March 6, 1965, pp. 1, 26.

Birritteri, Anthony. "Economic Development Efforts Make South Jersey Great." *New Jersey Business* 43, Spring 1997, pp. 30–38, 40.

"Bi-State Blue Crab Panel Approves Stricter Harvest Restrictions." *Bay Journal* 10, January–February 2000, p. 3.

Blair, Jayson. "Federal Order Activates L.I. Power Line." *New York Times*, August 17, 2002, pp. B1, B5.

———. "Giuliani Says He's Not Rushing to Close Deals on Stadiums." *New York Times*, December 26, 2001, pp. D1–D2.

———. "L.I. Power Officials Ask Federal Regulators to Order Activation of Undersea Line." *New York Times*, August 15, 2002, p. B5.

———. "Power Agencies' Plan to Merge Draws Mixed Reviews of States." *New York Times*, August 22, 2002, p. B2.

Blankenship, Karl. "Bay, Long Island Sound Take Sharply Divergent Cleanup Paths." *Bay Journal* 11, April 2001, pp. 1, 12–13.

Blumenthal, Ralph. "Byrne Again Opposes Port Unit: Vetoes Its Plan for Bus Projects." *New York Times*, June 22, 1977, pp. 1, 36.

"The Boom Belt: There's No Speed Limit on Growth Along the South's I-85." *Business Week*, September 17, 1993, pp. 98–102

Boulard, Garry. "Wine Wards: To Ship or Not to Ship." *State Legislatures* 23, October–November 1997, pp. 12–19.

Boyle, James E. "The Relation Between Federal and State Taxation." *The Annals of the American Academy of Political and Social Science* 58, March 1915, pp. 59–64.

Bradbury, Katharine L, Yolanda K. Kodrzycki, and Robert Tannenwald. "The Effects of State and Local Public Policies on Economic Development: An Overview." *New England Economic Review*, March/April 1997, pp. 1–12.

Braden, George B. "Umpire to the Federal System." *The University of Chicago Law Review* 10, 1942, pp. 27–48.

Brandon, Craig. "Butt Smugglers." *Times Union* (Albany, NY), June 24, 1993: 1, A9.

Brown, Ernest J. "The Open Economy, Justice Frankfurter, and the Position of the Judiciary." *Yale Law Journal* 67, December 1957, pp. 219–39.

Brown, Peter A. "Big Business Exploits War Between the States for New Jobs." *Times Union* (Albany, NY), February 6, 1994, p. B3

Bruce, Andrew A. "The Compacts and Agreements of States with One Another and with Foreign Powers." *Minnesota Law Review* 2, 1919, pp. 500–516.

Bruckner, John R. "Ideological Conceptions of Progress and Political Participation and Their Effect on State Economic Development Policy: A Case Study of the Kentucky-Toyota Venture." *Southern Political Review* 21, Spring 1993, pp. 219–37.

Brutus. "14 February 1778." Ralph Ketcham, ed. *The Anti-Federalist Papers and the Constitutional Convention Debates*. New York: New American Library, 1966, 302–04.

"Budget Roulette." *Times Union* (Albany, NY), October 25, 2001, p. A10.

"California Lottery Faces Trial on Prizes." *Times Union* (Albany, NY), December 22, 2001, p. A3.

Calvo, Cheye. "Regulating without a Net." *State Legislatures* 28, March 2002, pp. 28–33.

Carlton, Dennis W. "The Location and Employment Choices of New Firms: An Econometric Model with Discrete and Continuous Endogenous Variables." *Review of Economics and Statistics* 65, 1983, pp. 440–49.

Campbell, Tom. "State Alcohol Laws Shaken: Ban on Wine, Beer Shipments Unconstitutional, Judge Rules." *Richmond Times-Dispatch*, April 1, 2002, p. 1.

Carman, Ernest C. "Should the States Be Permitted to Make Compacts without Consent of Congress?" *Cornell Law Quarterly* 23, February 1938, pp. 280–84.

Carpenter, A.C. "Some History and Functions of the Potomac River Fisheries Commission." *Commercial Fisheries News*, September 1976, p. 4.

Carroll, James and David Moss. "Sports Stadiums and Public Financing." *State Government News* 45, June/July 2002, p. 17.

"The Casino Jinx." *New York Times*, November 29, 2001, p. A34.

"Casinos: Not a Solution for Buffalo's Economic Woes." *Empire State Report* 27, September 2001, p. 16.

Cason, Mike, Dave Hendrick, and Kelli Dugan. "City Gets $1B Plant." *Montgomery (AL) Advertiser*, April 2, 2002 (Internet Edition).

Celler, Emanuel. "Congress, Compacts, and Interstate Authorities." *Law and Contemporary Problems* 26, Autumn 1961, pp. 682–702.

Cerf, Christopher D. "Federal Habeas Corpus Review of Nonconstitutional Errors: The Cognizability of Violations of the Interstate Agreement on Detainers." *Columbia Law Review* 83, May 1983, pp. 975–1028.

Chapin, Tim. "The Political Economy of Sports Facility Locations: An End-of-the-Century Review and Assessment." *Marquette Sports Law Journal* 10, Spring 2000, pp. 361–82.

Chapman, Marguerite A. "Where East Meets West in Water Law: The Formulation of an Interstate Compact to Address the Diverse Problems of the Red River Basin." *Oklahoma Law Review* 38, Spring 1985, pp. 1–112.

Cheit, Ross E. "State Adoption of Model Insurance Codes: An Empirical Analyses." *Publius* 23, Fall 1993, pp. 49–70.

"Chester, VA." *The Washington Post*, July 19, 2002, p. A15.

Chi, Keon S. "State Business Incentives: Options for the Future." *State Trends Forecasts* 3, June 1994, pp. 1–31.

———. "Interstate Cooperation: Resurgence of Multistate Regionalism." *State Government* 63, July–September 1990, pp. 59–63.

Christian, Nichole M. "2 Winners Share the Biggest Lottery Jackpot in U.S. History." *New York Times*, May 11, 2000, p. A25.

"Cigarette Shoppers and Smugglers Hit the Road to Avoid Taxes As Excises Climb." *Tax Foundation Tax Features* 42, August 1998, pp. 2–3.

Clark, Thomas R. "The Effect of Violations of the Interstate Agreement on Detainers of Subject Matter Jurisdiction." *Fordham Law Review* 54, October 1986, pp. 1209–238.

Clines, Francis X. "U.S. Acts to Protect Embattled Horseshoe Crab." *New York Times*, August 9, 2000, p. A12.

Coffee, Hoyt E. "States, Provinces Luring High Tech with Broad Array of Incentives." *Site Selection* 37, June 1992, pp. 564–65.

Cohan, Paul. "Supporting the Home Team." *State Government News* 39, May 1996, pp. 19–22.

Coleman, Randy. "W.Va. Governor Signs Video Poker Legislation." *Union Leader* (Manchester, NH), May 9, 2001, p. A9.

Colgan, Charles S. "Internationalization of the Governor's Role: New England Governors and Eastern Canadian Energy, 1973–1989." *State and Local Government Review* 23, Fall 1991, pp. 119–26.

Collins, William F. and Ryder, Sarah L. "Current Issues in State Taxation of Multinational Corporations." *Proceeding of the 90th Annual Conference on Taxation 1997*. Washington, DC: National Tax Association, 1998: 147–62.

"Compact at Center of Budget Talks." *Keene (NH) Sentinel*, November 18, 1999, p. 4.

Conant, James B. "How the Compact Can Assist the Universities." *The Educational Record* 47, Winter 1966, pp. 99–105.

"Congressional Cowardice." *New York Times*, July 18, 2002, p. A20.

"Conn. Governors Signs 61–Cent Increase in Cigarette Tax." *Union Leader* (Manchester, NH), March 1, 2002, p. A2.

"Conn. Joins New York to Sue Midwestern Power Plants." *Union Leader* (Manchester, NH), November 30, 1999, p. A3

"Conn. to Send 500 Inmates to VA to Ease Overcrowding." *Union Leader* (Manchester, NH), October 26, 1999, p. A3.

"Connecticut Drops Challenge to Coastal Fish Law." *Bay Journal* 11, May 2001, p. 8.

"Connecticut Suit Challenges Constitutionality of Fishing Quotas." *Bay Journal* 10, November 2000, p. 5.

Conway, Joseph P. and Raphael Hurwitz. "New York City's Delaware River Basin Supply: A Case Study in Interstate Cooperation. In *Proceedings of the Symposium on International Transboundary Water Resources Issues*. Bethesda, MD: American Water Resources Association, 1990: 439–52.

Considine, John L. "Cigarette Smuggling Big Business. *Knickerbocker News* (Albany, NY), January 22, 1971, p. 16A.

Cooper, Alan. "Out-of-This-World Taxes Are Voided: Satellite Devices Levy to Be Refunded." *Richmond Times-Dispatch*, April 20,2002, p. 1.

Cooper, Michael. "Bloomberg Has His Doubts on Stadiums." *New York Times*, December 7, 2001, p. D9.

————. "Cigarette Tax, Highest in Nation, Cuts Sales in City." *New York Times*, August 6, 2002, pp. B1, B7.

"Cooperative Agreement on North Branch Potomac Signed." *Potomac Basin Report*, November–December 1993, p. 4.

Cotorceanu, Peter A. "Estate Tax Apportionment in Kansas: Out with the Old, in with the New." *The Journal of the Kansas Bar Association* 70, October 2001, pp. 28–36.

Courant, Paul N. "How Would You Know a Good Economic Development Policy If You Tripped Over One? One Hint: Don't Just Count Jobs." *National Tax Journal* 47, 1994, pp. 863–81.

Cox, Gail D. "Change of Course: Status Quo Threatened on America's Most-Litigated River." *National Law Journal* 16, September 13, 1993, pp. 1, 36.

Craig, Steven G. and Joel W. Sailors. "Interstate Trade Barriers and the Constitution." *Cato Journal* 6, 1986–87, pp. 819–35.

Crary, David. "Cigarette Taxes Help Spawn Illegal Trade." *Union Leader* (Manchester, NH), July 14, 2002, pp. 1, A6.

Crihfield, Brevard and Reeves, H. Clyde. Intergovernmental Relations: A View from the States." *The Annals of the American Academy of Political and Social Science* 416, November 1974, pp. 99–107.

Croce, Bob. "Firebirds Moving Home Base to Vermont." *Times Union* (Albany, NY), May 14, 1994, pp. 1, A7.

"Cross-Border Shopping by Beer and Cigarette Buyers Highlights Tax Competition Among States." *Tax Features* 45, June–July 1999, p. 6.

Crowe, Kenneth C., II. "Pair to Answer Liquor-Smuggling Charges Today." *Times Union* (Albany, NY), June 9, 1994, p. B7.

———. "Policy a Roadblock to Speeding Truckers." *Times Union* (Albany, NY), August 26, 2001, pp. E1, E11.

———. "State Stockpiling Contraband Liquor." *Times Union* (Albany, NY), December 9, 1993, pp. B1, B11.

Cuomo Comes Out of the Bullpen in Late Pitch to Save A-C Yankees." *Times Union* (Albany, NY), March 20, 1994, pp. 1, A5.

"Cuomo, Puerto Rico Governor Sign Pact." *Times Union* (Albany, NY), August 16, 1994, p. B2.

"Cuomo Warns N.J. to let Yankees Alone." *Times Union* (Albany, NY), October 7, 1993, p. B2.

Dabsen, Brian, Carl Rist, and William Schweke. "Business Climate and the Role of Development Incentives." *The Region*, June 1996, pp. 47–49.

"Dairy Compact Offers Farmers Stability, Pataki Says." *Times Union* (Albany, NY), July 27, 2001, p. B2.

Dao, James. "Congress Weighs Bill to Expand the Cartel Letting Northeast Dairy Farms Set Prices." *New York Times*, May 2, 1999, p. 53.

———. "Indians Offer State a Share of Monticello Casino Profits." *New York Times*, March 2, 1995, p. B6.

———. "States Joining in Combating Illegal Guns." *New York Times*, April 26, 1993, pp. 1, B7.

Davidson, Donald. "Political Regionalism and Administrative Regionalism." *The Annals of the American Academy of Political and Social Science* 207, January 1940, pp. 138–43.

Derthick, Martha. "Federalism and the Politics of Tobacco." *Publius* 31, Winter 2001, pp. 47–63.

Dewan, Shaila K. "Cigarette Tax Would Cost State Millions, Critic Says." *New York Times*, March 2, 2002, p. B6.

———. "This Week, New York Plans to Join Multistate Lottery." *New York Times*, May 12, 2002 (Internet edition).

Diaz, Elvia and Pat Flannery. "Phoenix Out of the Race for Stadium." *Arizona Republic*, February 21, 2002 (Internet edition).

Dickinson, John. "The Functions of Congress and the Courts in Umpiring the Federal System." *The George Washington Law Review* 8, June 1940, pp. 1165–179.

Dodd, Alice M. "Interstate Compacts." *U.S. Law Review* 70, October 1936, pp. 557–78.

Doig, Jameson W. "Coalition-Building by a Regional Agency: Austin Tobin and the Port of New York Authority." In Clarence N. Stone and Heywood T. Sanders, eds., *The Politics of Urban Development*. Lawrence: University Press of Kansas, 1987.

Donovan, William J. "State Compacts As a Method of Settling Problems Common to Several States." *University of Pennsylvania Law Review* 80, 1931–1932, pp. 5–16.

Dougherty, Pete. "The Yanks Are Going to Norwich." *Times Union* (Albany, NY), March 15, 1994, pp. 1, A7.

Drahozal, Christopher R. "On Tariffs v. Subsidies in Interstate Trade: A Legal and Economic Analysis." *Washington University Law Quarterly* 74, Winter 1996, pp. 1127–192.

Dunbar, Leslie W. "Interstate Compacts and Congressional Consent." *Virginia Law Review* 36, October 1950, pp. 653–63.

Dunham, Allison. "A History of the National Conference of Commissioners on Uniform State Laws." *Law and Contemporary Problems* 30, Spring 1965, pp. 233–49.

Durant, Robert F. and Holmes, Michelle E. "Thou Shall Not Covet Thy Neighbor's Water: The Rio Grande Basin Regulatory Experience." *Public Administration Review* 45, November–December 1985, pp. 821–31.

Dutton, D. Ben. "Compacts and Trade Barrier Controversies." *Indiana Law Journal* 6, 1940–1941, pp. 204–19.

Dwyer, Laurence. "Border Battle." *Boston Globe*, February 20, 1983, p. 21.

Eager, Bill. "Vermont Milk Legal in New York." *Times Union* (Albany, NY), June 11, 1994, p. B2.

Earle, Ralph III. "Northeast Promotes Recycling Markets." *State Government* 63, July–September 1990, pp. 64–66.

Eaton, Leslie. "Ruling May Erode Longshoremen's Grip on Ports." *New York Times*, May 16, 2001, pp. B1, B6.

Eckel, Mike. "Northeast Interstate Dairy Compact Dries Up." *Union Leader*, September 28, 2001, p. B2.

"The Economic War Among the States." *The Region*, June 1996, pp. 2–66.

"Education Finance Features of Act 60, as amended." *VCCT Bulletin* (Vermont League of Cities and Towns), August 2000, pp. 1–15.

"The Effects of Land-Based and Riverboat Gaming in New Orleans." *Louisiana Business Survey* 28, Spring 1997, pp. 2–11.

Eichorn, L. Mark. "Cuyler v. Adams and the Characterization of Compact Law." *Virginia Law Review* 77, October 1991, pp. 1387–411.

"Electronic Cash Exchange Developed for Trading Recyclable Commodities." *EPA Activities Update*, April 17, 1995, p. 3.

"Employees of Professional Sports Franchises Paying Income Taxes in Up to 20 State As State Governments Compete for Funds." *Tax Features* 46, Summer 2002, pp. 4–5.

Engdahl, David E. "Interstate Urban Areas and Interstate 'Agreements' and Compacts': Unclear Possibilities." *Georgetown Law Journal* 58, March–May 1970, pp. 799–820.

Engelbert, Ernest. "Federalism and Water Resources Development." *Law & Contemporary Problems* 22, Summer 1957, pp. 325–50.

Enos, Gary. "Big Breaks Lure Plant to Ky." *City & State* 10, June 21, 1993, pp. 1, 22.

"EPA & States to Restore Great Lakes." *EPA Activities Update*, April 17, 1995, p. 1.

Erhardt, Carl. "The Battle Over 'The Hooch': The Federal-Interstate Water Compact and the Resolution of Rights in the Chattahoochee River." *Stanford Environmental Law Journal* 11, 1992, pp. 200–28.

Erskine, Michael. "Commission OK's Arena Fund Package." *Commercial Appeal* (Memphis, TN), May 9, 2002 (Internet edition).

Eule, Julian N. "Laying the Dormant Commerce Clause to Rest." *The Yale Law Journal* 91, January 1982, pp. 425–85.

Evans, David. "Contest Offers Mislead Entrants." *Times Union* (Albany, NY), August 25, 1994, p. C9.

"Extension of Interstate Compact to Conserve Energy." *Congressional Record*, May 2, 1979, pp. S5192–94.

"The Eyes of Taxes: They're Upon You If You Buy VT Booze." *Times Union*, December 26, 1972), 1, B10.

Fahey, Tom. "Northeast States Eye Prescription Buying Pool." *Union Leader* (Manchester, NH), December 15, 2002), p. B3.

Faison, Seth. "Newark Residents Accused of Taking New York Welfare." *New York Times*, March 3, 1994, pp. 1, B2.

Fand, Beth E. "Lotteries Are Hitting Jackpot." *Trenton Times*, July 23, 2002 (Internet Edition).

Farnsworth, Clyde. "Canada Cuts Cigarette Taxes to Fight Smuggling." *New York Times* February 9, 1994, p. A3.

Farrell, Chris, "The Economic War Among the States: An Overview." *The Region*, June 1996, pp. 4–7.

Faught, Albert S. "Reciprocity in State Taxation As the Next Step in Empirical Legislation." *University of Pennsylvania Law Review* 92, March 1944, pp. 258–71.

"Favoring Dairy Farmers Over the Poor." *New York Times*, August 12, 1996, p. A14.

"Federal Limitations on State Taxation of Interstate Business." *Harvard Law Review* 75, 1961–62, pp. 953–1036.

"Federation of State Medical Boards." *Congressional Record*, November 24, 1993, p. E 3052.

Fenton, John H. "Officials of Mass. and N.H. to Study Liquor Price War." *New York Times*, December 14, 1969, p. 73.

Ferguson, Doug. "Federal Judge Rules Killer Must Serve New York Sentence." *Times Union* (Albany, NY), October 19, 1993, p. 1.

Filzer, Paul N. "Revenue Sharing Compacts . . . May Help in Getting Approval for Off-Reservation Casinos." *The National Law Journal* 18, September 11, 1995, pp. B5–B6.

"Finding the Forum for a Victory." *The National Law Journal* 13, February 11, 1991, pp. S3–S4.

Fingeret, Lisa. "The Big Apple Needs to Grow." *Financial Times*, June 4, 2002, p. 12.

Firestone, David. "Black Families Resist Mississippi Land Push." *New York Times*, September 10, 2001, p. A20.

———. "State Lures Good Jobs, but Companies Worry About Workers." *New York Times*, January 28, 2002, p. A8.

Fisher, Daniel. "Football Team Valuations." *Forbes* 170, September 2, 2002, pp. 70–73.

Fisher, Peter S. and Alan H. Peters. "Tax and Spending Incentives and Enterprise Zones." *New England Economic Review*, March–April 1997, pp. 110–18.

———. "Taxes, Incentives and Competition for Investment." *The Region*, June 1996, pp. 52–57.

Fisher, Ronald C. "The Effects of State and Local Public Services on Economic Development." *New England Economic Review*, March/April 1997, pp. 53–67.

Flannery, Pat. "Stadium Site May Go to Voters." *Arizona Republic*, May 1, 2002 (Internet edition).

Florence, M. Taylor. "Using the Interstate Compact to Control Acid Deposition." *Journal of Energy Law & Policy* 5, 1985, pp. 413–46.

Florestano, Patricia S. "Past and Present Utilization of Interstate Compacts in the U.S." *Publius* 24, Fall 1994, pp. 13–25.

Foderaro, Lisa W. "Line Drawn in Water Against a Predatory Fish." *New York Times*, October 5, 2002, pp. B1, B2.

Fois, Robert A. "Albany's Last Resort: Casino Gambling." *Empire State Report* 27, December 2001, pp. 21–24.

Frankfurter, Felix and Landis, James M. "The Compact Clause of the Constitution: A Study in Interstate Adjustments." *Yale Law Journal* 34, May 1925, pp. 685–758.

Franklin, Ben A. "Christmas Cheer Is Smuggled Out of Washington." *New York Times*, December 24, 1969, pp. 1, 11.

Freedman, Eric. "6 States Sue EPA Over Acid Rain." *Knickerbocker News* (Albany, NY), March 20, 1984, p. 5C.

Fricano, Mike. "Jackpot Dreams Coming Closer to Home." *Times Union* (Albany, NY), May 16, 2002, pp. 1, A5.

Frickley, Philip P. "The Congressional Process and the Constitutionality of Federal Legislation to End the Economic War Among the States." *The Region*, June 1956, pp. 58–59.

Friedman, Barry. "Valuing Federalism." *Minnesota Law Review* 82, December 1997, pp. 317–412.

Frothingham, Stephen. "Plenty of Summer for Everyone." *Union Leader* (Manchester, NH), May 1, 2001, p. B1.

Fruchtman, David A. "State Apportionment Factor Consequences of Section 338(h)(10) Election." *Business Entities* 3, May/June 2001, pp. 30–35.

Gallagher, Hubert R. "Work of the Commissions on Interstate Co-operation." *The Annals of the American Academy of Political and Social Science* 207, January 1940, pp. 103–10.

Gallagher, Jay. "Gambling Deal Marks Flawed Process." *Times Union* (Albany, NY), October 28, 2001, p. A11.

"Gambling Fever." *Keene (NH) Sentinel*, September 1, 2001, p. 6.

"Gambling Now Third Largest Source of Revenue for R.I." *Union Leader* (Manchester, NH), February 18, 2002, p. B3.

Gausman, Carlton J. "The Interstate Compact as a Solution to Regional Problems: The Kansas City Metropolitan Culture District." *Kansas Law Review* 45, May 1997, pp. 987–1020.

Gearing, Dan. "Brattleboro, Keene Court Giant C&S." *Sunday Sentinel* (Keene, NH), March 24, 2002, pp. 1, A3.

———. "Insurance Heads Moving South." *Keene (NH) Sentinel*, March 27, 2002, pp. 1–2.

Gibeaut, John. "Skybox Shake Downs." *ABA Bar Journal* 84, June 1998, pp. 68–73.

Gillette, Clayton P. "Business Incentives, Interstate Competition, and the Commerce Clause." *Minnesota Law Review* 82, December 1997, pp. 447–502.

Goble, Dale D. "The Compact Clause and Transboundary Problems: 'A Federal Remedy for the Disease Most Incident to a Federal Government.'" *Environmental Law* 17, 1987, pp. 785–813.

Goldman, Ari L. "Low Fares Cited As Carey Vetoes PATH's Budget." *New York Times*, February 11, 1982, p. 1.

Goodman, Leonard, Miranti, Paul J. Jr. "The California Method of Taxing Nonresidents in New York." *Journal of State Taxation* 9, Fall 1990, pp. 31–44.

Goodnough, Abby. "Interstate Competition for Teachers from Abroad." *New York Times*, July 18, 2001, p. B9.

Gootman, Elissa. "Idea of Electricity Cable Under the Sound Is Revived." *New York Times*, December 13, 2001, p. D5.

"Governors, Premiers Wrap up Conference with Pact Signing." *Union Leader* (Manchester, NH), July 19, 2000, p. A3.

"Governors Sign Fish Ladder Pact." *Community Affairs* (Pennsylvania Department of Community Affairs), May–June 1993, p. 3.

Grad, Frank P. "Federal-State Compact: A New Experiment in Co-Operative Federalism." *Columbia Law Review* 63, May 1963, pp. 825–55.

Grant, Daniel R. "The Government of Interstate Metropolitan Areas." *Western Political Quarterly* 8, March 1955, pp. 90–107.

Graves, W. Brooke, ed. "Intergovernmental Relations in the United States." *The Annals of the American Academy of Political and Social Science* 207, January 1940, pp. 1–218.

———. "Influence of Congressional Legislation on Legislation in the States." *Iowa Law Review* 23, May 1938, pp. 519–38.

Gray, Jerry. "States with Acute Smog Problem Sign Ozone Pact." *New York Times*, August 5, 1992, p. A18.

Grecco, David J. "*Oklahoma Tax Commission v. Jefferson Lines, Incorporated, 115 S.Ct. 1331 (1995)*." *Duquesne Law Review* 34, Fall 1995, pp. 139–62.

Greenhouse, Linda. "Court Ruling Over Dividends Pains Albany." *New York Times*, March 31, 1993, pp. 1, B7.

Greer, William R. "New York Joining Jersey to Combat Sales-Tax Evasion." *New York Times*, June 7, 1985, pp. 1, B5.

Grodzins, Morton. "Centralization and Decentralization in the American Federal System." Robert A. Goldwin, ed. *A Nation of States*. Chicago: Rand McNally & Company, 1963, 1–23

"Gulf of Mexico Plan to Reduce Nutrients 30% Is Finalized." *Bay Journal* 11, March 2001, p. 3.

Gulick, Luther. "Reorganization of the State." *Civil Engineering* 3, August 1933, pp. 419–26.

Gurwitt, Rob. "The Riskiest Business." *Governing* 14, March 2001, pp. 19–22.

———. "Shaking the Stadium." *Governing* 15, April 2002, p. 80.

Gushman, J.L. "The Sales Tax and Interstate Commerce." *Law Journal of the Student Bar Association of the Ohio State University* 2, February 1936, pp. 260–73.

Guy, David J. "When the Law Dulls the Edge of Chance: Transferring Upper Basin Water to the Lower Colorado River Basin." *Utah Law Review* 1, Spring 1991, pp. 25–54.

Haag, Gary L. "The Natural Gas Property Tax/Severance Dilemma: Are They One and the Same?" *Tulsa Law Review* 24, Summer 1989, pp. 661–73.

Hanley, Robert. "County in New York Gets New Jersey Help in Opposing Power Plant." *New York Times*, February 2, 2001, p. B10.

Harberson, Albert. "Licensed by the States: Keeping Driver's Licenses in the Hands of the States." *State Government News* 45, August 2002, pp. 20–25.

Harlin, Kevin. "Pataki Looks to Expand Discounted Electricity." *Times Union* (Albany, NY), March 6, 2002, p. E4.

————. "Region Consortium Formed to Lure Research Funds." *Times Union* (Albany, NY), December 12, 2001, p. E1.

Hanley, Robert. "E-Z Pass Survives Rush Hour on Turnpike." *New York Times*, October 3, 2000, p. B5.

————. "7 Northeastern Governors Seeking Uniform Minimum Drinking Age." *New York Times*, December 6, 1983, pp. 1, B4.

————. "With Ease Comes Expense: E-Z Pass Starts on Turnpike, but So Do Toll Increases." *New York Times*, September 30, 2000, p. B5.

Hansen, Deborah A. "State Efforts toward National Crime Control." *State Government* 63, July–September 1990, pp. 72–79.

Harmon, Amy. "U.S. Says Dissenting States Can Pursue Microsoft." *New York Times*, April 16, 2002, p. C10.

Hartmann, Ray. "Loving the Cardinals As They Are." *New York Times*, March 26, 2002, p. A25.

Hawkins, Wilbur F. "The Lower Mississippi Delta: A Region in Transition." *State Government* 63, July–September 1990, pp. 67–70.

Hellerstein, Walter. "Commerce Clause Restraints on State Taxation: Purposeful Economic Protectionism and Beyond." *Michigan Law Review* 85, February 1987, pp. 758–69.

————. "Commerce Clause Restraints on State Tax Incentives." *The Region*, June 1956, pp. 60–63.

————. "Commerce Clause Restraints on State Tax Incentives." *Minnesota Law Review* 82, December 1997, pp. 413–46.

————. "Complementary Taxes As a Defense to Unconstitutional State Tax Discrimination." *Tax Lawyer* 39, 1985–86, pp. 405–63.

————. "State Taxation of Interstate Business: Perspectives on Two Centuries of Constitutional Adjudication." *Tax Lawyer* 41, 1987, pp. 37–81.

Henckel, Mark. "Montana Now Among States Looking to Courts to Maintain Water Levels." *Billings Gazette*, May 13, 2002 (Internet edition).

Henry, Diane. "Interstate Police Force Urged to Combat Cigarette Smuggling." *New York Times*, March 26, 1975, p. 31.

Henry, Toby. "Farmers Fight for Their Future." *The Sunday Sentinel* (Keene, NH), September 2, 2001, pp. 1, A6.

Henszey, Benjamin N. and John E. Tyworth. "Income Taxation of Interstate Motor Carriers: A Need for Equity and Uniformity." *Transportation Law Journal* 17, 1988–90, pp. 281–320.

Herbert, H. Josef. "Court Upholds EPA Regulation Requiring 19 States to Control Power Plant Pollution." *Union Leader* (Manchester, NH), March 4, 2000, p. A2.

————. "6 Northeast States Push Midwest Smog Rules." *Union Leader* (Manchester, NH), July 22, 1998, p. A5.

Heron, Kevin J. "The Interstate Compact in Transition: From Cooperative State Action to Congressionally Coerced Agreements." *St. John's Law Review* 60, Fall 1985, pp. 1–25.

Herszenhorn, David M. "Rowland Details $771 Million Plan for Hartford Riverside." *New York Times*, March 4, 2002, p. B3.

Herter, Christian A. "New Horizons for States." *National Municipal Review* 46, April 1957, pp. 174–80.

Hicks, Chester. "Play Ball!" *State Government News* 43, June/July 2000, pp. 20–22

Hill, Gladwin. "U.S. and States Move on Program to Protect Tahoe." *New York Times*, June 9, 1981, p. B9.

Hill, Kim Q. and Patricia A. Hurley. "Uniform State Law Adoptions in the American States: An Explanatory Analysis." *Publius* 18, Winter 1988, pp. 117–26.

Hill, Michael. "After a Quarter-Century, We Still (Heart) That Ad Slogan." *Times Union* (Albany, NY), May 13, 2002, p. B5.

Hoffer, George E. and Michael D. Pratt. "Do State Variations Make a Difference to Interstate Carriers?" *State Government* 58, 1986, pp. 158–63.

Hoffman, David K. "State Income Taxation of Nonresident Professional Athletes." *Tax Foundation Special Report*, July 2002.

Hoffman, Kathy B. "New York Ranks Third for Economic Growth." *Times Union* (Albany, NY), January 2, 2002, p. E1.

Hoyt, Henry M. "Corporation Regulation by State and Nation." *The Annals of the American Academy of Political and Social Science* 38, July 1908, pp. 235–39.

Hu, Winnie. "Stock Exchange May Move Some Operations to New Site." *New York Times*, July 25, 2002, p. B5.

Hull, Cecil H.J. "Delaware River Basin Water Resources Management." *Journal of the Water Resources Planning and Management Division, ASCE* 104, November 1978, pp. 157–74.

——— . "Implementation of Interstate Water Quality Plan." *Journal of the Hydraulics Division, ASCE* 101, March 1975, pp. 495–509.

Humbert, Marc. "Governor Says Cuomo Letting Personal Bias Drive Grasso Case." *Times Union* (Albany, NY), October 13, 1992, p. B2.

Hummer, Paul M. "Insurance Catches Up to Internet Revolution." *National Law Journal* 22, March 20, 2000, pp. B9, B15.

Humphrey, Theresa. "States Agree to Share Unclaimed Payments." *Times Union* (Albany, NY), January 7, 1995, p. B2.

Hurewitz, Mike. "Gold in the Green Mountains?" *Times Union* (Albany, NY), February 12, 1995, pp. 1, A10.

Ihlanfeldt, Keith R. "Ten Principles for State Tax Incentives." *Economic Development Quarterly* 9, November 1995, pp. 339–55.

"Interstate Commerce and State Power." *Virginia Law Review* 27, November 1940, pp. 1–28.

"Interstate Compacts As a Means of Settling Disputes Between States." *Harvard Law Review* 35, 1921–1922, pp. 322–26.

"Interstate School District Opens Today Despite Debate Over New Curriculum." *Union Leader* (Manchester, NH), August 28, 2000, p. A7.

Jackson, Robert H. "The Supreme Court and Interstate Barriers." *The Annals of the Academy of Political and Social Science* 207, January 1940, pp. 70–78.

Jackson, Vicki C. "Federalism and the Uses and Limits of Law: Printz and Principlews." *Harvard Law Review* 111, June 1998, pp. 2180–259.

Jehl, Douglas. "Atlanta's Growing Thirst Creates Water War." *New York Times*, May 27, 2002, pp. 1, A8.

———. "Development and a Drought Cut Carolinas' Water Supply." *New York Times* August 29, 2002, pp. 1, A16.

———. "U.S. Approves Water Plan in California, but Environmental Opposition Remains." *New York Times*, August 31, 2002, p. A8.

Jennetten, Peter R. "State Environmental Agreements with Foreign Powers: The Compact Clause and the Foreign Affairs Power of the States." *National Environmental Enforcement Journal*, November 1996, pp. 3–24.

Johnson, Kirk. "To City's Burden, Add 11,000 Tons of Daily Trash." *New York Times*, February 25, 2001, pp. 1, B4.

Johnson, Lester. "No Maine Potatoes in Idaho?" *Congressional Record*, June 15,1959, p. A5127.

Johnston, David C. "Musical Chairs on Tax Havens: Now It's Ireland." *New York Times*, August 3, 2002, pp. C1, C3.

———. "Officers May Gain More Than Investor in Move to Bermuda." *New York Times*, May 20, 2002, pp. 1, A13.

———. "States Say Bill Would Open Bermuda-Like Tax Loopholes." *New York Times*, July 18, 2002, p. C4.

———. "U.S. Corporations Are Using Bermuda to Slash Tax Bills." *New York Times*, February 18, 2002, pp. 1, A12.

———. "Vote on an Offshore Tax Plan Is Roiling a Company Town." *New York Times*, May 9, 2002, pp. 1, C14.

Jones, Benjamin J. "Interstate Compacts and Agreements: 1978–79." *The Book of the States: 1980–81*. Lexington, KY: The Council of State Governments, 1980: 596–603.

———. "Interstate Compacts and Agreements." *The Book of the States: 1992–93*. Lexington, KY: The Council of State Governments, 1994: 648–60.

Jones, Benjamin J. and Duane Osborne. "Recent Developments in Interstate Compacts and Agreements." *The Book of the States 1988–89*. Lexington, KY: The Council of State Governments, 1989: 465–67.

Jones, Benjamin J. and Deborah Reuter. "Interstate Compacts and Agreements." *The Book of the States: 1990–91*. Lexington, KY: The Council of State Governments, 1990: 565–67.

Jones, William R. "Increasing State Taxing Power Over Interstate Commerce." *Tulsa Law Journal* 32, Fall 1996, pp. 75–99.

Judson, C. James and John Creahan. "Supreme Court Prohibits Restrictions on Interstate Waste." *Journal of State Taxation* 11, Spring 1993, pp. 1–8.

Judson, Frederick N. "The Extent and Evils of Double Taxation in the United States." *The Annals of the American Academy of Political and Social Science* 58, March 1915, pp. 105–11.

Judson, George. "Weicher Signs Agreement with 2 Tribes on Casino Gambling." *New York Times*, April 26, 1994, pp. B1 and B7.

"Justice Department Sides with NH Workers at Shipyard . . . if It's Not in Maine." *Union Leader* (Manchester, NH), October 24, 1996, pp. 1, 16.

Kasler, Dale. "San Diego Attempts to Make Water Deal Work." *Sacramento Bee*, August 28, 2002 (Internet edition).

Kearney, Richard C and John J. Stucker. "Interstate Compacts and the Management of Low-Level Radioactive Wastes." *Public Administration Review* 45, January–February 1985, pp. 210–20.

Kennedy, Randy. "I-95, a River of Commerce Overflowing with Traffic." *New York Times*, December 29, 2000, pp. 1, B6.

———. "Two-Story Buses Fare Poorly in Pollution Tests." *New York Times*, January 8, 2000, p. B5.

Kenney, Douglas S. "Institutional Options for the Colorado River." *Water Resources Bulletin* 31, October 1995, pp. 837–50.

Kenyon, Daphne A. "Theories of Interjurisdictional Competition." *New England Business Review*, March/April 1997, pp. 13–28

Kershaw, Sarah. "Senecas Sign Pact for Casinos in Niagara Falls and Buffalo." *New York Times*, August 19, 2002, p. B5.

Ketterer, James. "It's Outta Here." *Times Union* (Albany, NY), January 29, 1995, pp. B1, B3.

Kihss, Peter. "New York and Jersey Agree to Cooperate in Regional Program to Reduce Air Pollution." *New York Times*, December 4, 1980, p. B3.

Kilborn, Peter T. "Vermont Spending Plan Seems to Help Schools." *New York Times*, January 31, 2001, p. A11.

Kincaid, John, ed. "American Federalism: The Third Century." *The Annals of the American Academy of Political and Social Science* 509, May 1990, pp. 11–152.

"Kittery Ends Free Ride for Illegally Registered Cars." *Union Leader* (Manchester, NH), March 21, 2002, p. B1.

Koch, Robert E. "Keene 'Best Choice.'" *Keene (NH) Sentinel*, April 2, 2002, pp. 1, 5–6.

———. "C&S Courting Both Keene and Brattleboro." *Keene (NH) Sentinel*, October 17, 2001, pp. 1, 2.

Koch, Robert E. and Dan Gearino. "Keene Lands C&S Complex." *Keene (NH) Sentinel*, April 1, 2002, pp. 1–2.

Kocieniewski, David. "Newark Stadium Bill Dies in Final Session." *New York Times*, January 8, 2002, p. B5.

Koselka, Rita. "The Fight for Jobs." *Forbes* 154, January 31, 1994, pp. 69–72, 77, 80.

Krasner, Jeffrey. "Drug Research Giant Heads to Cambridge." *Boston Globe*, May 7, 2002, p. 1.

Krugman, Paul. "The Great Evasion." *New York Times*, May 14, 2002, p. A10.

Labaton, Stephen. "States to Regulate Money Transfers." *New York Times*, January 22, 1990, p. D2.

Landsberg, Mitchell, Alan Abrahamson, and Seema Mehta. "NFL Stadium Plan Outlined." *Los Angeles Times*, May 16, 2002 (Internet edition).

Lathrop, Douglas A. "Professional Sports & Public Funds: The New England Patriots Seek a New Stadium." *Comparative State Politics* 20, October 1999, pp. 29–40.

Laski, Harold J. "The Obsolescence of Federalism." *The New Republic* 98, May 3, 1939, pp. 362–69.

Leach, Richard H., ed. "Intergovernmental Relations in America Today." *The Annals of the American Academy of Political and Social Science* 416, November 1974, pp. 1–169.

———. "The Interstate Oil Compact: A Study in Success." *Oklahoma Law Review* 10, August 1957, pp. 274–88.

"Legal Problems Relating to Interstate Compacts." *Iowa Law Review* 23, 1937–1938, pp. 618–35.

Lemov, Penelope. "The Untaxables." *Governing* 15, July 2002, pp. 36–37.

Levy, Clifford J. "2 States to Join in System to Stop Fraud in Welfare." *New York Times*, March 30, 1994, pp. 1, B5.

Lewin, Tamar. "At Core of Adoption Dispute Is Crazy Quilt of State Laws. *New York Times*, January 19, 2001, p. A14.

Lewis, Judy J. "Severance Taxes As an Offensive Weapons: The Forbidding Legacy of *Wyoming v. Oklahoma.*" *Journal of Natural Resources & Environmental Law* 9, 1993, pp. 149–66.

Liepas, Algirdas M. "Water Law: Discrimination Against Interstate Commerce in Ground Water for Economic Reasons." *Land and Water Review* 19, Summer 1984, pp. 471–83.

Lipton, Eric. "Guiliani Says That He Lacks Power to Take Over Airports." *New York Times*, March 29, 2001, p. B4.

Little, Gregory G. and Brian V. Otero. "Firing Back When AGs Wage War." *National Law Journal* 25, September 16, 2002) B9, B12.

Lockhard, William B. "State Barriers to Interstate Trade." *Harvard Law Review* 53, June 1940, pp. 1253–289.

Lopez, Salvador and Jorge Martinez-Vazquez. "State Corporate Income Taxation: An Evaluation of Formula Apportionment System." *Proceedings of the 90th Annual Conference on Taxation.* Washington, DC: National Tax Association, 1998: 155–62.

Lord, William B. and Douglas S. Kenney. "Resolving Interstate Water Conflicts: The Compact Approach." *Intergovernmental Perspective* 19, Winter 1993, pp. 19–23.

"Low-Level Waste Controversy." *State Legislatures* 20, September 1994, pp. 30–31.

Lueck, Thomas J. "New York Buys Ads Charging 'Raid' of Company by Connecticut." *New York Times*, October 11, 1994, pp. B1, B5.

Macey, Jonathan R. "Federal Deference to Local Regulators and the Economic Theory of Regulation: Toward a Public-Choice Explanation of Federalism." *Virginia Law Review* 76, March 1990, pp. 265–91.

Macey, Jonathan R. and Geoffrey P. Miller. "The McCarran-Ferguson Act of 1945: Reconceiving the Federal Role in Insurance Regulation." *New York University Law Review* 68, April 1993, pp. 13–87.

Mahtesian, Charles. "How States Get People to Love Them." *Governing* 7, January 1994, p. 44.

———. "Romancing the Smokestack." *Governing* 7, November 1994, p. 38

———. "Saving the States from Each Other." *Governing* 10, November 1986, p. 15.

"Maine Investigates Illegal Resale of Massachusetts Megabucks Tickets." *Keene (NH) Sentinel*, April 10, 1984, p. 14.

"Maine and NH Say Shipyard Vital to Defense." *Union Leader* (Manchester, NH), March 18, 1994, p. 7.

Mansfield, Harvey C. "Intergovernmental Relations," in James W. Fesler, ed., *The 50 States and Their Local Governments*. New York: Alfred A. Knopf, 1967: 158–99.

Maremont, Mark and Gary Putka. "Tyco Ex-CEO Is Indicted for Failure to Pay Taxes." *The Wall Street Journal Europe*, June 5, 2002, pp. 1, A4.

Marsico, Ron and George E. Jordan. "New Life for Arena in Newark." *State-Ledger* (Trenton, NJ), August 23, 2002 (Internet edition).

Martin, James W. "Tax Competition Between States." *The Annals of the American Academy of Political and Social Science* 207, January 1940, pp. 62–69.

Martinez, Deborah. "Soldiers Bolster Security at Arsenal." *Times Union* (Albany, NY), October 20, 2001, p. B1.

"Mass. Lawmakers Dropping Plan to Leave the Northeast Dairy Compact." *Union Leader* (Manchester, NH), July 18, 2000, p. B3.

Mass Starts Crackdown on Illegal NH Plates." *Union Leader* (Manchester, NH), May 9, 1995, p. A10.

"Mass Tax Is Good News: Cigarette Buyers Pour Into N.H. *Keene (NH) Sentinel*, January 4, 1993, pp. 1, 5.

"Massachusetts Reimburses New Hampshire." *Worcester Telegram* (Worcester, MA), December 5, 1959, p. 5.

"Massport Urges Travelers to Use Regional Airports." *Telegram & Gazette* (Worcester, MA), January 5, 2001, pp. E1, E3.

Matthews, Olen P. "Judicial Resolution of Transboundary Water Conflicts." *Water Resources Bulletin* 30, June 1994, pp. 375–83.

Matzer, Maria. "N.Y.P.D. Freebie." *Forbes* 155, April 10, 1995, p. 22.

Mauro, Frank J. and Glee Yago. "State Government Targeting in Economic Development: The New York Experience." *Publius* 19, Spring 1989, pp. 63–82.

Maynard, Micheline. "A Pension Fund Chief Bets on US Airways." *New York Times*, October 5, 2002, pp. C1, C3.

"The Mayor Taxes Will Power." *New York Times*, July 2, 2002, p. A20.

Mays, Amanda. "Innovative Tools for Economic Growth." *State Government News* 45, May 2002, pp. 17–18.

McAllister. "Court, Congress, and Trade Barriers." *Indiana Law Journal* 16, December 1940, pp. 144–68.

McCabe, John M. "Uniform State Laws: 1988–1989." *The Book of the States: 1990–1991*. Lexington, KY: The Council of State Governments, 1990, 405–16.

McCool, Daniel. "Intergovernmental Conflict and Indian Water Rights: An Assessment of Negotiated Settlements." *Publius* 23, Winter 1993, pp. 85–101.

McCormick, Zachary L. "Interstate Water Allocation Compacts in the Western United States: Some Suggestions." *Water Resources Bulletin* 30, June 1994, pp. 385–95.

McCray, Sandra B. "Federal Preemption of State Regulation of Insurance: End of a 200 Year Era?" *Publius* 24, Fall 1993, pp. 33–47.

McCulloch, Anne M. "The Politics of Indian Gaming: Tribe/State Relations and American Federalism." *Publius* 24, Summer 1994, pp. 99–112.

McDowell, James L. "The Politics of Trash: Solid Waste Disposal, the Interstate Commerce Clause, and Congress." *Southeastern Political Review* 27, December 1999, pp. 725–44.

McElhenny, John. "Senate: Mass. Should Withdraw from Dairy Compact." *Union Leader* (Manchester, NH), May 18, 2000, p. A12.

McKay, Jim. "Revitalizing the Roadways." *Government Technology*, March 2001, pp. 52, 54.

McKeon, Michael. "Steinbrenner Wants A-C Yankees to Stay Put." *Times Union* (Albany, NY), March 22, 1994, pp. 1, A8.

McKinley, James C., Jr. "Gambling Expansion Is Part of Albany Budget Agreement." *New York Times*, October 24, 2001, pp. D1, D5.

McKusick, Vincent L. "Discretionary Gatekeeping: The Supreme Court's Management of Its Original Jurisdiction Docket Since 1961." *Maine Law Review* 45, 1993, pp. 185–242.

McLaughlin, Gerald T. and Neil B. Cohen. "Revised U.C.C. Art. 9, Part 2." *National Law Journal* 23, January 22, 2001, p. B5.

McLaughlin, Susan. "The Impact of Interstate Banking and Branching Reform: Evidence from the States." *Current Issues in Economics and Finance* 1, May 1995, pp. 1–5.

McLure, Charles E., Jr. "Severance Taxes and Interstate Fiscal Conflicts." *Texas Business Review* 56, July–August 1982, pp. 175–78.

Meislin, Richard J. "10 States Link Efforts to Hunt Tax Cheaters." *New York Times*, January 17, 1986, p. B1.

282   *Bibliography*

Meissner, Frank. "Consumer Protection or Butter Politics?" *Cartel* 3, October 1952, pp. 49–55.

Melder, F. Eugene. "Trade Barriers Between States." *The Annals of the American Academy of Political and Social Science* 207, January 1940, pp. 54–61.

———. "Trade Barriers and States Rights." *American Bar Association Journal* 25, April, 1939, pp. 307–09.

Mikesell, John L. "Lotteries in State Revenue Systems: Gauging a Popular Revenue Source after 35 Years." *State and Local Government Review* 33, Spring 2001, pp. 86–100.

Miller, Fred H. "The Uniform Commercial Code: Will the Experiment Continue?" *Mercer Law Review* 43, No. 3–4, 1992, pp. 799–823.

Miller, Jerry. "N.E. Governors, Canadian Leaders Gather." *Union Leader* (Manchester, NH), June 7, 1995, p. A7.

———. "NH Tourist Office Getting Aggressive." *Union Leader* (Manchester, NH), April 4, 2002 (Internet Edition).

Millman, Joel. "Visions of Sugar Plums South of the Border." *Wall Street Journal*, February 13, 2002, pp. A15–A16.

"Miss America: Atlantic City Gets Pageant 1 More Year." *New York Times*, December 28, 2001, p. D5.

Moffitt, Donald. "More States Cancel Inventory Tax on Items for Sale Elsewhere." *Wall Street Journal*, January 25, 1964, p. 1.

Money, Jack. "State Ready to Sue Texas Over Water." *The Oklahoman*, August 27, 2002 (Internet edition).

Moore, Doug. "City Moves Stadium Deal Forward." *St. Louis Post Dispatch*, September 24, 2002 (Internet edition).

Morais, Richard C. "Casino Junkies: The Latest Gambling Wave Has a Silent Partner: Governments Throughout the Country are Hooked." *Forbes* 169, April 29, 2002, pp. 66, 68, 70.

———. "New York State of Mind." *Forbes* 169, April 29, 2002), p. 68.

Morris, Dvid and Daniel Kraker. "Rooting the Home Team: Why the Packers Won't Leave: And Why the Browns Did." *American Prospect Magazine* 40, September–October 1998, pp. 38–43.

Mott, Rodney L. "Uniform Legislation in the United States." *The Annals of the American Academy of Political and Social Science* 207, January 1940, pp. 79–92.

Mountjoy, John J. "Adult Compact Version 2.0." *State Government News* 45, August 2002, pp. 26–27.

———. "State Solutions." *State Government News* 45, June/July 2002, pp. 14–16.

"Moving Toward Online Sales Taxes." *New York Times*, September 3, 2001, p. A14.

Murphy, Blakely M. "The Administrative Mechanism of the Interstate Compact to Conserve Oil and Gas: The Interstate Oil Compact Commission: 1935–1948." *Tulane Law Review* 22, December 1947, pp. 384–402.

Muys, Jerome C. "Interstate Compacts and Regional Water Resources Planning and Management." *Natural Resources Lawyer* 6, Spring 1973, pp. 153–88.

Myers, Steven L. "Giuliani Says Connecticut Broke Truce." *New York Times*, October 14, 1994, pp. B1, B6.

Nachtigal, Jerry. "Arizona Goes all Out to Entice Wealthy Seniors to Retire There." *Sunday Sentinel* (Keene, NH), March 9, 1997, p. C6.

Nadleman, Kurt H. "Full Faith and Credit in Judgments and Public Acts: A Historical-Analytical Reappraisal." *Michigan Law Review* 56, 1957–58, pp. 33–88.

"Nationwide Crackdown on Funeral Homes That Fail to Provide Required Information Launched by FTC with State Attorneys General." *FTC News Notes* (Federal Trade Commission), July 3, 1995, p. 1.

Naujoks, Herbert H. "Compacts and Agreements Between States and Between States and a Foreign Power." *Marquette Law Review* 36, Winter 1952–1953, pp. 219–47.

"Nebraska Rejects Compact." *State Government News* 42, June/July 1999, p. 6.

Nesbit, Justin M. "Commerce Clause Implications of Massachusetts' Attempt to Limit the Importation of 'Dirty' Power in the Looming Competitive Retail Market for Electricity Generation." *Boston College Law Review* 38, July 1997, pp. 811–50.

Netzer, Dick. "An Evaluation of Interjurisdictional Competition Through Economic Development Incentives," in Daphne A. Kenyon and John Kincaid, eds., *Competition Among State and Local Governments*. Washington, DC: The Urban Institute Press, 1991, pp. 221–45.

———. "Reinventing the Port Authority." *City Journal* 6, Summer 1996, pp. 77–89.

"New England Leaders Tout Regional Airports." *Union Leader* (Manchester, NH), November 24, 1999, p. A8.

"New Hampshire Goes to High Court in Lobster Dispute." *New York Times*, June 7, 1973, p. 43.

"New Lottery Debuts in New York." *Legislative Gazette* (Albany, NY), April 15, 2002, p. 2.

"New War Between the States." *New England Business Review*, October 1964, pp. 2–7.

———. Part II: State Loans and Loan Guarantee Programs." *New England Business Review*, December 1963, pp. 1–5.

———. Part III: Municipal Bonding for Private Industry." *New England Business Review*, July 1964, pp. 2–7.

———. Part IV: Tax Exemptions and Concessions." *New England Business Review*, October 1964, pp. 2–7.

"NH Commissioner Critical of Vermont Seal of Quality." *Union Leader* (Manchester, NH), October 6, 1993, p. 14.

"NH, Maine Face Off Over Snowmobile Trail Rights." *Union Leader* (Manchester, NH), April 23, 2001, p. B3.

"NH, Maine, Vt. Joining Forces on Health Care." *Union Leader* (Manchester, NH), November 11, 1993, p. 9.

"NH Powerball Cuts Into Vt. Lottery Sales." *Union Leader* (Manchester, NH), January 19, 1996, p. A9.

"NH-Vermont Solid Waste District Chief Under Fire." *Union Leader* (Manchester, NH), April 17, 2000, p. B1.

Nice, David C. "Cooperation and Conformity among the States." *Polity* 16, Spring 1984, pp. 494–505.

———. "State Participation in Interstate Compacts." *Publius* 17, Spring 1987, pp. 69–83.

Nimmer, Raymond T. "UCC's Art. 2 Gets Revised to Fit the Information Age." *National Law Journal* 14, November 15, 1993, pp. 32–34.

"NMFS Rescinds Implementation of Horseshoe Crab Moratorium; Virginia Closes Fishery As of October 23." *ASMFC Fisheries Focus* 9, November 2000, p. 4.

Nodel, Bobbi. "Washington Expands Lottery Lineup Today." *Seattle Times*, September 4, 2002 (Internet Edition).

North Carolina-South Carolina Seaward Boundary Agreement." *Congressional Record.*, September 29, 1981, pp. H6667–668.

"Northeast Battles Midwest Smog." *Times Union* (Albany, NY), August 8, 1997, p. A3.

"Northeast States Ask Clinton to Press Midwest on Air Quality." *Times Union* (Albany, NY), August 15, 1997, p. A16.

Northrop, Vernon D. "The Delaware River Basin Commission: A Prototype in River Basin Development." *Journal of Soil and Water Conservation* 22, March–April 1967, pp. 58–61.

"N.Y.P.D. Freebie." *Forbes* 155, April 10, 1995, p. 22.

"NY Sewage Treatment Plant to Install BNR, Boost Bay Efforts." *Bay Journal* 9, March 1999, p. 3.

"N.Y.-N.J. Tax Pact Targets Cheaters." *Knickerbocker News* (Albany, NY), February 21, 1986, p. 5A.

Nyhan, David. "Applying the Brakes to a New State Auto Emission Standard." *Boston Globe*, November 25, 1992, p. 17.

N.Y.'s Gambling Fever. *Times Union* (Albany, NY), October 28, 2001, p. B4.

Odato, James M. "Coalition to Sue over Expansion of Gambling." *Times Union* (Albany, NY), January 29, 2002, p. B3.

———. "Compact Clears Way for Casinos." *Times Union* (Albany, NY), August 19, 2002, pp. 1, A5

———. "Court Battle Heats Up over Mega Millions Game." *Times Union* (Albany, NY), May 9, 2002, p. B2.

———. "Pact to Expand Gaming Draws Closer to Reality." *Times Union* (Albany, NY), October 2,3 2001, pp. 1, A9.

———. "State Betting on Casino, Video Lottery Revenue." *Times Union* (Albany, NY), March 10, 2002, p. 26.

———. "State Expected to Hit $1B Jackpot." *Times Union* (Albany, NY), October 26, 2001, pp. 1, A13.

Odato, James M. and Jay Jochnowitz. "All Bets Placed on Gambling." *Times Union* (Albany, NY), October 25, 2001, pp. 1, A6.

————. "State's Newest Budget Deal Plans for Gambling Profits." *Times Union* (Albany, NY), October 24, 2001, pp. 1, A11.

Oden, Michael D. "The Horse Before the Cart: Toward a More Rational Management of Economic Development Incentives." *Texas Business Review*, June 1999, pp. 1–3.

"Official Recommendations of the United States Commission on Interstate Child Support." *Family Law Quarterly* 27, Spring 1993, pp. 31–84.

Olsen, Daryll and Walter R. Butcher. "The Regional Power Act: A Model for the Nation?" *Washington Public Policy Notes* 12, Winter 1984, pp. 1–6.

"One Last Squeeze Play." *Times Union* (Albany, NY), December 29, 2001, p. A6.

"Ontario Takes Acid Rain Case to United States Supreme Court." *Background* (Ontario Ministry of Municipal Affairs), March 16, 1987, p. 11.

"Pataki Unveils Plan to Fight Welfare Recipients' Double-Dipping." *Times Union* (Albany, NY), September 10, 1995, p. D4.

Patchel, Kathleen. "Interest Group Politics, Federalism, and the Uniform Laws Process: Some Lessons from the Uniform Commercial Code." *Minnesota Law Review* 78, November 1993, pp. 83–164.

Perez-Pena, Richard. "In Albany, Getting Serious About Casinos." *New York Times*, October 20, 2001, p. D1.

————. "Competition Fierce for Stake in New York Gambling Market." *New York Times*, December 17, 2001, pp. F1, F4.

————. "Court Upholds Law to Repeal Commuter Tax." *New York Times*, April 5, 2000, pp. B1, B7.

————. "Deal Brings Indian Casino in the Catskills Closer to Reality." *New York Times*, November 16, 2001, p. D8.

————. "Despite Economic Dip, State Needs More Power Plants, Group Says." *New York Times*, March 28, 2002, p. B5.

————. "Gambling Bill Is Questioned on Constitutional Grounds." *New York Times*, October 26, 2001, p. D6.

Perez-Pena, Richard and James G. McKinley Jr. "Casino Deal Emerges As Fiscal Crisis Looms." *Times Union* (Albany, NY), October 21, 2001, pp. 1, A4.

Perlman, Ellen. "Buying It Better." *Governing* 8, August 1995, pp. 61–62.

————. "Vintage Politics: The Complexities of Shipping Chardonnay Across State Lines." *Governing* 9, December 1995, p. 47.

————. "Dancing Around the Dumps." *Governing* 8, August 1995, pp. 48–51.

Petersen, John E. "Interstate Meat Markets: The High Price of Buying Jobs." *Governing* 7, October 1993, p. 60.

Pierce, Sarah B. "State Taxation: Unitary Business/Formula Apportionment Tax Accounting Method." *Georgia Journal of International and Comparative Law* 23, Spring 1993, pp. 89–110.

Pitcher, Robert C. "The International Fuel Tax Agreement: Are There Lessons Here for Sales and Use Taxation?" *State Tax Notes* 20, March 12, 2001, pp. 887–91.

Pitzl, Mary J. and Tom Zoeliner. "Hull, Tribes OK Gaming Deals." *Arizona Republic*, February 21, 2002 (Internet edition).

Plungis, Jeff. "Nations Within a State." *Empire State Report* 19, October 1993, pp. 31, 33–35.

Post, Paul. "I Love NY Again." *Empire State Report* 27, July–August 2001, pp. 27–30.

Postrel, Virginia. "A Look at Wine Sales over the Internet Shows the Price of Some Regulations in the Name of Consumer Protection." *New York Times*, July 17, 2003, p. C2.

Potoski, Matthew. "Clean Air Federalism: Do States Race to the Bottom? *Public Administration Review* 61, May/June 2001, pp. 335–42.

Powell, Thomas R. "Indirect Encroachment on Federal Authority by the Taxing Powers of the States." *Harvard Law Review* 31, 1917–18, pp. 321–72 and 572–618.

"The Power of the States to Make Compacts." *Yale Law Journal* 31, 1922, pp. 635–39.

"Powerball Fever Proves Too Much for Greenwich." *Union Leader* (Manchester, NH), August 24, 2001, p. A18.

"Powerball Politics." *Times Union* (Albany, NY), September 11, 2001, p. A8.

Price-Waterhouse. "Voting with Their Feet: A Study of Tax Incentives and Economic Consequences of Cross-Border Activity in New England." *The State Factor* 18, August 1992, pp. 1–60.

———. "Voting with Their Feet II: The Economic Consequences of Cross-Border Activity in the Southeastern U.S." *The State Factor* 19, August 1993, pp. 1–68.

Prichard, James. "No Rescue for Life Savers Employees." *Times Union* (Albany, NY), April 14, 2002, p. F2.

Prokesch, Steven. "New York, Seeking Taxes, Follows Shoppers Across Hudson." *New York Times*, December 9, 1992, pp. B1, B5.

Pulley, Brett. "Exchange Delays Vote to Move As New York Adds Incentives." *New York Times*, October 12, 1995, p. B5.

———. "New York Makes Staying Put Irresistible to Coffee Exchange." *New York Times*, October 13, 1995, pp. B1, B3.

Quint, Michael. "Met Life Asked for $10 Million." *Times Union* (Albany, NY), February 7, 1994, p. B5.

Rael, Jason M. "Down in the Dumps: Can States Regulate Out-of-State Waste Flow and Survive the Commerce Clause?" *Natural Resources Journal* 38, Summer 1998, pp. 489–507.

Redburn, Tom. "New Flare-Up in Region's Border Wars Kills an Oft-Ignored Truce." *New York Times*, October 16, 1994, pp. 37, 42.

Reeves, Hope. "Read Their Lips: No Taxes." *New York Times*, July 8, 2002, pp. B1, B6.

Regan, Donald H. "The Supreme Court and State Protectionism: Making Sense of the Dormant Commerce Clause." *Michigan Law Review* 83, May 1986, pp. 1091–287.

"Region's Economic Competitiveness Ranks High." *Union Leader* (Manchester, NH), April 11, 2002, p. A13.

"Regional Education: A New Use of the Interstate Compact?" *Virginia Law Review* 34, 1948, pp. 64–76.

Revesz, Richard L. "Rehabilitating Interstate Competition: Rethinking the 'Race-to-the-Bottom' Rationale for Federal Environmental Regulation." *New York University Law Review* 67, December 1992, pp. 1210–254.

"Revision to Blood Alcohol Concentration (BAC) for Recreational Vessel Operators." 66 *Federal Register* 1859, January 10, 2001.

Revkin, Andrew C. "In New Tactic, State Aims to Sue Utilities Over Coal Pollution." *New York Times*, September 15, 1999, pp. 1, B5.

"Rewriting the Rules." *Government Technology*, January 2001, pp. 50–52.

Ribstein, Larry E. and Bruce Kobayaski. "An Economic Analysis of Uniform State Laws." *Journal of Legal Studies* 25, January 1996, pp. 131–87.

Riggs, Russell W. "Radioactive Waste Compacts for the Northeast States." *State Government* 63, July–September 1990, pp. 80–82.

Ritchie, Bruce. "Counties Protest River Talks." *Tallahassee Democrat*, July 16, 2002 (Internet Edition).

Roach, Thomas A. and Lydia P. Loren. "State Licensing of Out-of-State Wholesale Distributors: An Undue Burden on Interstate Commerce." *Food, Drug, Cosmetic, and Medical Device Law Digest* 13, January 1996, pp. 21–25.

"Roadblocks Used by State to Shut Off Tax-Free Liquor." *Knickerbocker News* (Albany, NY), February 9, 1966, p. 6A.

Robbins, Jim. "Farms and Growth Threaten a Sea and Its Creatures." *New York Times*, April 2, 2002), p. F3

Robbins, William. "3 Million Chickens Destroyed in Bid to Halt Spread of Virus." *New York Times*, November 28, 1983, pp. 1, B11.

Roberst, W. Lewis. "The Right of a State to Restrict Exportation of Natural Resources." *Kentucky Law Journal* 24, March 1936, pp. 259–71.

Rockefeller, Nelson A. "An Act Concerning N.Y.'s Ratification of a Compact Relative to the Development of the Delaware River Basin Water Resources." *Public Papers of Nelson A. Rockefeller 1961*. Albany: State of New York, n.d. 427–30.

Rodriguez, Daniel B. "Turning Federalism Inside Out: Intrastate Aspects of Interstate Regulatory Competition." *Yale Law and Policy Review* 14, 1996, pp. 149–76.

Rogers, Lindsay. "The Power of the States Over Commodities Excluded by Congress from Interstate Commerce." *Yale Law Journal* 24, May 1915, pp. 567–72.

Roos, Norman H. and William E. Bandon, III. "Acts Seek Uniform 3–Policies." *National Law Journal* 23, November 27, 2000, pp. B 11, B13, B15.

Rosenbaum, David E. "Congress Is Urged to Block Use of Offshore Income Tax Shelters." *New York Times*, May 18, 2000, p. C4.

Routt, Garland C. "Interstate Compacts and Administrative Co-operation." *The Annals of the American Academy of Political and Social* Science 207, January 1940, pp. 93–102.

Royster, Judith V. and Rory S. Fausett. "Control of the Reservation Environment: Tribal Primacy, Federal Delegation, and the Limits of State Intrusion." *Washington Law Review* 64, July 1989, pp. 581–659.

Rubin, Edward L. and Malcom Feeley. "Federalism: Some Notes on a National Neurosis." *University of California Los Angeles Law Review* 41, April 1994, pp. 903–52.

Rulon, Malia. "Great Lakes Report Faults Pace of Cleanup Efforts." *Times Union* (Albany, NY), September 13, 2002, p. B2.

Rychlak, Ronald J. "Lotteries, Revenues, and Social Costs: A Historical Examination of State-Sponsored Gambling." *Boston College Law Review* 34, 1992–1993, pp. 11–81.

Sack, Kevin. "Will Nashville Say No to N.F.L. Team? Maybe." *New York Times*, May 3, 1996, pp. 1, A26.

Sagan, John R. "Severance Taxes and the Commerce Clause: *Commonwealth Edison v. Montana.*" *Wisconsin Law Review* 1983, 1983, pp. 427–52.

Sandomir, Richard. "New Stadiums Slip Far Down on the List of Priorities." *New York Times*, September 20, 2001, p. A24.

Schemo, Diana J. "For Oklahoma's Teachers, Big D Is Dollars (and Dallas)." *New York Times*, July 6, 2002, p. A7.

Schuck, Peter H. "Some Reflections on the Federalism Debate." *Yale Law and Policy Review* 14, 1996, pp. 1–22.

Schwarcz, Steven L. "A Fundamental Inquiry into the Statutory Rulemaking Process of Private Legislatures." *Georgia Law Review* 19, Summer 1995, pp. 909–89.

Scott, Michael J. "Attention Emall Shoppers!" *State Government News* 42, May 1999) 26–27.

Seabrook, Charles. "Is Atlanta Drinking the Future Dry?" *Atlanta Journal-Constitution*, May 15, 2002 (Internet edition).

Scott, Dana. "State Taxes Helped Drive Out KeyCorp, Riley Says." *Times Union* (Albany, NY), February17, 1994, p. C10.

"Scott Paper Leaving Philly for Florida." *Times Union* (Albany, NY), March 14, 1995, p. B12

Seldin, Chris. "Interstate Marketing of Indian Water Rights: The Impact of the Commerce Clause." *California Law Review* 87, December 1999, pp. 1545–580.

Shaffer, Anita T. "Officials Foresee More Millions to Fix E-Z Pass." *The Times of Trenton* (NJ), May 22, 2002 (Internet edition).

Shahrokhshahi, Kaveh. "The Constitutionality of a Federal Ceiling on State Severance Taxes." *Santa Clara Law Review* 23, 1983, pp. 867–98.

Shanker, Vijay. "Alcohol Direct Shipment Laws: The Commerce Clause and the Twenty-first Amendment." *Virginia Law Review* 85, March 1999, pp. 353–83.

Sheehan, Jan. "Growing (Like) Crazy." *Colorado Business Magazine*, February 1995, pp. 32–38.

Shenon, Philip. "Home Exemptions Snag Bankruptcy Bill. *New York Times*, April 6, 2001, pp. 1, A19.

———. "Home As Shield from Creditors Is Under Fire." *New York Times*, April 4, 2002, pp. C1, C6.

Sheppard, Doug. "Streamlined Project Moves Ahead with 2001 Agenda." *State Tax Notes* 20, March 12, 2001, pp. 874–78.

Sherk, George W. "Resolving Interstate Water Conflicts in the Eastern United States: The Re-Emergence of the Federal-Interstate Compact." *Water Resources Bulletin* 30, June 1994, pp. 397–408.

Shlaes, Amity. "Let America's Corporations Off the Tax Leash." *Financial Times*, May 28, 2002, p. 19.

Shores, David F. "State Taxation of Interstate Commerce: Quiet Revolution or Much Ado About Nothing?" *Tax Law Review* 38, Fall 1982, pp. 127–69.

"Siblings Claim Final Share of Powerball." *USA Today*, August 31, 2001, p. 3A.

"Sick Chickens Force Quarantine in PA." *Knickerbocker News* (Albany, NY), November 5, 1983, p. 2A.

Silverman, Gary and Edward Aiden. "Tyco Chief Charges Highlight Havens." *Financial Times*, June 5, 2002, p. 24.

Simon, Bernard. "In Men's Clothing, More and More of the Labels Say 'Made in Canada.'" *New York Times*, March 23, 2002, p. C2.

Simpson, Aaron H. "The New Hampshire/Vermont Solid Waste Project: Is There a Solution?" *Vermont Law Review* 20, Summer 1996, pp. 1091–1135.

Simpson, Glenn R. "Complicated Tax Code Is Cited for Driving Companies Out of U.S." *Wall Street Journal Europe*, June 6, 2002, p. M6.

Sims, Calvin. "Port Authority Seeks $1 Rise in Bridge Tolls." *New York Times*, November 21, 1990, pp. B1, B6.

Slayden, James L. "Railway Regulation in Texas." *The Annals of the American Academy of Political and Social Science* 32, July 1908, pp. 225–34.

Smith, Michael E. "State Discrimination Against Interstate Commerce." *California Law Review* 74, July 1986, pp. 1203–257.

Smothers, Ronald. "Arena Plan for Newark Is Said to Stall on Insurance." *New York Times*, May 2, 2002, p. B5.

———. "As It Turns 80, the Port Authority Looks to Its Roots to Find Its Future." *New York Times*, April 30, 2001, pp. B1, B8.

———. "As McGreevey Unveils a Plan for Nets Arena, Critics Scoff." *New York Times*, May 9, 2002, pp. B1, B5.

———. "DiFrancesco Adding Projects to Widen Arena Bill's Allure." *New York Times*, September 6, 2001, p. B6.

———. "Fury Over Tolls Aside, Port Authority Has Major Building Plans." *New York Times*, January 29, 2001, p. B3.

———. "McGreevey's Pledge on Arena Leaves Opponents Unswayed." *New York Times*, May 10, 2002, p. B4.

———. "Nets and Devils Owners Close Offices in Newark." *New York Times*, July 12, 2002, p. B5.

———. "Newark Approves Arena Financing Deal." *New York Times*, August 24, 2002, p. B4.

———. "Port Authority Approves Budget, Putting Capital Plan in Motion." *New York Times*, February 23, 2001, p. B4.

———. "Port Authority Increases Tolls and Train Fare." *New York Times*, January 26, 2001, pp. 1, B8.

———. "Using Niceties, Not Power Plays, to Win Bergen County Support for a Newark Arena." *New York Times*, May 27, 2002, p. B5.

Smyth, Patrick and Jim Cusak. "Ireland to Sign Up to Closer EU-Wide Police Links." *Irish Times*, May 30, 2000, p. 9.

"South Carolina to Restrict Its Nuclear Dump." *Governing* 13, August 2000, p. 64.

Spengler, Joseph J. "The Economic Limitations to Certain Uses of Interstate Compacts." *American Political Science Review* 31, February 1937, pp. 41–51.

Spindler, Charles J. "Winners and Losers in Industrial Recruitment: Mercedes-Benz and Alabama." *State and Local Government Review* 26, Fall 1994, pp. 192–204.

Sporza, Daniel. "Turnpike Lends Snarled E-Z Pass $30M." *The Record of Bergen County* (NJ), September 25, 2002 (Internet edition).

Starr, Joseph R. "Reciprocal and Retaliatory Legislation in the American States." *Minnesota Law Review* 21, March 1937, pp. 371–407.

Stashenko, Joel. "Business Council Joins Push for Power Plants." *Times Union* (Albany, NY), August 7, 2001, pp. E1, E4.

———. "Instant Games a Boon for Lottery." *Times Union* (Albany, NY), May 1, 2002, p. B6.

———. "State Validates Tax on Some Natural Gas Importers." *Times Union* (Albany, NY), October 28, 2001, p. F1.

"State Attorneys General Launch Investigation of Cable Industry." *Times Union* (Albany, NY), November 18, 1993, p. D8.

"State Pioneers Tax Change for Visiting Athletes." *New York Times*, August 4, 1994, p. B2.

"State Won't Become NJ's Power Broker." *Times Union* (Albany, NY), July 22, 1995, p. B2.

"States Act to End Long Oyster War." *New York Times*, June 14, 1964, p. 55.

"States Agree to NOX Reductions: Benefits to the Bay Are Uncertain." *Bay Journal* 4, November 1994, p. 4.

"State's Concession May Cost $3 million." *Keene (NH) Sentinel*, May 9, 1996, p. 14.

"States Impose Quarantines on California Produce." *Keene (NH) Sentinel*, July 20, 1981, p. 5.

"Status of Indian Gaming Compacts." *Governors' Bulletin* 27, December 6, 1993), insert page.

Steinhauer, Jennifer. "Giuliani Loosened Ball Clubs' Leases Days Before Exiting." *New York Times*, January 15, 2002, pp. 1, B4.

———. "Mayor Says There's No Money to Build 2 Baseball Stadiums." *New York Times*, January 8, 2002, p. B3.

Steinhauer, Jennifer and Richard Sandomir. "Let's Play Two: Giuliani Presents Deal on Stadiums." *New York Times*, December 29, 2001, pp. 1, D6.

Stern, Eric. "County Balks at Stadium Money Unless Parks Get Some." *Post Dispatch* (St. Louis), February 16, 2002 (Internet edition).

——. "County Council OKs Extending MetroLink into Shrewsbury. *Post Dispatch* (St. Louis), August 14, 2002 (Internet edition).

Stern, Sol. "No to Sports Stadium Madness." *City Journal* 8, Autumn 1998, pp. 77–88.

Strunsky, Steve. "Pact Between New Jersey and Netherlands Will Mean Cleaner Air for State." *New York Times*, December 24, 1999, p. B6.

Suggested State Legislation Program for 1957. Chicago: The Council of State Governments, 1956.

"Suit to Void Gambling Law Could Bar Seneca Casinos." *Times Union* (Albany, NY), August 20, 2002, p. B2.

Sullivan, Joseph F. "Federal Judge Voids New Jersey Rules Against Out-of-State Milk." *New York Times*, April 19, 1990, pp. B1, B5.

——. "Trenton Sues Freeloaders on Insurance." *New York Times*, February 28, 1992, pp. B1, B4.

Sundeen, Matthew and Cheryl L. Runyon. "Interstate Compacts and Administrative Agreements." *State Legislative Report* 23, March 1998, pp. 1–12.

Swartz, Jon. "Scandal-Plagued Execs Build Palaces." *Times Union* (Albany, NY), July 15, 2002, p. A5.

"Taking Care of Business: State and Local CIOs Assume Greater Roles in Economic Development." *Government Technology*, November 2001, pp. 34–35.

Tannenwald, Robert. "Massachusetts' Tax Competitiveness." *New England Economic Review*, January/February 1994, pp. 31–49.

——. "State Regulatory Policy and Economic Development." *New England Economic Review*, March–April 1997, pp. 83–99.

Tatarowiecz., Philip M. "An Analytical Approach to State Tax Discrimination Under the Commerce Clause." *Vanderbilt Law Review* 39, May 1986, pp. 879–960.

"A Taxation Milestone." *Government Technology*, June 2002, p. 10.

Tenenbaum, David. "Whose Trash Is This? Flow-Control War May Get Costly." *City & State* 11, January 1994, p. 30.

Tinsley, V. Randall and Larry A. Nielsen. "Interstate Fisheries Arrangements: Application of a Pragmatic Classification Scheme for Interstate Arrangements." *Virginia Journal of Natural Resources Law* 6, Spring 1987, pp. 263–321.

Tracy, Paula. "Maine Now Charging NH Snowmobilers $66." *Union Leader* (Manchester, NH), January 4, 2002, p. A7.

——. "NH Businesses Change Market Strategy." *Union Leader* (Manchester, NH), October 30, 2001, p. A3.

"Trouble with Trash." *New York Times*, July 13, 2002, p. A10.

"2-State Pact Bars Double Taxation." *New York Times*, February 9, 1958, p. 22.

"2 States to Allow New York Business." *Times Union* (Albany, NY), October 14, 1995, p. B8.

"2 Teens in Smart Case Move to Maine Prison. *Keene (NH) Sentinel,* October 6, 1992, p. 5.

"230-Year Border Fight Settled by Maine and New Hampshire." *New York Times,* July 11, 1974, p. 18.

Uchitelle, Louis. "Cincinnati's Revival Sags Under Weight of Falling Revenue." *New York Times,* November 3, 2001, p. A8.

"U.S. and Florida Fight Texas and California Over Citrus Shipments." *New York Times,* February 16, 1988, p. A13.

Usborne, David. "Dennis the Dealmaker Given a New Nickname: The Artful Tax Dodger." *The Independent* (London), June 6, 2002, p. 3.

Vairo, Georgene M. "Removal Update." *National Law Journal* 24, July 15, 2002, p. B11.

Van Alstyne, William W. "International Law and Interstate River Disputes." *California Law Review* 48, 1960, pp. 596–622.

Vawter, Wallace R. "Interstate Compact: The Federal Interest." In Task Force on Water Resources and Power, *Report on Water Resources and Power.* Washington, DC: U.S. Commission on Organization of the Executive Branch of the Government, 1955: 1683–702.

Verhovek, Sam H. "Texas Caters to a Demand Around U.S. for Jail Cells." *New York Times,* February 9, 1996, pp. 1, A24.

"Vermont Looks for Way to Keep Liquor-Buyers from Going to N.H." *Keene (NH) Sentinel* January 12, 1996, p. 9.

Vest, Robert E. "Water Wars in the Southeast: Alabama, Florida, and Georgia Square Off over the Apalachicola-Chattahoochee-Flint River Basin." *Georgia State University Law Review* 9, 1993, pp. 689–716.

"Virginia General Assembly Takes Steps to Leave ASMFC." *Bay Journal* 5, March 1995, p. 13.

"Virginia Legislature Approves Subsidies to New Disney Park." *New York Times,* March 14, 1994, p. A15.

Voit, William K. and Gary Nitting. *Interstate Compacts & Agencies.* Lexington, KY: The Council of State Governments, 1998.

Waits, Mary J. "Building an Economic Future." *State Government News* 38, September 1995, pp. 6–10.

Wald, Matthew L. "California Car Rules Set As Model for the East." *New York Times,* December 20, 1994, p. A16.

———. "Court Backs Most E.P.A. Action on Polluters in Central States." *New York Times,* May 16, 2001, p. A24.

———. "E.P.A. Urges Compromise on Auto Pollution Rules." *New York Times,* September 14, 1994, p. B4.

———. "Governors Agree on Auto Standards." *Times Union* (Albany, NY), October 30, 1991, p. B10.

———. "Weicker Drops Out of Regional Clean-Air Program." *New York Times*, November 8, 1991, p. B5.

Warren, Barry P. "Assessing the Policy Implications of State Incentives: Firm Specific Vis-à-Vis Economic Growth Strategies." *Economic Development Review* 14, Spring 1996, pp. 47–50.

Wasylenko, Michael. "The Location of Firms: The Role of Taxes and Fiscal Incentives," in Roy Bahl, ed., *Urban Government Finance Emerging Trends*. Beverly Hills: Sage Publications, 1981: 155–90.

———. "Taxation and Economic Development: The State of the Economic Literature." *New England Economic Review*, March/April 1997, pp. 37–52.

Watson, Douglas J. and Thomas Vocino. "Changing Intergovernmental Fiscal Relationships: Impact of the 1986 Tax Reform Act on State and Local Governments." *Public Administration Review* 50, July/August 1990, pp. 427–34.

"Web Sale of Tobacco Costing States." *Boston Globe*, August 13, 2002, p. B2.

Wechsler, Herbert. "The Political Safeguards of Federalism: The Role of the States in the Composition and Selection of the National Government," in Arthur W. MacMahon, ed., *Federalism: Mature and Emergent*. Garden City, NY: Doubleday & Company, Incorporated, 1955, 97–114.

Wehrwein, Peter. "State Officials Unhappy About Pollution Trading." *Times Union* (Albany, NY), February 11, 1993, p. B1.

Weiner, Joann M. "Formula Apportionment and Unitary Taxation: What Works and Doesn't Work." *Proceeding of the 90th Annual Conference on Taxation*. Washington, DC: National Tax Association, 1998:233–38.

Weiner, Tim. "Water Crisis Grows Into a Test of U.S.-Mexico Relations." *New York Times*, May 24, 2002, p. A3.

———. "U.S. Reaches Partial Deal with Mexico Over Water." *The New York Times*, July 5, 2002, p. A14.

Weissert, Carol S. and Jeffrey S. Hill. "Low-Level Radioactive Waste Compacts: Lessons Learned from Theory and Practice." *Publius* 24, Fall 1994, pp. 27–43.

Welch, Susan and Cal Clark. "Interstate Compacts and National Integration: An Empirical Assessment of Some Trends." *Western Political Quarterly* 26, September 1973, pp. 475–84.

Werden, Gregory J. "Market Delineation under the NAAG Horizontal Merger Guidelines: Realties or Illusions?" *Cleveland State Law Review* 35, 1986–1987, pp. 403–22.

Wigmore, John H. "The International Assimilation of Law: Its Needs and Its Possibilities from an American Standpoint." *Illinois Law Review* 10, January 1916, pp. 386–98.

Wilgoren, Jodi. "Facing New Costs, Some Smokers Say 'Enough.'" *New York Times*, July 17, 2002, p. A14.

———. "Midwest Towns Feel Gambling Is a Sure Thing." *New York Times*, May 20, 2002, pp. 1, A14.

Wilkinson, Charles F. "Western Water Law in Transition." *University of Colorado Law Review* 56, Spring 1985, pp. 317–484.

Williams, Stephen F. "Severance Taxes and Federalism: The Role of the Supreme Court in Preserving a National Common Market for Energy Supplies." *University of Colorado Law Review* 53, Winter 1982, pp. 281–314.

Winkle, John W., II. "Dimensions of Judicial Federalism." *The Annals of the American Academy of Political and Social Science* 416, November 1974, pp. 67–76.

Wise, Charles R. "The Supreme Court's New Constitutional Federalism: Implications for Public Administration." *Public Administration Review* 61, May/June 2001, pp. 343–58.

Wollenberg, Elmer. "The Columbia River Fish Compact." *Oregon Law Review* 18, 1939, pp. 88–107.

Yardley, Jim. "New York's Sewage Was a Texas Town's Gold." *New York Times*, July 27, 2001, p. A12.

Zielbauer, Paul. "In Connecticut, Governor Signs 61–Cent Cigarette Tax Increase." *The New York Times*, March 1, 2002, p. B8.

———. "Prisoner's Death Renews Call to Stop Exporting Connecticut Convicts." *New York Times*, April 7, 2000, p. B5.

Zimmerman, Joseph F. "Child Support: Interstate Dimensions." *Publius* 24, Fall 1994, pp. 45–60.

———. "Congressional Regulation of Subnational Governments." *P.S.: Political Science & Politics* 26, June 1993, pp. 177–81.

———. "Dimensions of Interstate Relations." *Publius* 24, Fall 1994, pp. 1–11.

———. "Federal Judicial Remedial Power: The Yonkers Case." *Publius* 20, Summer 1990, pp. 45–61.

———, ed. "Federal Preemption." *Publius* 23, Fall 1994, pp. 1–121.

———. "Federal Preemption: A Recommended ACIR Research Agenda." *Publius* 14, Summer 1984, pp. 175–81.

———. "Federal Preemption Under Reagan's New Federalism." *Publius* 21, Winter 1991, pp. 7–28.

———. "Federal Preemption of State and Local Government Activities." *Seton Hall Legislative Journal* 13, No. 1, 1989, pp. 25–51.

———. "Federally Induced Costs." *Federally Induced Costs Affecting State and Local Governments*. Washington, DC: U.S. Advisory Commission on Intergovernmental Relations, 1994, 33–39.

———. "Financing National Policy Through Mandates." *National Civic Review* 81, Summer–Fall 1992, pp. 367–73.

———. "Fiscal Implications of Federal Mandates." *Diskussionsbeitrage*. Siegen, Deutschland: Forschungs-Schwepunkt Historische Mobilität under Normenwandel, Universität Gesamthochschule Siegen, December 1987, entire issue.

———. "Frustrating National Policy: Partial Preemption," in Jerome J. Hanus, ed., *The Nationalization of State Government*. Lexington, MA: Lexington Books, 1981, pp. 75–104.

———. "Interstate Cooperation: The Roles of the State Attorneys General." *Publius* 28, Winter 1998, pp. 71–89.

———, ed. "Interstate Relations." *Publius* 24, Fall 1994, pp. 1–114.

———. "Introduction: Dimensions of Interstate Relations." *Publius* 24, Fall 1994, pp. 1–11.

———. "National-State Relations: Cooperative Federalism in the Twentieth Century. *Publius* 31, Spring 2001, pp. 15–30.

———. "Maximization of Local Autonomy and Citizen Control: A Model." *Home Rule & Civil Society*. Kujike, Abiko, Japan: The Local Public Entity Study Organization, 1999, pp. 175–89.

———. "Obstacles to Establishment of Interstate Compacts," in Deirdre A. Zimmerman and Joseph F. Zimmerman, eds., *The Politics of Subnational Governance*. Washington, DC: University Press of America, Incorporated, 1983, pp. 71–77.

———. "Preemption in the U.S. Federal System." *Publius* 23, Fall 1993, pp. 1–13.

———. "Regulacio Federal Dels Governs Estatals I Locals Dels Estats Units D'America." *Seminari sobre la Situacio Actual del Federalisme als Estats Units D'America*. Barcelona, Spain: Institut d'Estudis Autonomics, Generalitat de Catalunya, 1991, pp. 70–98.

———. "Regulating Intergovernmental Relations in the 1990s." *The Annals of the American Academy of Political and Social Science* 509, May 1990, pp. 48–59.

———. "The Silent Revolution: Federal Preemption." *Diskussionsbeitrage*. Siegen: Forschungs-Schwerpunkt Historische Mobilität under Normenwandel, Universität Gesamthochschule Siegen, September 1988, entire issue.

———. "Trends in Interstate Relations: Political and Administrative Cooperation." *Book of the States: 2002 Edition*. Lexington, KY: Council of State Governments, 2002, pp. 40–47.

Zimmermann, Frederick L. "Intergovernmental Commissions: The Interstate-Federal Approach." *State Government* 42, Spring 1969, pp. 129–30.

———. "The Role of the Compact in the New Federalism." *State Government* 43, Spring 1970, pp. 128–35.

———. "A Working Agreement." *National Civic Review* 58, May 1969, pp. 201–05, 232.

Zimmermann, Frederick L. and Richard H. Leach. "The Commissions on Interstate Cooperation." *State Government* 33, Autumn 1960, pp. 233–42.

Zolkos, Rodd. "California Tax Still Irritates Great Britain." *City & State* 5, September 26, 1988, pp. 1, 25.

Unpublished Materials

"Agreement Between the State of New York Department of Social Services and State of Rhode Island Department of Human Services." Albany: Department of Social Services, n.d.

"Air Quality Planners Release List of Potential Emission Control Regulations." News release issued by the Metropolitan Washington Council of Governments, July 1, 1993.

Bennett, Lynne L. "The Economics of Interstate River Compacts: Efficiency, Compliance, and Climate Change." Unpublished Ph. D. Thesis, University of Colorado, Boulder, 1994.

Booker, James F. "Economic Allocation of Colorado River Water: Integrating Quantity, Quality, and Instream Use Values." Unpublished Ph D. Dissertation, Colorado State University, Fort Collins, 1990.

Bowman, Ann O'M. "Interstate Interactions: Cooperation, Competition, and Conflict." Paper presented at the annual meeting of the Midwest Political Science Association, Chicago, April 27–30, 2000.

——— . "State-to-State Relationships in the U.S. Federal System." Paper presented at the annual meeting of the American Political Science Association, San Francisco, September 1, 2001.

"Cooperative Fire Control Agreement between Northeastern Forest Fire Protection Commission and Forest Service, United States Department of Agriculture." Warner, NH: The Commission, 1996.

"Cooperative Fire Control Agreement between State of New Hampshire and Forest Service, U.S. Department of Agriculture." Warner, NH: The Commission, 1983.

"Cooperative Fire Control Agreement between the State of New York and the Forest Service." Albany, NY: Department of Environmental Conservation, 2000.

"Cooperative Fire Protection Agreement for the Northeastern Coordination Center Between the Northeastern Forest Fire Protection Commission, State of Maine, U.S. Forest Service, U.S. Fish and Wildlife Service, U.S. National Park Service, and U.S. Bureau of Indian Affairs." Warner, NH: The Commission, 2001.

Doig, Jameson W. and Mary H. Durfee. "Resolving Cross-Border Hostilities in the U.S. and Canada: What Roles for Expertise, Insulated from the 'Hurry and Strife of Politics?'" Paper presented at the annual meeting of the American Political Science Association, San Francisco, August 31, 2001.

Duryea, Christopher J. "The Emergency Management Assistance Compact: An Analysis of the 'Issues.'" A research paper prepared for an American federalism seminar, Rockefeller College, State University of New York at Albany, December 7, 1999.

Eglene, Ophelia. "Interstate Cooperation in the Area of Air Pollution: The United States and the European Union Cases." A research paper prepared for a seminar on American Federalism, Graduate School of Public Affairs, State University of New York at Albany, Autumn 1999.

Featherstone, Jeffrey P. "An Evaluation of Federal-Interstate Compacts as an Institutional Model for Intergovernmental Coordination and Management: Water Resources for Interstate River Basins in the United States." Philadelphia: Unpublished Ph. D. dissertation, Temple University, 1999.

———. "Interstate Organizations for Water Resource Management." Paper presented at the annual meeting of the American Political Science Association, San Francisco, September 1, 2001.

Florestano, Patricia S. "Interstate Compacts: The Invisible Area of Interstate Relations." Paper presented at the 1993 annual meeting of the American Political Science Association, Washington, DC, September 3, 1993.

———. "State Legislatures and Interstate Relations: Assessments of Formal and Informal Instrumentalities by Southern Legislative Leaders." Institute of Urban Studies, University of Maryland, College Park, September 1978.

"Governor Pataki, Governor Dean, EPA Sign Lake Champlain Plan." News release issued by the Office of New York Governor George E. Pataki, October 28, 1996.

Herring, John H. "The Management of Major Interbasin Water Transfers." Unpublished Ph. D. Dissertation, Cornell University, 1995.

Hill, James P. "Managing the Nation's Water without Washington: The Interstate Compact Experience." East Lansing: Unpublished Ph. D. dissertation, Michigan State University, 1992.

Hines, James B., Jr. "Altered States: Taxes and the Location of Foreign Direct Investment in America." National Bureau of Economic Research, Incorporated. Working Paper No. 4397, July 1993.

Hoskins, Joseph A. "An Introduction to a Study of the Commerce Clause of the United States Constitution." Washington, DC: Unpublished Master of Laws Essay, Georgetown University School of Law, 1939

"Interstate Air Pollution Compacts in Relation to the Air Quality Act of 1967." Washington, DC: U.S. Department of Health, Education, and Welfare, 1968.

Lamana, Michael. "Motivations for the Creation of Interstate Compacts: The New York Experience." Unpublished Ph. D. Dissertation, State University of New York at Albany, 1971.

———. "Nature of Federal Involvement in the Delaware and Susquehanna Interstate River Basin Compacts." State University of New York at Albany, 1981.

Lee, Seung-Ho. "Federal Preemption of State Truck Size and Weight Laws: New York State's Reaction and Preemption Relief." Unpublished Ph. D. Dissertation, State University of New York at Albany, 1994.

Letter from Massachusetts Governor Michael S. Dukakis to President John C. Hoy and Dr. Melvin M. Bernstein of the New England Board of Higher Education, May 3, 1990.

Letter to Governor Christine Todd Whitman of New Jersey from Governor Mario M. Cuomo of New York Dated March 6, 1994. Available in the New York State Library archives, Albany, NY.

Littlefield, Douglas R. "Interstate Water Conflicts, Compromises and Compacts: The Rio Grande, 1880–1938." Los Angeles: Unpublished Ph. D. Dissertation, University of California, Los Angeles, 1987.

McCormick, Zachary L. "The Use of Interstate Compacts to Resolve Transboundary Water Allocation Issues." Unpublished Ph. D. Dissertation, Oklahoma State University, 1994.

"Members Certify GLBA Reciprocity Requirement Met." A news release issued by the National Association of Insurance Commissioners, September 11, 2002.

"New England Board of Higher Education: A Fact Sheet." Boston: 1999.

"New Report Shows Success Story in Air Pollution Trading." News release issued by the Ozone Transport Commission, Washington, DC, March 27, 2000.

"News release from the Office of Governor Mario M. Cuomo of New York, February 23, 1983."

"Northeast Governors Petition EPA to Control Air Pollution." Press release issued by the Office of Governor George E. Pataki of New York, August 14, 1997.

"A 100–Year Tradition of Excellence." Unpublished fact sheet issued by the National Conference on Uniform State Laws, Chicago, IL, n.d.

Palmore, Joseph F. "The Not-So-Strange Career of the Interstate Jim Crow: Race, Transportation, and the Dormant Commerce Clause, 1878–1946." Unpublished Master of Arts Thesis, University of Virginia, Charlottesville, 1998.

Press release issued by the Office of Governor Nelson A. Rockefeller, Albany, NY, September 29, 1972.

Press release issued by the Office of Governor Nelson A. Rockefeller, Albany, NY, February 11, 1973.

"Regional Dairy Quality Management Alliance Implementation Plan Year 2000 and Beyond." Albany: New York Department of Agriculture and Markets, n.d.

Spill, Rorie L. and Ray, Leonard. "Getting Better with Age? Investigating the Differential Success of the States in the Courts of Appeals." Paper prepared for presentation at the National Conference on Federalism and the Courts, University of Georgia, Athens, Georgia, February 23–24, 2002.

"Statement to Accompany the Report of the Free Joint Conference Committees on Coal Taxation." Helena: Montana Legislative Assembly, April 16, 1975.

"Uniform State Laws: What Are They?" Unpublished fact sheet issued by the National Conference on Uniform State Laws, Chicago, IL, n.d.

Vestal, T. Edward. "An Analysis of the Commerce Clause As It Affects States Desiring to Prohibit Solid Waste Imports." Unpublished Master of Law Essay, University of Houston Law Center, 1995.

Winders, Edward E. "Public Authorities in New York State: The Interdependent Governmental Roles of the New York State Thruway Authority." Unpublished Ph. D. Dissertation, State University of New York at Albany, 1998.

Zimmerman, Joseph F. "Changing United States Federalism by Congressional Preemption." Paper presented at the annual conference of the American Politics Group, University of West of England, Bristol, January 5, 1996.

––––––. "Federal Preemption Under Reagan's New Federalism." Paper presented at the annual meeting of the American Political Science Association, Atlanta, Georgia, September 1, 1989.

———. "Federal Regulation of State and Local Governments in the United States." Paper presented at the Institut d'Estudis Autonomics, Barcelona, October 9, 1990.

———. "Federalism in the United States." Paper presented at Moscow State University, June 4, 1990.

———. "Federalism in the United States: The Preemption Revolution." Paper presented at the Maxwell Graduate School, Syracuse University, October 25, 1990.

———. "Federalismo E O Sistema Fiscal Urbano." Paper presented at a conference on federalism, Brasilia, Brasil, November 16, 1984.

———. "Föderalismus in Der Bundesrepublik Deutschland." Paper presented at the Maxwell Graduate School, Syracuse University, October 7, 1993.

———. "Formal and Informal Interstate Administrative Cooperation." Paper presented at the annual meeting of the American Political Science Association, San Francisco, September 1, 2001.

———. "Interstate Cooperation: The Roles of the State Attorney General." Paper presented at the annual meeting of the American Political Science Association, Washington, DC, August, 18, 1997.

———. "President Reagan's New Federalism." Paper presented at the Universität Hamburg, July 5, 1988.

———. "Resolving Interstate Tax Disputes: Reciprocity, Congressional Preemption, and Judicial Decisions." Paper presented at the annual meeting of the American Political Science Association, Chicago, September 2, 1995.

———. "The Silent Revolution: Federal Preemption." Paper presented at the annual meeting of the American Political Science Association, Washington, DC, September 4, 1988.

Index